D1035851

The British

PORTRAIT OF A PEOPLE

Books by Anthony Glyn

ELINOR GLYN: *A Biography*

PEMBERTON LTD.

I CAN TAKE IT ALL

KICK TURN

THE TERMINAL

THE SEINE

THE DRAGON VARIATION

THE BRITISH

The British

PORTRAIT OF A PEOPLE

by Anthony Glyn

Childe Rowland to the dark tower came,
His word was still, Fie, foh, and fum,
I smell the blood of a Britishman.

SHAKESPEARE, *King Lear*

G. P. Putnam's Sons
New York

Published simultaneously in Canada by Longmans Canada Limited, Toronto.

Library of Congress Catalog Card Number: 73-127717

Second Impression

PRINTED IN THE UNITED STATES OF AMERICA

Author's Note

This is a personal book and in no way an official publication. But I should like to record my thanks to Her Majesty's Government, the Central Office of Information and, in particular, to Mr. S. Hart-Still, for supplying me with a mass of statistics and information without making any suggestions about how I might use them.

Contents

1. The Britishman 11
2. The Melting Pot 16
3. The Cult of the Loser 25
4. The Thin Red Line 36
5. A Tudor Day 47
6. Puddings and Pies 57
7. The Drinking Man and His Image 75
8. "A Nice Cup of Tea" 98
9. Animals as Gods 110
10. The Happiest Years of Their Lives 123
11. The Antifamily 145
12. And So to Bed 160
13. Very Private Lives 176
14. The Funny Side 190
15. Fair Play 204
16. The Sporting Life 220
17. Men at Work 235
18. Chairmen and Clubmen 249
19. The Glory of the Garden 264
20. Wanderlust 284
21. To the North 300
22. Smith, Macdonald and Jones 330

23. The Tip of the Iceberg 350
24. As Others See Us 358
25. Blindfold into the Seventies 363
Appendix: The 100 Names to Drop in Britain 371
Index 373

The British

PORTRAIT OF A PEOPLE

I

THE BRITISHMAN

⁂ The title of this chapter perhaps requires some explanation. It is an attempt to describe, in a single telegraphic word, a subject of Her Britannic Majesty, an inhabitant of the United Kingdom of Great Britain and Northern Ireland. The name of the country itself is daunting enough—the clumsy invention of a clumsy monarch, King James I. The full name is, of course, used only on official documents such as passports; normally it is shortened to either the United Kingdom or Great Britain, both unsatisfactory. The phrase "United Kingdom"—and there are, after all, other united kingdoms in the world—is usually applied to delegates at the United Nations, as in "The United Kingdom delegate defended the British record in Singapore," a confusing sentence in an already confusing situation. The phrase "Great Britain" invites and often gets the tart question "What's so great about it?" It also positively encourages the slogan "Keep Britain Great." With traditional modesty the inhabitants usually refer to the country as Britain, although in French this becomes Bretagne or Brittany. An American travel agency tactfully refers to the whole area as the British Isles. The French, Italians, Spaniards firmly call it all Angleterre, Inghilterra, Inglaterra even if they are referring to Scotland or Wales.

The point may best be illustrated by the difficulties of a traveler in finding the telephone number of the British consul in, say, Beirut. French, Italian, Swedish travelers will know immediately where to look for their consulate in the tourist directories or the telephone book, but the British traveler is less fortunately placed. He will look first under *B* for Britain and, failing that, will try *G* for Great Britain and then *U* for United Kingdom. Still balked of success, he will probably try *E* for England, *A* for Angleterre, perhaps *I* for Inghilterra. He will wonder how you spell Britain in Arabic. He will probably give the whole thing up. It would take a fine leap of his imagination for him to realize that he should all along have looked under *R* for Royaume-Uni.

The same difficulties, of course, are met by the citizens of another great multiracial country, the United States of America. I recall a dialogue in Yugoslavia between Mr. Arthur Miller and a local young admirer and the boy's consternation on discovering that the famous playwright did not live in America, as he had supposed, but in the States. Or the United States, or the U.S., or the U.S.A. The Soviet Union, a country where Russian is merely the name of a language, has, of course, the same problem for the same reason.

But even if we agree that the country where I was born is most conveniently referred to informally as Britain, what are its inhabitants called? An American critic once referred to me as "a witty Englishman," and leaving aside the arguable question of wit, and despite the fact that I have a little English blood, I did not recognize myself. To have called me a Scotsman would have been misleading, even though I have more Scottish than English blood. It would have suggested a predominantly Scottish angle in my work; anyway I have been to Scotland only three times in my life, and I am not entitled to wear a kilt.

On the continent of Europe we are called *les anglais, die Engländer, los ingleses*. But this distresses us a good deal. One of the British characteristics is that we are usually prouder of being Scottish or Welsh or Irish than of being English. Or, equally, of being a mixture, such as most of us are. British schoolboys love to boast to one another about being partly Scottish, partly Irish, partly French, partly Norwegian. Even strangers in trains, in Britain usually the most uncommunicative of people, will burst to tell you about their American grandmother, their wife's Swedish aunt. Such people are not adequately described by the word "Englishmen," *anglais, ingleses.*

The country is now acceptably called Britain, despite the complications of Bretagne and cars on the Continent labeled GB. The inhabitants are reasonably called British. But what is the singular of British? How does the individual describe himself? The press tries with the word "Briton," everything else failing. Britons, we read in the holiday headlines, are fighting forest fires on the Costa Brava, being buried by avalanches in Switzerland, being arrested for undisclosed activities in Tangier, flocking abroad in greater numbers than ever before. But the word has never caught on except in popular headlines; it is never used in ordinary conversation. Britons, to me and to practically everybody else, were rather uncivilized people who wore woad and fought the Romans under Boadicea. Racially, linguistically, culturally, they had almost nothing in common with the present British. The refrain of the old song "Rule Britannia"—"Britons never, never shall be slaves"—illustrates the poet's dilemma as well as reaffirms the importance of human liberty. Britons in the history books were almost always slaves. Shakespeare, at the start of the seventeenth century, suffered from the same problem. The lines from *King Lear* which are quoted on the title page of this book illustrate the point very clearly. The fairy-tale rhyme which Edgar misquotes requires correctly the word "Englishman." But Shakespeare set his tragedy in pre-English Britain. Furthermore, the new king was a Scot, King of Scotland as well as of England, engaged in composing the cumbersome title for his new united kingdom referred to earlier in this chapter. Shakespeare, more ingeniously and neatly, coined the word "Britishman."

It is my contention that, for practical convenience, the word needs to be revived, whether it be spelled in one word or two—

though logic would suggest that it follow the pattern of Englishman and Irishman. I feel that Britishman is a needed word at the present time, in the same way that the British people have been, and still are, needed people. The Britishman is different from—it would be presumptuous to say greater than—the Englishman, the Scotsman, the Welshman, the Irishman. Whether he is more than the sum of his parts is a matter of personal opinion. But he is certainly different, immediately recognizable, readily identifiable wherever in the world he may be found. We all have our mental picture of the typical Britishman, but just what his personal mixture of races is will be known only to himself and his close relations.

I should perhaps declare my own interest in the matter before going any further. Like most Britishmen, I am a mixture of many races. I have already admitted to some Scottish blood, Highland for those who care; Buchanan on my father's side, Sutherland on my mother's. I have an English grandfather, an Irish great-great-grandmother, Canadian great-grandparents, some very distant French cousins, a Welsh surname. My paternal great-grandfather came from the Baltic state of Courland (now Lithuania), a penniless refugee from the persecution of Catherine the Great. According to family tradition, he was by birth a Baltic baron, but in exile he did not confine himself, like other aristocratic refugees, to teaching dancing and languages. His success in business suggests Jewish or Armenian descent, perhaps the latter, to guess from the surname which he adopted. Settled in the West Indies, he married a Creole girl from Martinique. Judging from the ring that he gave her, an emerald from Russian Georgia set in a circle of Brazilian diamonds, he was much attached to her. A marriage of the Old World and the New, it was a happy one. On the other side I claim English royal blood. Three of my great-aunts were beheaded on Tower Green. Two were aunts by marriage; one was a blood relation. Two were beheaded with an ax, one with a sword. All three were briefly queens.

I am thus a typical Britishman. I was born in London and educated in England. I served in the Welsh Guards during

World War II. I have learned six languages, two of them dead. I have lived in six different countries. I feel at home everywhere. I am completely British.

But to answer a question is always to pose another. To tie on a label is not the same as opening the suitcase. Who is a Britishman? What is he like? What makes him like that? It is the question that everyone asks himself, and never more often than in this century, never more anxiously than in this new decade of the 1970's—the oldest and newest question in the world: Who am I? What am I?

This book is an essay in discovery. I hope that the intended lightness of the treatment will not completely mask the seriousness of the theme.

2

THE MELTING POT

⁂ The Britishman is unmistakable, easily identifiable by those who have seen him only in caricature. Among foreigners he stands out as clearly and recognizably as if he were carrying a paper bag covered with a Union Jack, as indeed in the 1960's he, or she, often was. He is perhaps seen at his clearest abroad, surrounded by the men and women of other nations. You do not have to approach within earshot of his voice to know that he is British. You have only to see him sporting a mustache and a regimental tie, with a dignified, courteous, world-weary manner, stalking like a pelican up the steps of the nearest embassy or high commission to sign the book, while his wife in her large white hat, waits in the car. Or on another level, you may find him on the hotel terrace drinking beer or perhaps a beer (a wealth of class distinction lies in the use of the indefinite article there), while his wife, in a blue cotton frock, newly out of boarding school, tells the family at the next table that the frescoes (or, as it may be, the ski runs) are jolly good. Or, on another level, you may find him and his wife sitting in a bar beside a warm sea; he will be wearing gray flannel trousers, a tweed coat, an open-necked white shirt with a collar tucked over the collar of the coat; she will be patting her perm; both, at one o'clock in the afternoon on a hot Mediterranean day, will be drinking tea. You do not need to glance at the newspapers they have with them to know that they are not Americans or French or Germans or Scandinavians or Italians. They are unmistakably, confidently British.

The homogeneity of styles has misled many foreign observers and commentators into thinking that, racially, we all are the same. It is supposed that we are uniformly of Anglo-Saxon origin, part of the vast Teutonic racial group, but conditioned by damp gray weather and an island existence into a variation—and not a very different one at that—of the Anglo-Saxon persona. It has often been asserted that the British and the Germans are cousins, a point which has caused much political confusion. The French usually refer to the British and the Americans as *les Anglo-Saxons,* implying that the people of both nations are descended from one single ancestor and not, at that, a very remote one.

But this is to ignore all the strains in the British heredity save one. Many peoples and races have gone to the making of the modern American, and up to a point, the same may be said of the modern Frenchman. The Britishman is no different, as even a quick glance at his history will show.

Starting at the point when Britain first became an island, the original Britishman was Neolithic Man. He came from France or North Africa or Spain and is usually referred to as an Iberian. He lived in thatched huts which were sometimes built on piles over lakes, and he was essentially a farmer. As he also built, for religious purposes, the circles of huge stones at Avebury and Stonehenge, he was evidently the first engineer as well.

About 2000 B.C. a new wave of invaders flooded over southern Britain from the Continent. These were metalworkers, and they brought with them the skill of smelting bronze. The first wave of Celts arrived about 600 B.C. They were tall and fair with light eyes, and they were known as Gaels. A bellicose people, fond of fighting and armed with iron weapons, they easily conquered and enslaved the Iberians, though they later intermarried with them. The second wave of Celts, called the Brythons, came 200 years later. These Celts were smaller and darker, the forerunners of the modern Welshman, and they drove the Gaels into the northern part of the island—traces of Gaelic customs and language can still be found in western Scotland. A third wave of Celts, the Belgae from the lower Rhine, arrived about 150 B.C. and settled in southeastern Britain. Julius Caesar, a century later, found the Belgae, whom he had been fighting in northern France, in Britain, too, and noted the similarity of the buildings and the landscape. He wrote:

> The inland part of Britain is inhabited by those who, according to tradition, were born in the island itself, while the maritime part is occupied by a people from the lands of the Belgae. These had invaded the country for the purpose of war and plunder, and are frequently known by the names of the places from which they originally came. Their war over, they stayed on and settled and began to cultivate the lands. The number of the people is countless, and their buildings very numerous, for the most part very like those of the Gauls, and they have a great number of cattle. They use either brass or iron rings of a specified weight as their money.

The picture of the early Briton is fairly clear: a peasant-farmer, wearing woad, fighting tenaciously against Roman invaders, both the slave raids of Julius Caesar and the more long-lasting, more important conquest which started A.D. 43. Throughout the long, prosperous and civilized occupation by the Roman legions the Britons remained, by and large, hungry slaves waiting on their Roman masters. Of course, many Britons benefited by the occupation. They became Romanized, living in villas, enjoying their baths and their wine. Some even became kings under their Roman overlords. There was no question of protecting the local culture, as the Romans had done in Greece or in Palestine and as the British were later to do in India, Nigeria, and elsewhere. In Britain there were only the Roman civilization and the barbarians, and when the legions were withdrawn A.D. 410, there was no one in Britain capable of organizing, administering and defending a new, young, independent country.

The exception, perhaps, was King Arthur, that legendary figure who has haunted the imagination of writers for centuries. He and his knights, with their Welsh names, were probably Romanized Britons, organizing sporadic, ineffectual, but gallant resistance in places as widely separated as Cornwall and the West Country, Wales and Scotland. The last fight of Arthur in the west has epic stature, the Trojan War of Britain, though personally I am always puzzled by the legends themselves, by the concentration on court etiquette and tournaments, and adultery, and the Holy Grail and occasionally a sinister and probably symbolic Black Knight in the forests; puzzled by the lack of any reference to the great enemy in the east, the Saxon hordes that were beginning to sweep over the country. The Knights of the Round Table seem to have been a very inward-looking group.

What is certain is that the Roman civilization and the traces of British and Celtic culture were swamped and largely obliterated by the Saxon hordes. Britain or, more exactly, England was for the first and also for the last time in its history, a mainly Anglo-Saxon country, a peasant society speaking a Germanic language, groping the way through barbarism and cruelty to another civilization, which was finally achieved under the great King Alfred.

Then came the Danes, another Teutonic invasion, but by racially different people. Denmark is a long way from Saxony, and the Danes and Vikings had very different characteristics from the Saxons who had preceded them. Even now, this can be noticed. A Britishman descended from Danes in Yorkshire is likely to be different from his neighbor in East Anglia, Essex, Sussex or Wessex. For one thing, he is likely to have more of the Viking sense of feasting and to be a heavier eater and drinker. Perhaps because of this, his expectation of life is shorter.

King Alfred defended mainly in the south, and the Danish invasion was concentrated in the north of England, so that in the end Alfred had to recognize Danish sovereignty over that part of the country, the Danelaw, the word which still exists and is still used. But Danish tribes came south, too, and the effect is noticeable even to this day in the Hampshire village where I have lived for many years. A tribe from Jutland settled in the area between Alton, Winchester, and Petersfield. This had previously been occupied, rather unexpectedly, by the Celts, who, despite the close proximity of Winchester and King Alfred's court, had remained in Wessex throughout the Saxon conquest. The two races can be clearly identified to this day. The Jutes are tall, blond, blue-eyed, working mostly on the farms, taciturn, practical, fond of sport and physical achievements. The Celts, living alongside them, are small, dark, wiry, quick of speech, resourceful. They are usually skilled men, plumbers, telephone engineers, craftsmen, and many of them are still called Arthur. Even though they and the Jutes have been living in the same village, peaceably, for hundreds of years, it is rare even now for a Celt and a Jute to marry.

In 1066 the Normans conquered the country, and everything was changed forever. The Normans were, of course, originally Vikings, but two centuries of contact with the French culture and intermarriage with the French had changed them drastically. They brought with them their own hierarchy, their own culture, their own language. They imposed the feudal system on Anglo-Saxon and Danish England. Enthusiastic Christians, they built vast cathedrals and abbeys. Naturally restless people, they turned English eyes toward the glitter of foreign possessions and the lure of Crusades. But the division inside the country was easy to see. On top of the Celts, the Anglo-Saxons and the Danes, there was now a different race ruling on every level from the king to the country squire. The Anglo-Saxon laborer, still speaking his Germanic language, worked for his lord in the fields and on the battlegrounds and, in the few moments he was allowed to himself, tilled his own strip of land. His Norman overlord feasted in his castle, plotted for power, went on Crusades, and, above all, spoke only French. Between the two there was almost no communication. Even by the thirteenth century we find that the king, Edward I, spoke only

French, as did the putative founder of British democracy, Simon de Montfort.

It was several centuries before the two languages, Anglo-Saxon and French, blended to form the English language. The Battle of Crécy in 1346 was a turning point in language, as well as in the techniques of war. The English archers who won the day spoke only Anglo-Saxon, and several different dialects of it, and so could not communicate with the English knights, who spoke only French. King Edward III, who was watching the battle from a nearby windmill, saw the disadvantages of this; he also felt it a pity, in a patriotic Francophobe period, that his knights could speak only the language of their enemies. On his return he encouraged the court and nobility to learn Anglo-Saxon, and in 1362 he ordered that it should be used in the lawcourts. He was also helped, if it can be so termed, by the great wave of bubonic plague called the Black Death which swept over Europe in 1348 and killed off a third of the population of England, including many educated French-speaking priests who acted as tutors to the children of the nobility. New priests were hastily ordained from the humbler Anglo-Saxon-speaking masses and taught their own language to their charges.

Gradually the new language emerged, the common everyday words being usually of Anglo-Saxon origin, the longer and more abstract words coming from the French. Henry IV was the first King of England to use English as his native language. The court by then spoke the language so fluently that Chaucer, the first great writer in the English language, could read his *Tales* aloud at court and be sure that none of his shafts of wit were misunderstood.

The two languages had blended, but the two nations stayed apart far longer. It was rare for a Norman to intermarry with a Saxon or Dane. Not only was custom and prudence against it, but also class distinction. A Norman lord did not marry a Saxon girl, though he might summon her to his bedroom in his castle.

The consequences of this division and the resentment it necessarily brought about lasted longer even than the division in languages. The English Civil War in the seventeenth century was not only a clash between King and Parliament, between royal authority and democracy, but also a resurgence of the centuries-old Saxon hostility to the Norman, and the two words were often and openly used at the time. Indeed, one may regard Cromwell's victories as the final Saxon revenge for the defeat at Hastings.

The Norman Conquest was the last. After 1066 no other nation has succeeded in forcing its way in by violence to take over the country, though many have tried. But the foreigners still come, this time as refugees or guests, each adding his little contribution to the British character and way of life. Bohemian Protestants; French Huguenots, fleeing from the persecution of Louis XIV; Flemish weavers from the Spanish Netherlands; Russians, like my great-grandfather, escaping from tyranny; French aristocrats smuggled away from the Terror, though these were not particularly numerous and few remained in England after the Battle of Waterloo. The Jews found the British more appreciative of their talents than most host nations and have, in the end, become better integrated in Britain than in any other country. Those coming from central Europe settled mainly in London and Leeds. The Scots, bringing with them a different history, and a different tradition, came south of the Border in search of work; the Irish crossed the sea also in search of wages, settling permanently in big cities like London and Birmingham or else coming in search of temporary work and returning home at Christmas and other holidays. Other Irish reached Liverpool, Manchester or Cardiff on their way to America and then found that, for various reasons, including shortage of money, they were unable to go any farther and remained there. Of the Celtic races round England, the Welsh alone seem to have stayed firmly within their principality, until driven to emigrate by the Depression.

At the turn of the century the Italians started coming, mainly as waiters, but later, as they prospered, becoming restaurant keepers and hoteliers. Greeks, Cypriots and even some French came for the same reason. To walk through Soho today is to catch a glimpse of the huge melting pot that is London and to wonder again at the blending process which will turn these disparate elements eventually into typical Britishmen, indistinguishable from the others.

All these immigrants were from Europe. Immigration from continents outside Europe, in particular from Asia and Africa, hardly existed before World War II, though there have been for centuries small and ancient colonies in the ports, descendants of seamen, lascars, stevedores. In some cases the families date back to the early tea trade or even farther beyond. One thinks in this connection of the Chinese in Limehouse and Liverpool, of the Negroes in Tiger Bay, Cardiff, and of South Shields on the Tyne, the largest Arab colony in the kingdom, though the word "Arab" in this context is a little misleading.

But the large-scale and more controversial immigration of immigrants from outside Europe only began after the last war. The pioneers were, perhaps, the young West Indians who came over to join the British armed forces during the war, in particular the RAF, and sent back glowing accounts of the opportunities in Britain to their friends and families at home. Soon the ships and the planes were bringing in West Indians, mostly Jamaicans, by the hundreds and thousands, looking for work and homes. They tended to settle in the larger cities, in particular South London, Birmingham, Manchester, Bradford, and have already made a considerable impact on life in those crowded and rather grim areas.

The Asians came later: Pakistanis from their own poor country; Indians expelled by the leaders of the new, young African countries, where they had been living and trading for generations. These Asian immigrants, bringing as they do new religions, new social customs, and new languages into Britain, may well, if they merge with the surrounding population and do not remain in self-contained communities, cause the greatest change in the image of the Britishman since the Norman Conquest.

No doubt there are many more still to come, even though Britain is now the fourth most crowded country in the world. Only Japan, Belgium and Holland have a higher density of population. For Britain, long before the discovery of America, was the America of Europe, the farthest point west, where men were driven by invaders from the east; the land of the free, where refugees could find sanctuary and the hungry and disappointed could find hope. As has been shown, this tradition has continued, even after the great waves of immigration into America. And it is to be hoped that it will continue, although for reasons of overcrowding the numbers have had to be restricted. But it will be a sad day for the British if the people of other nations no longer wish to come and live with us, if Britain is forced like Canada and Australia to advertise for immigrants.

3

THE CULT OF THE LOSER

So all day long the noise of battle roll'd
Among the mountains by the winter sea....

The words are from one of the great poems in the English language, Tennyson's *The Passing of Arthur*. Tennyson wrote it at the height of the power and glory of the British Empire, and the battle he chose to write about was a defeat: the great Battle in the West, the final eclipse of civilization.

The battle itself is not gone into. All we know is that King Arthur and his knights, heavily outnumbered, fought to the last, till only Arthur himself, mortally wounded, and one knight, Sir Bedivere, survived. After that follow, at some length, their symbolic and rather complicated efforts to return the magic sword Excalibur to the Lady of the Lake. In the end, Arthur, the Once and Future King, sailed into the west in a mysterious boat, leaving his knight, Sir Bedivere, alone on the hostile and wintry shore, the image of isolation and defeat.

It is interesting to compare this poem with the masterpiece of another imperial poet laureate, Virgil. The Roman poet laureate was required, both by his muse and by his imperial patrons, to glorify the new Empire, to sound a note of victory and a hope for even greater triumphs in the future. The very idea seems alien to the British. It is impossible to imagine a British poet writing the *Aeneid.* The only part of the epic which seems tolerable to the Britishman, whether he be scholar or schoolboy, is the Dido episode: forsaken Dido, another loser, another defeat.

The heroic loser, the man who, outnumbered and outgunned, still manages an epic last stand before the end, this is the character which has excited British imagination and admiration throughout history. It has, of course, to be a gallant defeat, and not one brought about by incompetent planning or mismanagement. The surrender of Singapore in the last war has inspired no sagas or legends. The hero has to be brave and skillful, faithful unto death, but outnumbered and, in the end, doomed.

Tennyson, in another of his poems, the popular ballad *The Revenge,* spelled the myth out very clearly. Sir Richard Grenville, trapped at the Azores by a huge Spanish fleet, refused to fly and abandon his sick men. Instead, in his one small ship, he took on the whole Spanish fleet, fifty-three high-built galleons, in a heroic, hopeless fight which doomed his men as surely as if he had abandoned them in Flores.

> And the sun went down, and the stars came out
> far over the summer sea,
> But never a moment ceased the fight of the one
> and the fifty-three.

The disparity of numbers is emphasized in verse after verse of the poem. The little *Revenge,* of course, fights on until her powder and her shot are gone and the vessel is all but a wreck. Sir Richard Grenville dies, proclaiming that he has only done his duty. He was, I understand, an uncouth and bad-tempered man, who liked chewing up the wineglasses when he drank. He had had a distinguished career as a sailor, commanding the fleet which carried Sir Walter Raleigh's first colony to Virginia, and was noted for his courage and resource on both land and sea. But it was his last hopeless battle, simply and purely lost without any compensating strategic advantages elsewhere, the last fight, which Queen Victoria's poet laureate wished to hold up to us for our admiration. And in this, of course, Tennyson perfectly caught the enduring mood of the British.

It wasn't only King Arthur and Sir Richard Grenville. Caractacus, the British king who twice raised an army and fought the Romans, lost and was dragged through Rome in the Emperor Claudius' triumph. But his name (in Welsh, Caradoc or Caradwg) is still a popular one for boys in Wales. The whole of British history is star-studded with glamorous losers—Boadicea, the defiant British queen, still rides across Westminster in her chariot, but the name of the Roman general who defeated her is now forgotten. One thinks, too, of Harold of England, desperately trying to hold off the Norwegians and the Normans on two fronts and finally falling a victim to the somewhat unsportsmanlike trick of shooting the arrows into the air. Hereward the Wake in the Fenland marshes; Owen Glendower in Wales; the Duke of Monmouth, who could, perhaps, be called an incompetent and rather unattractive intriguer, but became heroic by his defeat and execution; Sir Walter Raleigh, not the ambitious flattering courtier of his younger days, but the grizzled and defeated explorer; the Earl of Strafford; Mary Queen of Scots, and indeed all those whose lives were ended on the block.

Above all, there was Bonnie Prince Charlie, the young and romantic hero, the inspiration of a thousand legends and books, who was sufficiently defeated at Culloden, so that we may now forgive him for having died in exile and not on Tower Hill.

All these last were rebels against the existing power, and their causes did not always commend themselves to everybody. It was their defeats that made them admirable. British admiration, however, could also be freely given to explorers and soldiers cut off and outnumbered far from home; Henry Hudson in North America, Captain Cook in the Pacific, Gordon at Khartoum, and perhaps the most extraordinary case of all, General Smuts, who fought at odds against the British, was defeated, and later became more beloved and admired in Britain than he ever was in South Africa.

Martyrs, if we assume that their premature and unpleasant deaths were evidence of defeat, have always been admired by the British, far more than the kings or the governments that ordered their torture or execution; we recall in particular Thomas à Becket, the Tudor archbishops and bishops, the Tolpuddle martyrs, who pioneered trade unionism, and especially Guy Fawkes. It is not only their fortitude in their subsequent sufferings, though this was often enormous, which commands our admiration, but the fact that they lost. Had Guy Fawkes succeeded in his destructive mission to blow up Parliament and survived, we would probably not now remember him affectionately every November.

Failing defeat in battle, a retreat is the next best thing, and the British dwell lovingly on the retreats in their military history. Sir John Moore's long and brilliantly executed retreat across Spain to Corunna, ending most happily with the general's own heroic death, is much more to British taste than Wellington's later victories at Salamanca and Vittoria. The retreat from Mons in 1914 is spoken about in quite a different way from the later, muddy slogging at Ypres. The same may be said of Kut in Mesopotamia.

But perhaps the clearest example of all is Dunkirk. The retreat of the British Army to Dunkirk and its subsequent evacuation are recalled more lovingly than the same Army's later and more successful achievements in Normandy. Arnhem is remembered, but the precisely planned and executed crossings of the Rhine at Rees and Emmerich are forgotten. A large part of the admiration of Field Marshal Auchinleck is due to the fact that, like Moore and Gort before him, he commanded a British army on a long retreat, this time across the North African desert, finally turning at bay at Alamein. This is the classic British military operation, and we are not wanting in military historians who assert that Auchinleck's defensive battle at Alamein was a finer military achievement than Montgomery's clear-cut victory on the same site a few months later. Indeed, one of the problems in public relations which the more successful British generals have had to face—Cromwell, Marlborough, Wellington, Kitchener, Haig, Montgomery—is that they did not have the required tragic heroic image.

Captain Scott of the Antarctic, on the other hand, had many problems to face, but public image was not one of them. Indeed, it is hard to imagine a more perfect British hero. His difficulties in mounting and financing his expeditions were worthy of Raleigh, and when he finally reached the South Pole after immense suffering and resolution, it was only to find that Amundsen had got there first. Struggling back to base, short of food, in conditions requiring the maximum possible courage and endurance, he died a few miles from safety, leaving diaries whose literary quality was such that extracts from them were reprinted in the *Oxford Book of English Prose.* The shaping of the story was perfect. It might have been devised by a film scriptwriter and indeed has been used for such purposes. It can safely be assumed that Scott's name will be revered, even adored, long after the names of the successful Mount Everest expedition or the later trans-Antarctic expedition are forgotten.

What is this cult for the loser which is so instinctive and all-pervasive, dominating even sport, where the ostensible object, like that of war, might well be thought to be to win? Many a young and attractive tennis player, American or Australian, male or female, has been surprised by the clear partisanship of the Wimbledon crowd, unexpected and displeasing, in view of the famous British passion for fairness and fair play. The partisanship will not, of course, extend to booing or jeering or throwing tomatoes—such behavior is to be expected only in Spain or Latin America. But the young player will not fail to notice that the applause given to his or her opponent is a good deal greater than he or she earns by even the most brilliant services, that a murmur of sympathy goes up when a good shot by the opponent just fails to go in. "What," the young hero or heroine asks himself, "has gone wrong? Why don't they like me? Is it political? Have I broken some local, obscure rule of court manners?"

The answer, of course, is no. The crowd is simply on the side of the loser, particularly if the loser has some disadvantages, is older or perhaps a stateless alien searching for a country or, best of all, limping. No young hero or heroine, however handsome and talented, can hope to gain a British crowd's sympathy against such odds, though he or she can recover a lot of goodwill by seeming modest and engagingly diffident in the moment of victory, warmly embracing and congratulating the opponent, bowing correctly to royalty present, accepting a cup with endearing shyness and later, on television, speaking steadily about the wonderful performance of his or her opponent. The most popular postwar figure to appear at Wimbledon was undoubtedly Jaroslav Drobny, an exiled Czech who, for much of the time, played in Egyptian colors, but nevertheless seemed to embody, in British eyes, all the best characteristics of British sportsmanship. Tournament after tournament he would battle on, indomitably, usually against players far younger than himself, often upsetting well-known form to the delight of the crowd, struggling wearily through some of the longest matches in the whole history of lawn tennis, only to lose finally somewhere around the semifinals. The Wimbledon crowd took Old Drob to their hearts, and there were mixed feelings when he dented his image by finally winning the tournament.

But this is only to repeat the question, not to answer it. Why do the British love a loser more than a winner? Why is there the automatic sympathy with the defeated, with the underdog, with the oppressed? Why should the British, during the long history of European politics, have always thrown in their lot with the smaller nation, the one most likely to be defeated, the one least likely to succeed? It is a policy, incidentally, which has led to an automatic balance of power and which has, on the whole, preserved the independence of the European nations throughout the centuries. But it was not adopted as a pragmatic foreign policy. It was followed instinctively. British sympathy and support always went to the weaker nation, perhaps only temporarily weaker, to the country most likely to lose. This often produced sudden changes from one ally to another, but there was no need to make speeches explaining these shifts to the country.

All Britishmen are deeply suspicious of victory and the victorious. To exult over a fallen foe is, to the British, profoundly distasteful. As for a Roman triumph, with a conquering general riding through the streets of Rome in his chariot, his highborn enemies and captives driven before him with whips like slaves, even the idea is unbearable. Or again, Hitler dancing in triumph as he surveyed surrendered Paris. Or Mussolini proposing to ride in triumph through the streets of Alexandria on a white horse—though this, at least, to their great delight, the British were able to thwart.

The same reaction takes place in the more modest world of sport. The British are, perhaps, the most sport-conscious nation in the world, but winning and losing are to them the least important part of it. Sitting one morning in an American coffee shop, I overheard two girls talking.

"I just love a man who wins," said one girl.

And her friend echoed her, "So do I. A man who goes all out and wins."

My British soul was deeply shocked.

Cricket, even more than lawn tennis, probably provides the best example of the cult. Although in theory cricket is one side of eleven playing another side of eleven, in practice, at any given moment, it is one man against eleven, one batsman against a bowler and ten fieldsmen, the heroic batsman thus being satisfactorily and reassuringly outnumbered. The batsman is, of course, required in theory to make runs, to help win. But the hearts of the public really go out to the man who is playing for a draw, the man who, in a lost and hopeless position, has to stay at his post until the close of play and thus deny the opponents their victory. Like Horatius on the bridge, he has to hold the ranks of Tuscany at bay for many hours; like the sentry at Pompeii, he has to remain faithful unto death, or at least until half past six.

My own most enduring memories of cricket matches are of moments like this: Watson and Bailey batting through the long afternoon at Lord's, defying fast bowling, slow bowling, the new ball, with no hope of winning for England, no thought except to stay there until the end. Or Washbrook coming out to bat for England at Manchester, when England had lost her first three wickets for a miserable seventeen runs—Washbrook the famous England opening batsman, now long past his prime and virtually in honored retirement, a team selector, an elder statesman. His return to the side had been controversial. Some felt that a selector should not select himself; others that an older man, whose reactions were no longer so fast and who no longer felt able to be an opening batsman, should not be included in any England side. And then, at the moment of crisis, he walked out of the pavilion, down onto the ground, his home ground, his cap pulled over one eye as always, the crowd clapping him all the way. No one dared expect too much. He stayed in, with his captain, Peter May, all through the long afternoon until stumps were drawn. He scored ninety-nine runs, missing his century by one run. Ninety-nine! It was wonderful! To have succeeded in scoring his century would have made his heroic performance a little less moving, a little less memorable. But which side in the end won the match, I can no longer recall.

Or best of all, perhaps, Cowdrey coming out to bat for England with a broken arm. In the first innings, a fast ball had broken his arm. He had retired hurt, left the ground and gone to the hospital, where his arm had been set. Then he returned to the ground, in case he still might be needed to help save England. He was needed, and he came out to bat again, as the afternoon shadows spread across the turf. In great pain, unable to hold the bat with both hands, unable to score runs, he was still able to hold up his end, to help his side to remain undefeated at the close of play.

It is at moments like this that a Britishman's eyes mist over, a lump grows in his throat, and he chews, by mistake, through the handle of his umbrella.

It is instructive to compare a Britishman's emotion—strongly controlled emotion, of course—at moments like these with his amused disdain for medals, the pride and glory of other armies. In the last war, photographs of German, Russian, Italian marshals festooned, apparently from neck to ankle, in medals would cause happy laughter in British Army messes. At the same time, the War Office had to issue an order that all ranks would wear the decorations, medal ribbons, wound stripes, long-service bars and other insignia to which they were entitled. Failure to do so would constitute the crime of being improperly dressed. It is not an order which one can imagine being issued in any other army. To ask, say, a Finn how he won his medal is to be given an accurate account of a notable feat of arms. The man is justifiably proud of his exploit and of the medal he won. But if you ask a Britishman how he won his Military Cross or his Distinguished Flying Cross, you will be told that he got it by mistake, that it was meant for somebody else, that they all were issued with the rations. A friend of mine, a wartime RAF officer, was one of the famous Dambusters, and he was awarded a very high decoration for his part in that desperate raid. A little while later he returned to his old school, Eton, for an afternoon to see some old friends. It was a warm summer's day, but he wore his RAF greatcoat the whole time so that nobody would see the new medal ribbon on his chest. Nobody was particularly surprised at this. After all, the English summer weather is changeable, or perhaps he felt that the brass buttons on his RAF tunic underneath were insufficiently polished. It was only later that the true reason was discovered. He was killed later in the war, and the story of his greatcoat was recalled in his obituary notice, with general understanding and approval. We were as proud of him for his modesty as for his gallantry.

At the end of the war, the War Office complained that few people had bothered to claim the campaign stars and medals which they were entitled to. There were apparently thousands of them awaiting distribution in a vault somewhere. They asked would all those entitled to them claim them forthwith. The request was ignored by most people, including myself. We had other things on our minds at that time. Finally, in the summer of 1949, my own campaign stars reached me, although I had sent in no application. I suppose they were trying to clear the vault. I was at the time office manager of a company in what is now Guyana, and I opened the unexpected official parcel with some curiosity. Never having seen them before, my secretary and I inspected them with some interest. Then, not knowing what else to do with them, I put them in the drawer of my desk. I suppose they may still be there.

It was a British poet, once again writing at the height of Victorian imperialism, who wrote the famous and revealing lines:

> If you can meet with triumph and disaster
> And treat those two impostors just the same....

Kipling's words found an echo in the breasts of his countrymen. But other nations, perhaps more wisely, know that triumph is not the same as disaster, for triumph is the result of talent and careful planning and much arduous work, while disaster, particularly military disaster, will lead only to conquest and possible enslavement. It is only the British, free of foreign conquest for 900 years, who can take such a detached view.

Occasions such as coronations may be celebrated with all the pageantry at Britain's command; there is no defeated enemy to feel sorry for. But a victory must be played down. If it must be celebrated at all, then let it be done as a funeral. In 1805 the populace of London far preferred mourning at Nelson's funeral to celebrating the great and decisive victory at Trafalgar. The French, who know well the difference between triumph and disaster, celebrate November 11 as a national holiday with fireworks and processions. It is called *Jour de la Victoire*. But the same event in London, Remembrance Day, is treated as the biggest and saddest funeral of all. The queen and members of the government, all dressed in solemn black, lay wreaths on the Cenotaph, the bands play Chopin's "Funeral March," the pipers play that most moving of Scottish laments "The Flowers of the Forest." Across the country, church congregations sing "O, Valiant Hearts" with bowed heads and mumble, "We will remember them."

The inscription on the War Memorial in Liverpool sums up accurately the British attitude to victory: "And the victory that day was turned into mourning unto all the people."

Perhaps the most bizarre example of the British wish to turn an occasion for rejoicing into a funeral is the annual cup final at Wembley. Everyone has come to be happy; the two competing football teams, after hard and muddy struggling through the winter games, have finally reached the final, the smooth green turf of Wembley, the May sunshine. Whatever the result, all the players will receive a finalist's medal from the queen, who is present. The spectators are happy, too, all 100,000 of them. Somehow, by fair or less fair means, they all have got tickets. The massed bands play in the center of the ground before the game starts and everybody sings, and the song they love best to sing is the evening and funeral hymn "Abide with Me."

> Swift to its close ebbs out life's little day,
> Earth's joys grow dim, its glories pass away,
> Change and decay in all around I see,
> O, Thou Who changest not, abide with me.

This chapter started with a quotation from a sad poem of defeat, and with a sad poem of victory it seems appropriate to conclude it.

4

THE THIN RED LINE

☙ Of course, you cannot lose all the time and remain independent as a country, still less acquire a large empire. At some stage a clear and decisive victory has to be won. The British, it has often been said, like to lose every battle till the last, and indeed this is just how the British would wish it to be, retreating, outnumbered, turning at bay, just—and only just—holding the position, and then finally securing, rather reluctantly, the victory required for peace and independence.

Better still if the winner can manage to bring it off against great odds. A Britishman does not enjoy the thought that his enemy is smaller or weaker than he is. Given a choice, he would prefer to be the smaller and weaker, winning by daring and resource alone. It is his Jack-the-Giant-Killer complex, and the legend of Jack-the-Giant-Killer, from far back in the British race memory, provides a valuable clue to much that is instinctive in British policy at home and abroad. The story itself is probably based on the struggles of the Celts to outwit their heavyweight Saxon conquerors.

The sight of a large, powerful country, bullying or attacking a small neighbor is, of course, one which angers many other nations besides the British, but the British carry this attitude much further. Conquerors from Genghis Khan onward arouse less admiration in Britain than in many countries. Julius Caesar, outnumbered in Gaul but outwitting the tribes, playing them off against one another, winning by his dash and his resource, is a sympathetic hero. The later Caesar, the founder of imperial Rome, is much less sympathetic. The young General Bonaparte in Italy, outmaneuvering the powerful Austrians, "lightning among the hills," in Belloc's applauding phrase, commands far more admiration than the later emperor with his Grand Army. Even Churchill fell a victim to this attitude. The Winston Churchill of 1940 at bay, growling defiance, was exactly the image which the British would have chosen above all others for themselves. The Churchill of 1945, the victorious war leader, was much less to their taste, and he was immediately voted out of office.

But, as previously remarked, victory is essential to survival and independence. All the British ask is that there should not be too much of it, that it should be won against odds and preferably by a very narrow margin. "The thin red line" (the phrase was coined by the *Times'* war correspondent in the Crimea) must always be thin. Wellington's remark after Waterloo—"It was a damned close-run thing"—struck exactly the right note, and Montgomery after Alamein would have been well advised to repeat it.

Drake and his little ships taking on the high-built galleons, the might of Spain, were another classic example of the Jack-the-Giant-Killer complex. Or Nelson, usually outnumbered and outgunned, fighting the combined fleets of France and Spain. Clive and Wolfe against odds, operating far from home. General Wingate and his Chindits, fighting behind the Japanese lines in Burma; the Light Brigade at Balaclava—though this episode can hardly be termed a victory and, in any event, must be regarded with very mixed feelings. The point to remember is, of course, that there were only 600 of them.

Best of all, perhaps, was the Battle of Britain, for this was a battle, a moment in time, which every Britishman can think about without mixed feelings. Churchill, with his instinctive sense of the right words at the right moment, focused attention above all on the fewness of the RAF pilots involved, not so much their gallantry, or their exhaustion, or their tactical skill, or the excellence of the Spitfire as a fighter plane. It was the fewness which the British wished to remember, and "The Few" will remain so nicknamed forever. "We few, we happy few, we band of brothers," as Henry V may or may not have said before the Battle of Agincourt. Shakespeare was cleverly sugaring the unpalatable pill of a victory in an unnecessary and imperialistic battle. Crécy, seventy years earlier, with its handful of British archers defying the might of French chivalry, was a more satisfactory military episode, but the whole of the Hundred Years' War, whatever the legal or dynastic ins and outs, was in essence an imperial war of aggression. With the war won, and Henry VI crowned King of England and France, the English rapidly lost interest in their new empire, hardly bothering to defend the French possessions. The new hero, of course, was Joan of Arc, for British heroes and heroines do not necessarily have to be British.

Churchill, not a man to relish defeat, nevertheless included in a book of essays on his favorite historical characters portraits of Joan of Arc, George Washington and William the Conqueror. William the Conqueror was, of course, hardly carrying out a heroic, outnumbered defense (Churchill also included Harold among his favorite characters). But the expedition from Normandy was, by any standards, a risky and hazardous one, sufficiently so for William to scrape in as a hero. Joan of Arc, of course, was a natural for the list, a winner against odds, a leader who checked, quite rightly, English imperialist ambitions, a girl and a martyr, too. It is no wonder that the British admire her so warmly. (One may, however, wonder whether, if General de Gaulle were compiling a list of his favorite historical characters, he would feel compelled to include, say, Wellington.)

Equally popular is George Washington, a classic British hero. His legend, though probably not the political future of his new country, would have been bettered, however, if he had been killed dramatically in his hour of triumph. General Smuts in South Africa was another who fulfilled all the ideal requirements. His attitude, too, to medals was entirely in the British tradition. Later in his life, when he was an admired statesman and a warm friend of Britain, he was showered with honors and decorations. But though he accepted these, he preferred not to wear them. He wore few medals on his chest, but those he did wear always included the two medals he won fighting against the British. The British found this very endearing.

More recent heroes include Field Marshal Rommel, the Desert Fox, at first sight rather a surprising choice. For much of the time he was far from outnumbered, advancing strongly, and had he achieved his purpose, the war would no doubt have been lengthened by several years. But his type of warfare, the brilliant handling of small groups, was just the type of fighting the British admire most. Add to this the defeat, a long retreat and a premature death, and the legend is complete. A biography of him written by a British author was a best seller in Britain a few years ago. (In passing, one may wonder if a German author will ever write a biography of Montgomery and if such a book would be a best seller in Germany.)

Both George Washington and Jan Smuts have statues in London, one in Trafalgar Square, the other in Parliament Square. I cannot recall a memorial to Joan of Arc in England, but Shaw's perennially popular play perhaps counts as one, and it is not impossible that one day there may be a statue of Rommel in London. Should this happen, it will no doubt be erected by the Old Comrades of the Eighth Army or the descendants of those who fought against him. Gandhi's centenary was celebrated by a big meeting and concert in the Royal Albert Hall in London at which speeches paying tribute to his achievement were made by the Prince of Wales, the Prime Minister, and Lord Mountbatten. It was a remarkable tribute to the man who ended the Indian Empire, and nobody thought it the least odd.

The admiration for Washington and Smuts (not to mention Joan of Arc) was not, however, due only to their personal qualities and achievements. There was also the feeling, stronger now than ever before, that they were in the right, and the wars in which they were involved were among the most unpopular ever undertaken by the British. The British pride themselves on being underdogs and the friends and allies of underdogs. To find themselves the large imperial power, bullying and making war on small, outnumbered groups of colonists, was deeply repugnant to them. The image of the ally of the weak, the protector of the oppressed, was severely tarnished. It was the British role in history to block other people's imperial ambitions and thus maintain the balance of power. What on earth were they doing, then, sending troops to shoot at American or South African farmers?

Both wars were strongly opposed by many people inside Britain. Many people sympathized with the American colonists, either because of their genuine grievances or simply because they were American colonists. It can be fairly said that the British fought the war in a halfhearted way, and indeed, rarely in any war have commanders been less successful or more ready to surrender.

Fortunately, the British lost the war. Their *amour propre* was, to some extent, salvaged. They could begin repolishing their traditional image. But in South Africa the British won—a temporary, evanescent victory, as it now turns out, but at the time, it seemed solid enough. But once again there was strong opposition to the war in England, particularly from the Liberals, the "Little Englanders," who believed that the British should confine themselves to their own island. The British, as a whole, preferred to think about and celebrate the few occasions when British troops were cut off and besieged at Mafeking or Ladysmith (or in Lucknow, during the Indian Mutiny—another unpopular military operation) rather than remember Kitchener's tough and methodical mopping-up operations. The dismay the British felt at finding themselves in such an unsympathetic role lasted only a short time, however. Thirteen years later, they were happily back in their preferred role, defending little Belgium from the might of imperial Germany.

But feeling as they did, and always have, about empires and

conquest and underdogs and losers, how then did the British themselves manage to acquire a vast empire? The question may be fairly asked. And having acquired it, how did they manage to live with themselves and their new image? Was it simple hypocrisy, a tacit admission that an empire is a fine thing, as long as it is your own? Is it the other person's empire which must, in the end, be dismembered and eliminated? The accusation cannot be hastily dismissed. There are many who would support it, both inside Britain and outside, and never more so than in these days of disillusion. But the cult of the loser and the underdog goes very deep, and it can be held with, I think, greater justice, that the true reason, the true answer to the double standard, is both more fundamental and less cynical.

To have set out, in cold blood and glory, to acquire an empire, like Napoleon or Hitler, would have been unthinkable, even to the most jingoistic British patriot. The British Empire, as has often been remarked, was acquired in a fit of absentmindedness or, if not absentmindedness, then at least largely by accident. The Indian Empire grew out of a commercial venture, the East India Company. Canada was annexed as part of an outflanking operation against the French, a strategic move in the perennial attempt to encircle and contain French military ambition in Europe. Australia was a far, forlorn shore, to which convicts could be transported without fear of their escaping home. Expansion in Africa, Cecil Rhodes' dream of the red strip on the map all the way from the Cape to Cairo, began as a railway engineer's project, the Cape to Cairo Railway. In the railway age, British engineers, like their American and Russian colleagues, wished to build railways stretching as far as possible into the distance, connecting coast to coast and shore to shore. The Cape to Cairo Railway fulfilled these ambitions in a way that the line from London to Aberdeen could not. From there, the dream was transmitted, by Cecil Rhodes and others, into the imperial concept of the Thick Red Line, a concept which, of its nature and timing, could, and did, only last a few years.

The Empire won and consolidated, the British reconciled

themselves to the idea in various ways. Some—many, in fact—particularly schoolchildren, gloated over the amount of red on the map, on the queen's possessions encircling the globe, on which the sun never set—an unfortunate phrase, even for the euphoria of the Diamond Jubilee. Others had misgivings, particularly the "Little Englanders," and there were several, especially writers, who asked when the sun would begin to set and who speculated what would happen "when the Rudyards cease from Kipling, and the Haggards Ride no more." Kipling himself sounded this note strongly in several places, in particular in "The Recessional," and those who imagine that the too-often quoted words "Lest we forget" referred to soldiers killed in battle should reread the original poem.

But the majority took the view that British rule was wholly beneficial to the local inhabitants, wise, peace-keeping, paternalistic, and that this rule was carried out by the British often at considerable sacrifice to themselves, as part of their moral duty to mankind. Indian durbars were all very well, with crowns and elephants and jeweled howdahs, but the British preferred the idea and the phrase of the "white man's burden." It was not a governor general who was the symbol of the Empire; it was the district commissioner, harassed, overworked, with his solar topee, his khaki shorts and his pipe, administering a vast territory, keeping the peace among bickering tribes who spoke no English, suffering from malaria, and with the next Britishman several thousand miles away.

But it was a viceroy, that splendid and eloquent figure Lord Curzon, who made the point so clearly and so majestically. In a speech he said: "The Almighty has placed your hand on the greatest of His ploughs, that somewhere you have left a dawn of intellectual enlightenment where it did not exist before." Such sentiments and such language, sincere enough at the time, are now regarded with the gravest suspicion. Nobody today could think Curzon's thoughts, much less utter his words. Empire has become a dirty word. But it could be that the pendulum has swung too far and that the truth lies somewhere between Curzon's magniloquent pretensions and the modern intellectual sneers.

It is interesting in this connection to quote the views of the South African writer Laurens van der Post, who admits that he speaks as a man who was defeated by the British, as a member of a conquered race, who was brought up to hate the British and came to love them. Questioned on the radio about Britain's imperial power by an interviewer, Cliff Michelmore, who took the normal, ashamed attitude, he replied, "I think the answer to that is that they left those countries much better than they found them. I went round India only eighteen months ago and lived with the Indian Army and in the Indian villages, and I was terribly moved to find how the voice of England still speaks in the literature and poetry, and what is good about the English political tradition still appeals to men of imagination. We are living in a very difficult moment of time. It is not peculiar to Great Britain. We are living in a moment when people have had to lose faith in the old before they could have faith in the new, but I think that the most telling examples, for me personally, are examples from British history and the histories in which British history is rooted, the Judaic, Greek, Roman histories."

Of course it can be argued, and not only by BBC interviewers, that many of the former British colonies are not now in a very happy state and that a considerable part of the blame for this must lie with the British. But for once it is not very easy to be wise after the event. Did we govern too firmly, impose alien British ideas and cultures too tenaciously, so that the local inhabitants had little chance of growing up politically, economically, and artistically and were therefore unprepared for independence and democracy when it finally hit them? Or were we, on the contrary, too self-effacing? One thinks perhaps of Lord Lugard, the influential British governor in West Africa, in this connection. Far from bringing a dawn of intellectual enlightenment, were we not so keen to preserve the local social systems, tribal customs, castes, religions and languages that at the end, the peoples were left exactly where they had been when we arrived, unable to communicate with each other in English, or indeed in any common language, and therefore resuming their tribal wars at once?

The point is debatable. What is certain is that the Curzonian ideal was too exalted for many men to live up to. As time went by, the highminded and selfless idealists were replaced by others, more venial, more grasping.

But despite the decline in ideals, the Empire was still cohesive enough to survive two world wars, in which so many other traditions and ambitions foundered. Indeed, one can maintain that the ties were strengthened at Vimy Ridge and Gallipoli, the Western Desert and the Rhineland. I was myself brought up in a most Empire-conscious family between the wars. My father was, among other things, an adviser on colonial trade for the government, and he was always addressing imperial chambers of commerce. My mother was a vice-president of the Royal Empire Society and an active organizer. We lived in a world of imperial economic conferences and imperial study groups and lectures on imperial defense, in the latter case without ever mentioning who or what the enemy might be. There was no suggestion that the whole system was on its final legs, no admission that its days were numbered.

It is not part of my intention to be a new Gibbon, to write an extended *History of the Decline and Fall of the British Empire*. That will be a different book, written at a greater distance from the event. But the immediate causes of the end of the Empire are clear enough to anyone: the new nationalisms, the new racialisms, the shift in the balance of world power, the wish to be as independent as one's neighbor. To this I would like to add another reason—economics. A British economist has recently written:

> In the East, for example, it does not always seem to be realised that help must be mutual if it is to be long sustained. If Ceylon complicates British defence communications with Malaysia, Australia equips her Air Force from the U.S.A. (ruining the British Aircraft industry at a stroke) and Singa-

pore threatens to ban our exports, it becomes rather hard financially for Britain to bear the main burden of defending these countries. At the same time, Britain is buying most of their products and has been finding funds for their development projects too. Britain has supplied twelve per cent of all the paid-up capital of the World Bank from which India, Australia and Japan have been the biggest borrowers.

To some extent, no doubt this "take all and give nothing" attitude is a retribution for Britain's failure to develop the Commonwealth between the wars, when the chance was there. It is a tragedy that the blinkered orthodoxy of our economists in those years led us to believe that we could not afford to invest in the Commonwealth. We can see now that if we had done so with more energy, we would have cured our own slump as well as putting purchasing power into the pockets of good customers.

The last flicker of the British Empire (or Commonwealth and Empire, as it had come to be called) was probably the coronation of Queen Elizabeth II. The citizens of London cheered the detachments from overseas who marched through the streets in the procession and who had come of their own free will to take part in the great occasion. The prime ministers, still only a few, walked together up the nave of Westminster Abbey to take part in the service. The Queen of Tonga, riding in her open carriage through the rain, was the heroine of London. The Empire, it seemed, in transforming itself into a Commonwealth, was taking on a new lease of life.

But it was not to be. The idea of a regular conference of Commonwealth prime ministers, a truly multiracial, multicontinental gathering, was a hopeful possibility. Views could be exchanged about foreign policy and defense, constructive suggestions made about trade and finance. Perhaps it was too ambitious an idea for the times. Perhaps it could only have worked in an earlier century. As is now sickeningly well known, Commonwealth prime ministers do not exchange constructive proposals or agree on policies. Instead, they vie with one another in seeing who can be rudest, in the hope of gaining prestige at home and even of winning the honorary but coveted title of the Personality of the Conference.

Perhaps it is time to write finis to the whole experience. A growing number of people, myself included, believe that the Commonwealth should now be finally and formally wound up and the tumult and the shouting allowed to die.

5

A TUDOR DAY

☙ I was curious to see the Tower of London again, that majestic fortress, that unequaled monument to human suffering and the struggle for power. It is by far the biggest tourist attraction of Britain, the most widely visited building in the kingdom. Foreigners pour in in their thousands, every London schoolchild is taken to see it at one stage or other.

But few Londoners go there after the age of eleven. Many Britishmen never visit the site at all, and this is a pity because the great fortress really demands an adult eye, a historian's knowledge.

It was strange to see it again. Many buildings, many sights unvisited for a long time seem smaller, less impressive than the childhood memory. Not so the Tower. It still broods there beside the Thames, huge, formidable, glowering, the four little cupolas on the white Tower adding a frivolous note which seems to make the rest grimmer, more macabre.

It was a Saturday afternoon in November, and I walked under the thick Towers, the Middle Tower, the Byward Tower, the Bloody Tower. The place swarmed with children, climbing up the stairs of the Bloody Tower, trying to identify the spot where the strangled princes may, or may not, have been found, scampering along Raleigh's Walk, with tourists being led around in groups by yeomen warders, those beefeaters who have become so strangely the advertising image of Britain. And today there were in addition, and to the general surprise, several hundred people formally dressed, the ladies in feather hats and fur coats, the men in gray top hats and morning coats. I was one of them. I, too, was going to a wedding in the Royal Chapel of St. Peter ad Vincula.

I was early, and to pass the time, I went into the White Tower and looked at that marvelous collection of armor, tooled and worked as carefully as if it had been jewelry, standing in solemn lines under the massive walls.

I looked, too, at the execution block and ax which is said to have been used for the beheading of Lord Lovat in 1747 and, in that grim inner chamber where the daylight hardly enters, at the thumbscrews and the gibbet and the model of the rack and a particularly subtle instrument of torture called the Scavenger's Daughter. Here, or in the dungeons below, an unknown number of men and women had died, secretly executed or stretched too far on the rack, or had moldered away in damp cells.

I came out onto Tower Green, into the gray daylight, and went to the site of the scaffold, that patch of ground where, it is said, no grass would ever grow. Now it has been paved. It was here that the scaffold was occasionally built for private executions—not that they were so very private, for the Tower was a palace and a fortress, as well as a prison, and there were a large number of soldiers and servants able and indeed eager to come and watch the spectacle.

But executions here were a rarity. Normally, they took place outside the Tower, on the permanent scaffold on Tower Hill, under the orders of the sheriff of London and in full sight of the entire populace. All told, seventy-five men were beheaded there, starting with Sir Simon Burley in 1388 and finishing with Lord Lovat in 1747. They were all of noble rank, and they had all been attainted or condemned for high treason. After the execution, the head was left on a pike on the scaffold, but the body was brought back to the Tower in a cart and buried in St. Peter's Chapel.

Inside the Tower, on the Green, only seven people were beheaded, and only two of them were men. One was Lord Hastings, who was summarily executed at the orders of Richard, Duke of Gloucester, later King Richard III. His words according to Shakespeare were: "I shall not dine till I have seen his head." The other was the Earl of Essex. It was a last gesture on the part of Queen Elizabeth that her onetime favorite should be allowed to die in comparative privacy.

The other five executed were all women, the three young queens—my great-aunts, those three silly girls—and two peeresses who were also convicted of treason.

The wedding guests were now assembled around the scaffold, reading the inscription and grimacing.

I glanced up at the damp, lowering sky. It was All Souls' Day, the feast of the dead, and a suitable day for remembering.

"Just the same sort of weather as at Lady Jane Grey's execution," I remarked to my neighbor, as we shuffled into the chapel. "That's the bell that tolled all the time."

"S-sh!" he rebuked me, "Not now!"

The royal chapel is a graceful Tudor building. Before the altar, where the bridal couple were shortly to stand, lie (in the words of Stowe, writing in the reign of Queen Elizabeth I) "two Dukes between two Queens—to wit, the Duke of Somerset and the Duke of Northumberland between Queen Anne and Queen Catherine, all four beheaded." But today the chapel was full of flowers, and we wedding guests smiled and nodded at one another in greeting.

The bride arrived, all white satin and tulle, followed by small children in red velvet. We rose to our feet and began to sing "Praise my Soul, the King of Heaven."

There were, I reflected, eighty-two headless skeletons buried under the floor, over which she now walked so happily. I was in a macabre mood. My thoughts, I admit, were not entirely concentrated on the charm and future happiness of my bridal cousin, who was now taking vows and receiving a ring at the altar steps. My mind strayed continually to the five ladies who had been beheaded a few yards away on the Green.

For Anne Boleyn there must surely be much sympathy. She was certainly an adventuress, an attractive brunette with big dark eyes, desired by the king. But she refused him, she would not let him have what he wanted, until she was sure that he was going to marry her.

King Henry VIII was a man who did not care to be frustrated, and his irritation simmered inside him, hidden, turning sour despite his pleasure at her coronation and the birth of her child, Elizabeth, waiting for her to put a foot wrong.

It seems that when the abyss suddenly opened before her feet, on May 1, 1536, she was completely unprepared. At a tournament at Greenwich she happened to drop her handkerchief. The king took it to be a signal to a lover and was overcome by Othello-like jealousy. He rose abruptly and left the tournament to general consternation. His queen remained behind, and she never saw him again.

She was arrested and taken to the Tower and there charged with treason, infidelity and incest with her brother, Lord Rochford. Throughout her trial in the Tower, throughout the interrogation by the judge, who was her uncle, the Duke of Norfolk, she protested her innocence and begged to be allowed to see the king. In one interview, she felt, she could explain everything and win him around. But she was refused the opportunity. In any event, it is doubtful if she could have succeeded. The king was by then bored with her, waiting to be rid of her. He wished to marry Jane Seymour.

There was little direct evidence against her, but there was much prejudice. She had failed to produce another child. She had miscarried once and had had one still birth. She had many enemies. Her brother, Lord Rochford, was sent to the scaffold for treason and incest, on evidence largely provided by his wife. There were other stories of infidelities and lovers. There was also her trick of keeping her fourth finger crossed over her little finger. This was to hide a growth on her little finger, which was thought to be an embryonic extra finger and which made many people suspect her of being a witch.

It took only nineteen days to bring her from the tournament to the scaffold. As there was, at the time, no experienced headsman in the Tower, an executioner was brought over from Calais, and in the continental style, he preferred to use a sharp sword.

Catherine Howard, two queens and six years later, can also truly be called an adventuress. She was barely educated and came from a poverty-stricken home, where her father spent much time hiding from his creditors. Her face, it seems, was not particularly pretty, and it is difficult to see why Henry chose her as his fifth wife. Perhaps he liked her high-spirited, willful, confident manner. She was a Catholic and a Howard, and he was at the moment trying to appease both. Or perhaps he was affected by her sexiness. She was strongly sexed, and later she admitted having had several lovers before marrying Henry. Was it this, perhaps, that made her risk everything, made her throw everything away, when she finally reached the throne? Were her sexual needs so great and the syphilitic king no longer able to satisfy them? She herself denied it later, but it is hard to know what other interpretation can be put upon the secret messages and trysts with Culpepper, often late at night.

Her imperious manner she kept to the last. On the night before her execution, she commanded that the block be brought to her in her room, so that she might practice laying her head across it—possibly the most gruesome rehearsal ever held. She was still only twenty-one.

Jane Grey, my distant kinswoman, as every schoolboy knows, was only sixteen when she was brought to the scaffold. Since she usurped the throne, she may perhaps be called an adventuress, too, but she had a very different character from her predecessors on the Green. Quiet, studious, devout, she longed for a life of study and prayer and only reluctantly agreed to her husband's and father-in-law's plans that she should be proclaimed queen.

Why, I wondered, was she not pregnant by the time she was

brought to execution? Her life might then have been spared. Certainly she saw little enough of her husband during her nine days' reign, as he was at Syon House, sulking that he had not been proclaimed king. But there were opportunities for her to conceive, both before and afterward. One can hardly think that she was too young. Perhaps the marriage was deliberately left unconsummated. Jane as a mother might not have suited the ambitious plans of her father-in-law, the Duke of Northumberland. Or perhaps Jane's own mind was fixed too firmly on other things—on chapels and libraries.

Unlike Queen Catherine, she spent the night before her execution in almost continual prayer, and she went out to the scaffold with the firm conviction that she was to be a martyr for the cause of Protestantism.

As for the two peeresses, one can feel little sympathy for Jane, Viscountess Rochford. It was her evidence which had helped send her husband and his sister, Anne Boleyn, to the block. And later, as the confidante of Catherine Howard, she had helped to arrange the assignations, the exchanges of messages and tokens, which were to be so incriminating. Then, when the horror of her situation finally and belatedly dawned on her, she went out of her mind. And she was still mad when she was brought to the block, a few minutes after Catherine Howard's head had rolled across the scaffold.

The bridal couple had now finished taking their vows and had withdrawn to the vestry, together with their close relations, to sign the register. The rest of us sat down and listened to an anthem.

I meditated on the fifth lady to be buried under the chapel floor. Margaret, Countess of Salisbury, was the last of the old Plantagenet line and thus a possible danger to the Tudors. But her principal fault in the eyes of King Henry VIII was that she was a Catholic and, still worse, the mother of Cardinal Pole, who was later to be Archbishop of Canterbury under Queen Mary. Her son, indeed, had written a tiresome essay condemning the king's divorce and had sent it to the king. And though

Lady Salisbury dissociated herself from this paper, she remained suspect.

At other times, she was showered with honors and was created Countess of Salisbury in her own right. But at court she was thought to be a center of Catholic and antiroyal intrigue, and in due course she was brought to the Tower and attainted for treason. She was not executed, however, and remained there for two years. But in 1541 Sir John Neville led a rising against the king in the north of England, and it was decided to execute Lady Salisbury summarily under the Bill of Attainder which had been passed earlier.

There was no time even to build a scaffold. The block was laid on the ground, and the old lady—she was then sixty-eight—was brought out. Normal scaffold etiquette was to mount the steps of the scaffold, pale, dignified, resigned, and then from the rails to address the crowd briefly, acknowledging your guilt or protesting your innocence, or sometimes, in rather muddled speeches, both at once. You then forgave and tipped the headsman, who was standing there in his hideous black mask. You partially disrobed to leave your neck bare and then knelt before the block, muttered a brief prayer and laid your head across it.

According to the popular account of the episode, Lady Salisbury flatly refused to do any such thing. Those were the actions of traitors, she said, and she had committed no treason. She would not lay her head on the block; it was up to the executioner to get her as best he could.

A dreadful scene then followed. She dodged around the block while the headsman chased her, taking swipes at her with his ax. She was old and encumbered with skirts, and he got her in the end, splitting her skull with his ax, so that the blood poured through her gray hair. The crowd was appalled. The people had come expecting, indeed hoping for, horrors, but they had imagined nothing as dreadful as this. A few seconds later, Lady Salisbury's head was off.

Such a desperate defiance of authority was typical of a special type of Britishwoman who has existed through the centuries. One cannot imagine a similar scene being played on the guillotine. Lady Salisbury, clearly, was an example of a British archetype, tough, formidable, dominating even in the most adverse circumstances, refusing to compromise, refusing to give in. The species has been constant across the centuries all the way from Boadicea resisting the might of Rome to Dame Irene Ward, the veteran Member of Parliament, recently making a protest demonstration in the House of Commons against the government's suppression of the views of backbenchers. One thinks of Florence Nightingale summoning the Prime Minister to her bedside; Gertrude Bell fighting her way up the Finsteraarhorn in a blizzard; Flora Macdonald in Scotland rescuing Bonnie Prince Charlie after the Battle of Culloden and rowing him to safety over the sea to Skye; and, especially of countless schoolmistresses and nannies quelling rebellious natives or rioting tribesmen in defense of their young charges. Lady Salisbury's courageous and hopeless defiance was only another example, and it was justly and rightly admired.

The anthem was finished; the organist struck up Mendelssohn's "Wedding March"; the bride and the bridegroom came down the aisle smiling happily, faintly pursued by the small children. We followed them out.

I remarked brightly to my neighbor, "No sign of Anne Boleyn's ghost today."

"Hush!" he said, rebukingly, "Not now!"

Indeed, Queen Anne's ghost is said to walk in the chapel and on Tower Green on certain occasions, but the whole question of ghosts and the Tower has been somewhat confused by the song of Stanley Holloway:

> With her head tucked underneath her arm,
> She haunts the Bloody Tower.

A friend of mine, who was once an officer in the Coldstream Guards, was on one occasion lieutenant of the Guard of the Tower and it was his duty, wearing his bearskin gray overcoat and Wellington boots, to make his round of the sentries. He admits now that he found it an unnerving experience to cross Tower Green in the silence of one o'clock in the morning, and he would stamp his feet and clank his sword on the ground to encourage himself.

One night one of his sentries saw smoke issuing from one of the cannon which stand around the White Tower. The smoke gradually took shape in the form of a human figure. Since the cannon had not been fired for several hundred years, the sentry was puzzled. He continued on his beat to the corner, where he found the other sentry patrolling the other side of the Tower and summoned him. The other sentry also saw smoke issuing from the cannon, but the shape that it took in the air seemed to him to be different. At this point both sentries decided to call out the Guard.

The Guard arrived in a hurry and was rather cross to find that it had been turned out in the middle of the night to investigate a ghost, particularly since the smoke from the cannon had now blown away. My friend investigated the stories in greater detail later and was inclined to believe them, particularly since the two accounts of the incident were slightly different. At any rate he felt it his duty to report the story next day to the lieutenant governor of the Tower.

"Ghosts? Nonsense!" the lieutenant governor said briskly. "The sentries must have seen the smoke coming from the guns."

The reply and the attitude were particularly British: the matter-of-fact acceptance of and manner of dealing with both history and the supernatural.

Avoiding the crowds queuing to see the crown jewels, I found myself talking to a skiing girlfriend of the bride's. Together we drove in a car to the House of Lords, where the wedding reception was being held.

In the sixteenth century it was customary to go from the Tower to Westminster by closed barge for trial and probable condemnation. The prisoner and escort would then return to Traitors' Gate and the Tower, the headsman carrying the ax before the prisoner, the blade pointing toward him to indicate to the watching crowds that he was to die. But in the twentieth century it seemed more appropriate to make the journey in a small Mini.

In the House of Lords, in the gallery behind the woolsack, we queued to kiss the bride and join the other champagne drinkers already arrived. Above me on the walls were portraits of the three unfortunate young women I had been thinking about earlier in the day: persecuted Queen Anne, promiscuous Queen Catherine, pious Queen Jane. I nodded at them and moved on down the gallery. It had been a Tudor day.

6

PUDDINGS AND PIES

☙ Following the events of the previous chapter, Harrison Ainsworth's romance *The Tower of London* was in my mind. It contains the following passage:

> The repast consisted of a cold chine of beef, little the worse for its previous appearance at the royal board; a mighty lumber pie, with a wall of pastry several inches thick, moulded to resemble the White Tower, and filled with a savoury mess of ham and veal, enriched by a goodly provision of forcemeat balls, each as large as a cannon-shot; a soused gurnet floating in claret; a couple of pullets stuffed with oysters, and served with a piquant sauce of oiled butter and barberries; a skirret pasty; an apple tansy; and a prodigious marrow pudding. Nor, in this bill of fare, must be omitted an enormous loaf, baked expressly for the giants, and compounded of nearly a bushel of mingled wheaten flour and barley, which stood at one end of the table, while at the opposite extremity was placed a nine-hooped pot of mead—the distance between each hoop denoting a quart of the humming fluid.

The question of Ainsworth's reliability as a chronicler of Tudor manners being left aside, the point, whether Tudor or Victorian, is clearly made. The British have been famed throughout the centuries as huge eaters. The size and the shape of Henry VIII's armor provide, perhaps, a more accurate measurement of Tudor appetites. In later centuries there are moments in fiction, in particular the novels of Henry Fielding, which provide further evidence, and for those who have not read the novels, the recent and popular film of *Tom Jones* reiterated the point. The British were huge eaters. They enjoyed their food and the pleasures of the table.

It was, of course, a Viking tradition, the trencherman boasting truthfully of the vast amount of roast beef and fowl and pie which he could eat. The Vikings went to France, as well as to England, taking with them their admiration for great appetites and great meals, a tradition which still continues in Normandy. From Normandy the Vikings, transmuted now into Normans, conquered England, bringing their habits with them, so that it was not only the Danish areas in the north but the whole of the ruling class of England which were proud of the size of their appetites. The stomach of William the Conqueror was famous at the time and has passed into history, as have those later royal stomachs of George IV and Edward VII.

The tradition of huge meals found perhaps its climax in Edwardian days and had its consequence in the ample figures of the eaters. My wife's grandfather, a very short man, weighed 280 pounds; my own grandfather, a taller man, weighed 100 pounds more, and the king himself was known informally to his friends as "Tum-tum." Fullness of girth was a matter for pride, and a gold watch chain or Albert would be hung across it to draw attention to the area.

Both in London and in country houses, Edwardian hostesses organized large and interminable meals for their guests. At Easton Hall in Essex, the home of the Earl of Warwick, where my grandmother was a frequent visitor, they ate a thousand eggs a week. Not all, of course, were eaten by the guests, a considerable number were consumed by the household staff and by their friends in the nearby village, but the guests themselves got through a considerable amount. I myself can remember English country-house breakfasts in the 1930's, the great sideboards with the chafing dishes kept warm by blue and smelly methylated flames. Even then, even during the Depression, the choice was bewildering: porridge, scrambled eggs, boiled eggs, sausages and bacon, kippers, ham, deviled kidneys, perhaps half a cold grouse, a large choice of marmalades. Not all of it was eaten, of course, for by then the British appetite was starting to fail, but it was still provided as a matter of etiquette. In one country house in Wales, three separate breakfasts were provided for each guest to choose from. A dozen poached eggs were served automatically every day; should nobody happen to want them, they were thrown away. A few miles away, unemployed miners were living on tea and bread and margarine.

It seems now like another world—not merely the social mores of our grandparents, but an experience within living memory of many of us. It is not only that the social inequality is now unthinkable. It is also that we can no longer imagine wishing to put so much food inside us or to spend so much time in doing it.

Some time during this century the British nation lost its appetite. An Edwardian courtier once said to his king, "Tum-tum, you are very fat!" And the king, a genial man, did not take it much amiss. One cannot imagine a similar remark ever being made to the next King Edward (now the Duke of Windsor), who, all his life, has preserved a slim, boyish figure. When Prince of Wales, he often refused lunch, to the dismay of hostesses who were trying to entertain him. As a gesture of renunciation it would have been incomprehensible to his grandfather.

By 1966 British wages had risen by 600 percent over their prewar level, but the Ministry of Agriculture found, with some surprise, that the Britishman was eating less beef than he had in prewar days, 10 pounds a head less each year. He put less butter on his bread, less bacon on his breakfast plates; he ate less fish, less mutton and lamb, less fresh fruit. True, he ate more pork, much of it processed in the form of pork pies or sausages, more chicken, more eggs, more canned fruit—all cheaper foods—and these filled the gap. But the fact remains that, despite an enormous increase in wages, in general standards of living, and in the amenities of life, the average Britishman was eating no more than he had during the Depression. Recently the downward trend seems to be accelerating. In 1958 he spent five shillings and threepence in every pound on food. By 1968 he was spending only four shillings and twopence. He was keeping his money for other things. James Thurber has said, "Seeing is deceiving, it's eating that's believing," and by this standard we must believe that something very strange happened to the British during this century, a symptom, or perhaps a cause, of many other reappraisals and changes.

The reasons are a matter for conjecture. In the upper classes, in the country-house set, it is all fairly obvious. First there was the war, which requisitioned their homes, removed their servants, and imposed food rationing. Then, after the war, there was the continued scarcity of servants and the acceptance of the burdens of income tax and surtax, which were expressly designed to bear most heavily upon the rich and the nearly rich. There are, of course, areas where the old traditions are still maintained. We read in the newspapers about the Duke of Marlborough's dinner parties, the soufflés prepared by a French chef. Sir John Vanbrugh designed Blenheim Palace with a fine disregard for time-and-motion study; the kitchens are a long way from the dining room, separated by drafty, stone-flagged passages. A number of footmen are, we understand, required to hold the various doors on the way open for the chef or his assistant, sprinting like an Olympic runner, so that the soufflé may travel from the oven to the table in the shortest possible time and without having fallen in a draft. But such achievements are unusual in the modern world.

It is not everyone who can manage to live in the style of Blenheim Palace. The owners of a country house these days live in a few rooms; the rest of the house is either open to the public or converted into apartments, depending on its age and interest. Servants who would have prepared and served and washed up the huge meals have gone to work in shops or offices or factories. It is one thing to instruct the cook and the butler on the dinner party they are to serve; it is quite another to prepare and serve it yourself. I recall a sharp controversy in my family. Some held that the lady of the house should see the cook every morning after breakfast in the kitchen, discussing the affairs of the kitchen and casting a keen, though tactful, eye over its running. The other point of view, represented by my mother—who had been brought up in the French tradition, where the lady breakfasted in her bedroom, probably in bed—was that the men should be left alone downstairs over their deviled kidneys, to discuss the day's sport, without frivolous feminine interruption. Obviously, therefore, the cook would come to see her in bed, to discuss the day's menus. The mistress would visit the kitchens, at rare and irregular intervals at some other time of day.

But of course, once you have to cook your own breakfast, the whole problem, the whole controversy, fades rapidly into oblivion, as does the wish for a large breakfast. Better, and easier, are cornflakes, a boiled egg, a Continental breakfast, bringing back perhaps memories of French or Swiss hotels, and, finally, simply a cup of coffee, which is all one finds one needs these days.

But the impoverishment of the upper classes does not provide the only reason for the increasing starvation of the British nation. The decline of the fabulous and now almost unbelievable standards was not fully compensated by a raising of standards among those who had previously been undernourished. For instance, we each now eat four and a half pounds less of butter in a year. Margarine, once the symbol of those on the dole, is now more popular than ever before, and its consumption has gone up by 33 percent from its level during the Depression. Some of this, of course, may be due to astute advertising. We are assured hourly on television that modern margarine is indistinguishable from, and indeed often better than, butter. Some of it may be due to the fear of coronary thrombosis, which is thought by some to be linked with eating animal fats. But the true reason, of course, is simply that margarine is cheaper, and the British are reluctant to spend money on food.

Food, indeed, is felt by many Britishmen to be an unnecessary evil, and the less of it, the better. The strong British streak of Puritanism is responsible for some of this. Shakespeare could write affectionately of Falstaff and his appetites, of the judge "in fair round belly, with good capon lined," but less than a hundred years later Oliver Cromwell preferred to fast on Christmas Day. After the Restoration there was a return to good living, and Samuel Pepys was able to write, "Strange to see how a good dinner and feasting reconciles everybody." The two traditions have continued in British life ever since, sometimes alternating, sometimes coexisting, complementing each other.

At the moment the Puritan streak seems to be in the ascendant, and it is a matter for conjecture if the longing for great meals will ever return. Britishmen now tend to boast about how little they eat and not how much, how few meals a day they require and not how many. Like cats, they do not like to be seen eating, except in a public restaurant by other diners. Curtains have to be drawn across the windows so that they cannot be watched at meals by passersby in the street outside and envied or perhaps despised. Parents of an overweight child, even though the reason be glandular, will feel bitterly ashamed. Mothers and nurses have fallen gleefully on the austere and partly misunderstood doctrines of Dr. Truby King, the New Zealand expert who campaigned against overfeeding babies. Children in old stories who stole apples from orchards, no doubt in a subconscious wish to get some vitamin C and balance their diets, were soundly beaten. Chocolates were regarded with suspicion and kept only for special occasions. Indeed, the three great Quaker families who founded the British sweet industry, the Cadburys, the Rowntrees and the Frys, felt so guilty about their businesses and their contribution to the national economy that they devoted most of their wealth and their time to public philanthropy.

Rationing imposed during the last war was hardly resisted at all. The British public was only too happy to be ordered to eat less and to spend less on food. The black market, which played such an important part in other war-ravaged countries, was barely noticeable in England. When I once asked a Frenchwoman about the black market during the German occupation, she said, "But, of course, we had to have a black market. We could not live on the rations." The British saw it differently, and the reasons were not entirely patriotic. Several years after the war, some members of the British Labour government suggested that rationing might continue forever. Was not rationing by book, it was asked, more equitable than rationing by price?

But this was going too far. In a world which had given up rationing, the British did not like to feel that they were still regulated by small books and smaller coupons. They liked to feel that they were free to buy beef and butter even if, in the event, they did not choose to do so. It was displeasing to be told by the Ministry of Food how much of the weekly meat ration would be issued in the attractively sounding "canned corned beef" and how much in the repulsively sounding "carcass meat." Still worse was it for the conservatively minded lovers of plain fare to be issued with such bizarre rations as reindeer steaks, whale steaks and the previously unheard-of fish called snoek. The Labour government was voted out of office, rationing was abolished, but the food on the table, apart from the elimination of reindeer, whales and snoek, did not change very much.

It was another Labour government which, for reasons of austerity, abolished the businessman's expense-account lunch, except in certain cases where export orders were involved. Britain was the only major commercial country to do so, but the move met with almost no opposition, even by businessmen themselves. Many businessmen feel guilty at eating big lunches at the taxpayer's expense, but the question of expense is largely irrelevant. Other than on rare occasions, the Britishman feels guilty about eating a big lunch at all. He is puzzled at the habit of, say, the Swiss, of closing their offices at noon every day and returning home for a substantial lunch. He prides himself on only needing a sandwich in the canteen, at the pub around the corner, even at his desk, and when you visit him in his office later in the afternoon, he will often find occasion to mention this. For, except in some parts of the North of England, where the Viking tradition survives, the British now disapprove of food. Perhaps this is a reemergence of the Puritan streak, or a reaction against earlier centuries of gluttony, or both.

What has remained unchanged throughout the centuries is the British suspicion of fancy food. The great feasts, the whole roast oxen, the sides of beef, the saddles of lamb, the legs of pork, the York hams are, in essence, plain food. The Britishman is sure that fancy food, messed-about food, is bad for you, and this certainly goes back much farther than Cromwell and the Puritans. Chaucer writes disapprovingly in the *Canterbury Tales* about the five ostentatiously new-rich tradesmen who brought a townsman with them to cook spices and stews. Everything about him, we are to infer, was unwholesome:

> They had brought a Cook with them, just for the occasion, so that he could boil chickens with their marrow-bones, sharp seasoning-powder and aromatic root. He was not slow in recognising a draught of London ale and knew how to roast, steam, boil and fry, make stews and bake a pie nicely. To me, however, it seemed a great pity that he had an open sore on his leg. As for minced chicken blancmange, well he could cook that with the best.

In *Wuthering Heights,* the child was given oatmeal porridge, "and nowt else," and therefore, because it was plain, grew strong and healthy. More recently, it was widely believed in Scotland that porridge with milk and, of course, sugar were bad for you (porridge is a plural noun in Scotland), but made with plain water and eaten with salt, they were a grand food and built fine lads. As we now know, such a diet causes rickets. The French have long understood British tastes in cooking. Food *à l'anglaise* means cooked in the plainest possible style. *Pommes à l'anglaise* means plain boiled potatoes. They knew how suspicious the British were of sauces, of anything which might conceal the taste or the quality of the original ingredients.

A reaction, however, set in under that Francophile King

Edward VII. Hostesses employed French chefs; their husbands were on cordial terms with the headwaiters and chefs of the most famous restaurants in Paris and the South of France. Sauces and soufflés were served in stately homes. But except in the few homes and a few London restaurants, this trend did not survive the First World War. However, it has, to some extent, revived in recent years, with the new passion for Continental holidays and may be particularly found in the stockbroker belts of Surrey and Cheshire. There young housewives, still wearing their Mediterranean suntans, their kitchens full of strings of Breton onions, will thumb through the recipes of Mrs. Elizabeth David, the leading British cookbook writer, will grow limp with the effort of making cannelloni or paella and, in an endeavor to regain the holiday spirit, will probably put far too much garlic into everything. When their husbands give them a break and take them out to dinner, it will probably be to the new little Italian or Dutch restaurant which has just opened in their town. Whether this neocosmopolitanism will survive the ingrained British distrust of fancy food, the continued reemergence of Puritanism, has yet to be seen. Certainly, it has caught on only among certain areas and classes. It is reassuring, though also a little saddening, to overhear a pretty girl in a bikini on a Mediterranean beach confiding to her friend, in her North Country voice, that she can't wait to get back to egg and chips and a proper cup of tea.

The great change in British eating habits was no doubt started by the Industrial Revolution. In an agrarian society, food seemed to be free, though it might take time and work. Vegetables were grown in the garden; a pig was kept. Home farms provided the eggs and the beef and the milk for the big house. It was available even if a man did not own it or grow it himself; it was often given to him as part of his wages, the final residue of the feudal system. But when the Britishman went to live in towns, everything changed. Food was no longer available; it had to be bought with money earned in some job, money which, in the opinion of the earner, could be better spent on something else. One of the problems which employers and governments have to face is that an employee or a schoolchild will go without, rather than spend money on something so unnecessary as a decent meal. One can admire the various ingenious attempts which have been made—subsidized canteens, luncheon vouchers,* cheap school meals, free milk in schools—to persuade the Britishman and his child to eat something sometime.

Food may be a necessary evil, but it is at least necessary. What the Britishman really asks is that it should not cost too much. Money is for things like cars, television sets, clothes, drinks, theater parties, holidays, refrigerators, electric hedge cutters and so on. More than a quarter of every pound the Britishman spends goes on his home. But money spent on food is often thought, privately, to be money wasted. A good wife, a good housekeeper, can manage on very little and prides herself on it. During the Depression the near-starving families were being continually lectured by social workers on how to make their money go further. During the last decade, two acquaintances of mine, one a doctor, the other a civil servant, carried out prolonged tests on their own bodies to prove that the human machine could work perfectly satisfactorily on a diet composed exclusively of, in one case, oatmeal and cod-liver oil and, in the other case, spaghetti and iron pills. In both cases the points were made, but in both cases the various committees involved felt that this was going too far and that even with the maximum possible publicity such a diet was unlikely to be acceptable in general, even to the economy-minded British housewife.

The answer to the dilemma was, of course, cheap food, and a cheap food system has been officially adopted ever since the repeal of the Corn Laws in 1846. This has led to some strange government policies. Instead of tariffs or price-support agreements, farm subsidies have been preferred. Dumping of surplus produce by other countries has been encouraged, and British prices have been held down to this competitive level, offset by payments to the farmers. This produces the incongruous situation in which the government thinks it frankly an economy to

* These are provided by some employers and are exchangeable in restaurants.

import food from abroad, and a recent disastrous outbreak of foot-and-mouth disease in cattle was hailed in some quarters as a national blessing because of the millions it saved in farm subsidies. Only a very strange economy indeed, one feels, could manage to find comfort in such a horrible plague. But then there are many economists who feel that British agriculture should be discontinued totally and all food imported from abroad.

To walk around a branch of the International Stores (and what chain store was ever more appropriately named?) is to wonder at the vast distances that British food has traveled before it reaches the kitchens. Beef from the Argentine, lamb from New Zealand, bread made from wheat originating in Canada, bacon from Denmark, sardines from Portugal, eggs from Finland, strawberries from Holland, even Cheddar cheese from France—and the list continues a very long way. "It all comes from abroad these days," said a woman, moving around the counters beside me. British farming, already the most highly mechanized in the world and already producing the largest crop per acre, could, it is estimated, be expanded to produce another hundred million pounds' worth of produce a year. The effect on the balance of payments problems would be considerable. But the snags are daunting: either a large increase in the national allocation for farm subsidies or a general increase in prices, both for home produce and for dumped produce from abroad. This would simply result in the British family's buying and eating less food. For what Britishman would not willingly give up his breakfast or his lunch, or both, to save up for a new car or a holiday on the Costa Brava?

But of course, a certain amount of food, unwelcome though it may be, does still find its way to the Britishman's table. It will probably be imported, processed, deep frozen in the supermarket and known in the official jargon as convenience food, and it can be itemized and described. Breakfast, in the traditional sense, has almost entirely disappeared. Instead of the original kedgeree and kippers, a bowl of cornflakes will now suffice. A Continental breakfast of bread and jam is both more sophisticated and more laborsaving. Or perhaps simply a cup of tea or a cup of coffee (depending on the breakfaster's social class) will suffice. A large proportion of British schoolchildren, it has been revealed, go to school each morning without any breakfast inside them.

For the midday meal, a greater variety of trends is apparent, and here at once the question of class raises its head. It is indeed impossible to write about British eating habits, or indeed about the British at all, without bringing in the question of class differences. Other nations, of course, have their class differences, equally firm and clear to the knowledgeable eye, but perhaps no other nation parades them as publicly as the British. The Frenchman, whether he be a marquis or a taxi driver, will refer to his midday meal as *déjeuner*. The German, however he places himself in the social scale, will call it *Mittagessen,* but in Britain the great divide between those who call the midday meal lunch and those who call it dinner is unbridgeable. (When I was working on a West Indian sugar estate, I found that many of the senior staff, following old plantation tradition, referred to the midday meal as breakfast, though it was a substantial meal with meat, often preceded by rum punch or gin swizzles. The laborers in the cane fields, for some reason, referred to the midday meal as tea. The rest of the staff referred to it as lunch or dinner, depending on their family background, and the possibilities for confusion were therefore almost unlimited.)

The essential difference between lunch and dinner is largely a question of name. The man who eats "lunch" may have it at his club, if he is lucky enough to have a club near his office: an excellent meal of potted shrimps, roast lamb, and Stilton. Or he may have a plate of cold roast beef and Russian salad at the nearest pub, eaten at a counter while those waiting for his stool breathe down his neck. If the local pub does not boast a snack bar, lunch may be, more simply and cheaply, a sausage roll or a Scotch egg, with a pint of beer. It may be a plate of stew in the office canteen, should such a thing exist, or it may be a slice of overdone roast beef in a small, cheap restaurant which accepts luncheon vouchers, or, simplest and cheapest of all, it may be a sandwich, bought in the pub or brought from home and eaten at the office desk. By sandwich I do not mean a French sandwich, a fresh, crusty loaf filled with Camembert; still less an American sandwich, a hot turkey sandwich with mashed potato, gravy, and cranberry sauce, a giant club sandwich or even a triple-decker. I mean two slices of thin presliced bread, joined together by a thin slice of canned gristly ham or perhaps only by a meager spread of meat paste.

His employee, eating his dinner in the factory canteen, will be having a hot, cheap, subsidized meal of stew and plum duff, washed down with tea; or egg and chips in a roadside drive-in; or, if he is far from base, sandwiches, those great social levelers.

Their wives, whether they call it lunch or dinner, will make do with a very light snack, at home or out at work (more than half the working women in Britain are married). At best, they will eat with the other secretaries at the little café around the corner, where they accept luncheon vouchers.

Tea, like lunch, is another source of social confusion. Care must be taken to distinguish between "tea" and "his tea," between "afternoon tea" and "high tea." I recall the distress of a Canadian friend, an impoverished music student, who, by way of returning some hospitality, invited my wife to tea at a famous London teashop and then, to the waiter's horror, ordered sausage and baked beans, when he should have ordered scones and small triangular sandwiches. But then, except for children, afternoon tea has largely ceased to exist. Served at half-past four, it is a gentle, though starchy, meal, with scones, hot buttered toast and Fuller's sugar-coated walnut cake. It exists now largely as a social occasion, probably on Sundays, and most of the food will probably be left because the guests—and the hostess herself—are dieting.

The other sort of tea takes place two hours later and is a much solider affair, indeed probably the main meal of the day. Frozen hamburger and chips (what the Americans call French fries and the French, *pommes frites*), egg and chips, ham and chips, sausage and chips, fish fingers and chips, followed by canned fruit and homemade cake and possibly a small piece of cheese. The whole will be washed down with great quantities of tea and consumed while watching television. When the day's viewing is over, a further light snack, called supper, may be eaten before going to bed.

But he who has had lunch in the middle of the day, and not dinner, will have dinner when he finally reaches home. This may vary a good deal, depending on whether there are guests, on whether his wife fancies herself on her cooking, on the size of the family budget, on whether he has children or not. It may be lasagna from the nearest Italian delicatessen, it may be a Spanish omelet, it may be cauliflower au gratin, it may even be a mixed grill, or it may, once again, be frozen fish fingers, served on a special table in front of the television set, another great social leveler. It sometimes seems to me that the whole British race lives exclusively on that strange dish, fish fingers.

The basic change in the British attitude to its meals is one not of taste or of appetite, but of self-esteem. A man no longer prides himself on his great appetite; he thinks more of the attractions of a youthful waistline. A woman no longer prides herself on her cooking; instead, she wishes to be admired for being a good "manager," for feeding her family as economically as possible, for not asking for an increase in the housekeeping money. Her husband, with other demands on his funds, is only too happy to go along with this. A lady of my acquaintance was quartering commandant of a military hospital during the war, and she prided herself on feeding her soldiers on only half the ration allowance to which they were entitled. This was, to her, good housekeeping.

It was possible, in the past, to compensate for economical managing and cheap ingredients by careful cooking; the cheaper cuts of meat, such as neck, could be concealed in shepherd's pie or stews or hot pots. But the average housewife nowadays rarely has the time or inclination for this. Other things come first. She probably has a job. Even if she hasn't, she is proud of her home. Stimulated by advertising, she wishes to be admired for her polished lino, her cared-for furniture, the whiteness of her children's clothes, her own appearance, the increasing freedom and opportunities of her life. She no longer wishes to be a drudge at the kitchen stove, and like her neighbors, she is quite content to feed her family on snacks. The one meal of the week which she is prepared to cook, in the old-fashioned sense, is the midday meal on Sunday, lunch or dinner, according to which side of the divide she places herself. She will cook this on Sunday morning, while her husband beds out the asters or polishes the car, depending on his circumstances, followed by a Sunday-morning drink, either in the local pub or with friends. It is most unlikely that either she or her husband will go to church, but it is possible that she will have guests, friends or relations, and her husband will entertain these with bottled beer or gin and tonics, according to the family's class, while the wife serves up.

The meal will no longer be roast beef, Yorkshire pudding (or popover), roast potatoes and cabbage, followed by apple pie. It will now almost certainly be roast chicken with frozen chips and frozen peas. The swing from beef to chicken is fairly recent. It is due partly to the wish to manage economically (chicken is cheaper than beef) and partly to the fact that in past, feudal days, chicken was associated with the gentry, and therefore, today it has some value as a status symbol. But the change also explains, perhaps, the increasing anemia of the British people. The matron of a large London maternity hospital told me that most of her patients were anemic when they were admitted and had to be given iron pills. Game, in the form of roast pheasant, partridge, duck, venison and so on, may be served at the tables of those who call the meal lunch. The bird or the beast will almost certainly have been shot by the man of the house or a friend on a previous Saturday. But game will never be found on the tables of those who call the midday meal dinner. The man of the household does not go out shooting; his wife and children do not like the taste of game, and it is not acceptable, even as a status symbol. Servants, it was explained to me when I was a boy, would never eat game; it could only be served in the dining room. In the servants' hall, they had to have "butcher's meat," which had been bought with money. It was part of their wages; they would not want pheasants which had been shot for nothing. As advice it was not really very helpful; servants and servants' halls hardly exist today, but eating game is still part of the great divide.

After the roast chicken, today's housewife will serve not apple pie, but canned or bottled fruit, perhaps with ice cream or with frozen pink mousse. One of the slogans at the British Pavilion at the 1967 Montreal Expo was "We believe in puddings." But except in the North of England, this is rather misleading. Except sometimes in institutions, gone are the days of spotted dick and black treacle, of apple charlotte and plum duff. Puddings require too much work, and anyway they are fattening. The housewife, however, may well bake a cake from time to time, since this can be offered to friends and neighbors who drop in for morning coffee and given to the children when they return home from school. If she has the time, she may also bottle fruit and make jam, since these are both ways in which she can pride herself on her economical managing and prevent perishable fresh fruit from being wasted.

The great meal of the year, the one to which the British housewife is prepared to give her time and energy without any stint, is Christmas lunch or dinner. She may spend five hours preparing this meal, perhaps more if she is entertaining a large family party and has a big turkey to cook. The meal is standard in every household: roast turkey, stuffed and served with all the trimmings, followed by plum pudding served in flames, with brandy or rum butter, followed by mince pies, cheese, stone ginger, sweets, and anything else she can think of. It is her great triumph, the culinary achievement of the year, but not one which she or her family would expect her to repeat for a long time. I was talking once to a young man in a pub in Hampshire, and he expressed the strong opinion that all pubs should be closed by law on Christmas morning. "You go into a pub, just meaning to have a pint and say Merry Christmas, and then you meet some of your mates and you have another pint or two, could be six or seven, and then you go home to your Christmas dinner and you just don't fancy it. Perhaps you throw up all over the table, and that sort of puts people off. I mean, it's not fair on your Mum, is it? She's been cooking that dinner since six o'clock in the morning. They really ought to make a law, shutting the pubs on Christmas morning. I mean, you owe it to your Mum, don't you, after all that she's done. Christmas night, of course, you can have as many pints as you like, it's all over by then. See what I mean?" I saw what he meant.

It is unlikely that he or, for obvious reasons, his Mum would have been to church. The favorite British church service of the year, the one that brings in even the most tepid among the faithful, is the annual Harvest Festival Service. This is essentially a pagan festival, though the rejoicing is now couched in formal terms of gratitude to the Almighty. The churches will be filled with flowers and fruit, giant vegetable marrows, chosen wholly for their weight and size, sheaves of corn, great loaves, fresh and crusty, perhaps six feet long. Both the loaves and the sheaves of corn have to be carefully arranged beforehand by the churchwardens or the rector, for neither is readily available in the world of the combine harvester and the wrapped sliced loaf. But the effort is gladly made, recalling fleetingly, nostalgically, the lush, fertile landscapes and harvest fields in the pictures of Constable and Samuel Palmer. But then, with typical Britishness, the matter is quickly forgotten, the congregation returns home to its roast broiler chicken and canned peaches, and the decorations of the church—the flowers, the fruit, the vegetables, the bread—are sent to the local hospital. Plenteousness is not a subject that the Britishman wishes to think about for very long.

Visiting gourmets from abroad often say kindly that British food at its best has been, and sometimes still can be, the best in the world. Indeed, can a greater meal be devised than half a dozen Whitstable oysters, roast grouse and Stilton? It is a meal which I have only eaten once in my lifetime, but in these meager days one may perhaps briefly cast a nostalgic backward glance at those great British dishes which are now seen so rarely: roast sirloin with horseradish sauce, roast saddle of lamb with red currant jelly, roast leg of pork with crackling and apple sauce, roast venison, spotted dick, Devonshire cream, treacle tart, angels on horseback, toast and dripping, pigs' trotters, brawn, cockles, tripe and onions, Lancashire hot pot with red cabbage, haggis. Shall we ever see them again, or is it fish fingers forever? It is a long way both in time and in thought from Falstaff to Twiggy, both essentially British characters, typical of their time, and as we measure the distance from steak, kidney, lark and oyster pudding, Dr. Johnson's favorite dish, to the television snack, we may chart, rather sadly, the changing face of Britain.

7

THE DRINKING MAN AND HIS IMAGE

As with food, so with drink. It is a long way from the stirrup cup to the breathalyzer, but the reasons for the changes in drinking habits are slightly different from those in the eating habits and revealing perhaps in a different way.

The tradition, once again, starts with the Vikings. A whole roast ox needs many gallons of ale to wash it down. A man was as proud of his thirst as he was of his appetite. The baron in his castle with his hogsheads of ale is a familiar figure in the British race memory. Quantity, rather than quality and the appreciation of taste, was the point, and the drink was beer or, to give it its older and more poetic name, ale. French or Spanish wines, Bordeaux or sack, were acceptable, but were not always available in the quantities required for such Gargantuan and exemplary drinking. Mead, a medieval drink made from honey, was also on tap, but like wine, it was more for sipping than for gulping. It can still be found occasionally in Britain and I have myself drunk it—a sweet, pleasant drink, but it would be difficult to imagine drinking a whole gallon of it at a sitting.

Shakespeare looked back on the old tradition in two of his plays. Falstaff, as might be expected, praised the virtues of sherris-sack:

> Skill in the weapon is nothing without sack, for that sets it a-work; and learning a mere hoard of gold kept by a devil, till sack commences it and sets it in act and use. Hereof comes it that Prince Harry is valiant; for the cold blood he did naturally inherit of his father, he hath, like lean, sterile and bare land, manured, husbanded and tilled with excellent endeavour of drinking good and good store of fertile sherris, that he is become very hot and valiant. If I had a thousand sons, the first humane principle I would teach them should be, to forswear thin potations and to addict themselves to sack.

Hamlet, however, a more austere man, did not much care for Viking drinking habits.

> (A flourish of trumpets, and ordance shot off, within.)
>
> HAMLET: The king doth wake to-night and takes his rouse,
> Keeps wassail, and the swaggering up-spring reels;
> And, as he drains his draughts of Rhenish down,
> The kettle-drum and trumpet thus bray out
> The triumph of his pledge.
>
> HORATIO: Is it a custom?
>
> HAMLET: Ay, marry, is't:
> But to my mind, though I am native here,
> And to the manner born, it is a custom
> More honour'd in the breach than the observance.
> This heavy-headed revel east and west
> Makes us traduced and tax'd of other nations:
> They clepe us drunkards. . . .

The Viking tradition not only was instinctive, the reaction of a lusty and vigorous people, who knew they were on top of the world, but were always uncertain of the future, the next day, the next meal. It was also an unconscious protection against the danger of drinking water, a prudent one in an age of plagues. In the Middle Ages we hear that: "Not a man ever tastes water, save for a penance." More recently, my father-in-law, who never touched water in his life, was so appalled to hear that his son at Eton was being forced to drink water that he sent him a barrel of beer, so that the boy and his friends might be spared this terrible danger. The housemaster thanked my father-in-law politely, but what happened to the beer is not known. It did not reach the boy and his friends, who were only thirteen at the time.

The drinking man's image, then, was one of being able to drink huge quantities, and the result was inevitably a great deal of drunkenness, especially among the upper classes, who could afford the beer. To be as drunk as a lord was entirely proper, and the lesser classes, of course, followed the jolly example, as and when they could. But by the Renaissance a new image was developing. Wine was becoming the upper-class drink rather than ale or mead. The aristocracy still prided themselves on their thirst and their great capacity for liquor, but they also prided themselves on how well they could hold it. It was no longer right to be as drunk as a lord; instead he was expected to hold his wine like a gentleman. Cassius, in *Othello,* is not admired for his weak head, for the ease with which Iago makes him drunk. Marlowe, killed in a tavern brawl, was not respected for his drinking habits any more than for the company he kept. Falstaff was giving way to such fastidious characters as Mr. Bingley and Mr. Darcy.

However, provided it was unaccompanied by drunkenness, heavy drinking was still a matter for pride. In the eighteenth century, to be a one-bottle man was to have a somewhat feeble, namby-pamby public image. Better a two-bottle man, like William Pitt the Younger. Better still a three-bottle man, even if it led inexorably to gout. The bottles were of port, and there are few of us today who could drink two or three bottles of port in a sitting. Either, we feel, the bottles must have been smaller or the wine weaker, or else the British thirst, like the British head, is not what it was.

It was widely believed, too, that a considerable quantity of alcohol brightened and polished the wits instead of dulling them. Charles James Fox, perhaps the most dazzling of all political debaters, would drink heavily in his clubs before going down to the House of Commons to devastate his opponents. Lord Birkenhead, as celebrated as an after-dinner speaker as he was as a lawyer, always, it is said, spoke better if the wine had flowed freely at dinner. The same is reported of G. K. Chesterton. But once again the image is changing. Few politicians today would prepare for an important debate by drinking heavily, however strong their heads. If they did so, they would not expect to retain their reputation with their party and the public. Winston Churchill alone was not afraid to drink champagne before a great parliamentary occasion, and in this, as in so many other things, he was perhaps the last of his line.

But on other social levels the Viking tradition is still sometimes found. Sergeant majors still pride themselves on the amount of beer they drink on Saturday nights in the sergeants' mess. A brewer's drayman of my acquaintance, who of course receives a substantial quantity of free beer, both from the brewery and from the pubs where he delivers, would be ashamed not to drink at least twenty pints during the day. In a country pub, you may often hear a man boast of the occasions when he has drunk ten or fifteen Guinnesses during the evening, though I have noticed that such achievements are always in the past and that nowadays he seems to manage on two or three light ales. And it is to be noted that such heroic performances are achieved only with beer. The man who drinks a bottle of whisky a day does not boast of it, nor does he expect to receive any admiration. Nor does the image extend to women. Throughout the centuries, ladies have been expected to manage on a small glass of Madeira or a little ratafia, which have been superseded in the modern pub world by such mild drinks as shandy or Babycham, and a woman is expected to make one of these last the whole evening.

The instrument which has finally succeeded in tarnishing and blurring the Viking image is the car. The Vikings loved horses, as well as drinking, and indeed the two went very well together. They were part of the same legend, part of the cult of the conqueror, and until the last few years, the two cults have complemented each other. One thinks of hard riding and hard drinking, the stirrup cup at the meet, the hunting flask in the pocket, the potboy running out to meet the coach with steaming tankards, the drunken coachman himself, a perennial figure in British folklore. The whole idea of "one for the road" belonged to an age when it was unthinkable to mount a horse or the box of a coach completely sober. You rode or drove better, it was assumed, with some good wine or beer inside you, and, if the worst came to the worst, the sober horse knew the way home. All you had to do was remain in the saddle. But in the car age the two images finally clash. Statistics, breathalyzers, prosecutions are harassing the dwindling number who believe that they drive, as they ride, better after a couple of drinks. It is not the faithful sober horse but the faithful sober wife who gets the happy reveler safely home from the pub. Outside is a poster proclaiming: "If you drink, don't drive," and one wonders what the Saxon kings Hengist and Horsa would have thought of that.

Side by side with the Viking image of the British drinking man is another image: the connoisseur, the man who prefers quality to quantity, who knows his way around the vineyards and wine lists of the world and assumes that a glass of very good wine is better than a bottle of mediocre wine. It is not clear when he first appeared on the British scene; possibly he existed in Roman times, for, under the Roman Empire, Britain was celebrated for her excellent wine. One feels that the weather must have changed considerably in Britain since those days. A little wine is still made at Hambledon in Hampshire, but its owner often has to harvest his grapes in the most difficult circumstances. With the cooling of the British climate, the departure of the Romans, the arrival of the mead-and-ale-drinking Saxons, the connoisseur disappeared from the scene. He reappeared more definitively in the eighteenth century when the British took to traveling abroad for pleasure, as opposed to trade or military operations. The young scion of the big house would return from his grand tour of Europe an expert, not only on Italian painting and Greek statues, but also on wine. He would begin to collect a cellar of good Burgundies and Rhine wines. He would be proud to offer his guests only the best claret or Marsala. On the birth of his eldest son, a year or two later, he would lay down a case, or perhaps several cases, of vintage port, to be broached on the boy's twenty-first birthday.

It was an age of elegance, a time for the connoisseur, and the British were the wine connoisseurs of Europe, more even than the French or the Germans, or at least, they believed themselves to be so. They mispronounced, Anglicized and nicknamed their favorite wines: sherry, port, claret, hock (attributed to Queen Victoria, who could not stand hearing her butler coughing, "Hochheimer, my Lord?" right around the table), even Bungho, a Peninsular War corruption of the Portuguese *vinho*. In our own day we have the lovable Newts, Ernest Bevin's pronunciation of his favorite wine, Nuits St. Georges. The British not only bought the wines, but often bought the vineyards, too, settling locally and marrying the daughter of the next vineyard owner. The bulk of the wine produced in Jerez or Oporto is made and owned by Anglo-Spanish or Anglo-Portuguese families.

The houses themselves usually have British names: Cockburn, Dow, Graham, Williams and Humbert, Sandeman—though this is often denied locally. I have been assured in Spain that both Williams and Duff-Gordon are old Spanish names, and indeed by now they are. The drinks that they produce, too, are tempered specially to the British palate. Vintage port, such as is drunk in England by provosts in their colleges, or judges in their halls, or Guards officers in their clubs and messes, is difficult to find in Portugal or indeed anywhere outside Britain. It has become not only a British institution, but a British ritual. A lawyer, newly qualified for the bar, dines in his inn for the occasion. He and the other fledgling barristers are summoned to the high table, and there they stand in a line before the senior benchers. They are not, of course, invited to sit down, but each one is given a ceremonial glass of vintage port, which they drink, standing there, feeling rather foolish. Such consumption of port is naturally rather limited, and there are disquieting rumors that port itself is going out of fashion. In the universities the younger men prefer claret or white wine or even beer after their meal. The port shippers are making some effort to combat this by introducing port to a younger, more swinging generation, and it is to be hoped, in the interests of preserving a great drink, that they will succeed.

The arrival of the wine connoisseur led also to the appearance of his counterpart, the wine showoff, the wine snob, the wine bore. Usually less expert than the connoisseur, he is noted for his high-flown, precious diction and the mumbo jumbo which he has created around a simple pleasure. Several writers have had fun at his expense.

The wine snob is a peculiarly British invention. In France, such flights of fancy are firmly eschewed. Professional winegrowers, Chevaliers du Tastevin, use a tougher, more professional language. Perhaps the wine snob, as distinct from the expert, is on the way out. I seem to have met him more rarely in recent years.

The drinking man's image, then, has changed considerably with the centuries. The Viking has largely gone; the connoisseur is falling a victim to more austere times; the wine bore is more a subject for satire than for admiration. They have been, to a large extent, replaced by the families in the stockbroker belt who experiment with Continental cooking and learned to enjoy cheap local wines on their last holiday abroad. A glass of inexpensive vin rosé makes the homemade risotto or boeuf Stroganoff more enjoyable, more nostalgic. The cheap table wines now being drunk increasingly in Surrey and Cheshire are, like homemade movies, a pleasant reminder of the family's last Mediterranean holiday.

This, however, is not much of a drinking man's image. The true new image is something more sinister, the image of the man who needs a drink.

Alcoholism, as distinct from Viking and medieval roistering, was a product of the Industrial Revolution. In the misery and squalor and cold of the mill towns of the North of England, twopenceworth of gin was, in the saying, "the quickest way out of Manchester." After a couple of drinks on a Saturday, the city was no longer a cheerless prison; Glasgow belonged to you; the misery produced the consolation, gin or rum—particularly gin, known affectionately as Auntie's Downfall. Beer was weak, poor stuff which kept out little of the cold and hardly let you forget anything. It was better with gin; as the advertisement said, "Drunk for a penny, dead drunk for twopence."

The result was a wide and sudden spread of alcoholism among the working classes. One of the saddest consequences was the large and growing number of alcoholic children. Children were, perhaps, the principal victims of the Industrial Revolution, working unbelievable hours in mills and foundries, beaten, underclothed, underfed. It was hardly surprising that they, too, sought to escape from Manchester. There were no restrictions at all on the sale of alcohol to children until 1839, and then only to prohibit the sale of spirits to children under sixteen. A survey carried out in 1834 on fourteen London pubs, revealed more than 18,000 visits by children within the space of a week.

The Duke of Wellington was the first to do anything about it. In 1830 his government passed an act forbidding beerhouses to sell spirits. Almost overnight, Britain was changed back from a gin-drinking country to a beer-drinking country. A heavy beer-drinking country, it is true, and regarded indulgently by employers, who thought it kept the people happy. Many farm laborers received part of their wages in beer or cider. Pubs were used, not only as drinking places, but as pay offices, meeting halls, committee rooms, Army billets, all of which assisted the consumption of beer. Hangovers and absenteeism on a Monday morning (keeping Saint Monday, as it was called) became in some areas a ritual, but at least the move was in the right direction. Beer was less harmful than gin.

Further efforts were made later in the nineteenth century by philanthropists and social workers, by such bodies as the Band of Hope and the Church of England Temperance Society. All drink was forbidden in pubs to children under eighteen. Alcohol was taxed and became correspondingly more expensive, though, with rising wages, this was no more a deterrent to drinking than it is today. But the real deterrent was the improved conditions. Life was no longer so unendurable; there were better things to do in Manchester and Glasgow than sink into oblivion.

The North of England, as might be expected, is still the drinking heart of England. Salford, near Manchester, maintains its lead for the highest number of convictions for drunkenness, though many people might have guessed that Glasgow was a strong competitor. I have found Liverpool, when the pubs shut, to be a noisy city, though perhaps this was more due to teen-age Saturday night high spirits than to more traditional debauches. But the average British drinking man in this age is unlikely to be an alcoholic. There are estimated to be only 300,000 in Britain, and the number is thought to be decreasing. Certainly the number of cases of public drunkenness has gone down, though on special occasions the Britishman may pretend to be drunker than he really is, to make a party go or for the sake of Auld Lang Syne.

Historically, social tendencies tend to descend through the various class levels from Norman baron to Lancashire mill hand, but with alcoholism it is working the other way. Dying out in the working classes, it is growing among the middle levels. The car worker in Coventry, the farm worker in Martyr Worthy are likely to be fairly abstemious, enjoying an occasional pint of mild beer or a light ale. It is in the middle classes, the more affluent social groups, that the affliction now seems to be growing. It is the overworked and tired business executive, hard pressed and with many problems on his hands, perhaps insecure in his job, who succumbs most readily to the temptations of the saloon bar, the snuggery, the cocktail lounge, the nineteenth hole at the golf club. Never drunk, never sober, topping up throughout the day on pink gins and gin and tonics and whisky and sodas, he tries to screw himself up once again for the vital morning conference, for the crucial afternoon meeting, for the pages of figures and reports in his dispatch case. He risks daily the dangers of a breathalyzer test and a prosecution for drunken driving, or that one day he may go a little too far and that one of his superiors may notice what it is that keeps him going and disapprove.

This is rather a sad picture of the British drinking man—not at the moment, fortunately, a very widespread one. A jollier and more typical picture of the Britishman in his surroundings is seen in the local pub, that supremely British institution, which is neither a bar nor a club nor a café, but something all its own, which rarely survives transporting to foreign cities. Dr. Johnson wrote: "As soon as I enter the door of the tavern I experience an oblivion from care and a freedom from solitude." And most Britishmen, myself included, would heartily agree with him. The sense of peace, of relief, of refuge to be found in a British pub is not to be found in a London cocktail bar, no matter how smart and expensive, or in a hotel lounge, no matter how pleasantly furnished. A lot of a pub's charm is its feeling of coziness, of being hidden from the outside world, of providing the womb, to which, it is said, we all wish secretly to return. Certainly it must be enclosed, for the Britishman does not like to be seen drinking, except by his fellow drinkers. Even on summer days, the door must be kept shut, there must be net curtains over the windows, and at the first hint of dusk, curtains must be drawn. Frosted glass, bottle glass, bubble glass in the windows are useful in preserving the privacy of the British drinking man, especially in dark northern streets where the lights have to be on even at midday. Various explanations are suggested for this; a man does not like to be seen drinking, especially by Puritan or temperance-minded acquaintances in the street outside. Somebody may tell his wife that he stopped by on his way home from work for a pint. A visit to the pub is something about which he feels guilty and enjoys feeling guilty.

But the real reason is the wish for coziness, to shut out for a moment the outside world and to keep his thoughts and his eyes firmly inside the pub. In this he is the opposite of his French counterpart, who likes to sit outside on his café pavement, watching the world go by, even in quite chilly weather. In London streets the pavements are rarely wide enough for terraces, even if there should be any demand for them, but country pubs often provide a garden with roses or a lawn beside a river for their clients to use. However, even on a warm August evening, the British drinking man will prefer to remain in the dark saloon bar with net curtains over the windows and the empty grate, rather than take a few steps out onto a sunlit lawn, with roses and hollyhocks and the distant view of the South Downs.

We all have in our mind our picture of the ideal pub, whether in a city or in the country. It will be old, with great beams; there will be chintz curtains and a warm red carpet, a blazing fire. There will be Toby jugs on the mantelpiece, and the publican behind the bar, a genial and friendly man, will look rather like a Toby jug. There will be good company, and several friends who use the pub regularly will be already there. There will be a choice of beer, both draft and bottled, and it will, of course, stock our favorite beer. For my taste, this would be Bass, Worthington, Flowers or Whitbread, but others will have different preferences. It will serve hot and cold snacks, but it will not have a restaurant, as this moves it into a different category and attracts a different type of trade. The landlord will be glad to see everybody, a regular customer or stranger, whether he is drinking gin and tonic or light ale, whether he is spending a lot or a little. Other luxuries, such as ice, car parks and washing facilities, are desirable but not nearly so important.

A vivid description of this type of British pub, in the last century, was given by Thomas Hardy in *Far from the Madding Crowd:*

> Jacob, on receiving the order to see if the liquor was warm enough, placidly dipped his forefinger into it by way of thermometer and having pronounced it nearly of the proper degree, raised the cup and very civilly attempted to dust some of the ashes from the bottom with the skirt of his smock-frock, because Shepherd Oak was a stranger.
>
> "A clane cup for the shepherd," said the maltster commandingly.
>
> "No—not at all," said Gabriel, in a reproving tone of considerateness. "I never fuss about dirt in its pure state, and

> when I know what sort it is." Taking the mug he drank an inch or more from the depth of its contents, and duly passed it to the next man. "I wouldn't think of giving such trouble to neighbours when there's so much work to be done in the world already," continued Oak in a moister tone, after recovering from the stoppage of breath which is occasioned by pulls at large mugs.
>
> "A right sensible man," said Jacob.

It is possible, even in this age of diminished comfort, to find pubs all over the country which provide this standard of hospitality. But all too often, and increasingly, we are finding a very different sort of pub. This is a bleak and chilly place, with a small, all-night fire, smoldering in the grate, giving smoke but no heat. Instead of wooden benches and Windsor chairs, there are leatheretteen settees; the bar is made of plastic, and there are plastic flowers and brass Buddhas on the mantelpiece. Taped music has been switched on, rather too loud, playing the same tunes over and over again. There are plastic tiles on the floor instead of carpet. Everywhere there is a plethora of brewers' publicity knickknacks. The landlord will be a thin, sour man, more interested in the television set in his own rooms than his customer. When he does speak, it will be to grumble about his income tax or the small profit which he makes on a pint of beer. There will be strip lighting over the bar and only a small choice of beers and whiskies available. You will probably be the only customer, alone with the taped music and the distant sound of television.

Myself, I always imagine that I have visited more pubs in Britain than anyone not actively engaged in the liquor trade. For one who is neither a Viking nor an alcoholic, but simply a follower of Dr. Johnson, I reckon to have spent more of my time in pubs than any of my friends and colleagues. Indeed, I consider I have spent more time in pubs than anywhere else on earth except bed. And I think I could best give a picture of the British drinking man at his friendliest and indeed add some more vital touches to my portrait of the Britishman himself, by describing four typical but different, very different, British pubs.

The first one is in the City of London, just off Bishopsgate. Deserted in the evening, it is full at lunchtime with solicitors' clerks, small stockbrokers, bank cashiers, assistant managers of insurance companies, the lesser cogs in the great wheel of the City. The pub will be crowded, the voices clamoring; the talk may be of business, the ins and outs of normal commercial dealing, none of it particularly confidential or interesting. Or among friends, it may be about cars or gardening or holidays or families. Everybody stands, shoulder to shoulder, a drink in one hand, a sausage roll or a sandwich in the other. The publican will not be noticeably in evidence; the drinks will be served by a blond barmaid, who will chat up her regular customers as long as she has the time. The drinks will be mostly beer, probably bitter or Guinness, the bitter drunk out of a glass mug, the Guinness out of a glass like an inverted pear. The higher salaried, the wearier, those with bigger burdens on their shoulders may drink pink gins or gin and tonics or even whisky. No women will be present; the secretaries and the typists will be lunching at nearby cafés with their luncheon vouchers, sitting down and drinking tea or coffee. Across the room from the bar there is a buffet table with a white tablecloth, and behind it great ribs of rare beef and hams and a man dressed as a chef. Those with the money, the time, and the appetite will perch on high stools in front of the counter, if they can find a place. They will lunch off a plate of cold ham or tongue or pork pie with Russian salad and beets, followed by biscuits and cheese. If they are sophisticated, they may easily drink a glass of wine, probably Beaujolais, which is sold here by the glass. The pub may be very old or recently redecorated. It may have old glass in the windows or a modern plastic bar. But nobody will notice the decor; the place is much too crowded.

By way of contrast, my second pub is near the docks at Liverpool and accordingly frequented by dockers and seamen. It is fairly small, just three ground-floor rooms knocked together with plain wooden tables and benches. There is wallpaper on the walls, originally with a floral pattern of roses, but now faded with smoke and years to a tobacco-brown. Beside the bar is a very elderly upright piano; some of the ivory notes are missing; some of the notes do not sound. An elderly man is sitting there playing, banging out familiar songs. Everybody knows the words; we all sing, too. The songs are not, of course, drinking songs; this is not Munich. They are old favorites like "Daisy, Daisy" or sentimental Irish ballads like "The Rose of Tralee," for there are many Irish in Liverpool. Beside the bar there is a quantity of broken glass, not yet swept up, and I ask my neighbor, a burly docker, how it happened.

"Could be there was a fight," he answers laconically, but with friendliness. "But I didn't see nothing, and what you don't see you can't answer questions about. See what I mean?"

We talk instead about football. He is a faithful supporter of Everton as opposed to Liverpool and watches them every Saturday, traveling, if necessary, to the far end of the country and back after the match on the special train through the night. I ask him what his wife thinks of all this, and he answers: "Well, I don't ask her what she does in her kitchen. See what I mean?"

We continue talking about football, and I reveal that I am a supporter of Portsmouth. We buy each other pint after pint of beer until the towels are put on the beer handles and we are ushered out into the drizzling night.

The third pub is just off the Kings Road, in Chelsea, and here, for the first time, we meet the signs of class distinction. One door opens onto the public bar, used by thirsty tradesmen, plumbers, delivery men, wanting a quick light ale at the cheaper public bar prices, and never mind the amenities or the company. The other door opens on the larger and more important saloon bar, which is crowded. It is full of Toby jugs, and parchment lampshades and iron scrollwork, and empty bottles on shelves, lit artistically from underneath. In the evenings, particularly from nine o'clock onward, it is full of young people of both sexes, the girls in miniskirts, the men in dark suits. The place is solid with bodies, with talk, with smoke. It is difficult to find anywhere to stand, harder to fight your way through to the bar, impossible, if you should wish it, to sit down. The girls sip their Babychams or their Cinzanos and gaze brightly at the young men. The men are all drinking bitter out of pint glasses with handles, jogging one another's elbows. Some phrases are overheard through the din:

"Well, cheers everybody."

"Well, actually, I'm sort of sharing a flat with three other girls . . ."

"Anyway, I got it into this garage. I'd never been there before. And they said it was the petrol pump, and I said, 'I bet you a quid it's the carburetor!' I thought it was an easy way to make a quid . . ."

"Mummy told me I'd got to get a proper job, and I said, 'But this is a proper job . . .' "

Perhaps even more typically, this pub is best seen on a Sunday morning, for the Sunday morning drink is one of the great British rituals. After getting up late, cleaning and polishing the car, buying the Sunday papers, glancing at the front page, but not having time to look inside, the boys and girls will rendezvous at the pub, for more bitter and more Cinzano. The girls will still be in miniskirts, but the men will now be wearing dark-gray flannel trousers and blazers. The farewells will be brief:

"Come on, Sue. Drink up or we'll be late. Bye, Jane, bye Sarah. See you on Monday."

The young couple go out into the quiet Chelsea street. She ties a scarf over her long blond hair; he puts on a brown corduroy cap. They get into his Aston Martin, which is parked outside.

"I say, we'll have to step on it."

The quiet Chelsea street is shattered by the noise, as he revs his engine, and neighbors glare out of their windows. The sports car heads for the Thames Valley or Midhurst, to lunch with his or her parents.

My fourth pub—and the best of all—is a country pub. It may be an old pub, a centuries-old coaching inn, with a history going back to Magna Carta; it may be an old pub modernized with leatheretteen and plastic; it may be a Victorian pub made to look Tudor, with sham beams and copper bed warmers; it may be thatched and whitewashed and look out over the village pond or the cricket ground; it may have bright lights and a large car park and cater with grilled steaks for the passing trade; or it may be lost, alone in a quiet corner of the countryside beside a trout stream, so that only the expert ever find it. But one thing it must have: a group of regular customers, living in the village or nearby, who know each other, marry each other, share the same interests; an informal club of different ages, sexes, income groups. Without such a club, a country pub is not a country pub, no matter where it may be located. However well placed it may be on the main road, however capacious its car park, however tender its steaks, it will not attract the passing, carborne trade for long unless it can also produce the true country pub atmosphere, the group of local regulars.

Being a sort of club, the country pub serves many other purposes besides selling beer. It is a meeting place, a notice board, a sports selection committee room, a savings club, an insurance scheme. I have used my local pub as a telephone operator, an answering service, a bank, a taxi and a garage. The Thrift Club will meet in the pub once a week; each member will pay in a shilling or perhaps more. Three weeks before Christmas will be payout night, and each member will receive back exactly what he paid in, without fees and without interest. Much of this will then be spent on a pleasant evening's drinking. It is not a form of saving which attracts everyone in this age of inflation, but it still continues, appealing perhaps to those who feel daunted by modern economics. The Slate Club, a form of insurance club, where every member pays in a sum weekly, for the benefit of those who may fall on difficult times later, has largely died out, its functions having been taken over now by the state.

Above all, the country pub will be a sports club. The sport varies from area to area, from pub to pub. It may be racing and horses, or sailing, or fishing, or motor racing, or rock climbing. If the pub overlooks the village cricket ground, it is certain to be the headquarters of the local cricket team or club. There has long been an association in British minds between beer and cricket, as has been noticed by many poets. The beer and cricket school of English poetry was perhaps started by A. E. Housman, who wrote a lot about beer, or ale as he called it rather archaically, but little about cricketers, preferring sorrowful soldiers being executed. Edmund Blunden, J. C. Squire, and others, however, added the cricket, and until it was rescued by T. S. Eliot, it seemed at one time that English poetry would be confined forever to these two pleasant, but perhaps rather undemanding, subjects.

In the winter it will be football. The local team will not, of course, come in immediately after the game. They will be muddy and sweaty, and anyway the pub will not be open at that time. But they will turn up later in the evening, washed and brushed, to talk about the game. There will be talk about the big professional clubs, the big professional games, since the British are a nation more of football watchers than football players. Indeed, it is difficult to spend a great deal of time in a British country pub without learning a lot about football. During the Suez Canal crisis a man in my local pub said to me thoughtfully, "If you ask me, there are a lot of people in false positions at the moment." This, it seemed to me, was a penetrating comment on the international situation. "Take Arsenal," he went on, "they've no right to be as high as they are." And, of course, he was talking about league football. It is not done to discuss politics or religion in a British pub. Your friend and drinking partner may hold different views, and the last thing you want is to provoke an argument.

Most entertaining of all are the games which are actually played inside the pub, the greatest of which is darts. Darts is always fun, whether it is a lighthearted game between those who happen to be in the pub at that moment, or the more serious matter of a match against a neighboring pub, or the annual darts tournament. Strange cries echo across the room:

"How about Shanghai, Fred?"

"Proper whitewash, this is."

"Well, looks like mugs away, then."

Most extraordinary is the ability of the scorer; far from being an expert mathematician, he has probably had only the minimum education required for a farmhand. But in two seconds, he will be able to add 19 and 9 and double 13, subtract the total from the present score of 187, and inform the bewildered and probably inexpert player that he needs triple 19, double 18, and tops to go out.

Best of all, perhaps, is cup night, the night when the finals of the village darts tournament are played off. Except for those who are frankly out of their depth and have simply come for the fun, this is serious business; match temperament, match nerves are in evidence. Those who speak or move while the probable champion is throwing his crucial double will be scowled at. Good humor and joking will go on, especially while the somewhat inexpert ladies are playing. But for the men, it is different, and I have known a defeated player slam out of the pub in a temper, never to return. In a nation which admires good losers more than anything else, this was not a popular maneuver, and we were glad to see him go.

The matches finished, all is smiles; tensions are relaxed; the cups are filled by the winners, with strong and baffling mixtures, and are passed around for everyone to drink. Reeling slightly, we stagger out into the cold night at closing time. It has been a memorable evening, something unique in British folklore.

The mixed drinks are, of course, part of it, but normally the Britishman in his pub does not mix his drinks. He will stick to what he likes best, and in his choice we will notice further clear signs of class distinction. If the drinking man or his wife orders gin, with or without tonic or ginger ale, sherry, port, cider (except in cider country), Irish whiskey (except in such west coast cities as Liverpool and Bristol), he will probably be a member of the gentry or at least a "half sir." He will probably call his midday meal lunch. If he orders mild or stout, either straight or in bizarrely named mixtures such as Mother-in-law (old and bitter) or Grannie (stout and mild); if his wife or girlfriend asks for such terrible concoctions as lager and lime or port and lemonade or gin and cider or whisky-mac, then they are the other side of the great divide, and probably refer to their midday meal as dinner. If he drinks vodka, he will probably have been influenced by James Bond and be on the different side of the divide from someone who orders parsnip wine or cherryade. Bitter bestrides the line; formerly in the lunch camp, it stared across at mild in the dinner camp, but one of the signs of increasing prosperity has been the switch from the cheaper mild to the more expensive bitter, and a pint of bitter now gives no indication of its drinker's social standing. Nor does whisky as long as it is drunk plain or with water or soda, though never, of course, with ice. Many different brands of whisky will be available, and the customers will have strong views about the best, which he is prepared to defend to anybody. In Scotland, it is reported that a man drinks four times as much whisky in the year as his English counterpart, as might be expected in that cold, damp, whisky-loving land. But in no circumstances, in either country, will anyone ever refer to the drink as Scotch, a fact which sometimes confuses overseas visitors.

Another, more obvious sign of class difference can be seen in the various bars. As in London, the saloon bar, the lounge, or whatever it is called will charge higher prices and have a higher standard of comfort than the public bar, where there will be plain benches, lower prices and perhaps sawdust on the floor. The public bar was intended as a place where muddy and unwashed laborers could drink without offending or being embarrassed by the more sophisticated customer in the saloon, but few laborers now go into a pub in a muddy or unwashed state. When they arrive for their evening pint, they and their wives and girlfriends will be as smart as those who have spent their day in an estate agent's office. But then 90 percent of the British nation, according to a recent opinion poll, regard themselves as belonging to the middle classes. Except that you will never hear anyone ordering a gin and tonic in a public bar, there is now little outward difference between the customers on either side of the partition, and many landlords are getting away from the unwelcome and invidious distinction and knocking the two bars into one. There is only one type nowadays that a publican wishes to keep out of his house, other than the drunk or the quarrelsome. Each year in September, he will put in his window the sign NO TRAVELERS. In France the sign PAS DE TRAVELERS means that the landlord does not accept traveler's checks, but in England it means, in the most fastidious and oblique of euphemisms, that the landlord does not welcome gypsies, especially at hop-picking time. A friend of mine, a professional gypsy lover, has fought a long campaign against this discrimination.

"You needn't be afraid when they get their knives out," he said to me. "They only ever fight each other."

But the landlords, trying to keep a quiet house, prefer at the risk of possibly illegal discrimination to keep the gypsies away.

Apart from a common interest in sport, in darts, in a wish for pleasant social company, two things unite the British drinking men in their pubs, wherever they may be, in town or country, in the North or the South, in saloon bar, lounge, snuggery, dugout bar, or public bar. One is a connoisseur's knowledge of beer. The Britishman knows what he likes and why, and he is prepared to change his local pub if, for some reason, it suddenly no longer stocks his favorite beer. Discussion is expert and prejudiced, though of course never heated, on the merits and demerits of various drafts and kegs and stouts. This is the more proletarian counterpart of the wine connoisseur in London, for the British drinking man, whatever his social level, is almost always a connoisseur, though it is rare to find a beer snob or a beer bore.

The careful landlord, however, does well to look after his beer like an anxious hen, to make sure that it is in the best possible condition, that, if it is draft beer, it has had time to settle. If it is cold weather, it will be wise to keep a stove in his cellar, to prevent the beer getting too cold, as this will spoil the flavor. He has, on the other hand, to keep his lager chilled. An average pub will stock perhaps fourteen or fifteen types of beer. Not only does he have to know their requirements, but he has to remember all their different prices, at both public bar and saloon bar rates, and these are altered with every budget, even it seems, with every occasion that the Chancellor of the Exchequer makes a speech. Pity the poor landlord, then, and his barmen and barmaids, with a full Saturday night crowd, having to add up the price of a round of drinks comprising a pint of bitter, a half of bitter, a light ale, a Guinness, a Worthington, a whisky-mac and a Babycham, and give the exact change from a pound note. It is as fine an achievement as that of the darts-board scorer, and I have never yet met a landlord who gave wrong change.

The second thing that binds all drinkers together, whether they are in the public bar or the lounge, whether they are drinking lager and lime or sweet martini, are the licensing laws, those brutal interrupters of quiet pleasure or happy revelry. Dr. Johnson did not suffer under them, but one can well imagine the Great Cham's orotund and caustic comments if he had been ordered to leave his favorite tavern twice in a single day. But we can speculate:

> "Sir, is the world outside so contemptible that we have to be commanded to return to it every four hours?"
>
> "Sir, is the only sign an innkeeper wishes to see that of the back of his last guest?"

The British licensing laws were introduced during the First World War, after the Battle of Neuve-Chapelle. They were brought in to reassure the hard-pressed troops at the front that the munition workers back home were actually making munitions and not spending all day drinking. The laws were a temporary regulation under the Defence of the Realm Act, but they are still with us. The British are now resigned to them, to the anomalies, to the fact that the actual hours are controlled by magistrates who are often far from being expert on the problems involved and that the hours will vary from district to district, sometimes even from street to street. They cannot imagine a time when such a system did not exist or a country where such laws do not apply. On going abroad for the first time, they are astonished to find that bars are not ordered to close in the afternoon, that it is possible to obtain a glass of beer legally at four o'clock in the afternoon or at midnight.

Certainly the laws in Britain can be very inconvenient, especially for those who, because of a journey or hours of work, cannot fit in with the scheduled drinking hours. It is known that the licensing laws are disliked by tourists and indeed are thought to be the biggest factor, greater even than the weather, in preventing Britain from becoming a major tourist center. However, the landlords like them; they can get back sooner to their television sets. So do the Puritans, the temperance societies. It is to be questioned, in fact, if the licensing laws have had much effect on drunkenness. People do not often go to pubs to get drunk; the alcoholic swigs it down at home. A more important factor here is the wish of the landlord to keep an orderly house, not to get into trouble with the police, not to lose his license. But certainly the laws have had a great effect on drinking habits. The urge "not to waste good drinking time" is strong. Instead of leaving when the mood takes him, the Britishman now finds himself compelled psychologically to stay to the bitter end, till closing time. This makes for a crowded, though convivial, last hour, and indeed, the best point in favor of the licensing laws is that, by obliging people to drink at the same time, it has increased the clublike atmosphere of the local pub. A snag is that it encourages them to drink faster, knowing that the deadline approaches. One of the reasons for British drunkenness in Mediterranean bars is that the Britishman has been conditioned to drink faster than the tourists of other nations or the local population, subconsciously expecting a closing time, which then does not arrive.

Closing time itself is a British ritual, perhaps the bleakest and most unsympathetic of them all. The last orders are served, in the North of England the washing-up towels are hung on the beer handles, the main doors are opened, letting in a cold draft, most of the lights are turned out, and the landlord bustles about in the dark, collecting glasses, emptying ashtrays and calling, "Come along now, please." The harshness of this is peculiar to the Britishman. In other countries, when they close bars, they speed the few remaining guests on their way with greater tact and gentleness.

For a student of the British character, the episode of drinking-up time is very revealing. Until a few years ago the customer was entitled to order a drink right up to the moment of closing time, and indeed he often did. He then had to gulp it down in a few seconds. To drink it after closing time would be in breach of the law and might get the landlord into trouble with the police. Lord Butler, then Home Secretary, felt that this was a barbarous procedure and introduced a measure allowing fifteen minutes' drinking-up time. No further drinks could be ordered during this period, but drinks already in the hand could be finished at comparative leisure. The merits of this proposal were strongly discussed by the licensed victualers' associations, breweries, landlords, temperance societies, and the drinking public as a whole. The landlords, as might be expected, were not in favor of it. Finally, Lord Butler bowed to the protests and reduced drinking-up time from fifteen minutes to ten minutes, a compromise typically British in itself and which apparently answered some of the objections. It is interesting that at a time when Britain was suffering from so many major problems, of politics, of economics, of defense, this bizarre and minimal measure excited so much discussion. But then, it affected almost every British drinking man, since he has now been trained to stay until the end.

Closing time! Mugs of bitter are emptied, the darts put away. All but one of the lights are turned out; the party breaks up; friends say good-bye. The best of evenings, the most exciting of games, the warmth of friendship, the most splendid of thirsts all are abruptly cut short by the saddest and most brutal words in the English language: "Time, gentlemen, please."

8

"A NICE CUP OF TEA"

I like a nice cup of tea in the morning
Just to start the day, you see,
And then at half-past eleven
My idea of heaven
Is a nice cup of tea.
I like a nice cup of tea with my dinner,
And a nice cup of tea with my tea,
And when it's time for bed
There's a lot to be said
For a nice cup of tea.

☙§ The old song cannot quite be described as a proletarian British national anthem, any more than tea can truly be called the drink on which an empire was built. Neither the Plantagenets nor the Elizabethans had ever heard of tea. An exotic Oriental product, it arrived in Britain long after tobacco or potatoes. There is no mention of tea in Shakespeare. Marlborough's soldiers did not feel obliged to drink tea, to brew up, every few hours. Incredible as it may seem to us now, there was a time when the Britishman never drank tea, when he went to work or to war after a breakfast of steaks and ale.

Tea built no empires. It was, instead, the product of Empire, the largest stone in the crown of India. It can be called, after Boston, the drink that lost an empire. From an expensive, imported Eastern drink for the few, it spread in popularity outward and downward in society to become the national drink, to be classed with such institutions as the royal family and Windsor Castle and football.

Tea! The nectar of the common man, the indispensable drink which restores him when he is tired, revives him when he is depressed, consoles him when he is weary, stimulates him when he has to get up and go, relaxes him afterward when he wishes to rest and sleep, refreshes him when he is thirsty, warms him when he is cold, cools him when he is hot, brings back his appetite when he is jaded, brings out the flavor in the meal which he is eating and, at the end, rounds it off with a suitable afterglow. Tea, with which you celebrate a triumph, or welcome a stranger, or greet a return home to the fireside of the various members of the family. Tea, which sends you on your journey and which greets you on your return. Tea, without which a Britishman cannot exist for more than about three hours.

Tea, of course, exists and is available in many other countries besides Britain, and indeed there cannot be many countries in the world where tea is not drunk in some form at some time. But nowhere else in the world, except perhaps in the cousin countries of Australia and New Zealand, is tea drunk as it is drunk in Britain; nowhere else is it made in the same way, regarded with such reverence, drunk with such dedication. If tea, by some mischance of nature or commerce, were to cease to be available, the American or the Frenchman would be only mildly annoyed. But without tea, the Britishman would be unable to act, to think, even to live. To understand Britain, it is necessary to understand tea and, even more so, to drink it as the British drink it, hot, fresh, strong, milky and sweet, many, many times a day.

You start very early in the morning, as early as possible. The alarm bell shrills through the bedroom. The Britishman grunts and turns over in bed; his wife, aware of her social duties, gets up, goes to the kitchen, and puts on the kettle for early-morning tea. She brings it to her husband in bed. Blearily he sips the first cup, nibbles a biscuit, perhaps smokes the first cigarette of the day; then he has a second cup, a third and even perhaps a fourth. It would be out of the question to get out of bed until he has at least three cups of tea inside him. On Sunday morning, perhaps he may feel chivalrous; it may be his turn to get up into the cold flat or house, to make the tea, collect the newspapers from the doorstep, bring the tray to his wife in bed and climb back in beside her. There the couple will luxuriate, reading the *Sunday Mirror* and the *News of the World,* casting a few uneasy thoughts at the gardening, the car washing, the chicken roasting which lies ahead in the day.

Or perhaps the couple own an ingenious and comparatively inexpensive machine which makes the tea at the bedside at a prearranged hour. This means that neither husband nor wife need venture out in the cold and inhospitable day until they have several cups of tea already inside them. The machine, which is an elaborate form of alarm clock, heats the water, makes the tea and then, and only then, switches on the radio to wake the sleeping couple. The drowsy pair do not have to endure a moment of the new day, a bar of music, a word of the cheery announcer's voice, a sentence of the news, a prayer, without a gulp of the hot, sweet, indispensable nectar inside them. I do not know what the export figures or even potential are for this particular machine, but I would not personally wish to be an export salesman trying to sell such a product in America or France or Germany, countries where the population do not feel the overwhelming need to greet the new day and the return of consciousness with an immediate gulp of tea. But there is no doubt that in Britain the machine is very popular.

British hotels are, of course, conditioned to provide this service, sometimes to the surprise of foreign visitors, who do not understand what the hall porter is saying when he asks the retiring guest what time he would like his early-morning tea. Even greater dismay is felt by the Britishman venturing abroad for the first time, to Italy perhaps or to Spain, and discovering that no matter how new or luxurious the hotel, no matter how blue the view, how helpful the management, how glossy the travel brochure, the hotel is simply not organized to bring him the one thing in life which is indispensable.

It would be a mistake, however, to give the impression that every Britishman requires early-morning tea. For myself, I cannot stand the thought, much less the taste of the stuff, before four thirty in the afternoon. And here a class distinction once again is involved, between those who crave early-morning tea and those who disdain it. But the divide is a subtle one, the line an uncertain and wobbly line. It is not the same line which divides those who have lunch and those who have dinner. It can safely be said that if you have dinner in the middle of the day, you will also have early-morning tea, but the converse does not necessarily apply. Those who are going to have lunch are decidedly less likely to be addicted to the habit of early-morning tea, but it is possible to find people, like, for instance, my brother, who enjoy both.

A similar divide separates those who drink tea for breakfast and those who drink coffee for breakfast. But once again, the line is not exactly the same as that between lunch and dinner or between those who insist on and those who disdain early-morning tea. Once again, one can say that, if you call your midday meal dinner, then you will certainly require both early-morning tea and tea with your breakfast (assuming, that is, that you have breakfast). It is possible to have early-morning tea and then go on to coffee with breakfast, followed, of course, eventually, by lunch. It is possible, though rare, to have early morning tea, continue with tea at breakfasttime, and follow it eventually with lunch. It is possible—just—to disdain early-morning tea, to talk about lunch and still drink tea with breakfast. My father-in-law was one of these, but then he was a man of strong and individual tastes, in some ways an eccentric. But the line, wandering though it may be and sometimes difficult to trace, still exists. Officers in the British Army drink coffee for breakfast, and nothing else is provided; other ranks drink tea, and only tea. This is known, assumed, allowed for in the rations, taken for granted by catering officers and administration. I still recall my jolt of surprise during the last war when I found myself, during one battle, serving with a U.S. infantry division and discovered that all its members, officers and privates alike, drank coffee, something which an ordinary British soldier would never taste or indeed wish to. An exception to the rule, a further wiggle in the line, is provided by the children of the rich. These are required to adopt something of a double standard. During the holidays they will talk about lunch, and they will drink coffee for breakfast. But the young son in his expensive boarding school, in his dining room at Eton, will talk about boys' dinner and will drink tea with his breakfast. But then, as Nancy Mitford has pointed out, the British upper classes have always lumped together the children with the servants and regarded their young offspring as being of a lower social class.

Coffee, it is said, is much more widely drunk in the South of England than in the North. This is understandable. The managerial classes and professional groups tend to be thicker on the ground in or around London, going to France or Italy for their holidays. Their tastes will tend to be more sophisticated than those of people in Sheffield or Newcastle. If a family likes wine with its meals or garlic in its cooking, you can be pretty certain that it likes coffee for breakfast.

It is difficult at first sight to see why coffee should be regarded as a more exotic drink than tea. Neither is homegrown; both are imported from hot, faraway countries; both provide hot, stimulating drinks; both are difficult to make. The Americans have historic reasons for preferring coffee to tea. The reasons for the equally strong British preference are far more obscure. Perhaps there is a touch of chauvinism here, a subconscious connection between coffee and untrustworthy Europeans on the Continent who speak different languages and do not understand about plumbing. Or perhaps it is because British coffee is often so nasty, the coffee kept simmering in huge urns behind buffet counters till it has developed a completely different taste from the original coffee bean, the milk boiled and boiled or condensed and condensed till it, too, has changed beyond recognition. Or perhaps, and worst of all, the coffee may consist of three drops of coffee essence dripped into a tepid cup of warm water and milk. Alternatively, hostesses who serve coffee after lunch may make it themselves on the coffee table with glass tubes and methylated flames, for all the world as if they were schoolboys learning chemistry.This does, at least produce excellent coffee, but it consumes a great deal of time and conversation. Most British coffee, however, is either made in an ordinary kitchen saucepan and may be full of grounds or else is made in the cup from powder—instant coffee.

A new element in this rather discouraging scene was provided in the fifties and sixties by the arrival of espresso bars, which spread like a rash across London and other more sophisticated cities. This is not the moment to discuss their social importance, the part they have played in changing British tastes, in providing meeting places for young people. But one may, perhaps, think gratefully of those huge whistling Italian machines and the Italian coffee which they provide, the widespread promotion of coffee which is neither instant coffee nor stewed in an urn. One can be grateful to Italy for espresso or capuccino coffee, served perhaps with whipped cream, drunk out of shallow glass bowls in an exotic decor recalling probably the Mediterranean or Cuba or Polynesia, surrounded by palm fronds and bullfight posters and pictures of Positano and open Continental sandwiches. The drink obviously has to be coffee. To order tea in such a place would clearly be improper, and this in itself limits the potential clientele of such establishments to those on the coffee side of the divide.

However, we must return to tea, since, in a study of the manners and customs of the Britishman, tea is likely to be the more rewarding and revealing drink. Following early-morning tea and breakfast tea, there is likely to be a brief pause while the Britishman goes to work and his wife busies herself with her housework. But at eleven o'clock or thereabouts, it all starts again. The workingman will go to his canteen; on building sites men will stop work and brew up; the wives will sit down for elevenses. And in offices, fresh tea will be brought around to everyone. Since many British people nowadays omit breakfast, the midmorning tea, the office break, will probably be the first nourishment they have taken since the early-morning tea at the morning alarm bell, and it is welcomed especially gratefully. In offices, it is prepared by the junior member of the staff, the office girl, the junior copy typist. But it will be drunk by everyone from managing director to filing clerk. For once there is no divide. Whether you call your midday meal lunch or dinner, you will drink office tea in the middle of the morning and love every sip of it.

With your dinner, in the middle of the day, you will certainly need at least two cups of tea. How else to swallow that plate of sausage and chips, those chutney sandwiches? But here, of course, a class distinction is at work again. If you call the meal lunch, you will not drink tea. Instead, you will drink coffee, or beer, or even, on occasions, wine. Britishmen who still call it dinner and happen to be abroad, where they do not serve tea with meals, will go to a café or bar before their dinner and have tea as an apéritif and again afterward to have more tea instead of coffee and liqueurs. A few years ago a Spanish friend of mine opened a bar in a fishing village on the Costa Brava and was astounded when her British guests arrived in her bar after a morning's sunbathing and ordered tea.

"Tea!" she exclaimed to me. "They want tea at one o'clock in the afternoon, in this heat!"

"They are used to it," I said. "Why not?'

She shrugged. "They can have what they like, but why don't they want beer or wine or *aperitivos?* Even coffee? It is too hot for tea."

I told her, "Tea is to the British what coffee is to the Spanish." Had she never heard, I asked her, of a nice cup of tea? She was an intelligent woman and took the point rapidly. The next day in her window was a placard proclaiming: "A nice cup of tea." A few days later, prompted by some other customer, she added the words "like mother makes." Her customers from other countries read the notice with some bewilderment. She did not, of course, put up any notices advertising her coffee, in English or any other language. It was taken for granted by her Spanish, her French, her German customers that her coffee would be just as good as anybody's mother's.

Back in Britain, in the middle of the afternoon, comes another tea break. Once again, builders will brew up on their sites, factory hands will go to the canteen, secretaries will pause in their typing to sip the indispensable brew. In the civil service, afternoon office tea is served rigidly at three o'clock, and many offices follow this, though some prefer to leave it till half-past three or even four. The managing director is unlikely to get his cup of office tea till four or even four thirty. But then, having had a larger, or at least a later, lunch, he is unlikely to be in such desperate straits. At three o'clock, too, is the time when dainty teashops called Ann's Pantry or the Copper Kettle in cathedral cities or market towns will start serving tea and homemade scones to sightseers and shoppers. At half-past four ladies of leisure will have tea, possibly in one another's homes. This tea may be China instead of the normal Indian or Ceylon and may be accompanied by small sandwiches or little pink cakes depending on the appetite or the figure of the ladies in question. At half past six or thereabouts, the Britishman, returned from his work, will sit down to "his tea." With his substantial meal and keeping a wary eye on the television, he will drink several cups of tea. Four and a half hours later, as the day's viewing draws to an end, he will have tea once more, the last and perhaps the best cups of the day, relaxed and sleepy before the fire, watching the late-night news, the weather for tomorrow, the religious epilogue. His wife will empty the teapot, wash up the teacups and prepare everything for the first cups of tea early the next morning. During the twenty-four hours, pillow back to pillow, the Britishman will have drunk tea on, perhaps, seven different occasions, possibly twelve cups in all, perhaps more. Hospital nurses, it is said, drink up to twenty cups a day, but then they have a specially complicated life.

The tea will, of course, be very strong, very hot, very sweet, full of milk. However much milk is put in, the color will still remain dark brown. If the teapot has been allowed to stand "on the hob," the tea will have become stewed, taking on a color and a strength all its own. I recall a lecture given to us at the Officer Cadet Training Unit, Sandhurst, during the war, where I and many hundreds of others were learning to be officers. As a change from tactics and leadership, we were given a lecture by the master cook on cooking in the field. Most of the recipes he recommended to us I have long since forgotten, but I still remember vividly his recommendations on how to make tea in a bucket, the huge quantities of tea, milk and sugar required for this operation. We were lucky, he told us, to be soldiers, because we received then larger rations than civilians and could make a richer tea. We could put in twice as much milk and twice as much sugar in each bucketful. "In black, rich tea, a richer milk concealed," we murmured to one another in low voices, those of us who knew our Brooke. Personally, I regarded his recipes with some unhappiness, as I have the misfortune to like my tea weak with a slice of lemon, and this sort of tea is not often found in Army camps.

Of course iced tea, that refreshing American invention, will not be found anywhere at all, except perhaps in a few luxury hotels catering specially for American visitors. British tea is, by intention, hot and strong and sweet, and later in the war, in cold wet dawns in Belgium, I came for a while near to liking it. Weak tea with lemon is a social habit, not a morale builder, and I am able to sympathize with the British tourist abroad, enticed into Señora Lola's bar by the thought of a nice cup of tea and then finding to his consternation that she has merely put a teabag into a pot of hot water. His mother never made it like that!

Tea, it will be seen, is not only a restorative, a stimulant, a warmer, a cooler, a thirst quencher, an awakener, a nightcap, the consolation for a bad day, the indispensable adjunct for a good day, the great life enhancer, but also an addiction, as compulsive as smoking or gambling or drinking whisky. As addictions go, it is clearly harmless. More than that, it is positively nourishing.

But tea is something else as well to the British. It is not only a drink, a restorative, an addiction, but something else, something over and above all this. The act of making tea is important, as important as the tea itself. Instant tea, unlike instant coffee, has never achieved much popularity in Britain, largely because it does not provide the opportunity for exercising the ritual, for making tea in the proper manner. The teapot, rinsed and dried since it was last used three hours earlier, must be carefully warmed with hot water and then emptied, for tea leaves must never touch cold china. The tea must be carefully measured out in spoonfuls: one for each person, one more for the pot. The kettle must be boiling, but it must not be brought to the teapot; instead, the teapot must be taken to the kettle, and the water poured into the pot while it is still actually boiling. For the water to be off the boil by even a fraction of a degree would spoil the tea completely. The tea is then stirred briefly, the top put on the teapot, and the teapot put under a tea cozy to stand for a minute or two.

When the tea is ready, somebody will be invited to pour; the question of who should pour or be invited to pour is often a delicate one, concealing subtle nuances of family relationships or hospitality. The pourer will then pour milk from a little jug direct into the cold cups, quite a lot of milk. She will not inquire of a guest how much milk he or she likes. Naturally she assumes that her guest wants the best tea possible in the way she always makes it. A class distinction, however, is again involved here, between those who put the milk in first and those who add it later. The divide is roughly the same as that between those who take early-morning tea and those who do not. Finally, the tea is poured out, and the sugar basin is passed around, for adding the sugar is the one part of the tea ritual that the guest does for himself. The pourer will then add more water from the still-boiling kettle and put the teapot back under the tea cozy in preparation for the second cup. The ritual cannot be varied, and this is where Señora Lola in her Spanish bar is at a disadvantage. Whether her tea tastes as good as the tea we make at home is a matter of opinion; what is certain is that she does not and cannot provide the required ritual, without which tea is hardly tea.

The instinctive reaction of the British to make tea at all moments of crisis has often been remarked. It is partly the immediate urge for a hot sweet drink or perhaps the instinct of terrified lambs running to suck their mothers' teats. It is partly the wish to be busy, to have something to do during the emergency. It is partly the wish to restore common sense, to reintroduce a note of calm normality at a difficult time. But more than this, it is the unconscious feeling that one great event deserves another, and what could be greater than making tea?

A few years ago the early-warning system was installed in Yorkshire, and it was announced that it would provide four minutes' warning of the arrival of an atomic bomb attack. This was interpreted to mean that everybody would have four minutes' warning of their imminent death. Whether or not the news could or would be brought to everyone in the country during this time was not gone into. The point which was discussed in trains and pubs and letters to newspapers was how you would choose to spend the last four minutes of your life, knowing that they were the last four minutes. Various suggestions, solemn or frivolous, were handed out—suggestions of prayer or repentance, or having a last drink, or saying certain things which had never been said before and could never be said again. My favorite suggestion was from a lady who wrote to a big national newspaper saying that in those last four minutes she would gather her family and her animals around her and make tea, even though she knew that they all would be dead before the kettle boiled. It was an endearing and wholly British suggestion, and she herself recognized that it was the making of the tea, not the tea itself, which counted. I think perhaps she underestimated the difficulty of summoning her family and animals in such a short time. Children are notoriously difficult to bring to the tea table if it is not part of their regular routine. Dogs, hamsters and budgerigars can be assembled fairly easily, but cats are much harder, ponies almost impossible. But she was reacting to the great event, death, doomsday, the end of the world, with the greatest ritual she knew, making tea, and a worthy ceremony for that final event.

9

ANIMALS AS GODS

◆§ Animals in the British hierarchy would have, of course, an honored seat at the final tea table, the last of all Last Suppers. As many visitors to Britain have discovered, domestic animals have a place of high importance in British families, level with that of the breadwinner and the housewife and above that of the children, to whom animals, in most cases, are infinitely to be preferred. But in Britain there is more to animal loving than simply friendship and domesticity. To understand the role of animals in British life, it is important to realize that the animals have been in the past, and to some extent still are, gods.

Horse worship has existed for a long time in Britain. The white horses, those great galloping animals carved in the turf of chalk downs, which are seen so spectacularly by riders in the Vale of the White Horse or by those traveling by train from London to South Wales, are very old. Horse worship in Britain is often thought to have been introduced by the Saxons, in particular by their two kings, Hengist and Horsa, but there is reason to believe that the worship of horses existed in Britain a long time before the coming of the Saxons.

One may, perhaps, cite as an example the weird ritual of

the Mari-llwyd, which still exists in Wales. This takes place on Christmas Eve; a group of men—and only men are permitted to take part—arrive outside the front door of a house, one of them wearing on his head a white mask like a horse's head. The mask is, in fact, always made of a real horse's skull and covered with cloth ornamented with ribbons. Its jaws open and shut with strings so that the horse can bite. By tradition, the local boys join in, dressed up as foxes, squirrels and bears. The rest of the party sing a song to a strange, haunting tune, a sad repetitive melody from the dim pasts of time, as old almost as the Welsh mountains themselves. The verses are theoretically improvised on the spur of the moment; the words explain, in Welsh, that the visitors are weary travelers who can find nowhere to stay and ask if they may come in for some food and drink. The owner of the house, who has greeted them at his front door, then improvises a reply to the same tune, also in Welsh, giving a reason why he cannot ask them in. The group and their horse then explain that they are Mary and Joseph, that there is no room for them at the inn, and will the host not take pity on them? The word "Mari-llwyd" means Gray Mary, though some believe that the original name was Mario-llwyd, or Gray Death, referring to the dying year. The host then gives a fresh reason why he cannot ask them in. The dialogue continues as long as possible, each side trying to outlast the other. My grandfather-in-law, a fluent Welsh speaker, could, it is said, keep the unfortunate party outside for an hour or more, improvising verses. In the end, however, the host's ingenuity or skill at versifying gives way, and he is obliged to ask them in. The horse then scampers around the house biting all the girls, who run shrieking into distant corners, while the rest of the party ransacks the house, eats the Christmas dinner which is being prepared for the family and drinks all the drink that is to be found. By old custom, if they had found a bare larder, they would end by raking out the fire on which last year's Yule log was burning alongside the new one. This, of course, would bring a year's bad luck.

In modern times, of course, this terrifying experience is much watered down; the group are probably friends from the village, and everyone is glad to see them on the festive occasion. Few hosts in these days speak Welsh or have the special skill required to improvise verses on the spur of the moment. The girls, especially the children, love being chased by the horse, which bites their behinds and makes them squeal. Finally, the whole group, including the horseman, who is by now rather hot from his exertions, are offered beer and cakes and the general hospitality which is accorded to welcome groups of carol singers. They depart, wishing everyone a Merry Christmas, and move on to the next house.

But the origins of the ritual still remain baffling. Clearly, the lines about Joseph and Mary are a later interpolation. Joseph's donkey, once admitted, did not gallop around biting the inhabitants. The horse was obviously something to be feared, which should be kept out of the house as long as possible. Once let in, it would sack and devour everything that came in its way. Perhaps there is a relic of history in it: the Celts trying to keep out the Saxons with their horses; once let in, the Saxons would eat and drink everything in the home, burn everything, and carry off the women. If so, it is a legend of the Welsh marches—for the Saxons never penetrated deeply into Wales—a legend grown up out of border fighting and frontier incidents. Personally, I think that it is much older, a half-forgotten reenactment of a Druid midwinter festival, an echo of a time when horses were gods in Britain and much to be feared.

The exaltation of the horse, of course, continued with the superiority of cavalry. The man on the horse not only was bigger and more powerful, but could outpace and outmarch the infantry. Chariots were important to the early Britons. King Arthur's knights were well aware that their only hope lay in their horses. Once these were gone, they would be defenseless against the Saxons. The Normans carried on the tradition, and indeed, to this day, cavalry regiments take precedence over infantry regiments in the British Army. In point of military history, cavalry has had a very unequal record as against infantry. One thinks of Crécy, the English Civil War, Waterloo and the Crimean War. But none of these failures, even by the enemy, shook the British faith in cavalry, in horsemanship, and in the greatness of horses. The dream of cavalry only finally died amid the mud and machine guns of Flanders during World War I.

But the cult still goes on, in particular the association of horses with royalty and aristocracy. The queen still takes the salute on her birthday parade, trooping the color, on horseback. She does not stand by the mausoleum, like a Russian military leader. And indeed, throughout British history, kings have been expected to spend most of their time on horseback, usually hunting. Queen Elizabeth I made her most famous speech, addressing her troops at Tilbury, from horseback. King Charles I still hunted three days a week at a time when the political problems in his kingdom needed his whole attention. His principal enemy, Pym, the parliamentarian, spent no time on horseback. Instead, he worked twenty-one hours a day, plotting the king's downfall, and of course, the end was never in doubt.

Hunting, however, continued and still continues, though nowadays we tend to associate royalty more with racing, rightly called the sport of kings. King Edward VII was famous as a lover of the turf, and his great-granddaughter follows his example. Her husband, the Duke of Edinburgh, is reputed to play polo four days a week during the season, again a suitably royal sport. The prince's prestige would be much less great were he to play, for instance, association football four days a week. His son has already won a half-blue for Cambridge at polo, and this is entirely traditional and proper. It would not have been royal for Prince Charles to have won his half-blue at squash racquets or chess. And side by side with the ancient horse cults of hunting and racing, we now find the new and spreading enthusiasm for show jumping, gymkhanas, pony clubs, though one may note a sex swing here. We are at a time when many Masters of Foxhounds are women, when women show jumpers capture the headlines, when the country seems to be flooded with young girls in velvet caps and rosettes, dreaming and talking of ponies. It is clear that the worship of horses has moved a long way from the days of Hengist and Horsa.

One aspect, however, remains. The British still refuse to eat horsemeat, for reasons which they can never explain coherently. On the whole, the British are indifferent to what food they eat. Cows and pigs may be eaten as readily as lambs and chickens, but horses are taboo. There are no horse butchers in London, as there are in Paris. When the Irish wish to sell off their old horses, they have to send them to knackers' yards and slaughterhouses in Belgium. It would be unthinkable to send them to London.

Dogs are in a somewhat different category. They have never been gods, nor are they particularly royal, though British monarchs usually own and enjoy the company of dogs. King Charles II was so inseparable from his dogs that King Charles spaniels are still the only dogs permitted by law to enter churches and attend services. The dog has more the role of the wise and faithful friend, the acute observer, the domestic psychiatrist. A horse has a deep and sensitive relationship with its rider, and a dog in the same way understands the character of its master. But a dog is expected to do more than this. The British dog is supposed to be an instant and accurate judge of character, even with people whom it is meeting briefly for the first time. If, for some reason, a friend's dog takes a dislike to you, you have scored a black mark indeed. Your character, previously socially acceptable, is suddenly seen for what it really is, a thin veneer of politeness cloaking all sorts of unnamable and vile characteristics. It cannot be accepted for a moment that the dog might be wrong, that it might have made a mistake, that perhaps its own character might not be perfect.

The theory, of course, does not stand up to serious examination. It cannot be true, for instance, that postmen, who are more steadily attacked by dogs than any other profession, have in general worse or less trustworthy characters than other, less molested people—indeed all the evidence would point the other way. But the myth still continues. A dog's judgment is the litmus paper of your character and one from which there is no appeal. Arriving at the house of an acquaintance once, I met his dog for the first time, a huge Alsatian which threw itself on me, licked my face all over, covered me with mud and left me panting and battered. My host was delighted. I had received the highest testimonial that it is possible for a British-man to receive. He was proud to be my friend. I admit that, being British, I was pretty pleased, too.

Dogs, then, are to be treasured as the best of companions, the wisest of friends, the beloved member of the family. There are few men who will not risk their lives to save a dog from drowning or from a burning building. To avoid running over a dog in the street, they will swerve their cars abruptly, indifferent to their own safety, as well as that of others. When the Russians sent a dog up into space in a Sputnik, and it was realized that the dog could not be brought back alive, the British nation was reduced to a state of near hysteria. Even the *Sunday Times* published a poem on its front page, an ode to the dog, perhaps one of the worst poems it has ever published, though clearly deeply felt.

The connection of dogs with character is capable of extension. Not only is the dog supposed to understand the character of those it is meeting for the first time, but it is also believed to be able to influence their character for the better. There are few parents who do not believe that a dog's company is good for a child; probably the child will be given a dog at an early age, whether the child wants it or not. Should a dog not be possible, a cat, a hamster, a budgerigar will do, though obviously less satisfactory. Even the most unperceptive and self-centered of hamsters or budgerigars will, it is thought, teach the child responsibility, care for others, cleanliness, and, if the child is a girl, encourage the motherly instincts. The idea then spills over into other walks of life. Children's programs on television are largely about animals. The children's book section in bookshops is crowded with stories about animals, and it is hard indeed to find a book for an imaginative child who has other interests. The first time I was ever taken to the cinema was to see a film about elephants, called *Chang*. A few weeks later I was taken to see *Chang* again. Six months later it was discovered that *Chang* was on again in London, and so, of course, I was taken once more to see it. By now I was getting the idea about cinemas. They always showed you a film about elephants, called *Chang*.

The idea was, and still is, that if a parent concentrates a child's mind during all its waking hours on animals, natural, happy, innocent animals, this will provide fine character training. There is also the insidious hope that the child will learn naturally and quietly all it needs to know about the facts of life, without having to ask awkward questions or be instructed in embarrassing interviews. This theory does not always work out very well in practice.

Animals, however, not only are gods and friends and educationalists, but are also, traditionally, quarry, prey, food, and this brings in the inevitable distinction between the hunter and the hunted. The huntsman does not feel the same about his chestnut mare or his hounds as he does about the fox. A farmer or a gamekeeper will break a rabbit's neck without a thought but take immense trouble to take a thorn out of his retriever's paw. All animals are not animals; some are vermin. But even here, a large section of the British public has a soft spot even for vermin, for those animals which are less equal than dogs. This concern, however, is found mainly among town dwellers and those in the country whose daily work does not bring them into frequent contact with wildlife.

Town dwellers have a strong and nostalgic interest in the country, even when they have no intention of going to live there. Indeed their picture of the country and the countryside is far more romantic than that of the farmer or the farm laborer. The town dweller buys calendars showing plowed fields and thatched cottages. He reads country novels, he buys his children books about ponies, he is heartbroken at the thought that the red squirrel is dying out. He identifies with animals, irrespective of whether they are noble animals or vermin. For example, one may mention three works of literature: the late poet laureate John Masefield's long and popular poem *Rey-*

nard the Fox, in which the central and heroic character is a hunted fox; Henry Williamson's *Tarka the Otter,* the most popular book by this distinguished British novelist; and Kenneth Grahame's indestructible *The Wind in the Willows,* in which the central and lovable characters are Toad and Rat. The animals in all these three works are, strictly speaking, vermin, but the town dweller identifies with them readily, perhaps because he, too, somewhere in the psychological recesses of his mind, feels persecuted and hunted, deprived of his natural birthright in the country, or perhaps because he simply does not understand the social difference between a foxhound and a fox, between a spaniel and a rabbit.

Instead, he has a wide, generous, romantic love for all animals, wild and tame, hunters and hunted. He brings in laws about humane killers and traps so that even a dying stoat may not suffer unnecessary pain. He brings in private member's bills in the House of Commons about minor cruelty to animals; private member's bills are rarely about anything else. He organizes committees, protests, movements to protect rare species. He suspends the felling of timber in Forestry Commission plantations so that the mating habits of squirrels may not be disturbed. In the course of history he has succeeded in suppressing such traditional country sports as bullbaiting, bearbaiting and cockfighting. He keeps a wary eye on the way animals are treated in circuses. He writes letters to the newspapers, begging British tourists in Spain to boycott bullfights. He subscribes funds to the antivivisection campaign. In his view, the advances gained by medical knowledge cannot possibly outweigh the death and suffering of so many defenseless animals. He organizes campaigns and protests to suppress the coursing of hares and stag hunting. He cannot understand why country people, living in the country, surrounded by animals, should oppose him in so many of these humane measures. He cannot see that vermin are merely pests that cause damage and should be wiped out. He cannot understand that the only reason for the existence of a fox is to provide sport.

A sentimental animal lover, his views on most points are

diametrically opposite from those of the traditional British hunter or the hard-pressed British farmer. When it comes, however, to dogs, horses, cats and other domestic animals, he will be at one with his country cousin in wishing to give them as happy a life as possible. Both town dweller and countryman will join in supporting the various societies which exist to spread kindness to animals: the Royal Society for Prevention of Cruelty to Animals, the People's Dispensary for Sick Animals, Our Dumb Friends' League, and others. It is well known that at boarding schools the weekly chapel collection will be twice as high as normal if the benefiting charity that week is an animal charity.

The plight of British families emigrating to Australia or New Zealand is painful. Naturally no normal British family would dream of moving to the other side of the world, to start a new life, without taking their dog or cat or even, sometimes, their pony with them, since these are full members of the family. However, quarantine regulations prohibit the pets from traveling with the families, and these have to follow later on their own. There is a shortage of suitable ships, and at the moment there are 3,000 dogs and cats waiting to emigrate to Australia, while their frantic owners telephone from New South Wales or Western Australia, asking after the health and well-being of Rover or Whiskers. The families have probably traveled out on assisted passages costing ten pounds, but they will cheerfully pay another eighty or ninety pounds for their pet's journey. For this the animal will travel in first-class luxury, the dogs being walked around the decks by sailors, the cats having their own quarters, separate beds, toilet facilities and play areas. Nothing is too good for the British pet.

The Australians regard all this with some bewilderment. Not being crazy about pets themselves—only one Australian in ten owns one—they are at a loss to understand the Britishman pining for his dog. Nor are they keen to import foreign animals by the thousand into Australia. Why, they wonder, does the Britishman not abandon his dog in England and buy himself a new one when he gets to Australia? But to a Britishman this is unthinkable, as bad as leaving his babies behind. And it seems that the Australian is now resigned to importing a considerable number of treasured mongrels and pampered tabbies. But budgerigars may not be admitted in any circumstances, even though they are by far the most popular British pet.

The British not only are obsessed by animals, but are obsessed by birds too. The countryman, of course, likes to walk round his woods on a wet afternoon, a gun under his arm, shooting pheasants and partridges. Or, more profitably, to let off his woods to shooting syndicates in London and other big cities. This is not, in itself, a symptom of bird interest; it is simply the continuation of a traditional aristocratic sport, which is found equally strongly on the continent of Europe, especially in France, Germany and Spain. It is not especially British, though the recent comeback of shooting as a prestige sport can be associated with prominent politicians and certain political viewpoints. But this is not British bird loving. The enthusiastic bird watcher, lying camouflaged motionless for hours in a damp clump of bracken to observe the mating habits of a plover, has little in common with, and little respect for, the grouse-moor image.

The Britishman's interest in birds is something different, ornithological, romantic, poetic. He will study birds with a care and enthusiasm which he will probably not even give to his own family. He will buy expensive illustrated books about them, powerful binoculars so that he may watch their habits more intimately. He will record their song on tape recorders; he will collect their eggs, blow them, stuff them and lay them out in walnut cabinets. This habit, of course, carried to excess, is not likely to benefit future bird life in the country, so he passes laws protecting certain types of birds, prohibiting altogether the collection of some eggs, like plovers', and restricting the times when other eggs, such as gulls', may be taken. He will draw or paint birds or, failing artistic talent, will buy pictures of birds, usually by Peter Scott. Indeed, there cannot be many homes in Britain without a Peter Scott print on some wall. He will buy china birds and arrange them in the pattern of a duck flight on his walls. He will take bags of crumbs in order to feed the ducks on the pond in St. James's Park or the pigeons in Trafalgar Square. Equally, he will put up notices at Victoria Station asking the public not to feed the pigeons, because they are becoming a nuisance, a notice which is usually ignored by the bird-loving public.

He will anxiously read in the paper the news of a pelican in St. James's Park which may be ill. Should it die, he will demand that it be instantly replaced. He will admire the peacocks spreading their tails on the lawns of stately homes. He is proud of the fact that most of the swans in Britain are royal and the property of Her Majesty, and he will wish to know all about the annual ceremony of Swan-Upping on the Thames, when the swans are caught and marked with their royal mark. Every year he will write to the *Times* announcing that he has heard the first cuckoo of the year, and the *Times* will, of course, print his letter. This is something which is of traditional interest. He will also feel superstitious about birds. If he sees one crow, denoting sorrow, he will be depressed and look anxiously for a second crow, which will indicate joy. He believes that the day on which the rooks leave the rookery or the trees near his house, his luck will also leave. He entirely approved the fact that, during the war, even at a time when the submarine menace was at its height and the rations were the smallest in British history, a special meat ration was issued to the ravens at the Tower of London. These spooky birds have been in the Tower of London from the beginning, used throughout the centuries as scavengers, to eat and clean the corpses that remained exposed, and of course there is a legend that when the ravens leave the Tower, the Tower will fall.

But though he may be obsessed by such exotic birds as swans, peacocks and ravens, the Britishman's principal love and interest will be in the ordinary songbirds, blackbirds, cuckoos, thrushes, skylarks, wood pigeons. Normally stolid and undemonstrative, he will become openly sentimental at the sound of a songbird; he will break off in the middle of what he is saying to listen to the blackbird. He will choke with fury at the thought of the annual festival at Spoleto in Italy, where a hundred thousand songbirds are cooked and eaten in a week. Once, on holiday in Italy, I asked an Italian friend over a drink where was the best place to hear the nightingale. He replied, not without pride, that there were no more nightingales on the island of Ischia. They shot and ate them the moment they arrived. I instinctively exclaimed, "Oh, how sad!" and my friend became quite angry. It was all very well for us in a rich country like Britain, he protested, to worry about nightingales, but Italy was a poor country, and the people needed all the food they could lay their hands on. And it was also not easy to shoot a nightingale; it required skill and the Italians were proud of their skill, and had I merely come to Italy to criticize Italians? I let the subject drop. I saw at once that we were totally incapable of seeing each other's point of view. Two of the most famous poems in the English language are odes to songbirds. Italy, too, has a long tradition of great literature, but it is hard to imagine an Italian poet writing an ode to a nightingale or a skylark.

Above all, the Britishman will buy cage birds, and keep them in his home. He will watch them, feed them, worry over them and the legal size of their cages, enjoy the song of canaries, the clucking and love play of budgerigars. There are, it is estimated, five times as many budgerigars in Britain as there are babies. And here, perhaps, we find a clue to explain not only the falling birthrate but also the British obsession with animals and birds, the passion for pets, the belief that no family is complete without an animal or a bird. To the British, animals and birds are not only gods, hunters, quarries, friends, singers of beautiful music, symbols of joy and freedom, flying Peter Pans in a workaday world, but also emotional substitutes; they provide an outlet in a code of manners which discourages expressions of emotion. They fill a hollow in the British heart. The dog not only must retrieve pheasants and bark at unwanted strangers, but must become, and be made to realize that it has become, a full member of the family.

This is something new. Until the last century, dogs were

largely kept for work: sheep dogs, gundogs, watchdogs. A country squire some years back would never allow the dogs inside the house, because this would spoil them for their work. He could not endure to see a dog being fussed over, taught, for instance, to sit up and beg. You might throw a stick for it to retrieve, for this was part of the dog's training, but it must not be degraded with parlor tricks. The same scene occurs in Nancy Mitford's novel *The Pursuit of Love,* where the daughters of the house were afraid that the dogs, confined outside in their kennels, might become bored. If only, they thought, dogs could learn to read. Anthropomorphism was coming in. Dogs were becoming domesticated, turned from hunting animals to walking hearthrugs, house-trained, accustomed to travel by car, eating canned food with the rest of the family. Indeed, dogs have now become so humanized that we are beginning to find dogs with ulcers, dogs with nervous breakdowns, even homosexual dogs.

Companionship for the lonely, an outlet for suppressed affection, something somewhere to fill the emotional hollow in the British heart, these are the functions of animals and birds in British life. The pet itself does not necessarily have to respond, though horses and dogs are capable of showing affection, and lovebirds bestow it publicly on each other with a demonstrativeness which would be found embarrassing in human beings. But pets in general are not required to reciprocate. Cats, canaries, rabbits, hamsters, goldfish are not expected to acknowledge the love which is poured upon them. It is enough that they exist.

The love of animals, it is evident, is the consequence of the lack of communication inside the family, the shortcomings in overt, emotional relationships. Just why there should be a lack of communication, this emotional void, this passionate need for a new focus of affection, is a different question. The answer is to be found in a study of British family life, its relationships and its conflicts, its totems and its taboos, and, above all, in the British attitude toward children, the key to a whole series of relationships.

10

THE HAPPIEST YEARS OF THEIR LIVES

Italians, according to Dr. Hugo Mancaldi, consider that cruelty to children is more typical of the British than of other races. It seems to them that the British are abnormally fond of animals and abnormally mean to children. Most Britishmen would retort that the truth is slightly different, that Italians are abnormally harsh to their animals and overfond of their children to the point of spoiling them. Either way, the points are supported by facts. During 1968 the Royal Society for the Prevention of Cruelty to Animals received a total of 703,387 pounds in legacies; by contrast, the National Society for Prevention of Cruelty to Children (and the absence of the word "Royal" in its name should be noted) received only 308,600 pounds. It is certain that a story of an animal being maltreated will cause the average Britishman fury to the point of apoplexy, while a similar story of cruelty to children will evoke a much less vivid reaction. Recently in New Zealand, the British were called "a nation of baby-bashers," and the charge cannot be lightly brushed aside.

In one year the National Society for the Prevention of Cruelty to Children dealt with more than 32,000 cases involving almost 93,000 children. The actual figure is probably much higher, including, as well, cases discovered by local authorities and police and an unknown number which can never be discovered. Prosecutions are rare; the only witness is usually the child himself, who is often unable to give coherent evidence. Convictions are even rarer. Unless the case is specially outrageous, judges and magistrates are loath to impose punishment on parents, who will probably be let off with a caution. At the back of the magistrate's mind is probably the British thought that a father has a right to beat his children, and a good beating never did a boy any harm yet, that the boy probably deserved it and, in any event, that he oughtn't to make a fuss. Should the case, however, be one of cruelty to animals, the magistrate's reaction will be quite different. He will give the accused a homily about kindness to animals and pass a much more severe sentence, probably prison.

The problem is not a new one. Dickens was among the first to draw attention to these miserable cases and to arouse the conscience of the nation. In his favorite novel, *David Copperfield,* he described the schoolmaster, constantly caning the boys during lessons:

> I should think there never can have been a man who enjoyed his profession more than Mr. Creakle did. He had a delight in cutting at the boys, which was like the satisfaction of a craving appetite. I am confident that he couldn't resist a chubby boy, especially, that there was a fascination in such a subject, which made him restless in his mind, until he had scored and marked him for the day. I was chubby myself and ought to know.

Of course, by Dickens' standards, things have improved, though experts estimate that the number of cases, uncomfortably high in any event, is continuing to rise. The problem is not, in its extreme examples, unique to Britain. Other nations have their cases of child cruelty, though perhaps not in quite the same numbers. It is no doubt a problem of social change and flux, of psychological stress and of maladjusted marriages. The very young husband and father, his life full of problems and changing ideas, living in one room with a baby who cries all day and all night, until he finally loses his temper and picks up the poker—cases like this occur in many countries. But the British are, perhaps, less ashamed of them than other nations.

A few years ago, a play put on in London contained a famous scene in which a gang of louts stoned and killed a baby in his pram, for no very good reason. The scene was, of course, intended to shock and succeeded. The critics were appropriately censorious of the playwright's bad taste. Recently the play was revived in London. By then, with the yearly escalation of violence in the world, the shock had worn off. This time the play was praised by the critics, its merits were appreciated, and the baby-stoning scene was found to be acceptable and relevant. The point is, of course, that the play was written by a Britishman and performed in London.

However, by way of consolation, one may point out another play, Agatha Christie's *The Mousetrap,* which has now been on in London for seventeen years. With more than 7,000 performances, it is the longest-running play ever. The reasons for this amazing run continue to defeat observers of the British scene. How could an ordinary detective play, however competent, attract such an enormous and faithful public? But when the whodunit trappings are removed, the play is essentially about child cruelty. Perhaps its success is a sign that somewhere down in the British conscience something is stirring.

The problem is sometimes regarded as a social evil, sometimes as a symptom of the times, or perhaps as a necessary expression of personal violence. In the eyes of the world, it is deplorable. The British attitude, however, is a little different. Certainly the British do not approve of killing babies in a temper or beating small daughters with red-hot pokers; such punishments are excessive. But there remains, all the same, in the back of the mind, the thought that it is better to be too harsh than too lenient, that to spare the rod is to spoil the child, and the idea of a spoiled child is far more reprehensible to the British than the idea of an unhappy child. Parents have, it is thought, not only the right but the duty to discipline their children. To this is added the parallel thought that a beating is, in the long term, beneficial to the victim and that everybody has to learn sooner or later "to take his medicine," and the sooner, the better.

"Discipline starts in the first hour of the baby's life"—the quotation is from a book on baby care for young mothers. A firm attitude has to be taken from the start and continued unremittingly. The child should be put in his pram at the end of the garden, so that he will not only get fresh air but also be out of earshot. Should the mother happen to hear the baby crying, she must resist the temptation to pick the baby up, to kiss, or cuddle, or comfort him. The secretary of the National Marriage Guidance Council said recently in London, "We are brought up in this country, in the main, to avoid physical contact with one another, at any rate until marriage. Babies after the first year or two are not encouraged to cling to their parents, to be cuddled by them, to sleep with them. Little boys, especially, are actively discouraged from making physical contact when in need of comfort. Too often they are pushed away from mother and father with the words, 'Big boys don't cry. Cheer up,' when what they need is a comforting arm and no words at all." But the British believe that the child must not be kissed or comforted, since that would be bad for the character, turning him perhaps into that ultimate horror, a spoiled child. Indeed, cuddling may encourage a little boy to become effeminate, perhaps even latently homosexual.

Italian and Spanish mothers, who love to kiss and cuddle their children of both sexes, would not begin to understand such an attitude and such an argument. All around them are men, of undoubted masculinity and virility, who were well cuddled and kissed as children, and indeed the Latin races are perhaps the least effeminate in the world. The British, however, stick firmly to their point of view. It is their duty to make men of their children; the child of either sex must be hardened, toughened, taught the need for self-discipline. In Victorian times, children were beaten frequently and with much righteousness to cure them of the great sin of self-will, but in these days a greater crime is thought to be weakness.

If a child falls off his pony and hurts himself, he must not be sympathized with; he must not be allowed to show pain or fear. He will already have learned, painfully, that in no circumstances must he cry. Instead, he must be put straight back on the horse, and the phrase "straight back on the horse" is a familiar one in British family life. The example is set at the highest level. Both Prince Charles and Princess Anne have broken noses, the one gained from a Rugby tackle, the other from a fall from her horse while jumping. And the whole British nation, including, of course, their parents, was proud of them for this.

The theory descends no doubt from the Greek stoics and the Roman matrons so much admired by British schoolmasters. The Teutons, too, believe in being firm with their children, and no doubt the Saxons brought this with them when they conquered Britain. But above all, the tradition is due to the Normans, to whom physical courage and physical achievement were the great qualities. The ultimate disgrace was to die in bed. Battle, tournaments, even execution, were preferable to that. The idea still continues, and many parents today would repeat unconsciously the Norman ideal. They would prefer their children to die in a battle, a revolution, on a mountain, in a sailing boat, on the hunting field, in a car crash even, to dying in a bed, even after perhaps a lifetime's work and achievement.

Roger McGough, the contemporary Liverpool poet, has made the point clearly:

> Let me die a youngman's death
> not a clean and in-between-
> the-sheets, holy-water death,
> not a famous-last-words,
> peaceful, out-of-breath death.

Much can be done to train British children for their tough destiny, and not merely in negative ways like withholding sympathy or visible signs of love. I myself, being as a child small and undersized, had a particular dislike for gym and boxing, for which I had no aptitude whatever. I was therefore given as Christmas presents dumbbells and Indian clubs to improve my biceps, chest expanders to improve my chest and a special course of boxing lessons, though my nose bled very easily and copiously, the consequence of a sporting accident in my extreme youth. Conversation during the holidays was entirely about football and athletics. I was cross-examined about my performances and lectured on my athletic future in the most painstaking way. My scholastic achievements were of little interest. I had to be hardened and toughened, and when it was seen that I did not greatly enjoy the procedure, efforts all around were redoubled.

British children, it has been said, should be seen and not heard. This is not strictly true; the true Britishman feels that children should not be seen either. A lecture each holiday on fortitude, fitness and trying hard at games is almost all the parental contact required. It must not be thought that this is the result of indifference, that the parents simply do not care what happens to their children. On the contrary, British mothers worry over their children far more than doting Mediterranean parents. While the baby is still in the womb, they will study books on baby care. Later they will anxiously study more books, magazine articles and the reported speeches of experts in case they might inadvertently be doing the poor children some irretrievable harm, and they are reassured to read that they are doing quite right in having as little to do with the children as possible and in leaving all problems to qualified professionals, such as schoolteachers, psychologists and educationalists. The parents will then start to worry about whether they are choosing, if a choice be available, the right school.

It sometimes seems that parents at, say, a Chelsea dinner party are incapable of discussing any topic except their children's schools. Over the ratatouille the debates rage, day school versus boarding school, state school versus private school, grammar school versus comprehensive school, and various combinations of these possibilities. These dilemmas, of course, occur in other countries, but not with the same intensity or the same agony, nor do so many of the parents of other nations consider that boarding school is the ideal form of education. Expensive boarding schools—known so curiously as public schools—started as tribal fetishes for the upper classes, and the idea has spread down into the middle classes and seems likely to spread even further. A large section of the British people now believes that a child cannot emerge into satisfactory manhood or womanhood unless he has been at a boarding school from the age of eight till eighteen. To afford the large fees, parents will make great sacrifices, get into debt, and almost bankrupt themselves to make sure that they are doing the right thing.

The school's the thing, particularly if it has a long tradition and is known to produce a good type of boy. On its reputation and on his performance while there, he will be judged by his friends, his family and his future employers. Such schools have always believed that football and Christianity, Latin and the cane provide the finest character training for a British boy and have applied these principles as single-mindedly and toughly as possible.

We may perhaps speculate whether any other country, any other nation, would tolerate, much less create, such harsh institutions for their children as British boarding schools. A boy's first week at his preparatory school is likely to be the most traumatic experience of his life, one for which he is, at the age of eight, totally unprepared. Until that moment, he has not realized that there are so many people in the world who wish to hit him and to hurt him and that they will be given ample opportunity to do so, both by day and by night. *Tom Brown's Schooldays* described, no doubt faithfully, the public school of his day, and though things are evidently not as savage now as they were then, they have not yet changed in their essentials.

The ferocious beatings inflicted by one boy on another, by school prefects, or captains of houses, or members of the Eton Society on younger boys, for relatively minor offenses or perhaps for shortcomings of character, are without parallel anywhere in British society. In no state school, approved school, borstal, or prison would a boy be given seventeen strokes of the cane (a heavy knobbly cane), for cheekiness to another boy. But in public schools these measures have been approved, partly because they keep discipline effectively, partly because they teach senior boys responsibility and a sense of authority, and particularly because a good beating is supposed to be good for boys, whether deserved or not.

A Spanish friend of mine was, as a boy, sent to a British boarding school by his Anglophile parents. A foreigner, speaking very limited English, he was, of course, given an even worse time than is usually accorded to new boys, and he still recalls the amazed horror of his first term. When he returned to Spain at the end of the term, he did not, of course, make any complaint to his parents; he had already learned the British school code that in no circumstances must you ever complain to anybody, masters, parents or school inspectors, about anything—and anyway his parents would not have believed him. Instead, he used his imagination and bought a flick-knife, which he concealed under his shirt. When he returned to school, he explained to the other boys in his now-improved English that he was really a Spanish gypsy and an expert knife thrower, though he had killed four men in accident while learning his art. The credulous boys believed him and now listened in awe as he recounted in the dormitories gory details of his career. As long as he kept his knife with him (not always easy while playing games), he was now safe. The other boys thought it more prudent to bully someone else. The headmaster, had he known the full story, would no doubt have been delighted; in one term his school had taught the boy self-reliance. What else are schools for?

The British public schools have evolved from the medieval and Renaissance grammar schools, but the ideas which have inspired them for the last century are usually attributed to Dr. Thomas Arnold, the famous headmaster of Rugby. His belief in the importance of religion, the classics, corporal punishment and stoicism was inherited from earlier centuries, though he restated the ideas with force and clarity. His special contribution to educational theory was the prefect system, the concept of hierarchy, the idea of putting older boys in supreme and almost godlike authority over younger boys, in the interests of both. His theories, as has already been shown, are still widely held and supported.

A change may, however, be coming with the new and progressive ideas to make the public schools coeducational. Girls at Eton, Winchester, Charterhouse and elsewhere will, if they are treated on equal terms with the boys, have considerable impact on the attitudes of those schools. British parents often think that their daughters are sons, weaker inferior sons. But occasionally the truth dawns, and they are usually treated a little more gently than boys. Whatever Dr. Arnold would have thought of girls at Rugby, and whatever effect they may have on the characters of the boys, it seems probable that their presence will have a perceptibly softening effect on the traditional harshness of public school life.

However, it is not to be imagined that they will succeed in making the places any warmer. Girls' boarding schools are deliberately as cold as boys', and cold is thought to play an important part in the training of a British child, boy or girl. Not in Britain the warm, stuffy schools of France, the central heating of the United States. British dormitories are unheated. Changing rooms are not heated. Gloves must not be put on chilblained hands. At Gordonstoun school in the north of Scotland, where both Prince Philip and Prince Charles were educated, the boys wear shorts and take cold showers even in the winter terms. At night, all windows are opened wide in the dormitories, and no boy is, it is said, permitted more than two blankets. This is a matter not of neglect, but of deliberate policy; cold, hard conditions are thought to produce tough, reliable leaders. The connection is, in some way, attributed to Plato's philosophy.

The importance of cold as a discipline is deeply entrenched and will probably survive the arrival of girls to share their brothers' Spartan training; girls are, in fact, better adapted to endure cold than boys. But the other disciplines are gradually being eroded and softened. The medieval or perhaps Victorian custom of fagging is being gradually abolished; under this system small boys act as servants, errand boys and, indeed, slaves in their spare time to the senior boys, under threat of painful punishment. So is the beating of one boy by another. So, at heart, is the whole of the prefect system.

These changes have been urged for some time by the Ministry of Education, though it has little power in the matter. Public opinion and the changing mood of the times are perhaps a more potent factor, especially when a number of enlightened headmasters have been appointed to some of the leading schools. But the liberal reforms still meet with a good deal of resistance from all sides. The prefects naturally oppose an end to their power and authority, and to be fair, it is hard to see how they can maintain discipline without an effective deterrent. The masters are naturally reluctant to see the buck, which the prefects have carried so happily for so long, passed back to them. How indeed are they themselves to carry it in more enlightened times? Even fagging is still defended by the small boys, the very people whose lives are made unhappiest by it. The reasons given are ingenious: that it teaches service and self-reliance. But the truer quality is endurance; the boys are enduring everything, waiting for the moment when they in turn become fagmasters and prefects and can hand on to others some of the misery and humiliation which has been inflicted on them.

Above all, the parents resist the changes, the parents who have passed through the same educational technique thirty years earlier and are now paying a great deal of money to give their children the same training. The modern father is suspicious of the new liberal trends. There was nothing wrong with the old ones, he feels, and is he not the living proof of it? Among the new ideas he is desperately afraid that his son may turn out sissy, effeminate, perhaps homosexual, or even, and worst of all, a bespectacled intellectual. An acquaintance of mine, a well-known novelist and critic, who believes firmly in Latin and the cane, cannot conceal his dismay. The tides are certainly changing, but there are still many people who have no wish to make the British public school any easier for the theoretically pampered boys who are privileged to go there.

These disciplines are, of course, only inflicted on boys and girls at boarding schools. Those at day schools, living at home, have an easier time of it, and the schools, seeing their pupils for only a few hours a day, will tend to concentrate more on work than on character training. (An exception is the steady refusal of teachers to intervene in cases of playground bullying or rowdiness; the children must learn, however painfully, to look after themselves and "find their places naturally in a social group.") Dr. Arnold's theories have never really percolated to the teachers and parents of children at day schools, and it is to be hoped they never will. The parents, too, will probably belong to lower social and income groups. They will have neither the means nor the wish to send their children to boarding schools. But the idea of the value of boarding schools as such is creeping down through the middle classes, and more and more parents are coming to feel it their duty to find the money somehow to send their children to boarding school. The effect of this trend on the British people has yet to be ascertained.

When the Labour government was elected to office in 1964, it was confidently expected to abolish the public schools or at least to modify them severely. There had been many threats and warnings given against them, and they were in many ways anathema to the whole spirit of Socialism. They perpetuated class and the idea of an elite; they were patronized only by the rich and the moderately rich, together with a few carefully selected boys on scholarships or grants; they were barely under the control of the Ministry of Education. But to the surprise of almost everyone, the government dropped its hostility to the public schools and concentrated instead on abolishing the grammar schools, those honored day schools. It had been thought that these were exactly the type of school which would appeal most to a Socialist government in a modern technological world. The grammar schools are often of very ancient foundation, though many are modern; they are housed in mellow Tudor buildings or Victorian Gothic palaces or contemporary glass cubes. They are free, open to anyone, boy or girl who has the brains to get in. They are the poor boy's road to success and intellectual achievement. They provide the vast majority of university students. They are still the brains trust of the country, far more than the public schools, where the emphasis is still largely on sport and character. How, it was asked, could any government abolish them?

There should, in fact, have been no surprise. Old though they may be, the grammar schools represent something very un-British in British life. They provide the idea of an intellectual elite, of a trained expert, and the Britishman regards these with deep suspicion. Brilliance is something he does not much care for. At a public school the boys will stay more or less together intellectually. They will not be encouraged to streak out far in front or, to be fair, to lag too far behind. They will be molded by the ideas of the school and will form a team, admirable to British ideas. They will be kept together, as a pack of hounds is controlled by an expert huntsman, and they will turn out the right type of boy or girl.

The grammar schools cut right across these deeply ingrained ideas. Further, it was discovered that they were by no means classless. The children of middle-class parents tend to pass the entrance examination more easily than those from working-class homes. This was an upsetting discovery; the grammar schools, being more numerous than public schools, were even more of a factor in preserving class differences. Therefore, under a Labour government, they had to go. The return to power of the Conservatives is likely to reprieve only a few of the most famous schools.

In their place there are to be large comprehensive schools, catering for a thousand or more children of all types and levels. In creating these, the British are, in fact, reverting to the ideas of the public school. The children will learn from one another as much as from the teachers. Nobody will get too far ahead or behind; the most skilled teachers, it is proposed, will concentrate on the less skilled boys and girls and on their weaker subjects. Team spirit will have been reconstructed, and the pack will stay together. Whether this system will have a beneficial effect on university standards later is very doubtful, but this is not a problem which is likely to cause the average Britishman to lie awake at night with worry.

Education for most of the British will come to an end when the boy or girl is eighteen, if not earlier. Enough time and, in the case of boarding schools, money has been spent; there are younger children to be considered. The object of a public school education is not to learn anything useful or indeed to learn anything at all. It is to have the character and mind trained, to have the right social image, and to make the right friends. All these objects should have been achieved by the time the boy or girl is eighteen. There is no point in going on any longer.

Universities, therefore, play a far smaller part in British life than they do in other countries. It is impossible to think of ambitious American parents, whatever their social level or income, refusing to send their children to a university or college. College is to them the really important part of their children's education, the experience which will launch them on the world and without which they will have little chance of making their mark in any sphere. Things are very different in Britain. I did not go to a university, nor did my brother or father or mother or uncles or cousins or any member of my family (with the recent exception of my daughter). Nor did any member of my wife's family, nor any of my friends or contemporaries. The very idea was hardly mentioned and never discussed. Education after the age of eighteen is not a normal part of the British way of life, unless it is a training for a technical or professional qualification—though recent heavy competition for the limited number of university places suggests the small beginnings of a change of attitude.

The reasons for this prejudice are various. Money has already been mentioned. A girl of my acquaintance won a place at London University, but she refused it because she felt she could not allow her father, who had already paid for ten years of boarding school, to spend any more money on her. State grants are generous and provide full tuition and maintenance, but they are only available to parents with small incomes, and it is their children who provide the bulk of British students, thus causing something of an educational imbalance in the nation. Even here the parents may discourage the boy or girl from trying for a university place, pointing out that it is high time he or she found a job, earned a wage, and contributed something to the family income.

A further reason, more difficult to eradicate, is the belief that a university education is a waste of time, teaching nothing that anybody could possibly need to know and taking up time and effort which could be more usefully spent elsewhere. Further than this, it is often felt that universities are positively harmful, giving wrong ideas, teaching the wrong subjects, undermining the characters of the students and giving them a false and premature idea of their own importance. Recent events in the student world have only tended to harden this attitude, of which the most colorful exponent is Prince Philip, Duke of Edinburgh. In a recent speech he pointed out proudly that he had never been to a university and added the sarcastic comment, "And a fat lot of harm it did me!" He was, of course, making a joke at his son's expense, his son being a Cambridge undergraduate, but it was a revealing and pointed remark. It was also one of the most popular public utterances he has yet made. My mother made the same point, rather more gently but equally firmly, when she said, "One does rather feel that universities undo all the good the school has done."

This traditional attitude is now coming into sharp conflict with new ideas imported from abroad. Intellectuals and eggheads, so long despised, are becoming influential. Expert opinion is sought and is available on almost every subject. Academic brilliance is coming into fashion. Professors and lecturers have invaded the Britishman's home as television and radio personalities. How is all this to be reconciled with his distrust of universities and his belief in team spirit? In a competitive world, it is clear that technological and academic standards are rising daily, and the British have no wish to be left behind in the international race. The Britishman is proud of his universities, as of all his institutions, and he hopes that they will remain among the best in the world, even if he would prefer his own children not to go to one. But who, then, is to go? This is the educational dilemma of 1970 and one which will have to be resolved during the decade ahead.

One major tradition of upbringing remains unaltered; bestriding all types of school, all classes, all income groups is the discipline of hunger. Not only is this too thought to be a valuable part of character training, but it has the added point that hunger is supposed to be good for the health of growing children. Spanish mothers will pinch their children's legs and arms to show the visiting British tourist how plump and well fed their children are. The British tourist will grimace and find it hard to make a polite reply. British children are expected to be lean; to be plump is to be overfed and unhealthy.

A recent laboratory experiment on rats disclosed that rats which were starved in their early youth lived longer than other rats. The connection was immediate in the minds of the scientists and sociologists analyzing the experiment. Would Britishmen, too, not live longer if they were given less to eat in their early youth? In the end, the experiment was thought to be inconclusive; the rats were found to be not essentially healthier, but merely to develop more slowly and later. But the first reaction was revealing, giving a sudden glimpse of the secret fear at the heart of every Britishman, the fear that his children might have too much to eat.

The tradition goes back a long way. Wordsworth in *The Prelude* described his hungry childhood and claims that this was responsible for his good health in later life:

> Our daily meals were frugal, Sabine fare!
> More than we wished we knew the blessing then
> Of vigorous hunger—hence corporeal strength
> Unsapped by delicate viands; for exclude
> A little weekly stipend, and we lived
> Through three divisions of the quartered year

In penniless poverty. But now to school
From the half-yearly holidays returned,
We came with weightier purses, that sufficed
To furnish treats more costly than the Dame
Of the old grey stone, from her scant board, supplied.

We are also given many interesting glimpses of the traditional attitude in nineteenth-century novels. In George Macdonald's *The Princess and Curdie,* when the young miner, Curdie, after working all day in the mines, settled in to work all night as well (as he often did), his supper was a lump of bread. He was twelve. In Frances Hodgson Burnett's *The Secret Garden,* the poor family's twelve children "scarce ever had their stomachs full in their lives. They're as hungry as young hawks and foxes." Their mother was proud of their health and vitality and claimed that they grew fat on the fresh air of the moors. The author compared them favorably with the children of the rich house (who were well fed and therefore inevitably unhealthy).

In *Jane Eyre,* the porridge was burned one day in the orphanage, and having nothing else to give the children to eat, the woman in charge raided her secret store and produced some cheese. The visiting clergyman scolded her severely for giving them such rich food, which would, of course, spoil their characters.

"And there is another thing which surprised me: I find in settling accounts with the housekeeper, that a lunch, consisting of bread and cheese, has twice been served out to the girls during the past fortnight. How is this? I look over the regulations and I find no such meal as lunch mentioned. Who introduced this innovation and by what authority?"

"I must be responsible for the circumstance, sir," replied Miss Temple, "the breakfast was so ill-prepared that the pupils could not possibly eat it; and I dared not allow them to remain fasting till dinner-time."

"Madam, allow me an instant. You are aware that my plan in bringing up these girls is, not to accustom them to habits of luxury and indulgence, but to render them hardy, patient,

> self-denying. Should any little accidental disappointment of the appetite occur, such as the spoiling of a meal, the under or the overdressing of a dish, the incident ought not to be neutralised by replacing with something more delicate the comfort lost, thus pampering the body and obviating the aim of this institution; it ought to be improved to the spiritual edification of the pupils, by encouraging them to evince fortitude under the temporary privation.... Oh, madam, when you put bread and cheese, instead of burnt porridge, into these children's mouths, you may indeed feed their vile bodies, but you little think how you starve their immortal souls!"

All this is fiction, although it indicates the attitude of the author, but many parallel cases can be found in real life. An uncle of mine was the child of a Norman family who had married into a Welsh farming family, and as a boy he was brought up on stern Norman principles, not being allowed, for instance, jam on his bread. One day his Welsh grandmother came to visit the family, bringing a cake for the boy, who was then seven. Cakes play an important part in the traditional life and culture of the Welsh and, indeed, of all Celts, and in bringing her grandson a cake, she was doing more than simply bringing him a treat. She had made the cake for him in her own farmhouse. She was, however, sternly told to take the cake away. She must never do such a thing again; such sickly food would inevitably ruin the boy's character and health. She left sobbing, carrying her cake with her, and never returned.

When the boy was older, he was sent to Eton, and his chief impression of Eton, judging from his later reminiscences, was one of hunger. The meals provided in his house were meager, and for obvious reasons, he was given no pocket money to buy extras in the various school shops. However, a godmother used to send him, secretly, sixpence a week, and this he would spend on toasted cheese, which he ate immediately before playing football. The indigestion this caused was enough to double him up with pain, but at least he did not feel hungry again for several hours.

My own father, from a different family but at the same school, some ten years later, had again hunger as his principal memory of his schooldays. On one occasion, scolded beyond endurance by his form master for his indifferent work, he burst out that he was too hungry to write Greek iambics. How could he compose Greek verse when all he could think about was his empty stomach? It was not a popular remark, and it was not sympathetically received.

In this century, things have undoubtedly improved. At any rate at that school, catering is more generous and more efficiently organized; the boys are provided with adequate pocket money to fill the gaps. But the tradition still continues. I recall a conversation during the last war between two Etonians, one still at school, the other who had just left and joined the Army. The Etonian asked what Army food was like. "Awful," he was told, "all stodge."

"Not worse than *m'tutor's?*" the boy asked incredulously (referring to schoolboys' dinner).

"Oh, that's just *not* food," the recruit replied.

These cases are taken from Britain's most exclusive school. But on other social levels things are not very different. A nutrition expert at London University has stated that thousands of British children are too hungry to learn when they go to school. In working-class families, according to statistics available, every fourth child goes so long without a proper meal that he can hardly concentrate on his lessons. These boys and girls, aged between ten and eleven, regularly fast for eighteen hours a day. They will have school dinner, a light snack or tidbit in the evening, no breakfast. For the last hour before the next day's school dinner they will be unable to concentrate on lessons or indeed on anything. The school dinner itself may not be a very large or nourishing meal, but at least it is hot and cheap and available. Many mothers, however, unable or unwilling to pay the small charge for each of their children, prefer to make sandwiches, bread with a scrape of meat paste and perhaps an apple or a tomato. The child will then have only one hot meal a week, the Sunday dinner. The gap has to some extent been filled by free school milk, which has obviously been of great benefit to young British bones and teeth, but the idea of free milk to children goes against the British tradition and has been much attacked. Although there is a national surplus of milk, the issue has now been stopped for children over the age of eleven, and eventually it is feared that it may be withdrawn altogether.

Various reasons are ascribed for this phenomenon of hungry children. Poverty is obviously one; even in the modern world and the welfare state there are families who do not have the money to spare for feeding their children adequately. Food faddiness is another, a misunderstood and half-forgotten idea of the importance of vitamins in life, the theory that a child can get all the nourishment he needs from a small piece of fruit. Indifference is another reason; the mother who vaguely assumes that the child is being adequately fed somewhere, somehow. If the child chooses not to hand in to the school the dinner money he has been given and prefers, in an austere world, to spend it on sweets and iced lollies and orangeade, the mother will not inquire. The British are the biggest sweet eaters in the world, and the child is as unwilling as his parents to give up his one luxury. A status symbol is involved here, too. An iced lolly is bought and sucked publicly, its owner will be envied by other less fortunate children, and the effect on his teeth is nobody's concern.

All these, however, are superficial reasons. Behind and below them all is the deep British feeling that a plump child is a spoiled child and a matter for shame and that a lean child is healthy, tough and likely to make his mark in the world, later on.

Linked with the admiration for cold and hunger is the deliberate withholding of sympathy to anyone who is hurt or ill, a no-nonsense attitude toward health in general. A distinguished British painter recalls that at his preparatory school he suffered severe stomach pains. The matron told him not to make a fuss. The pains got worse, so much so that, greatly daring, he asked for a doctor. Matron refused, telling him that he was a typical little crybaby and making a fuss about nothing.

He spent the night in agony. The next day he felt a little better, got up, and took the entrance exam for the Navy, which he passed successfully. He then collapsed and was finally removed to the hospital, where it was found that his appendix had burst, before the exam, and he had since developed acute peritonitis. He recovered in due course, but his health was so damaged that he could no longer hope to go into the Navy and eventually took up art instead. It was agreed by everyone, including, of course, his parents, that the school was in no way to blame for the unfortunate incident, and he himself, with British and good-humored phlegm, was inclined to attribute his later success to the incident, which both prevented his going into the Navy and gave him that resilience so necessary for a successful career in art. His health might have deteriorated; his character was saved.

A consequence of this attitude to children is an intolerance, a lack of frankness, a masking of emotions, a suppression of love, between parents and their children. It is fashionable for British parents to announce publicly and frequently that they do not like children. I once overheard a lady in a train in Surrey saying to a friend, "Don't imagine that I like children, just because I happen to have them. I much prefer animals." Her two small sons were present at the time and listening, but they did not seem unduly surprised. It was a sentence they must often have heard before. My own parents made no bones about the fact that they could not stand children, that they could hardly wait for me to be grown-up. "Thank goodness you've never been young," they would say to me, after one of my more precocious remarks. Conversely, the Jews in Britain, the Irish, and to some extent the Welsh are considered to be peculiar. "They're very fond of children, aren't they?" is a phrase often used about them, referring to this most extraordinary and regrettable tendency. How, it is implied, will their children ever grow up and take their place in the world, surrounded as they are with such open family affection?

To suit the Britishman, contact between parents and their children must be as reserved and formal as it can be made. If a child is unhappy, hurt, overworked, bullied at school, or hungry, he must not complain. He has to be very ill indeed before he dare mention it to his mother. An uncle of mine was caned severely fifty-seven times while he was at his preparatory school. The canings were administered, not for breaches of discipline, but for minor mistakes in Latin. In due course the master's sadism got completely out of hand, and he was sent to a lunatic asylum, but the boy, of course, never complained of his treatment to his parents.

But in the next generation the situation was changed the other way around. My uncle married and had a son. As he was convinced of the importance of games and sport in character building, and in life generally, he was particularly keen that his son should be a success in his school games. He organized special coaching in the holidays and provided his son with the best possible equipment. But despite all this, the boy seemed to have nothing to show for it and seemed to be a mediocre games player, a fact which saddened my uncle greatly, so much so that he even mentioned it once or twice to some other members of his family, though not, of course, to his son himself. In fact, though, the boy had achieved quite a success at games, winning both his cricket and football colors at Eton, but he never revealed this information to his parents, though it would have given them so much pleasure, and they died without ever knowing it. The boy did not do this out of spite; he was not a spiteful boy. Had he been asked a direct question, he would no doubt have replied truthfully, but as he was not asked a direct question, there was no need for him to say anything about it.

In the ideal British family, noncommunication among its various members should be as total as human ingenuity can make it. But surprisingly the consequences are not as uniformly harmful as might be expected. It has, it may be claimed, produced a nation of individualists. If you cannot rely on anyone else when you are in trouble, you learn to rely on yourself. As Churchill wrote, "The solitary tree, if it survives at all, grows strong," and the solitary, self-reliant Britishman has a capacity for independence, for thinking things out for himself, a feeling for innovation and experiment, a taste for travel and adventure. When we read, as we often do, in the *Times* an advertisement by a young man or girl who is willing "to go anywhere, do anything," we can guess exactly the sort of family he has come from and the training which has led him to this state. Many writers, too, have had lonely and unhappy childhoods which, though depriving them of human contacts, gave them time to reflect and to read. One may perhaps, in attempting to justify the British family life, point to the great body of English literature, which it has helped produce.

Whether the British attitude is the correct one is a matter of personal or national opinion; whether the stoic philosophy does, in the long run, benefit children's character, psychology and emotions, is arguable. But it seems clear that the effect on the parents themselves is damaging. To remove, to suppress, to deny, to cauterize a natural human emotion causes a variety of reactions, the most obvious and indeed the least harmful of which is the passion for animals. Something has to take the place of the lost children in the heart of the family. There has to be some outlet for parental love. If you may not show affection to your child, you must show it to your dog and indeed will be encouraged by everyone to do so. But whether dogs can fully replace children, whether love of an animal is, in the last resort, an adequate substitute, is a highly debatable question.

It seems to me and to other observers of the British family that the deliberate coolness and indifference between parents and children often spill out into coolness between the parents and the other adult members of the family and, most sadly, between the husband and the wife themselves.

11

THE ANTIFAMILY

The purposeful hardening of British hearts toward their children, the deliberate chilling of parental relationships, extends, of course, into other personal relationships. It is not possible to exude formal and polite iciness toward a son and daughter (who, despite appearances, may be, in fact, well loved) and then suddenly gush with warm affection toward a remote aunt who may have come to stay. Calculated undemonstrativeness once begun is hard to check. If you may not kiss your young son, you are certainly not going to kiss your niece, your cousin, your aunt, perhaps not even your mother. The children themselves will show casual indifference toward each other, and as they grow up into adult life, they will not, as might be expected, react violently against the tradition in which they were brought up, hugging and kissing their most remote relations. They will, in the strange manner of human beings, do unto others the unpleasant things that were done to them themselves. The cold British family is, against all arguments but of its very nature, self-perpetuating.

One may, perhaps, term the British family an antifamily, the epitome of family untogetherness, and it must not be thought for a moment that this is something of which the British are, or should be, ashamed. Once, on parade in the Guards Depot, I overheard the soldier standing to attention on my right answering questions from the inspecting officer. The officer asked if my fellow recruit was the brother of a man of the same name in the Grenadier Guards. The recruit replied, correctly and politely, that he simply didn't know and that he had had no contact with his brother for fifteen years. The inspecting officer nodded approvingly and passed on to look at my brasses and my boots. It is not a dialogue which one can imagine occurring in another army.

It is instructive to compare family habits elsewhere. According to Luigi Barzini, the Italian family is far more than a family; it is a harbor from which you set forth and to which you eventually return. It is a home, a refuge when you are wounded by life, a school, a hospital, an insurance policy, an orphanage, a poorhouse; it is also a channel of communication, an employment agency, a means of preferment and promotion, a bank, a board of directors, a political party. Luck strikes so rarely in Italy that the one on whom fortune has suddenly and inexplicably smiled is then expected to take care of his remote but less fortunate relatives to the fourth or fifth degree: his own distant cousins, his wife's remote cousins, anyone who can claim blood relationship, but who is, for one reason or another, less fortunate. To the Italians, one of the most extraordinary things about that extraordinary man Pope John XXIII was not that he was an insignificant son in a large, poor, peasant family in northern Italy, but that when he finally achieved the supreme position, he did not immediately ennoble his relations, give them rich sinecures in the Vatican, use his influence to find them powerful positions in the world outside, make sure they were well endowed with property and money; he merely invited them to dinner once a year. A British Pope, should there ever be another, would find himself obliged to do even less. It is doubtful if his brothers would even be invited to lunch.

At the other end of the scale of benefices, we find the vendetta, the duty to revenge injustices done upon relations, by further injustices done upon the relations of the original perpetrator or perhaps his remote collateral descendants. Nor is this attitude of family responsibility, for good or for evil, confined to Italy. It is to be found in all Mediterranean countries and also, though with less violence, in Teutonic countries such as Germany and Sweden.

A friend of mine, a Lebanese artist living in Paris, sent a quantity of her work to Beirut for exhibition in a local gallery. Works of art entering Beirut attract high customs duties, and my friend therefore asked a distant cousin of hers, who worked in a government ministry in Beirut, to go down to the docks, meet the ship, clear the pictures through the customs and use his influence to get the customs charges canceled. He meekly did all this, but as he was not a very senior official and as he worked in a ministry unconnected with customs, he was only able to get the customs charges halved instead of canceled, and my friend was extremely annoyed with him. She had expected that a cousin of hers would do better. To me, a Britishman, however, the remarkable part of the story was that he should be willing to use his influence in any way, to go down to the docks on a hot afternoon on behalf of a remote cousin whom he had never even seen.

By contrast, I can cite an experience of my own. I had mistakenly joined my family business, of which my uncle was chairman, and I found myself to be considerably underpaid. After a year, I ventured to ask my uncle for a raise. I pointed out that another member of the company, who was nobody's relation, had joined on the same day and was doing the same work. He was being paid almost double, although, unlike me, he had no family responsibilities. I asked that, as a measure of fairness, I should be paid at least the same as he was. My request was refused. It was pointed out to me that I was a member of the family and that I should therefore not expect the same treatment as others. Besides, my uncle ended up, to give me a raise would smack of nepotism, and that was something which he was not prepared to tolerate at any time in his company.

Looking back, however, I do not think he was trying to ease

me out of the company; he was merely doing his hard duty as my uncle. He seemed sad and disappointed when I resigned. "Nephews," as I later wrote in a novel, "in a British family business, start at the bottom and sink slowly."

Nepotism in British life is considered detestable. The thought that a man might be selected for being a relation of an important personage rather than on his own merits is repugnant to all right-minded Britishmen, even if his merits are demonstrably equal or even superior to those of the other applicants. Nothing made that otherwise adroit politician Mr. Harold Macmillan more unpopular in the country than when he filled his Cabinet with his relations. However competent and eligible they were, he would have been wise, in British eyes, to neglect them. A young Britishman does not expect any favor from his family, and equally he does not accept any responsibility for them. He would much prefer to pay higher taxes and have the welfare state look after them, should they be in need.

The reasons for this peculiarly British attitude are hard to discover. Perhaps there may be a clue in the fact that it is, in effect, an English rather than a British attitude. The members of Scottish clans have a strong sense of affinity, of belonging to the same family, even though, after many generations, their blood relationships may be fragile to the point of nonexistence. But the sense of tribal loyalty remains, a sense of the obligation to be one's brother's keeper. A Macdonald will feel concerned if he feels that another Macdonald is in distress or trouble and will feel obliged to do what he can to help, often to his great inconvenience. The same is true, to a slightly lesser extent, among Irish or Welsh families. It is only in England that family responsibility is strongly and deliberately denied.

The possible reason lies in the history of England, in the continuous waves of invasion which overwhelmed the country from Julius Caesar to William the Conqueror, but which never penetrated into the Celtic lands, where the families remained established, their traditions unbroken by foreign interference. In England, however, the tribal groups were being broken up continually by each new conqueror, their lands settled by small parties, haphazardly, from small ships, resulting in a thousand years of fragmentation of British family life.

The great Norman barons, with their feudal hierarchy, imposed a system of family influence on England, for a few hundred years, but this was not to do with togetherness; it was a power struggle based on the inheritance of land and carefully arranged marriages. The Earl of Warwick, the "Kingmaker" of the fifteenth century, was perhaps the greatest exponent of the rule of the family in English public life. He would have liked, he said, a dozen more daughters to be able to marry them off as and where it was politically necessary. The greatest, he was also the last. The Norman barons finally destroyed themselves in the Wars of the Roses, and the Tudor monarchs were careful to keep it that way. The rise to influence and therefore to wealth, at a Tudor court, required other qualities than merely lineage. There was a slight throwback to the idea of dynastic power in the eighteenth and nineteenth centuries among the influential Whig families, but this was only temporary.

The Norman system of primogeniture tended, in practice, to weaken the ties of kinship. The eldest son was the man who mattered; the others were small fry. The thing that counted was to preserve the continuity of the line, its independence, its pride and its power; the property, the manor, the farms. The estate must be kept intact, it must not be divided and later subdivided among dozens of descendants and relations. This idea continued into the twentieth century. It was known in legal terms as "making an elder son," and it meant, in effect, giving everything to the eldest son and providing practically nothing for the other children.

One may, in this context, note with some surprise the novels of Dorothy L. Sayers, whose hero, Lord Peter Wimsey, though a younger son, was at the same time extremely rich on inherited wealth. In an otherwise perceptive and observant author, this was an extraordinary touch of romanticism. My own grandmother, Elinor Glyn, equally romantic though perhaps less skilled in her prose style, nevertheless saw the theme more exactly. In her novel *The Career of Katherine Bush,* her ambitious and coldhearted heroine pounded her pillow in fury at having fallen in love with a younger son, who, whatever his charm, was and would always remain poor. Ruthlessly the girl crushed the signs of affection in herself, this unfortunate weakness, and by the end of the book had succeeded in marrying a duke, who, being an elder son, was of course rich and, by virtue of this and other attributes, was clearly destined to become a great statesman.

It was my grandmother who showed the greater realism. The elder son had it made, had it handed to him on a gold platter. The other members of the family, the younger sons, the daughters, the sons-in-law, the nephews, the cousins, the nieces' husbands, had to make their own way without any help or influence. They were never thought of as members of important families and therefore deserving of respect in their own right. They were instead "poor relations," snubbed and cold-shouldered when they revisited the family seat. They went into the Army, the Navy, the Church, the Law, all respectable professions but not exactly the same as being the Lord of the Manor. Failing all else, they emigrated to Canada, to Australia, to New Zealand, to South Africa, to the Colonies (as they were then called). Indeed, one may say that it was the younger sons of the great families who pioneered the British Empire and who spread the British culture and the English language around the world.

But whether they stayed at home and became "poor relations" or went abroad and became "colonials," they sank a little in class. They could no longer afford to send their children to the same schools; their language, their accents, became less noticeably aristocratic. They developed large, hard chips on their shoulders. In her novel *Mrs. Dalloway,* Virginia Woolf describes the plight of an impoverished cousin who is reluctantly invited to the party, but to whom nobody will speak:

> It made her timid and more and more disqualified year by year to meet well-dressed people who did this sort of thing every night of the season, merely telling their maids, "I'll

> wear so-and-so," whereas Ellie Henderson ran out nervously and bought cheap pink flowers, half a dozen, and then threw a shawl over her old black at the last moment. For her invitation to Clarissa's party had come at the last moment. She was not quite happy about it. She had a sort of feeling that Clarissa had not meant to ask her this year. Why should she? There was no reason really, except they had always known each other. Indeed they were cousins.

I can myself recall a discussion in the family about whether some cousins were "presentable" enough to be asked to Christmas dinner.

It was Lloyd George who first attempted to break the power of the big estates by introducing death duties. In 1925 the Property Acts were changed so that in the case of intestacy the estate had to be divided equally among all the children. This was a major alteration in social ideas, and though most owners of property did not, in fact, die intestate, the lawyers who guided them in drawing up their wills were themselves guided by the new laws. Younger sons and daughters, it was now thought, should have a reasonable share in the inheritance, though not, of course, an equal share. The more remote members of the family, nephews, cousins, in-laws remained, as always, in outer darkness.

The large country estates, the manorial properties, are now largely broken up, the farms sold off, the manor houses themselves divided into flats, rented to local auctioneers. But the continuing tradition may be seen clearly in businesses, particularly in such famous British family businesses as merchant banking. No chairman of a British company wishes to see the senior positions held by members of his family whatever their merits. His own elder son or, should there be none, his elder son-in-law will, of course, come into the business and be groomed from the start for stardom, though he may have to start at the bottom and win his spurs in the dreariest possible way. But his brothers and cousins, if they are wise, should look elsewhere for employment. If there is one thing that the old man at the top is afraid of, it is the accusation of nepotism.

If relations are not tolerated in family businesses, even less are they tolerated living in the family home. The idea of a whole family living together, in a manor house, farmhouse, or council house, is repugnant to the British people. In a recent court case a sister-in-law came to live with her family uninvited, presuming on being welcomed as a member of the family, as indeed she would have been in Italy or Spain or many other countries. The housewife, however, finally lost patience with her uninvited guest and strangled her with a scarf. At the trial, the jury strongly sympathized with the accused and recommended her to mercy. She received a prison sentence of only four years. The lesson was clear enough for all to see: You camp on your relations at your own peril.

The result has been, of course, smaller and smaller households, from the Norman Conquest onward, descending from castles to manors and finally to flats or apartments in the manors. The British were the first to invent the dower house, the house to which the lady of the manor was expected to move when her husband died. She was no longer supposed to stay in the big house.

In a Hampshire village, where I have lived for many years, the large home farm was intended to house many people of many generations, but the last farmer, unable to bear the company of his mother and his aunt any longer, divided the farmhouse so that he and his family might live in one part and the older generation in the other. This, however, was not far enough apart. Despite many hints and suggestions, the old ladies refused to move out of the farmhouse, where they had always lived, into the nearest town. He therefore had to move out himself. He gave up the farm and emigrated to Australia. It was as drastic as that.

The result of this untogetherness is that half of all old people in Britain live alone because their relations do not wish to see them, except on rare occasions such as weddings, funerals and Christmas dinner. The old people, usually short of money, short of food, short of heating, subject to sudden accidents and illness, whose long loneliness is eased only by a television set or a cat, are one of the great problems of Britain. It is not, of course, a problem unique to Britain, but it is probably more intense there than anywhere else in the world. It is a product of the deeply ingrained idea that a man is not responsible for his relations, young or old, that he should not want to see them more than once or twice a year and that, should they be invited into his home, they will, like the Furies, bring disaster in their wake.

It is not only the distant cousins, the old aunts, who are unwelcome in the home. It is young people, too, the children of the family. Some of them, as has already been mentioned, would have been at boarding school for two-thirds of the year, from the age of eight onward. But whether they have been in a day school or boarding school, they will be expected to leave home by the age of eighteen, at the latest. The bird-loving British people have an ornithological phrase for it: The young ones have to be thrown out of the nest and learn to fly by themselves. They may, if they are relatively unambitious, merely move to another house in the same town and become lodgers. Others may go farther away and find a bed-sitter in one of the big cities, where they will live a lonely but independent life. The luckier and better endowed ones will find perhaps two or three friends with whom to share a house or flat. They may revisit their parents for occasional and uncommunicative weekends and, of course, for Christmas and other formal family gatherings, but they will probably spend their holidays with one another, camping or skiing or digging up Mesopotamia, or walking across Turkey, or doing charitable works in the less developed parts of the world. Their parents will thoroughly approve and expect no more than an occasional postcard.

Should the young people be impatient and unable to wait until they are thrown out of the nest, they may run away early. Provided that the young Britishman or Britishwoman is over the age of sixteen and not, in the eyes of the police, "in need of care and protection," he (or she) has, it seems, an inalienable right to live away from his family from then onward, and nobody in Britain—parents, social workers or magistrates—would dream of questioning it.

Sometimes the children have moved out even before they were sixteen. A Hampshire friend of mine, now dead, once told me that he had joined the Army at the age of fifteen and had never gone home ever again. Another friend, a young Londoner, ran away to sea at the age of fifteen. Two years later, back in England, he returned briefly to his home, strolling in as easily as if he had merely been out to buy a packet of cigarettes. There was no tearful reunion, no wild celebration, no fatted calf. His parents merely looked up from their newspapers and said, "Hello, where have you been?" as if he had, indeed, been merely gone for half an hour to buy some cigarettes. They assumed, correctly, that he would, of course, not be staying more than a day or two.

When the young people marry, they immediately set up a home of their own. During their engagement, they will have to tramp the streets, looking for a house, a flat, a room, perhaps even a caravan on a caravan site. Should they, for some reason, be forced to share his or her parents' home for a few weeks or months before moving into their own, it is taken for granted by everyone that the young marriage will be doomed.

All this has been a great spur to housing. The Britishman will go without food, but he will not go without a home of his own, and the result is that the British are among the best-housed people in the world. Indeed, statistically, they have fewer people to a room than any other country. British children, no matter how young, never share their parents' bed or, indeed, one another's beds. From a very early age they are expected to have separate rooms. This is, once again, an inalienable right of British youth. The vast families of Italy or Spain cheerfully living, loving, eating, quarreling, sleeping all in the same room belong to another world. If, however, they go to boarding school, British children will live in dormitories with other young boys or girls of the same age. When they leave home, they may easily share their room with a friend. This is perfectly tolerable. It is done for friendship and convenience. It is only the members of your own immediate family with whom you must never share a room.

A moment of consternation and, of course, of many ribald jokes is likely to be the wedding night and the subsequent honeymoon. Not only is there suddenly someone else of the other sex in your room, your bed, your life, but, even more alarmingly, the other person will require to be spoken to at intervals. The nervous shyness of British honeymooners is often misinterpreted. It is rarely due to apprehension of the sexual act. Many couples will already be experienced, with each other or with others. Indeed every eighth bride will already be pregnant, the rate rising to one in four for teen-age brides. It is the outward signs of love which are so difficult for the British couple to manage: the caresses, the kisses, the fond words, the easy companionship.

Honeymoons are an integral part of the British way of life, as they are of many other races. Few newly married couples in Britain, however short of cash, do not afford themselves some sort of honeymoon. But it is the shyness, the tongue-tied embarrassment, the silence of British honeymoon couples which make them unique and unmistakable in whatever country they have chosen to visit. Indeed, for reassurance, for the feeling of safety in numbers, the British usually like to take their honeymoons in places where there are likely to be other honeymoon couples at the same time. Depending on the couple's financial means and in ascending order of wealth, the areas are likely to be: British holiday camps; Jersey; Majorca; and, finally, elsewhere beside the Mediterranean or in the snowy Alps. In Jersey, each Easter, there is a big honeymoon ball to which perhaps a thousand honeymooning couples go. The master of ceremonies may make some risqué jokes at their expense, but at least they will be reassured that there are others sharing their embarrassment. Outside the ballroom the couples can team up into parties, the bridegrooms can talk to one another and go swimming and drinking together. The girls can exchange details of their weddings and wedding dresses. Opportunities for conversation between the bride and the bridegroom can thus be, to the relief of both, much reduced.

A few years ago, I played the organ at the wedding of a young country boy, the son of a working-class family who had lived for some years in the cottage next door to mine. The boy was stiff and silent at the wedding, the bride sweet and pale, in a long white wedding dress, which she had made herself. After the wedding reception in the village hall, the young bridegroom went with his mates to play darts and drink beer in the village pub, while his bride meekly waited in his parents' home. He always played darts with his mates, he explained to me, every Saturday night and saw no reason to make an exception on his wedding day. The wedding night and the honeymoon would have to wait until later, and no doubt he and his bride were happy at the respite.

It should not be thought, however, that such shyness between the sexes is confined to the working classes. A few years ago, two young friends of mine who had both been at Eton with me and were both rich and titled, married beautiful, desirable, well-heeled girls in fashionable London churches on the same day, somewhat to the annoyance of their friends, who wished to attend both weddings. By a coincidence both honeymoon couples were booked to fly on the same flight to Paris that evening, and the society photographers were waiting at the airport in the hope of taking an entertaining photograph. They were lucky in this, as one of the couples was extremely late and caught the plane with only a minute or two in hand. The papers published the photograph the next day, the two couples sitting inside the plane, just beside the door. The two brides were sitting together talking, the two bridegrooms together behind them. No doubt both couples preferred to travel this way, but I could not help reflecting that an American or French bridegroom would not wish to sit beside somebody else, even an old school friend, on his honeymoon flight. It was no surprise to me when both marriages broke up a few years later.

It is not only British honeymoon couples who have nothing to say to each other. At mixed schools, such as grammar schools or comprehensive schools, the boys will never speak to the girls, will never become accustomed to speaking to girls. Brothers and sisters, too, usually have little to say to each other and are rarely seen anywhere together. Most saddening of all, perhaps, is the spectacle of a British date in a dance hall or ballroom. The men will stand at the bar and drink beer together, talking to one another; the girls, longing to dance, will be forced finally to dance with one another. Britain is perhaps the only country in the world where it is common and unremarkable to see girls dancing together, while their boyfriends stand at the side, drinking. When they go on a holiday to the Mediterranean in the summer, this re-pairing often causes some eyebrows to be raised in the nightclubs. The French, Spanish or Italian proprietor may indeed ask them to stop, but he will have misunderstood the situation. There is no hint of perversion in this regrouping. It is merely the most conspicuous and perhaps the most desperate display of British noncommunication between the sexes.

In the end the honeymoon will be over, the shyness will have worn off, but it will not be replaced by any natural or spontaneous relationship. The young couple may be deeply in love, but they both will take good care to hide it from the outer world, and from each other, too. When the children arrive, the couple will be careful not to show any affection, any weakness or "soppiness" in front of them. Sexual relations in bed may, and probably will, be normal, but social relationships between the couple and the rest of the house are likely to be polite but reserved. On one holiday in Austria a young British schoolgirl, aged eleven, confided to my daughter that the previous night she had seen her parents kiss. She had evidently been amazed and shocked by the sight. I had not noticed this memorable event, and I do not for a moment think that it was a very erotic kiss. On New Year's Eve, in Austrian ski resorts, there is likely to be a good deal of indiscriminate kissing between people who have only just met, and this festive occasion provided the opportunity and the excuse for this public act of affection. But the girl could not get over the sight. Never before had she seen her parents kiss each other, and she was likely to have to wait a long time, another year at least, before she saw such a sight again.

But if open affection is restrained, so also are open signs of hostility. Quarrels, open spoken quarrels, are rare in British households; the Mediterranean storm in a teacup is almost unknown. When I was living in Spain, the cottage next door, inhabited by a fisherman and his family, would from time to time shake with terrible family rows. Voices would be raised in anger, and the women would shout and bellow, the young girls cry. Terrible words would be used in the heat of the moment. *"Antipático!"* they would shout at each other. *"Antipática, tú!"* and what could be crueler than to tell anyone that he is antipathetic to you? When tempers and vocabulary were finally exhausted, silence would fall on the cottage, the complete silence of total sulks. One or the other of the family would creep out to tell me, in a low voice, how *antipático* another member was. Then, after three days, the storm would suddenly blow away. There would be a dramatic and equally noisy reconciliation, the little street would reecho to loud voices, laughter, and much audible kissing. *"Ah, simpático!"* they would all shout at one another, *"tú simpática!"* That is Spain. But in all the years I lived in an English village, I never heard a sound come from any other cottage. If any family quarrels were going on behind the net curtains—and by the nature of things and the law of averages, there must have been occasional moments of conflict, sometime, somewhere—the quarrels were carried on in icy silence, the form of quarrel which is most to the British taste.

From time to time one reads distressing stories in the British papers of couples who have lived together in the same house for ten or even twenty years without talking to each other. Neither side is willing to give way, to revert to normal social intercourse. Since there has been no obvious quarrel, there can be, therefore, no obvious reconciliation, and the couple continue to ignore each other, passing occasional written messages to each other or speaking through the children, about routine business matters. Divorce courts are sometimes called upon to rule whether such long silences constitute grounds for separation or divorce. But British law is firm and typical on the subject: As long as the husband provides a home and housekeeping money, as long as the wife cooks for the husband, neither party has any grounds for complaint.

Such drastic cases are fortunately rare, it is believed, though naturally there can be no statistical information on the subject. But the sex cold war has perhaps been brought to a finer art in Britain than in any other country. Men like to go as often as possible to a pub or club where their wives are not expected to follow them. The women, on the other hand, like to meet one another, to exchange news and chat at the Women's Institute or a baby clinic or launderette or even at a shop. When the man returns from work, commuting back from the City or bicycling from the nearby factory, he will read the paper, watch television, or go out for a pint. His wife will have learned, early in their marriage, not to bore him with details of her day. It is in this context that British addiction to television has to be seen. It has removed the last need for polite, formal conversation in the evening, much to the relief of all members of the family.

12

AND SO TO BED

The British are not generally thought of as being among the world's sexiest nations. They are not considered as being in the same class as the French, the Italians, the Spaniards, the South Americans or even the Swedes. It is sometimes said that the Britishman is a poor performer in bed. His virility is not so much in question as his technique, his competence, his experience and, above all, his interest. The Britishman, many foreigners tend to feel, is secretly rather bored by the whole business. The figures, however, seem to belie this. There are more British alive in the small overcrowded island than there are French or Italians or Spaniards, those sexy Catholic peoples living in much more spacious countries. Whatever else the Britishman may neglect in the matter, it does not appear that he has overlooked his breeding duties.

The misapprehension arises because the British so rarely speak about sex. It is not part of the British way of life. You may sit for hours in a pub or an office or a factory canteen or, come to that, in a British home without hearing the subject mentioned, even by indirect reference. Married couples do not speak about sex to each other; a recent questionnaire on sexual habits elicited this fact, though some of the women added: "If only we did!" Courting couples will not mention it, out of shyness or reserve. Parents will try to avoid the topic with their children. Children would die rather than ask their parents anything about it. Between married couples and their in-laws the subject is completely taboo. You do not speak about it to anyone of a different sex or a different generation. You are very reluctant to speak about it even to your doctor or, in desperation, to a marriage guidance counselor. You are much too shy. Only in closed circles where the members are all of the same sex and age-group will the subject ever be mentioned, and even here it will usually be done with fantasy or ribaldry: One thinks of the dormitories of boarding schools where the great and mysterious secrets are passed around in whispers and everyone, boy or girl, tries his hardest to conceal his ignorance on any point; one thinks, too, of officer's messes and, it is said, the Stock Exchange, where sex can at times be mentioned, lewdly and irreverently. From all these inner circles, strangers and members of the other sex are, of course, firmly excluded.

All this is very misleading for foreigners. The Frenchman puzzles over the British girl in a miniskirt: What is she doing; where does she belong in a sexless country? Is she a prostitute? Is she desperately trying to arouse desire in her boyfriend, the man in the street, any Britishman? The answer is no. He has misunderstood the social mores, the innocence and uniformity of fashion. The girl does not need to arouse sexy thoughts in her boyfriend. He has plenty of them already, but he will be careful not to show it. (The misunderstanding works both ways. When the girl goes on a holiday to Paris or Rome, she will, of course, wear her miniskirts because they are the only clothes she possesses, and anyway she would disdain to wear what is to her an unfashionable length. She is blithely unaware that her legs will be regarded as an open invitation to every wolf in the city. She will be shocked and indignant at being pinched and pawed and propositioned every time she sets foot in the streets. She will return home full of insular disgust, leaving behind her a renewed impression that British girls are frigid teases. The Channel will seem thousands of miles wide.)

The British may give the impression of being largely disinterested in sex, but in fact, they think about it a great deal. Exact information on the point is, of course, impossible, given the general lack of communication on the subject. But there are certain clues. One of them is books. Men will often write and publish what they cannot bring themselves to say, and English literature is among the sexiest in the world. It began sensationally with Chaucer, the first masterpiece in the English language and certainly one of the sexiest. *The Canterbury Tales* is obviously a book that British schoolboys have to study, not only for its literary and historical qualities, but because its original language is now almost incomprehensible and requires dictionaries and the whole apparatus of the discipline of translation. The difficulty arises in finding suitable tales and even passages for translation. The English master or mistress would rather leave the sex education of his pupils to someone else, probably the biology master or the school chaplain.

The tradition began with Chaucer; it continued vigorously throughout English literature. Shakespeare had it abundantly, as Dr. Bowdler, his emasculator, found to his cost. So did Marlowe, Webster and the Jacobeans. Much of the poetry of John Donne is bursting with sexual desire. So are the diaries of Samuel Pepys, whose famous phrase heads this chapter. The Restoration comedians touched new heights in sexy drama, but though there are still plenty of admirers of Wycherley, Congreve, Vanbrugh, Farquhar and the others, one can also feel that great drama requires something more than technique, dialogue, and single-mindedness. The sexual tradition suffered some degree of eclipse in the Puritanism of Victorian Britain, but it remained alive and underground, occasionally surfacing in such works as the anonymous *My Secret Life*. It erupted again in this century with D. H. Lawrence and his followers, whose books, if published at all, could only be published in Paris and smuggled back furtively to Britain by tourists. At the moment of writing, British literary sexuality has, in personages like Kenneth Tynan, reached new heights of intensity.

The preoccupation of British authors with sex is sometimes

hidden from those who study *The Merchant of Venice, Paradise Lost, Pride and Prejudice* and *David Copperfield.* The most famous lines of verse in English literature, "To be or not to be," which every French schoolchild has to learn by heart parrot-wise, whether he or she understands them or not, are for Shakespeare remarkably free of sexual allusions. Hence the French astonishment when they saw the recent film of Fielding's *Tom Jones.* "Why, it's just like Rabelais!" a Frenchman exclaimed to me. It was not thus that he had been taught to visualize the reserved British.

One may, in passing, add two further examples of British sexuality. One is the invention of the four-letter word, those picturesque monosyllables which are so freely used in Army barrack rooms, factory canteens, golf club bars and, increasingly, modern novels—though they may still cause, gratifyingly to the speaker, raised eyebrows when dropped into a predinner cocktail-sipping silence in a Belgravia drawing room. As words they are very old and have a natural appeal to a people who appreciate monosyllables and simple direct language, who are proud to call a spade a spade. The use of the words has, for obvious reasons, been taken up, too, in the United States, but it is difficult to translate them into any Romance language without losing the punch and the point. Mediterranean peoples may think as much as anyone about these matters, but they prefer to express themselves in more indirect and allusive phrases. This is one of the problems which French translators of modern British and American novels have to face.

The second example is Britain's most famous king, Henry VIII. He has been mentioned before in this book, and interest in him and his reign has never been greater than at the present time. He has left a permanent mark on English and European history and religion and legend. In two ways it was his sexuality which was the crucial factor rather than his Protestantism or his bloodthirstiness. Henry VIII was the first European monarch to marry for sex rather than for politics. The marriage (to Anne Boleyn) was certainly short-lived, but it gave an example which has been followed, sometimes intermittently, sometimes controversially, by monarchs and rulers ever since. King Henry was also the first and (it can be believed) the only English king to have contracted syphilis while on the throne. He was infected, perhaps deliberately, by a French lady during the diplomatic debauch known picturesquely as the Field of the Cloth of Gold. In several ways this was a crucial point in English history, and things might have turned out very differently in England and in Europe if the king had been as indifferent to sexual attraction as the British are sometimes thought to be.

You do it, you think about it, you write about it, you make films about it—but you do not speak about it. This is the British sexual code, and it must be admitted it is far from ideal. Even worse than shyness and noncommunication is the ignorance which is bred by such taboos. Queen Victoria, the famous case, knew so little about men that she did not know they shaved their chins. Her wedding night, it is said, was an amazing experience for her, but her ignorance did not prevent her from having nine children in due course. Some humbler couples, however, are less fortunate. According to the reports of social workers, a surprisingly large number of marriages are never consummated. Neither partner knows what to do, both are too shy to discuss it with each other or with any outsider, and the matter is left permanently in abeyance. A doctor in Blackpool, a seaside town favored by North of England honeymooners, has recently stated that he often receives visits from couples in difficulties on the third or fourth day of their honeymoon. The bride, blushing even more strongly than usual, waits in the waiting room, too shy even to enter the consulting room. The young bridegroom drags himself in to be told the facts of life and elementary sexual technique. The doctor sometimes sees the couple again later and notices that though still tongue-tied, they seem to be much happier.

Judging from the population statistics, it is obvious that despite ignorance and noncommunication, most marriages are successfully consummated. But it has often been felt that more information at an early stage would save a lot of problems later on. The difficulty lies in finding the right person and occasion to give the information, the generation gap, and the widespread reluctance of people to say or hear anything on the subject. I may perhaps quote my own experience in the matter.

At the age of twelve, on leaving my preparatory school, I was summoned to say good-bye to the headmaster. I had expected a homily on working hard and doing my best for the side. Instead, my headmaster, deeply embarrassed but doggedly doing his duty, told me about the breeding habits of daffodils and rabbits, ending with a somewhat incoherent account of how babies were born. I thanked him politely and got quickly out of his study. The information I had been given, though interesting, seemed to me then (and seems to me still) irrelevant to the hundreds of urgent problems facing me at that moment. Not being a biologist or gynecologist, I am still only theoretically interested in the matter. Of the process, in which I might one day be involved, of conceiving a baby, I was, of course, told nothing. Naturally I never asked my parents.

I had, however, innocently asked an adult a question about sex a few years earlier. At the age of eight I asked my governess, who was preparing me for my preparatory school (this was before the days of nursery schools) the meaning of the word "fornication." It was a word I had met in the catechism, and I had no idea I was speaking about anything sexual, or I would certainly have kept my mouth shut. The governess colored deeply, and speaking in a fast, flustered manner, she told me that the word meant eating meat that had been killed by strangulation, that it was a survival of an old Jewish eating custom and that it came from the Latin word *fornex,* meaning a throat. It was, I realize now, a remarkably ingenious explanation to be invented on the spur of the moment, and it satisfied me. It was, after all, no more extraordinary than all the other odd things small boys are expected to learn.

Since it was not a word in common usage, it was some seven years before I heard it again. This time it was while being prepared for confirmation, and my teacher was dwelling on the evils of sins such as fornication. I burst out that surely such things were out of date now, sir, and nobody paid any notice to them anymore. I was very severely rebuked for my impertinence and my immorality, and I suppose I was lucky that the matter went no further. Later the man, perhaps guessing that my intervention had been due to ignorance rather than plain wickedness, suggested that if there were any questions troubling me about sex, I was not to hesitate to ask him. But of course, I would have died rather than do such a thing. You do not talk about sex to people thirty years older, especially when they are bachelor clergymen. Like every other boy, I had learned all I needed to know about sex from my contemporaries, and the information, highly colored, inaccurate and boastful though it may have been, was at least freely available without embarrassment.

Sex education has moved some way since those days. Recently, as a parent I was invited to attend a "rehearsal" lecture at my daughter's school of the sex lecture shortly to be given to the girls. The lecture (given, curiously, once again by a clergyman) was extremely complicated, full of scientific words which were unexplained and unrecognizable diagrams. Had I not already been fully briefed, I would have found it hard indeed to follow, and I understand that the girls heard it in total silence the following day and avoided all comment. Also listened to in stony silence were the sex lectures given to the Army by visiting experts. No comments were ever made, no questions ever asked afterward. The British taboos run very deep.

At the present time the British Broadcasting Corporation, which has moved a long way since it was founded by Lord Reith, is running a series of sex talks for children. There are several advantages of having these on television: The children are not embarrassed by the familiar box; the lecturer is not embarrassed by having his invitation to ask questions received in total silence. The programs are of astounding frankness and show photographs and films of all aspects of sexual activity without any reticence. The programs are said to be designed expressly for eight-year-olds, and it is sometimes said that infants of that age are incapable of learning, much less of taking a personal interest in, the technical details. The view has been expressed that the BBC was less concerned with instructing the children than with shocking the parents.

One of the points of the BBC programs was that the words "love," "marriage" and "family" were never mentioned. Sexual activity was shown isolated from everything else, like swimming lessons. This, of course, is part of the modern denigration of married and family life, the new morality of which the BBC is such an ardent propagandist. But it is also typically British. The British have always tended to think of sex as something quite on its own.

It is amusing to consider the reactions of various races to sex, to tie labels onto different countries, even though this involves wild generalizations. The French are perhaps the only nation to identify sex with *l'amour,* to see it as an act of love. To the Italians it is more of an art, and in this they are following the traditions of their Roman ancestors. To the Germans and Austrians it is an act of aggression and domination, as Freud discovered in his rather specialized studies. To the Americans sex is a physical need or perhaps a status symbol or even a science (one thinks of college girls working out their orgasm averages). To the Moslem it is pride of possession; his women are beautiful chattels, like his carpets or his furniture. To the modern international man, sex is a form of scalp hunting or collector's instinct; playboys collect movie stars as well as Monets, and there is no reason to think that the Don Juan myth is peculiarly Spanish. But the British see sex as none of these things. They see it, of course and typically, as a sport.

"My favorite indoor sport." The phrase is often heard in officers' messes, one of the few places where, as has been mentioned, sex can be freely discussed. This puts sex in its place, along with snooker and table tennis. The tradition is obviously very old. In *King Lear* Gloucester describes the conception of his illegitimate son in the words "there was good sport at his making."

The Britishman's attitude to sport is one which deserves a

chapter to itself. But two aspects of it can be noted here: Sport must be played strictly by the rules, and it must be played hard, though not necessarily to win. His attitude to sex is no different from any other sport; it must be a good clean game.

Playing by the rules means to the Britishman straightforward sex. He prefers the normal orthodox sexual positions and is deeply suspicious of bizarre variants. Much of his inherent distrust of foreigners, indeed his racialism, derives from this. The phrases "damn gigolo," "filthy dago," "dirty wog" do not necessarily refer to bodily cleanliness. They refer rather to sexual technique, the thought that the other man, Mediterranean, Middle Easterner, or Indian, is not playing by the rules and is winning by a technical foul. There is naturally admiration for the black man and his famous sexual achievements, but these are clearly due, like his successes in the boxing ring or on the athletic track, to his fine physique. But the physique of Persians or Indians or Japanese is not usually particularly athletic, and their sexual successes, the Britishman assumes, must be due to those famous but secret love techniques which he so despises in principle. Books, both classic and modern, giving full details of Persian and Indian lovemaking are easily bought on barrows in the Charing Cross Road in London. But the normal Britishman would disdain even to look at them. They are bought, he assumes, entirely by foreign tourists, immigrants, dagos, wogs, gigolos and lesser breeds who do not understand the rules.

I may perhaps give an example of my personal knowledge. A colonel in the Brigade of Guards was fond of taking his family to eat at one of several Hungarian restaurants in London. He liked the food and the atmosphere, which reminded him of some pleasant experience in Budapest when he was young. He was, however, much less fond of the music. In particular, he could not stand the violinists, who, as part of their routine, would wander around the tables, playing romantically to the ladies. Knowing the colonel to be a distinguished and regular customer, the leader of the band would concentrate on his table, playing to the ladies on the low string, his bow moving horizontally, his eyes fixed deeply on theirs. The ladies found this romantic and rather enjoyable, but they soon learned to ignore the violinist, to scowl and wave him away. The colonel believed, perhaps rightly, that Hungarian gypsy fiddlers knew the secret note on the violin which would give women an orgasm, and he was not prepared to have his wife and daughters undergo that experience in a public restaurant, still less for them to be had by such a dirty underhand trick. When the violinist, not understanding, lingered too long at the table, the colonel knocked him down. The violinist, who despite his fancy dress was probably neither Hungarian nor a gypsy, was justifiably annoyed.

The Britishman's attitude toward perversion is a difficult one. Instinctively he distrusts someone who is not playing by the same rules. But he is tolerant, and he knows that the problem is ages old and will be with him permanently. He has therefore evolved an attitude of compassion; he will speak of homosexuals as if they were spastics—unfortunate, not altogether to blame, and a tragedy for all concerned. "I'm always so sorry for queers" is a phrase I have heard more than once in my clubs. By not being able to play football with the others, they are missing a lot of fun. At the same time he is wary; he suspects that the disease may be catching. He keeps them well away from his sons and daughters. He sups with a long spoon; he likes to keep them segregated in certain specific areas of life. He will condone homosexuality in actors or poets, but not in officers or merchant bankers. In history, homosexual kings have always had brief sad reigns and were usually murdered. What was all right for Francis Bacon was not all right for Edward II.

Sport does not only involve playing straight, but it also means playing hard, and here the Britishman scores. His single-mindedness, concentration and, possibly, his fitness combine to produce a fine sexual performance. A lady of my acquaintance who confesses to considerable international experience has stated that the British are the best lovers. She was referring, of course, to the physical act itself, not to the romantic paraphernalia which in other countries sometimes precedes it.

Afterward the Britishman expects to feel tired, and this conditions the pattern of his sexual activity. Friday night is traditionally pay night, and pay means beer which may possibly, though by no means always, arouse desire. It is thought that certain areas of Liverpool and Manchester favor Friday night. But in general the British prefer Saturday night for their sexual activity. The couple can sleep late on Sunday mornings and recover from their exertions. Sex also, then, fits well into the weekend sporting pattern, coming after the Saturday afternoon football or racing or tennis and before the Sunday morning golf or gardening or car washing.

This imposes a rhythm on British sex which is not found in other countries, where people make love as and when the mood takes them, and it is far different from the "on heat" rhythm of animals. The British rhythm is artificial and not necessarily the one best suited to individual needs. But the concentration of everyone on a single moment in time adds a touch of drama to something which might otherwise be a routine episode. The sensitive traveler, standing in a quiet London street at midnight on a Saturday night, can almost feel the week's suppressed sexual buildup bursting round him; he can almost hear the regular creaking of several million beds.

He will, of course, be a foreigner, and a romantic one at that. The normal Britishman will tackle the business much more prosaically. It is usually said, and probably rightly, that when he approaches his wife on a Saturday night, he will utter only one routine monosyllabic question, "Tired?" The sporting life continues; he might be asking her if she felt too tired for a last set of tennis. He is, of course, also checking tactfully that it is the right night in the month for her. But when Britishwomen dream of the Mediterranean, it is often about a tall thin Italian film star, playboy, count or waiter who will not begin the evening's lovemaking with the word "Tired?" Her husband, should he be aware of it, would ignore the comparison. No "dago" competition would make him say more at that moment. He does not make a speech before going in to bat at cricket. He does not make a speech before going into battle. Nor does he make a speech before getting into bed. His wife can, and probably will, supply the missing dialogue the next day by reading *Woman* or Georgette Heyer. But secretly she will be glad to keep this sort of thing for her dreamworld. Should her husband one Saturday evening start quoting D'Annunzio to her, she might feel inclined to panic or, worse still, to laugh.

He has, more or less, the same ideas about it all. He is not dismayed on Saturday nights to find his wife shiny with face cream, her hair carefully in rollers, wearing a flannel nightdress. Rather he feels reassured. These are her familiar sporting clothes; she is a sportswoman too; he thinks of her nightdress like his familiar friendly golfing jacket. If she were suddenly to appear in a see-through nightdress or baby-doll pajamas, he would feel very alarmed. What was she getting at? What did she suddenly expect from him? As it is, he inquires briefly if she is tired, gets into bed, turns out the light, thinks about Elizabeth Taylor or Brigitte Bardot and prepares to play a good innings. His wife may think about Marlon Brando or Serge Gainsbourg or even Clark Gable, should *Gone with the Wind* have been revived recently at the local cinema. But she will be relieved that her husband does not expect her to dress or to behave like a Southern belle or a model in St.-Tropez or a houri in a harem. Not only would this make her feel thoroughly silly, but it might inspire him to become obstreperous, to try out those love tricks which he might have discovered in Alexandria or Calcutta. She will also be grateful that he does not expect her to remove the nightdress, any more than he will take off his striped flannel pajamas. You do not play games in Britain naked. A relation of mine had, untypically, the habit of sleeping naked in summer. His wife complained bitterly about this to everybody, including myself. It was a major factor in the breakup of that marriage.

There is a second reason behind the British wish for formal, sober attire in bed. It is not only that the British wish to be correctly dressed at all times—other nations share this wish too—but that it is rather the assurance of fidelity. It is the visible proof that a woman is not setting out to make herself attractive to other men, even if the other man is at the moment her husband. There is a kinship here with the custom of certain African tribes, whose women blacken their teeth after marriage as a sign to the world that they are no longer available. In Britain it is thought to be disgusting for a woman to wear lipstick in bed even on Saturday nights. It might stain the sheets; it is the wrong sporting image (you do not wear lipstick on the hunting field). Worst of all, it would be a sign that she wished to be thought attractive, and who on earth could she be wanting to attract? Not, of course, her husband, whose amorousness she has only just got under control. Should she, as is possible, have a lover on a midweek afternoon, she would, of course, keep her lipstick on (and her flannel nightdress in the drawer). But here the circumstances would be quite different.

A wife's wish to "blacken her teeth" after marriage spreads, of course, far beyond the bedroom. During the daytime she may easily wear a tweed or tartan skirt, a twin cardigan set and two rows of pearls, possibly the most asexual clothing yet devised by the human species. Thus clad, she will feel safe to wear lipstick in public. Nobody will have any doubt about her virtue. On a lower class level a girl will wear a scarf over her head after she is married; a plain scarf, knotted under the chin and worn in the street, is a symbol of marriage as formal as a wedding ring. An unmarried girl does not wear a scarf over her head at any time. It might spoil her hairdo. The queen, embodying the whole society, often wears the whole lot together, and all the married women of Britain approve of her. They would wear the same in her place.

However, it is perhaps the forbidding clothes which have given the world the impression that the Britishwoman is, by and large, frigid. This is probably misleading, and there is no statistical reason to think that she is less able to respond physically than the women of other races. She is, of course, at heart a sportsman, too, but sport, as has been explained, is the companion of sex, not its substitute. Masters of Foxhounds, who nowadays are usually female, are popularly supposed to exclaim "Tally-ho!" as the orgasm overwhelms them. They have been much stimulated by hours in the saddle earlier in the day, and the bloodlust is upon them.

But the idea of frigidity dies hard. Masters of Foxhounds form only a small part of the population, and the stories may not be true. But then, nor may the stories about Britishwomen who are supposed to eat apples during copulation; it is never explained why they should so suddenly be aware of a vitamin shortage which has to be put right immediately. A fictitious character was the woman who thought out the Sunday meals during the Saturday night sexual activity. It was a time which, so to speak, she had to herself; at least no one was speaking to her. If for some reason the Saturday night routine did not take place, she would be faced by her kitchen on Sunday morning without an idea in her head. But whether this character was a figment of the author's imagination or whether she was based on a real person, only the author can know.

The facts suggest that such cases, even if they are true, are exceptional. The occasions when frigidity is made public, in divorce cases, in articles by marriage counselers, sociologists and doctors, suggest that such cases are unusual and unfortunate. There is no reason to think that the ordinary Britishwoman does not enjoy her sexual activity, provided it is not made too exotic, as much as the women of any other country. Sexual desire was the cause of the first English divorce, Henry VIII's, and infidelity is still the largest cause of divorce in Britain. (In passing, one may note the determined resistance to accepting divorce throughout the centuries of the Church of England, which was founded especially to sanctify a divorce. But with the recent, more permissive doctrines becoming more widely held among bishops and influential clergymen, the church is now reverting to its original intended role.) Sexual infidelity is now thought by many people not to be "immoral" in a marital context. Adultery is a more respectable matrimonial offense than cruelty or desertion. To maltreat your wife (or, sometimes, your husband) is ungentlemanly; to abandon her and leave her to starve is not to play by the rules. But to prefer another woman (or man) is something different. Sportsmen are always allowed to change their partners if they find the existing arrangement unsatisfactory. Who is to say, after all, which partnership is the "true" one? However, it should not be thought, the above remarks notwithstanding, that the British are a nation of adulterers. Most British married couples stay together, and the marriages work adequately, satisfactorily or even very well indeed. The reasons have been explained earlier. Both sides know the rules and are playing by them.

From all this derives one final point. You play by the rules, you play hard, but should you lose, you must at all costs be a good loser. The abandoned husband, the forsaken wife must above all conceal all traces of chagrin, jealousy or bitterness. He or she must keep a brave, unspiteful face to the world and speak about the supplanting man or woman with friendliness ("Such a nice girl; I do hope they'll be happy"). Anything less would be to let down the side, herself included.

Though violence and murders, which used to be rare, now increase yearly in Britain, as everywhere else, jealous crimes are still, as always, insignificant. The Britishman is amused that the French should have a special category of murder, the *crime passionel.* He is baffled by the crimes of honor in Corsica and Italy. In Lebanon most of the murders committed are for honor, a man killing his unfaithful wife and, occasionally, her lover too. The man will go to prison for life, and he knows this, confessing to his crime immediately. But his honor and, even more important, the honor of his family will have been saved. The visiting Britishman regards all this with astonishment. For him the violent jealousies of *Carmen* and *Cavalleria Rusticana* are (except among homosexuals) strictly for the operatic stage.

The point is that though he may be deeply mortified and hurt, his rules state clearly that he must in no circumstances show it, and in this he is the opposite of his Latin neighbors. The assumed nonchalance may mislead people who do not understand into thinking that he does not care. He is studiedly, pointedly casual about it all, and this is how he would wish it to be.

My grandmother, in her diaries, summarized in two adjectives the varying qualities of the men of different nations as lovers. For the British she wrote: "Casual and adorable." The juxtaposition is revealing. Throughout the love affair, from beginning to end, the Britishman has tried to be casual. For those who understand and appreciate the British style, this can be very endearing. But for those who want something more passionate and overtly committed, it can be too casual to be adorable.

13

VERY PRIVATE LIVES

⁂ The British are, perhaps, the loneliest people in the world. Many of them, in fact, live alone physically. The others, even at home or at school, are alone emotionally or intellectually. It is a country where the generation gap is accepted and, indeed, approved of; where baby-sitters, if they are available, have to be hired because relations will not help; where there is no one to confide in except the busy doctor and the Miss Lonelyhearts columns of the popular newspapers.

But if there is little contact between the members of a British family, there is even less between one family and another. The phrase "We like to keep ourselves to ourselves" is peculiarly British. The neighbors next door must not be encouraged into too great a familiarity, and they are of course adopting the same policy. They will be greeted politely when they are passed in the street. They may be invited in formally to occasional parties, for the British, surprisingly, are fond of formal entertaining. But otherwise they must be kept firmly on the other side of the garden fence or hedge.

John Evelyn the seventeenth-century diarist, wrote: "Is there under heaven a more glorious and refreshing object of the kind than an impregnable hedge?" The question could only, of course, have been asked by a Britishman. Other nations do not specially admire hedges or even possess many of them. One may travel for days through America or Russia or France or Spain or Italy without seeing a single hedge. It is possible for a nation to live without hedges, though the British find this hard to believe. And indeed, the hedge may well be thought to be the symbol of Britain, more than the rose, or the horse, or Britannia. The aircraft sinks through the cloud ceiling and suddenly below them, through the rain, the passengers see a countryside closely quartered with thick green hedges. It is hardly necessary for the captain to announce over the loudspeaker that they will be landing in a few minutes' time at London or Manchester. It is perfectly obvious from a quick glance, that the aircraft is not, by mistake, over France or Belgium or Holland.

Lord Keynes, the economist, stated at the start of the last war that Britain's wealth lay in her hedges, that no country could be poor with hedges like those, that by virtue of them, Britain was a rich country and could therefore certainly afford to fight a long and expensive war. Economically, the point is arguable; it is difficult to export or sell or exchange hedges. But patriotically he was on sure ground. He was touching, deliberately, a deep chord in the British heart. Agriculturally he was right, too, as many farmers have found, when they later gave way (against their better judgment) to the fashion of the moment and dug up their hedges to create larger and more economical field units.

Most of the precious hedges in England, however, do not divide one field from another, or protect the soil against erosion, or act as windbreaks or fertilizing agents. They are grown around houses, town, suburban or country houses, and their sole purpose is to keep the world out and preserve the privacy of the occupiers from prying eyes and passersby. The average home, particularly in the suburbs—and the suburbs now cover a vast area of the country—has a front garden with a lawn and flower beds, a back garden with vegetables. Around both there will be a hedge or, failing the hedge, a fence. The neighbors have to be held at their distance; the outside world has to be kept safely beyond the outer moat.

My cottage in a Hampshire village has, of course, a front hedge on the road, a back fence dividing me from the next property. It has, however, no side hedges. The gardens of the cottages, which are very old, are relics of the feudal strips, and on our side boundaries we have, not hedges, but nonhedges, imaginary hedges, which can be clearly seen in the mind's eye. Indeed, the boundaries are carefully marked on the land, every man cutting his grass or planting his vegetables up to the limit of his garden and not one inch farther. The imaginary hedges are as absolute and daunting as if they were made of prickly thorn. Should your neighbor be working in his garden a few feet away from you, you do not acknowledge his presence. You cannot see him through the hedge. Should you wish to speak to him, you go out through your own front gate, down the road, through his front gate, up his garden path, around to the back door, and knock on his kitchen door, a few feet from the point from which you started. Even small children, barely able to walk, are not allowed to play in the neighbor's garden or climb through the imaginary hedge, which they are perhaps too young to see. Should they stray even a few feet beyond the boundary, without any danger to themselves, they will be immediately hauled back by their parents with many apologies to the owner of the land where they have trespassed. A stranger who attempts to walk from one garden to another (perhaps someone from the Council Sanitary Department) will be politely but firmly invited to go around by the public road.

There are two motives behind these attitudes. One is a deep feeling for boundaries and, in the larger sense, for frontiers. You do not move your boundary or your frontier except by legal contract and with the agreement of the person concerned. British legal history is much occupied with boundary disputes, for the importance of these is far greater in British eyes than the value of the few yards of earth involved. In one of the most spectacular of recent cases, Mrs. Barbara Moore, famous for her long walks across Britain, threatened to starve herself to death over a boundary dispute, and when her husband, to avoid this catastrophe, gave way to the other party, after she had gone without food for several days, she was justifiably furious with him.

The other motive is the wish for privacy. Neighbors must be kept firmly on their side of the hedge. This is not done out of unfriendliness or hostility. The Britishman is probably on excellent terms with his neighbor, but social contacts will be formal, a result of specific invitation to visit. Casual contact is to be avoided. In *Pride and Prejudice,* Mr. Bennet (or Jane Austen, typically herself) was being cynical when he remarked to his daughter Elizabeth: "For what do we live, but to make sport for our neighbours, and laugh at them in our turn?" Naturally, you wish to protect your privacy, and you understand that your neighbor wishes equally to protect his. A hedge, after all, faces both ways.

The wish for privacy is very strong in the British heart. Early in the last war, a large number of young girls were called up for the Army and many served in the Anti-Aircraft Command. They had previously been telephonists, shopgirls, or engaged in other similar urban pursuits. The experience of an Army camp, of living in the country, of the manual work involved in antiaircraft units was quite new to them. A number of journalists descended on one camp to find a good story, to hear their reaction to their new life and, in particular, to get their complaints. The girls had, in fact, a good deal to complain about: The camp was not finished; the sanitary arrangements were elementary; the hours were long; there were problems about food and recreation. But the only complaint the journalists heard was of the lack of privacy. To sleep, dress, wash, manage their clothes and their appearance in public, never to be alone for one minute in the twenty-four hours—this was abhorrent to the Britishwoman. Compared with this, the mud, the isolation, the bucket latrines were trivial.

On a more civilized peacetime level, the need for privacy is still considered paramount. When I was living in Chelsea, my house had a back garden, which was separated by a low wall from the back garden of the house across the block. The family who lived in this house had a very small and engaging daughter, who often played in their garden and whom we had observed from our upper windows. One day, when we all were in our respective gardens, we remarked by way of conversation to our neighbor, how sweet the child was, how much we enjoyed seeing her play there. They were the first words we had ever spoken to our neighbor. She did not, of course, reply. Instead she scooped up little Sarah and carried her into the house. Two days later, workmen arrived and built a large wooden fence on top of the wall, so that we could no longer see into her garden from any window. She was, of course, quite right. In a moment of sentimental aberration, we had broken one of the great codes of British life. We had looked into her garden. We had admitted doing so; we had spoken to her. We had invaded her privacy. She naturally resented this, and she was willing to spend money to make sure that it never happened again.

The Englishman's home is his castle. The phrase is very old, and in its connotation it is untranslatable in any other language. The world must be kept beyond the gates. To admit a stranger is perhaps to admit an enemy. There is in the British a deep-seated race fear of the stranger who gains entrance to a home on some pretext and will then not leave but finally destroys the home or takes possession of it. This menace is subconscious but very real to most British people. Harold Pinter has demonstrated it most effectively in several of his plays. Unless they have been specially invited, visitors and, in particular, official visitors such as inspectors will be spoken to on the doorstep. They will not be invited to cross the threshold.

A recent example may serve to illustrate this. A village cottager came to call on his lord of the manor to ask his advice on a point which was troubling him. The relationship was not, in fact, as feudal as it sounds. The manor house had long since been divided into apartments; its owner was a busy lawyer who, among other things, was the local chairman of quarter sessions. The cottager, on the other hand, was not a tenant or employee of the manor. He worked on the railway and was a confessed and outspoken Communist, his principal enemy being the lord of the manor, whose advice he was now asking. The two men conversed long and seriously. The point troubling the railwayman was that the local sanitary authorities wished to send an inspector to inspect his lavatory. The railwayman contended that he had the right to refuse to admit the inspector. Wasn't his home his castle? he asked. Wasn't this his traditional right? The lord of the manor gave the matter the careful thought which his inquirer expected. Finally, he gave his opinion. In common law, undoubtedly, the railwayman was right, but recent statute law had given powers to local authorities, planning commissions and so forth, and probably the sanitary inspector did have a right to enter the railwayman's home and lavatory in the course of his duties. The railwayman expressed his thanks and went sadly away. The point of the episode is not in the mixture, piquant though it be, of feudalism and Communism, but the fact that even in a state-controlled and planned world, the Britishman expects that his cottage will remain inviolate.

Dropping in unannounced on friends, therefore, is not encouraged in Britain. The idea of keeping open house to all comers has never appealed. In earlier centuries it was, of course, permitted and indeed required of the country gentry that they should call on each other frequently and that their calls should be returned. But the calls themselves were rigidly governed by etiquette. Calls could be made only at certain times and by certain people. They must last only a short length of time and had, in due course, to be formally returned. Even in the eighteenth century the system did not find universal approval. Jane Austen described many such calls, with her usual cool detachment. Her view of the conversation of the callers was often less than enthusiastic, and she, like any other Britishwoman, would be happy at the thought that the system has now died.

It must not be thought, however, that the British are basically inhospitable. Indeed, they are one of the most hospitable of European peoples. It is perhaps a consequence of keeping strangers outside the gates that guests, when they do come and are admitted, are welcomed with unusual warmth. Such guests, however, have not dropped in. They have been specifically invited for a certain date or a certain event. They are not unexpected or unannounced. An exception used to be made for the friends and relations of earlier centuries, traveling from one part of Britain to another, who could not be allowed to face the dangers and the dirt of the local inn. But with the arrival of the modern hotel and modern transport, this obligation has, like the practice of calling, died. Jane Austen herself went to stay for long periods with her brother at Godmersham in Kent, but she was in no doubt that these visits were a charitable donation to a poor relation. They were also a token gesture from her sister-in-law, Elizabeth, who, in typical British fashion, refused to let Jane live permanently in the house.

British hospitality has seldom reached a more sumptuous point than the house parties of the Edwardian era, where large numbers of distinguished guests would arrive in a country house, complete with menservants, maidservants, and several trunks, to pass a Saturday-to-Monday, or perhaps a race week, in the costliest possible way. But these parties were, once again, the result of specific invitations to certain people for certain dates. A guest who overstays his welcome is as abhorrent to the British as a spoiled child or a starved dog. In the last two decades, middle-class British hospitality has been largely confined to a weekend with friends in their country cottage; small candlelit dinners in Chelsea or similar areas (where the guests will often include important business colleagues or superiors, to the dismay of the young hostess trying simultaneously to say the right thing, to look attractive, and to serve up coq au vin); the Sunday-morning visitors for sherry and gin and tonic (the modern equivalent perhaps of formal calling); and the ubiquitous and standardized cocktail party.

On a lower social level, hospitality is equally formalized. Dropping in is once again discouraged, but relations may be invited to stay for the weekend or to come over for Sunday dinner. The children of friends and neighbors may be invited to carefully prepared children's parties, and for these memorable occasions the front room, normally unused, will be opened, dusted and heated. On every level, the same etiquette applies. The invitation, formally given, comes formally to an end when the party is over. When the hospitality expires, or even earlier, the guests are expected to leave. The host wishes to reestablish his precious privacy for several more weeks or even months.

The Britishman's concern for his privacy extends far beyond keeping strangers on the doorstep or speeding parting guests. It applies particularly to a man or woman's personal appearance, his clothes, his hairstyle. Indeed, the British attitude to hair provides a revealing clue to character. The British are, of course, as capable as any other race of getting hysterical about the length of men's hair. Comments on the length of hair of certain pop singers or students is likely to be as forthright in Britain as in any other country, and indeed, the controversy, the intolerance may be traced back to the Roundheads in the Civil War or perhaps even farther. But even those who feel most strongly on the subject of male haircuts still have an overriding respect for the privacy of the wearer, a feeling that, in the last resort, his appearance is his own concern and nobody else's. Any violations of this rule will at once be reported in the daily press; a boy on the dole was ordered to cut his hair before he could be offered a job; a boy in a remand home awaiting trial had his hair cut compulsorily (he was in fact innocent, but he later took to crime, blaming the haircut for his lapses, and he was accordingly dealt with very leniently); the Sikh bus conductors were told to get their beards cut by the local transport authorities. In all these cases, the press and the public were solidly behind the boys or the Sikhs concerned. When a celebrated pop singer, who had, as much as anyone, popularized the present cult of long hair, was arrested on a drugs charge, the country held its breath in case some insensitive prison warder might cut his hair during the short period he was confined, and those who sighed with relief when he came out unscathed will have included many people who shared Cromwell's views about the right length of male hair. It was simply that they respected his privacy and felt that his appearance was his own business.

Privacy includes not only appearance, but personal life, political or religious opinions, income and even occupation. Two officers happened to meet again after a long separation. One asked the other what he was doing these days, and he received the reply, "Minding my own business, I hope." Most Britishmen would not answer quite so bluntly; they would evade the question, answer obliquely, mumble or give brief minimum information and then change the subject. The inquirer, even though he may be only making polite conversation, has no right to ask the question, has no right to intrude on their private life. I have often observed at my local railway station, in Hampshire, that when four Britishmen get into an empty train, they will, unless they happen to know one another already, choose to sit in separate compartments. They thus avoid the danger that one of the others might get into conversation with them. This would be most unlikely, but it is as well to make sure. The action is not caused by standoffishness, but by a respect for privacy, the other person's, as well as your own.

This idea is not shared by other races, where the four men would frequently choose to sit together, in the hope of starting a conversation. It is not, it seems, even shared by the Australians, though they have derived so much of their culture and attitudes from Britain. Perhaps they are, like Americans in the Middle West, surrounded at home by too much silence and isolation. Flying once to Moscow in an almost empty plane, I chose deliberately a window seat far from any other passenger and planned to spend the journey reading and briefing myself on certain aspects of the Soviet Union. I was, therefore, considerably annoyed when a fellow passenger, an Australian, changed his seat to sit beside me and tell me his life story. Every country, of course, has its quota of bores, but my resentment against the Australian was not due to the comparative lack of interest of his life story or to the fact that he was taking up valuable reading time, but that he was, uninvited, invading my privacy with his personality. I did not, of course, tell him my own life story or even why I was going to Moscow. I had no wish to intrude on his privacy.

With privacy comes silence. London and other busy cities are, of course, noisy with the roar of modern traffic. But many Britishmen do not feel the need for gratuitous background noise, for taped music or car radios to obliterate the silence which falls so heavily upon those who come from larger, more wide-open countries. The South African writer Laurens van der Post tells a story of a British sailor who, after long years at sea, had become used to solitude and quiet. When he retired, he emigrated to the Kalahari Desert and lived there by choice alone in the middle of the desert, in conditions of considerable hardship. He was perhaps the supreme example of a Britishman protecting his privacy from other people's noise, as well as from their company.

Proud possibly, unsociable certainly, reserved—indeed yes! And this is a quality on which the Britishman would naturally pride himself. Dame Rose Macaulay, in a splendid and striking phrase, wrote that we should consume our own smoke. It is not a phrase likely to find approval in countries where smoke is something to be used as a smokescreen.

It is sometimes said that the British are reserved to the point of insensitivity, but this is a misunderstanding of the British character. The British are not an insensitive nation. On the contrary, they are hypersensitive, unbearably sensitive, sensitive to the point of touchiness, and this, at least, is something which they have handed on to their Australian cousins. But this touchiness is carefully concealed from the outsider. To take offense, to complain, to kick up a fuss, to make a row, to cause a scene—all this is deeply distressing to the Britishman. He will prefer to keep silence and nurse his grievance in his heart. In the words of a romantic novelist, "not by the flicker of an eyelid did he show that the shot had gone home." This is the British ideal. He will smile, shrug, pretend not to hear, pretend to misunderstand, leave politely—and never return. And the matter can never be put right. As there has been no complaint, there can be no investigation, no inquiry, no apology, no compensation. The disagreement remains silent, concealed and permanent.

In a British pub, somebody may say something which offends one of the other customers. The speaker may be the landlord, a regular guest, or some casual drinker who happens to be passing by and has called in for a drink. The Britishman will notice the insult which may or may not have been intended. He may hesitate for a moment in what he is saying and then recover. He may go slightly red in the face, but otherwise he will give no sign. He will finish his drink, say good-night to all present and walk out forever. The other customers present will probably have noticed nothing. They will simply be surprised not to see him anymore in that pub. Encountering him later in the street, they may express surprise that they haven't seen him around lately. He will answer tersely, "Oh, I don't go there anymore," and he will not give any reason. The answer is sufficient.

Returning once to England after a prolonged spell abroad, I asked in my local pub what had happened to the local cricket club. I was told by a fellow drinker, "Oh, they don't come here anymore." I expressed surprise and asked if there had been a row. "No," I was told, "oh, no, nothing like that." Later it was admitted that there had been some discussion about which room the club was to use for its meetings, whether the members were to sit in a private room or in the lounge. In any event, the members of the club felt themselves slighted, and as a spontaneous and silent gesture, they all resolved never to set foot in that particular pub again. Henceforward, they, both as a club and as individuals, would drink elsewhere, which, as the next pub was two miles away, was no doubt greatly to their inconvenience, collectively and individually. But as no complaint was made, as there was no row, no scene, the matter could never be put right. Only a new landlord at the pub could, by his arrival, wipe the slate clean. The members would feel justified then in returning to the pub for an occasional pint. Their silent protest could be deemed to have lapsed. One of the problems which country publicans and owners of village shops have to face is that in the course of time and by the nature of human conversation, somebody sometime is bound to take secret offense and transfer his custom to the pub or shop in the next village or town, and after perhaps five years, the publican or the shopkeeper will find that most of his customers have gone elsewhere and he will never know why.

If the British find it hard to complain, they find it even harder to apologize. Most nations, most human beings, of course, find it difficult to admit a fault and to express regret, but the British find it harder than most. To apologize is to risk causing the very scene which was carefully skated over at the time of the incident. It is to endanger everyone's privacy by reviving old grievances, old insults. Since no complaint has been made, there is usually nothing to apologize for, and the Britishman with the grievance will be grateful for this. To receive an apology gratuitously, either explicit or implied, is as distasteful to him as to complain in the first place. "Let's forget it," is the British spoken reaction to a grievance—only, of course, that it is never either forgotten or forgiven.

All this helps explain perhaps the Britishman's reaction to bad service in hotels or restaurants or to bad plays, bad performances. Except on rare occasions, he does not boo in the theater, and when this occasionally does happen, the boos often come from an organized claque. He simply stays away. He does not whistle and jeer like an Italian crowd at the opera or a Spanish crowd at the bullfight. If the star cricketer scores a duck, if the highly praised footballer misses the goal, they will be allowed to leave the ground in heavy silence.

I may perhaps give two examples from my own experience of this British impassivity, this hatred of making a fuss. A few years ago I was spending a brief summer holiday on an Italian island. The hotel, a converted *palazzo,* had been recommended to us by a reliable travel agent, and indeed it had a superb view. Our room had a large terrace overlooking the bay, and though it had no private bathroom, as we had been warned, there was a bathroom nearby on the same floor. The owner of the hotel showed us with pride the room, the ceiling, the view, the terrace, the bath next door. It was only later that we discovered that the bath was pure window dressing, that it was unconnected to any plumbing. There was, in fact, no hot water anywhere, and it was obviously going to be difficult to wash. Being British, we naturally made no complaint, but the hotel proprietor, unable to bear the suspense, asked us after a day or two if we were enjoying our baths. We made noncommittal replies. He reverted to the topic several times during our stay, and each time we refused to be drawn into making a complaint. We washed as best we could, we had a good holiday, and the proprietor no doubt assumed that we had never even set foot in his beautiful bathroom. He must have been surprised that we did not return another year.

The other episode also centers on the ever-green subject of Mediterranean baths. Recently a middle-aged British lady was taking a holiday in a Spanish fishing village. The village, the beach, the shops, the hotel were entirely up to her expectations. Only one thing was wrong: the bathing arrangements. Her room had, as she knew, no private bath, but there was a bath on the same floor, and unlike my bath in Italy, this bath was connected to the plumbing. Only it seemed that the water was always cold. She hesitated for several days, wondering whether to make a complaint or not, and finally, since she spoke no Spanish, she approached the local representative of the travel agency, a friend of mine, and asked if he could arrange for her to have a hot bath. She agreed willingly to pay extra for this little luxury, and the representative duly spoke to the hotel proprietor. The proprietor was suitably astonished; who could possibly want a hot bath in Spain in July? The water was hardly cold in the pipes, and anyway there was the sea. However, he was a sympathetic and kindly man, and he valued both his British guests and the patronage of the travel agency. If *la inglesa* wanted a hot bath, then a hot bath she could have, and a date and a time were fixed for the event. Not trusting anyone else to do the job properly, he stoked the boiler himself, shoveling on more and more expensive coal, sweat pouring from every pore, sparing neither time nor expense to give the British lady what she wanted. At six o'clock he tapped at the lady's door and announced that her bath was ready. She thanked him politely, picked up her towel and her sponge bag and locked herself into the bathroom.

About an hour later, the hotel proprietor began to feel anxious, and he asked the British travel representative, who was in the hotel for the great event, if they should not tap on the door and find out if she was all right. The representative suggested that they leave it another ten minutes and, if she had still not emerged, they should perhaps go and find out the position. Ten minutes later the two of them tapped on the bathroom door. Was the bath all right? they called out. She called back that it was just right, that everything was fine, that she would be out soon. Fifteen minutes later she emerged, scarlet in the face like a tomato, thanked the two men for the bath and for the trouble they had both taken.

The proprietor shrugged and went back to the kitchen; the representative went on to another hotel. It was only as she was leaving the resort a week later that the guest confided to the representative what had really happened. On arriving in the bathroom, locking herself in, she had found indeed that the water was hot, gloriously hot, scalding. But she noticed for the first time that there was only one tap, the tap that normally ran cold and now ran boiling water. She was therefore in a dilemma; to go out from the bathroom and ask for a bucket or two of cold water would be to complain, and this she could not do, especially after everybody had taken so much trouble to help her. To abandon the bath and return to her room after a tactful interval would show defeatism, untypical of both her character and her race. The only possible solution—and the solution which she chose instinctively—was to run her boiling bath and then sit on the edge of the bath and wait for it to cool by the normal laws of nature. And on a July afternoon in Spain, hot water cools rather slowly.

14

THE FUNNY SIDE

◆§ The tourist in the bath, just referred to, was, of course, making a joke against herself. She was British, she had a sense of humor, and to a Britishman a joke, a funny story, or a humorous episode is a natural part of life, an essential part of existence. It is to his daily life what ketchup is to his food, what beer is to his drink, and indeed the analogy with beer is apt. A Britishman who does not like beer is as rare as a Britishman who cannot see a joke. And like British beer, British humor is warm, full, rich, something of a connoisseur's taste. It often does not travel well abroad, and conversely foreigners used to cooler, sharper tastes do not always appreciate it to the full.

Much of British humor, of course, is timeless and international, the common coin of world jokes. There are some episodes which will make a Britishman laugh heartily in tune with the rest of the world. To give a practical example, when I was a small boy, I attended a fair in South Wales, organized by the local church. The fair was held in a field outside the village and was attended by everyone from the village and by a number of visitors from farther off. An uninvited visitor, however, was a cow from the next field, which jumped the ditch and entered the ladies' lavatory, a rudimentary bucket and seat affair surrounded by canvas screens. The cow knocked the bucket over and emerged triumphantly, the lavatory seat on its horns like a crown. It then mingled with the other patrons of the fair, the ladies in their silks and straw hats, the farmers in their tweeds, pausing at intervals to eat the grass between the booths and then moving on to investigate the Aunt Sally or the coconut shies.* Since the cow had a willful and inquisitive nature, all efforts to drive it away were unsuccessful. So were attempts to remove the wooden crown from its head. The cow was in no mood to stand still, and in any event those trying to carry out this maneuver were almost helpless with laughter. When night fell and the fair closed, the cow was still proudly wearing its borrowed crown.

It was, of course, the most successful fair ever held in that village. But as an example of a humorous episode it was international more than British. The cow and the laughers were Welsh, but is there a country, a people in the world, with the possible exception of the Communist Chinese, who would not have found it funny? There are some jokes, some situations, which leap over all frontiers, and the British are no more impervious to them than any other race.

Satire, too, is international, an essential part of every major literature, all the way from Aristophanes to Art Buchwald, and the British have their full share of satirists, some, such as Swift, Pope and W. S. Gilbert, now classics, others, such as Evelyn Waugh and David Frost, more contemporary and therefore harder to judge. Circus clowns, too, are international and traditional, and the British clown varies in no way, either in appearance or in style, from his brother clowns in Russia or in Spain. But one may perhaps notice a slight difference in that supreme British clown Charles Chaplin. Many of his funniest scenes show the downtrodden little man pushing a cream bun in the face of the rich bully, scoring off the pompous, stealing the girl from the powerful and oafish other man. In these

* Fairground games. The player throws a ball to knock the pipe out of the mouth of a dummy figure called Aunt Sally or to hit a set of coconuts off their stands.

scenes, Chaplin is calling on the basic British Jack-the-Giant-Killer dream, a race memory of the small and clever Celts, outwitting the large and stupid Teutons who had conquered them. Except for this, Chaplin belongs in the international clown tradition, as indeed his life and career have belonged.

The original British humor, the older strand, was founded, like the humor of so many other peoples, on cruelty. The classic Punch and Judy show makes fun of a hunchback, who retaliates by beating his wife and throwing the baby out of the window. As a theme it is as gruesome as *Wozzeck,* but it used to be thought amusing. Cripples, hunchbacks, village idiots, Mongols were funny and to be laughed at. It was funny to throw eggs or tomatoes at a petty criminal, standing in the pillory or locked in the stocks. Times and tastes change, and we would not find it funny now. When, a few years ago, the Lord Chief Justice of England advocated in a speech bringing back the stocks and the pillory for petty offenders, ridicule being, in his view, the greatest of all deterrents, he was forgetting the changing outlook of Britain. A man in the pillory nowadays would not be laughed at or have eggs or tomatoes thrown at him. Instead, he would be given cigarettes and chocolate and tea by faithful girlfriends.

When William the Conqueror wished to raise a laugh, he had his enemies "pollarded"—that is to say, he cut off their hands and feet. This was a big joke, much appreciated by the onlookers. But if the British have changed in this, many other nations have not. During the last war, a Russian docker in Archangel happened to smoke in an area where smoking was prohibited. In punishment for this, his fellow dockers seized him, tied him, took down his trousers, and sat him on a large block of ice. They then stood around roaring with laughter at the ignominious and unfortunate man until he froze to the block and died. A British ship was in port at the time, and the crew was invited, as a gesture of hospitality, to come share the joke. But to modern British seamen there was nothing remotely funny about the spectacle, and they returned to their ship in disgust.

The British author Gwyn Thomas recently gave a lecture to a British audience on humor, in which he stated that the basis of all humor was cruelty and horror. The perfect funny story, he said, was about a woman jumping from the window of a blazing building into a fireman's net—only there was no net. However, when he told the story, it did not raise a laugh. The humor of horror is, of course, a perfectly valid form of humor, but it does not appeal to the modern Britishman. The cartoons of Charles Addams did not strike an answering chord, and indeed his work was not syndicated in British newspapers and journals. It was a specialized taste in Britain, for those with American connections and for those who read the *New Yorker*.

There is a type of humor which is specially and privately British. In many ways it is unique, unrelated to the humor of other countries, and it has certainly changed greatly since the Middle Ages. The change perhaps dates from the Renaissance and the arrival of the Welsh Tudors, who brought for the first, and perhaps for the last time, wit, subtlety and music to the court and to the great houses. Rough Viking jokes were not to the taste of the Elizabethans. Shakespeare's humor depended very little on horseplay. In this he had been preceded by Chaucer, who, in his sense of humor, as in much else, was ahead of his time and who foreshadowed the British satirical tradition. Henry VIII, half Welsh, half Norman, liked a boisterous joke against his friends or his enemies, but in his youth he also could appreciate a joke against himself, something which William the Conqueror would never have understood. The joke against oneself is arguably the basis for all the best British humor. It is ironic to think that it began in the reign of a king famed now for his cruelty.

With the Tudors also came the pun, the result of the Renaissance. The punning tradition goes back a long way, to Aristophanes perhaps or even farther. But it had been forgotten for many centuries, and it has now been forgotten again. Puns nowadays in Britain are the intellectual pastime of schoolmasters and professors, and crossword-puzzle composers. The puns which bedevil *Romeo and Juliet* are more likely to cause a groan than a hearty laugh. In recent years the pun has become the specialty of Irish writers, from James Joyce to Marshall McLuhan, but it still remains alien to the typical Britishman, who tends to regard puns as a tiresome affectation, a form of showing off which is too clever and not too funny.

Nonsense, to the Britishman, is a far more genuine strand of humor. One thinks in this connection of Lewis Carroll and Edward Lear. Nonsense is, of course, the *reductio ad absurdum* of incongruity. It is a Hungarian expatriate, Arthur Koestler, who has analyzed in detail the mechanism of the joke and has argued that the basis of humor is incongruity, the double reference, the phrase in its wrong context, the man in his wrong setting. Whether this is true of all humor everywhere is a debatable point. It is certainly true of British humor, and one may note happily that it is a fellow Hungarian in England, George Mikes, who has made such perfect use of the technique.

The incongruity joke leads naturally to the joke by understatement, very much a British specialty. We find it funny to refer to the *Queen Elizabeth II* as a paddle steamer, to call a Rolls-Royce a little runabout. The idea is to deflate, to cause, if possible, a feeling of anticlimax, which is an important ingredient of many British jokes. A man rescued from a blazing building will probably remark to the fireman, "Just as well you got me out when you did. I'd found I was right out of sunburn oil."

But the great British joke, perhaps the greatest British contribution to international humor, is the joke against oneself; the joke where the narrator is the silly ass, the fall guy, the sucker, and he knows it and can still find it funny and laugh at it—this is the antithesis of the cruel joke, unless it is regarded as an inverted cruel joke, a masochistic joke.

But this is, I think, to oversimplify. The joke against oneself is extremely British and has little to do with masochism. The chief object is to show that the narrator has a sense of humor, is an amusing raconteur, good company, but at the same time a nice chap without any wish to hurt, even inadvertently, anybody else's feelings. After all, if he tells a joke at somebody else's expense, somebody in the cocktail party, the pub, the club, the political meeting may be a friend of the person at whose expense the joke is being made. Faces may grow red, huffy words be spoken, tempers become troubled. The joke will have failed, and the speaker may incur the reproach, spoken or not spoken, "That's not very funny." It is always safer in Britain to make the joke against yourself, the one person who cannot take offense.

At a legal dinner on a local circuit, shortly after the last war, one of the speakers was a distinguished counsel. During his speech he poked fun at another member of the circuit who had been detained during the war, in prison, for pro-German sympathies, under Regulation 18b. The man himself, though released, was not present at the dinner, and there is no reason to believe that anybody else present shared his views. Some of them had had distinguished war records. But notwithstanding this and despite the distinction of the speaker, the jibe was much resented, and surprisingly for the self-contained British, the speech ended in uproar. There were cries of "Shame!" from all parts of the room, spoons were banged on the table, and the speaker was forced to sit down without saying anything more. He was of course, not invited to speak again. He would have been wiser, as everybody knew, to have confined his sardonic shafts of wit to jokes against himself.

The British pride themselves on their sense of humor. Not to have one is something which no Britishman will forgive in others or in himself. The man who is suspected of being without a sense of humor will be the first to protest that he, fortunately, has a great sense of humor, and in the end, if he says it often enough and tells enough jokes against himself, everyone may come to believe him. It is no more possible to admit to not having a sense of humor than it is to admit to being a bad driver or to being impotent. Objectively, there is no special reason why a sense of humor should be a necessary part of the human condition; many races do not require it as an essential part of life. It has been often observed that the Bible is very short on humor, both in the characters and in the writing. But the British are quite sure that humor is essential to the human makeup; indeed many would go further and say that a sense of humor is the greatest British national asset, worth more than any of the other qualities of the British character which are mentioned elsewhere in this book. British history, British culture, British industry, it is felt, were founded not so much on patriotism, or discipline, or hard work, or diplomatic skill as on a sense of humor. A joke is to the British a better call to arms than a bugle.

The result has been, unfortunately, to lower rather than to raise the standard of British humor. Too much too often levels down rather than levels up. The crudest joke told and heard often before will, unless it is at somebody else's expense, always raise a smile or a laugh; the hearer dare not risk not laughing, dare not risk the accusation that he is the one without a sense of humor. Political speakers know this well. A few jokes, however corny, and the audience will have to laugh with you or show themselves humorless. Nowadays they sometimes applaud instead of laughing, a less spontaneous reaction, but one which serves to show that the audience has taken the point, seen the joke, appreciated the wit of the speaker and acknowledged it, even if the joke was not funny enough to elicit an outright laugh.

The clearest-cut examples of all are the British joke clichés which are repeated endlessly in music halls (where these still exist), at seaside concert parties, at pantomimes, even on television. It is only necessary for a comedian to mention a kipper, a mother-in-law, a bailiff, a seaside landlady, a honeymooning couple or someone with a funny accent (from some other part of Britain or, better still, from abroad) and the audience will laugh automatically. It is partly, of course, a conditioned reflex, a Pavlovian reaction, but more important, it is the fear of appearing humorless to those sitting nearby. Clichés and repetitions are an essential part of the routine, the audience can quickly get the idea that it is being told jokes, and however bad or stale the jokes may be, it is required to laugh uproariously. It will invariably comply. The tradition, judging from some passages in Shakespeare, goes back a long way, and the idea of an unfunny joke becoming funnier by repetition may well be a legacy from pre-Elizabethan humor. Then, as now, the audience was a captive one, captive to the need to laugh publicly.

Queen Victoria's famous remark "We are not amused" amazed and shocked her people. Indeed, it is the only thing she ever said in her long life which is now generally recalled. It would be unthinkable for a Britishman to utter such words in any circumstances; Britishmen are always amused. But then, Queen Victoria was a German.

Humor, it seems, is a British institution, as much a part of British life as the royal family or the House of Commons or the local pub. But it is also a useful adjunct in social manners. To the laconic and reserved British, humor is a useful substitute for intelligent and thoughtful conversation. It passes the time of day sociably, good-humoredly. To meet a neighbor in the street and say merely "Good morning" is rather chilly and snubbing. It is politer to pause for a moment and exchange a few remarks on a neutral subject, such as the weather. Best of all is to make a joke about the weather, for the weather is something which is fair game, and of course, the joke does not have to be a fresh one. An old joke is safer; everyone knows exactly where he is. In Hampshire, in the winter, when an icy east wind blows across the Downs, a man stopping to speak to his neighbor in the street will remark, "It's a real lazy wind today," and the neighbor will reply, "It would sooner go through you than round you." Both neighbors will laugh in the friendliest way and move on, social contact fully established. Or the joke may be against yourself. The village postmistress may forget the date and write yesterday's date on the counterfoil she is making out. When the mistake is pointed out to her, she will not show any annoyance. She will laugh and say, "There, I've lost a friend" (the friend being the lost day), and those present, knowing the joke too, will laugh happily with her.

But if humor is desirable in normal social life, it is regarded as being completely essential at all moments of crisis. This is an instinctive reaction, perhaps indeed a panic reaction, and it applies to all sorts of Britishmen—Saxons, Vikings or Celts—from one class to another. It is often seriously misunderstood abroad. The flippancy of swinging London, obsessed with mini-skirts and hairstyles and gambling, is often criticized abroad as being frivolous, irresponsible, the visible sign of the final decadence of a great nation. In fact, it is more likely to be a clown's mask worn by people deeply anxious about the present and the future but obliged, both by their character and by their training, to laugh to the end. It is not in the British nature to sob with emotion, to beat one's breast in an agony of remorse or apprehension, to issue noble credos of faith in the future.

The reaction of the typical British businessman standing on a cold, crowded suburban platform waiting for a late, dirty train to take him to his office in the City on the Monday after the 1967 devaluation of the pound was not to whine, not to plan a social or economic revolution, not to make loud and pious resolves to work longer hours and export more. Things were too serious for that. It was no moment for high-flown oratory, for dust and ashes; the situation was too desperate. It was the moment for a joke. There was no other adequate reaction. A bitter joke, maybe, a savage joke, against the Britishman himself, his leaders, his advisers, but still a joke. Some foreign observers missed the point; the image of Britain sinking into the sea with a nervous giggle, the cliché about Nero fiddling, appeared almost daily in the foreign press, an analogy which showed partly a misunderstanding of Roman history and partly a misunderstanding of the British character. When a Britishman jokes all the time, things are desperate indeed.

It is, of course, possible at the right moment for the right man, using the right phrases, to provoke what is known as the Dunkirk spirit. Churchill used few jokes in his 1940 speeches, and the man being what he was and the occasion being what it was, this was allowed. His seriousness was admired, his heroic attitude, his grim, though romantic, determination. But it is not an attitude which the British can hold for more than a few weeks. Churchill, with his sure touch for public reaction, knew this. After 1940, his speeches became progressively lighter both in tone and in phrase, though not necessarily in thought or in content, till he finally achieved the typically British piece of rhetoric "Some chicken! Some neck!" The art of the British public speaker is to make his point without embarrassing his audience with sententiousness, and this perhaps is something which later politicians, calling regularly for a return of the Dunkirk spirit during the regular economic crises, would do well to bear in mind.

During a battle, the moment, so to speak, of total crisis, British dialogue is famous for its jokes, sometimes rather bad or forced jokes, but at least evidence of the speaker's wish to produce the right word on the right occasion. It is impossible to imagine a British soldier shouting sentences about *la gloire* or *la patrie,* or about victory for the heroic fatherland, or death to the Fascist hyena invaders. Far from inspiring anyone, such phrases would only make an unpleasant situation distinctly more unpleasant. The radio dialogues of Spitfire pilots during the Battle of Britain or between bomber pilots and base, when they were trying to bring their damaged planes home from a bombing raid on Germany, were lighthearted and slangy. Their sentences are not likely to find their way into the *Oxford Book of English Prose.* The orders of the day of Field Marshal Montgomery echoed deliberately the remarks of a school cricket captain in the pavilion. On a solemn occasion this was as far as he could go, as much as anyone could receive, but this is not to suggest that anyone, from the commander in chief to the rifle-bearing private soldier, underestimated the seriousness of the moment.

To recall a personal experience, during the German counterattack in the Ardennes in December, 1944, I was summoned as a liaison officer, in the middle of the night, to corps headquarters to receive orders. The battle, sometimes called the Battle of the Bulge, was going extremely badly for the Allies. It was thought that two German Panzer armies had broken through in the general area of the Ardennes and were likely to fan out behind the Allied lines, possibly recapturing Brussels and Antwerp, inflicting a tactical defeat on the British and the Americans which would have great positional and psychological advantages. On top of everything else, it was a cold, foggy night, and it took me several hours to reach corps headquarters. When I finally arrived in the early hours, there was obviously a great deal of tension in the air. The general was closeted with one of his senior staff officers, and I waited in the ops room till he was free, chatting, in a lighthearted way, of course, with the duty officer. Also waiting to see the general was a very senior artillery officer. He stood preoccupied, staring at the big map on the wall, lost in thought.

After about ten minutes, the senior staff officer came out of the general's caravan and paused in the ops room to greet the artillery officer, who was not only a friend but his equal in rank. I overheard their dialogue. The staff officer asked the gunner, "What is it that has two upsy-wupsies, four downsy-wownsies and a swishy-wishy?" The gunner, slightly bewildered at the change in his train of thought, confessed after a moment's thought that he didn't know. The answer indeed was simple: "A cowsy-wowsy." It is difficult to imagine senior German staff officers swopping somewhat juvenile riddles at a critical stage in the battle, but the British officers concerned were neither juvenile nor irresponsible. They were simply responding characteristically to an anxious moment.

Far from being a matter for apology, the British are proud of this reaction to a crisis. It is not only good manners, but evidence of high morale, refusal to panic, a great source of strength. The folk hero of World War I, the archetypal British Soldier, was not a romantic soldier poet, not, to quote Fitzgerald's phrase, "a football captain killed in battle," but Old Bill, the indestructible, undismayed character from Bruce Bairnsfather's cartoons. Old Bill in his steel helmet, his straggly mustache, his cape, gazing out through the rain at the mud of no-man's-land and finding it funny. The German High Command began to suspect that the British in their humor, in Bairnsfather, might have a secret weapon which they had taken so far too lightly. They therefore reprinted thousands of copies of a captured Bairnsfather cartoon and issued it to their own troops in an effort to indoctrinate them with humor. Old Bill sat huddled in his dugout beside a huge new shell hole. A new recruit just arrived for the first time in the front line asked him nervously what had made the hole. "Mice" was the laconic answer. (A classic example, incidentally, of the joke by understatement.) For the benefit of their own soldiers who might not get the point, the Germans added an explanation: "It was not mice; it was a shell." Old Bill was, of course, a fictional character. Whether he was modeled on millions of others or whether they modeled themselves on him is uncertain, but the officer who crawled forward through the barbed wire and the mud, across no-man's-land to within a few feet of the German trenches, with the sole object of taking down the score of the German Hymn of Hate when they sang it, was a real live person.

For once, in this book, there must be no mention of class distinctions, for the need to make a joke at moments of crisis is automatic at all levels. One can think of Charles II on his deathbed, murmuring, "I beg pardon, gentlemen, to have been such an unconscionable time a-dying"; or the dying Bernard Shaw telling his nurse that it was a great mistake to wash antiques; or the wounded soldier coming around from the operation in which his leg had been amputated murmuring dizzily, "Tell me, nurse, is it a boy?" down to the London gangster who was shot four times in the head and neck in a cellar, his friend killed before his eyes, before he fought his way out. Later, lying in hospital, critically ill, facing a number of serious charges, almost unable to speak, he yet managed to whisper to his wife, "I've got an awful sore throat. Can't think what gave it to me." Trapped miners, as if their circumstances were not already difficult enough, are expected to shout a nonstop stream of jokes at the rescuers trying to reach them. Mothers in labor are also expected to keep up a light repartee. British ambulance men have a carefully prepared line of jokes, enough almost for a professional comedian. British nurses in a children's hospital in South Vietnam, when guerrillas burst into the hospital and machine-gunned the operating room, are reported to have commented to each other, "Well, if this is war, it's not very nice, is it?" The reaction is pure routine.

The British attitude on the scaffold is revealing. The French aristo in the tumbril or on the guillotine preserved a stiff, calm, unsmiling dignity. The German generals who were strangled for their abortive attempt against Hitler in July, 1944, are reported to have called out slogans about their fatherland before they died. But the Britishman on the scaffold is, of course, required to make a joke. One thinks at once of Sir Thomas More, the most indefatigable of scaffold humorists. On his arrival on Tower Hill, he made a joke about the weather (what else?). At the foot of the rickety steps up to the scaffold he said to the commander of the guard, "I pray you, Master Lieutenant, see me safely up. For my coming down I will shift for myself." As he laid his head on the block, he made a further joke, about his beard. One thinks, too, of the more recent execution of John Amery, who greeted the public hangman with the words, "I've always wanted to meet you, Pierrepoint, but not in these circumstances." My aunt Jane Grey, however, whose humor was not her strong point, seems to have been an exception and does not seem to have attempted a joke in her scaffold speech, unless we count her schoolgirl howler, "I wash my hands in all innocence," a misquotation which must have made her tutor, the scholar Roger Ascham (who was reportedly present), shake his head sadly.

Speeches, in England, of course, are no longer made on scaffolds, but to the speaker the moment often seems to be equally critical. An immediate joke is called for, and no matter how stale or contrived the joke may be, the audience will laugh sympathetically. More practiced and therefore possibly less nervous speakers know that they have to be continually amusing, even on such unamusing occasions as the annual budget. Foreigners have often expressed surprise at the levity of British public speaking. To them, a serious public occasion demands a serious public oration.

A year or two ago I attended an international congress, whose theme was solemn, contemporary and rather erudite. The congress organizers had invited a number of experts, mostly professors, to come address us, and the whole affair was intended to be an important contribution to general thinking about the subject under discussion. But to me, the chief interest was in noting the different oratorical styles of the speakers and the impossibility, even in the age of simultaneous translation, of communicating with anyone except the speaker's own people.

The German professor read out a long lecture, without making any concessions to popular appeal, such as visual aids, topical examples or even changing the pitch or loudness of his voice. His compatriots listened to every word, but the rest of the audience became restive after the first hour. The Italian speaker, surprisingly for a delegate from a people famous for their showmanship, adopted the same manner. The French speaker concealed his argument in a cloud of apparently spontaneous rhetoric, which baffled most of his listeners and finally had them tiptoeing from the hall. The American spoke slowly, very thoughtfully and very seriously. But the British lecturer, alone, tried to make his contribution acceptable by a stream of anecdotes and jokes. Nobody, except the British contingent, laughed at these; perhaps they did not come over well in translation, or perhaps the audience had not come prepared to be amused. They decided, instead, that the speaker was being frivolous and so unworthy of their attention. They fidgeted, took off their headphones and began to talk among themselves. They did not realize that, stripped of its entertaining paper wrapping, the lecture was as serious and thoughtful as any of the others. The British speaker, however, knew this, and this was exactly why he had felt it his job to make his lecture on an unfunny subject as funny as possible.

15

FAIR PLAY

If, for some reason, a joke cannot be made at the speaker's own expense, it must be patently harmless, or should there be a barb in it, the victim must be clearly riding so high that he can laugh at it with the others. To make a joke about someone in misfortune is not only to be unfunny but, worse still, to be unfair. The tradition of not kicking a man when he's down is typically British, traditional and, indeed, instinctive. It comes as a shock to the Britishman to find that other nations do not always see things the same way. Luigi Barzini has written amusingly on the Italian preference for kicking a man when he's down. What better moment could there be to kick him? It would be foolish indeed to wait till he is back on his feet and able to kick back. No Britishman could begin to understand this attitude. The opponent, the enemy, must be given time to get back on his feet and recover, must be allowed a chance to kick back. Anything else would be not fair, and to be not fair is the worst, the most wounding, the most bitter accusation that a Britishman can make.

British children chant the phrase continually, everywhere, from smart and expensive preparatory schools at Ascot to the local primary schools in the big cities. The classroom, the corridors and the playing fields or playgrounds echo to the cry "It's not fair. That's unfair," and indeed schools often are unfair. The opportunities for privilege, preferential treatment, favoritism, bullying, gang warfare often produce unfair situations. But to the victim it is not the unmerited punishment, the caning, the bleeding nose or being suddenly dropped from a football side which hurts so much as the unfairness. A boy in his first term, meeting injustice for the first time in his life, protests instinctively and loudly against it.

The idea of fairness stems from the fundamental British assumption that there are rules for everything in life. Should somebody somewhere transgress or ignore these rules, a cry of "Unfair" will go up. Other parallel phrases may be used: "It's damned unsporting," or even "It just isn't cricket." Or perhaps, "He's just not playing the game." Listening to these complaints, a foreigner may sometimes wonder if the British do not regard everything—love, war, work, politics, careers, sex, life, death—as one big game for which the rules have been carefully laid down at some time in the past by a select subcommittee and which cannot be amended except at an extraordinary general meeting with everybody present and concurring.

For the British, nobody is exempt from the rules as they stand; nobody, even the boss, is allowed to make up rules as he goes along or to alter them to suit his convenience, a point which English kings, from King John at Runnymede to King Charles I at Naseby, had often to be taught by force. Magna Carta was only the first effort to force the king to play by the rules. Hampden's famous campaign against Charles I's tax called ship money was not an attempt to diminish the might of the Royal Navy; it was an instinctive protest against the king, who was making the rules up as he went along. The divine right of kings, even to those who believed most strongly in it, did not entitle the king to take an unfair advantage of anyone else. Indeed, in Britain, God Himself is required to be scrupulously fair, to play the game. The idea of an unfair God, so automatic in the Greek mythology, is unthinkable to the British, and several passages in the New Testament, particularly the parables, require a good deal of interpretation to be acceptable. The divine right of kings is, of course, no longer a battle cry, and much though the British may admire, respect and love their royal family, it is also a source of great satisfaction to them that the monarch is equally subject to the common law, that she pays the same taxes, that she plays by the same rules as anybody else.

The rules are, of course, known to everyone. Every Britishman "knows his rights" about almost everything. His knowledge of his position under even the most complicated law is remarkable. Should he find himself in a new situation, ignorant and at a loss, his first action will be to learn the rules. On joining or entering for the first time, a school, a company, a trade union, a club, a committee, the House of Commons, his immediate reaction will not be to show off, to make an impact, to display unique qualities of his personality; it will be to study the rules, learn them and then abide strictly by them. Should one of the rules not be to his liking, he will still accept it, though eventually he may start a small, tentative and probably unsuccessful movement to get the particular rule changed. Should the situation be such that there are no rules, these must be immediately drawn up. When he found himself the leader of a new people in a country without rules, it was the immediate reaction of George Washington, in many ways the most typical of Britishmen, to draw up a new set of rules, which would be respected and obeyed and amended only with the utmost difficulty.

On joining the British Army, a recruit is immediately given a lecture on the rules, not only of a soldier's duties and obligations under military law, but also of his rights. He will be told exactly what a sergeant may or may not do to him. Should his hair be cut slightly shorter than the authorized length, he will immediately complain, not only at the affront to his personality, but at the unfairness, the breaking of the rules by the camp barber. British criminals have an even more detailed knowledge of the rules; everyone will know exactly what the police may or may not do, what the rules of evidence are, the "judges' rules" about the admissibility of confessions, the limits of the prison governor's authority. Should a criminal be caught red-handed, he will probably say, "It's a fair cop." He then expects to receive a fair trial, and even if he is convicted and given a hard, but not unfairly hard, sentence, he will have no complaints. Everybody, himself included, has played strictly by the rules. It was a good game of cricket, and he just happened to lose. And as was explained earlier, it does not at all diminish a Britishman's self-respect to lose.

This respect for rules, for fair play, this instinctive acceptance of the umpire's decision or the judge's ruling are not to be confused with a respect for authority as such. The Britishman expects authority to keep to the rules, too. The idea of *l'état c'est moi* is repugnant. The rules, he feels, exist not to buttress and support the authority, but to control and harness it. Should the authority become tyrannical or unfair, as in the nature of things it sometimes does, then the rules are the weapons with which the little man will fight back for his rights. The laws in Britain are not or, perhaps one should say, should not be imposed from above to control and discipline the unruly population; on the contrary, they are stones in the sling of David with which the Britishman will fight back at authority, when he has a justifiable grievance; should authority have broken the rules and gone too far, then the nation will subsidize the little man in his battle for his rights. The introduction of the free legal aid service, which is now being further extended, is one of the most revealing examples of the British attitude to law and authority. There are not many governments in the modern world which would actually pay a small man to bring a case against them.

It goes, of course, further than this. Far from admiring authority, the British delight in their disrespect of it. Civil servants (and the name itself is typical of the basic attitude) are frequently caricatured in the press, on the stage and screen, and referred to by such undistinguished nicknames as Bumbledom. To catch out authority, if it should put a foot wrong, is a source of great triumph. Some of the most popular cases in

British legal history are those in which the small man fights authority with the full force of the law and wins: one may cite the Archer-Shee case, well known as the subject of Terence Rattigan's popular play *The Winslow Boy;* the Crichel Down case, where the dispossessed landowner succeeded in forcing the Minister of Agriculture to resign; the case of Timothy Evans, hanged for murder and later pardoned, after a long popular campaign on his behalf. On a lighter level, one may perhaps recall the story of the man in East London who added a room containing a lavatory, a shower and twin sinks to his home, but without previously obtaining planning permission. The local authority discovered this, and as the sanitary installations did not meet the required standards, he was ordered to take them out. Instead, the householder took the roof off the new lavatory. The room was then no longer a room within the meaning of the law, and the authority had no further power to interfere. The thought gave the man great pleasure as he took his shower in the rain.

This respect for rules is so deeply ingrained that it colors even the most unlikely events and situations. However furious two men may be with each other, they have to remember to hit each other only in accordance with the Queensberry rules. They must fight fair and not hit below the belt. Conduct between neighbors is closely regulated by the common law, which determines just how far a window may be obstructed, what sort of noise is legally a "nuisance" and when a householder has an "easement of eavesdrop" allowing his roof to drip onto the one next door.

Innocently, the British expect that the rules will apply in all countries and in all circumstances. When Iceland suddenly extended her territorial waters from three miles to twelve miles, a unilateral decision, the British protested. This was breaking the known international rules. When Iceland's case was upheld at the International Court of Justice in The Hague, the British were even more outraged. Somebody, it was felt, was making up the rules as he went along and being approved for it.

Contracts are regarded as binding in Britain; this is not the case in all countries. In *The Merchant of Venice,* Portia's plea for mercy got her nowhere. It was a fair cop for Antonio, and to plead for mercy came into the same category as arguing with the umpire. Portia's wriggling out of the contract on a quibbling point of law is also rather distasteful to the British mind, but the British usually console themselves with the thought that the original contract was not quite cricket, probably unenforceable in a British court and, therefore, itself a breach of the rules.

And as with contracts, so with treaties. It is understood and accepted that a rich, powerful country will wish to invade and conquer a smaller and weaker neighbor. This tendency, though regrettable, is time-honored and part of the rules of life. Nations have been invading and conquering each other since the beginning of the world, and though the British may rally to the defense of the attacked nation, they will do so in the sporting spirit of a weaker, but game, player taking on the new young champion. But should a treaty have been broken in the invasion, the sentiment will be very different. The Britishman will be outraged, will take up arms in anger. It is understood, though deplored, that from time to time the Germans will feel the need to invade Belgium and France. Such urges are part of the European pattern and are expected. What is not understood is a historic phrase like "Might is right" or "Just a scrap of paper." The enemy is not expected to tear up the existing rules or dictate a new set. If he should be unsporting enough to do so, he must be resisted to the furthest limit.

Once a war is started, even during the desperate and decisive business of a battle, both sides are expected to keep to what is known as "the rules of war." To be defeated in a fair battle by an enemy who is stronger or better equipped or better trained or better led is a matter for grief but not for complaint, but should one of the rules of war be broken, one of those rather artificial regulations dealing with the treatment of wounded or prisoners or civilians or ambulances or neutrals, then the Britishman will be moved to something approaching fury. Nothing made us angrier during the Normandy battle than a

Nazi section which arrived in the middle of a company of Grenadier Guardsmen, hidden in an ambulance; as the medical orderlies went forward, the soldiers jumped out with submachine guns and slaughtered everyone in sight, including several officers. Had the guardsmen been killed by mortar fire, the reaction would have been sorrow but not anger; soldiers expect to kill and be killed. But by using an ambulance as a stalking horse, it was felt the Nazis had broken the rules of war, and this was something which would not be forgiven.

In dealing with foreigners, in attempting to communicate with them, the Britishman is gravely handicapped by his sense of fair play. It is not only in the serious business of war, but in the lighter matters of trade, tourism and sport that he finds himself so easily misunderstood and misunderstands so easily back. The words "fair" and "fair play" are not easily translated into French or German or Italian or Spanish. Should an equivalent phrase be found, it would not convey the same meaning. A Spaniard does not expect fairness in life from anyone. A Spanish friend of mine, an old woman, the widow of a fisherman, found that she was entitled to a small state pension. The application, however, had to be made by a certain date, some eighteen months off. Prompted by me, she made her application out and sent it to the appropriate office. What happened after that is uncertain, as the office did not answer letters, accept telephone calls or receive visitors. It seems probable that the application remained on some clerk's desk. After eighteen months the old woman was told that her application was ineligible, as it had arrived too late for consideration. Being British, I was shocked by the unfairness of it all, but the old woman was resigned and uncomplaining; she had never expected fair dealing, in this or any other matter.

The game of cricket, that typically British invention, requires two umpires, who are normally provided by the home side, but are yet expected to behave with complete impartiality between the two teams. Errors of judgment are, of course, sometimes made, but the idea of an umpire who would deliberately give a wrong decision is unthinkable to the British cricketer. This idea of impartiality was exported by the British along with the game itself. Visiting British teams will find the same standard of impartial umpiring in Jamaica, Johannesburg, Sydney or Auckland as in England. But not in Pakistan. One of the several problems about playing test matches in Karachi or Dacca is that Pakistani umpires do not operate on the same principles and do not see their duty in the same light as the British visitors. It is difficult to make a Pakistani understand, much less agree with, the British principle of absolute fair play, and to be fair to the Asian civilization, it is difficult for the Britishman to understand that the Pakistani, operating on a different moral code, is not necessarily inferior.

For the British are proud of their passion for fair play, as proud as they are of their sense of humor. It is, to their mind, one of the great and vital strands of the British character, and the British contribution to world political thought and institutions stems from this confidence, this belief that a fair-minded people are usually right about everything. The Platonic ideal, the wise ruler, the great lawgiver, has no part in British thinking. The judgment of the common man is likely to be more reliable and in the long run sounder. Two burgesses summoned from each borough to parley with the king are likely to give better counsel than a cardinal or a justiciar. And from this simple idea the parliaments of the world have been descended. Twelve good men and true are more likely to produce fair justice than the most learned and experienced judges, and from this simple idea the jury systems of the world have been derived. There is an indestructible belief in common sense, the common man and the common law.

As a complement to this, there is an equally deep-seated distrust of experts. The expert witness in the box, who parades his knowledge on some technical point, will invariably be disliked by the jury and probably disbelieved. It is felt subconsciously that he is not playing quite fair. The pronouncements of experts on economics, sociology, criminology, drug taking, town planning and other similar contemporary problems are often disbelieved and discounted, particularly when their theories and their recommendations go against the instincts of the common man. The French concept of "my teacher knows what's right" has not traveled across the Channel. The British prefer to place their trust in "the reasonable man," a composite person who nevertheless exists legally and whose behavior and reactions in almost all circumstances can be worked out by learned judges.

It follows from this that a British court of law is a calm, unemotional place with common men applying common sense to discover the reactions of a reasonable man. It is a far cry from a murder trial I once attended in Corsica where the defending counsel made a long, sobbing speech about the geometry of the human soul. A far cry, too, from the court in India where the plaintiff sued for the return of a loan (which had, in fact, never been made) and produced fifty witnesses to testify that they had seen the loan being made. The defense used what was, as it transpired, the correct method. This was not to deny that the loan had ever existed, but to produce fifty-five witnesses who would, in their turn, swear that they had seen the loan being repaid.

During their long stay in India and other parts of Asia, the British finally learned to come to terms with the Asian concept of life, though not necessarily to agree with it or to adopt it. And now that so many Asians are coming to Britain the problem exists in the opposite sense and leads to many misunderstandings. A friend of mine, who works in the admissions department at a British university, has told me of overseas students who arrive in her office hopefully, but without the correct certificates or qualifications for entry. On finding themselves balked, they try to pass her, first a pound note, then a five-pound note and so on, the bribes being concealed in the palm of the hand and accompanied by a description of the importance of the applicant's relations in his home country.

I was present on one occasion at the ticket office of an independent airline in London. A visitor from overseas was trying to book a flight from London to Geneva. The ticket clerk told him that their airline had no services to Switzerland, but she gave him the address of two airlines which ran regular services to Geneva. The visitor did not believe her, but he understood well that she could not give way immediately, for her own self-respect. He therefore waited while I conducted my business and then tried again, this time with a bribe. When this too failed, he protested loudly and angrily about racial discrimination. It still had not occurred to him that the girl might be speaking the truth.

Such cases are, of course, exceptional. British fairness is often appreciated abroad, even by those who do not feel called on to emulate it. British football referees are widely in demand, especially in South America. The certificates of British auditors are accepted in many countries more readily than those of local firms. The British are, indeed, proud of their fairness, of their reputation for impartiality, perhaps too proud, with a self-congratulation verging on smugness. The British boy's celebrated description of his headmaster, "a beast, but a just beast," has always been approved. The boy's father felt satisfied that his son was at the right school. But an outsider may perhaps wonder if the phrase "a just beast" is not itself contradictory, whether beastliness can ever be justified by fairness, or justice, or anything else. One may wonder, too, if in the modern world, fairness is always enough.

The British have a theory that wrongs and injustices are accidental, and that, if brought to light, they will be immediately put right, and that often the best way of doing this is by that unique British institution, a letter to the *Times*. The citizens of other nations do not feel called upon to write indignant letters to *Le Monde* or the *Neue Zürcher Zeitung* or the Los Angeles *Times,* pointing out grievances and injustices, and indeed such action would be unlikely to prove very effective. But the British have a steady confidence that to draw public attention to a grievance is to cause it to be put right immediately. It sometimes still works, though not as frequently or effectively as in the past. In the modern age, stronger measures are required in Britain, as elsewhere.

The difficulty is that the rules are changing, are being

changed every year, in response to new theories about society, morals, economics, religion. Penalties for breaking the rules have become as outmoded as protectionism or virginity or other similar words from the past. Fairness itself has in many cases been replaced by egalitarianism. This is not the place to discuss the merits or otherwise of new codes of behavior, whether they are a step in the right or the wrong direction, but the reasonable man is often bewildered by these changes in the rules, which have been made in his name, but often without his agreement or even his understanding. They are the work of experts—in economics, sociology, criminology, environmental design, marriage—and the reasonable man distrusts all experts on principle. Further, he is often bolstered in this distrust by the failure of the experts' plans to work out as confidently forecast. At the same time he remains a law-abiding citizen, anxious to play by the rules, the same rules that everybody else is playing by or should be playing by. He is thus in a dilemma. Should he continue to follow the old rules, which have been tested by time, but which do not necessarily suit the modern world? Or should he work by the new ones which often seem to offend his common sense, his deep-rooted feeling for fairness?

The dilemma is perhaps best illustrated by the British attitude to taxation. The British have always been celebrated for their conscientious payment of taxes. It may confidently be said that, in this respect, they have been more punctilious than any other nation in the world, including the Germans. The Britishman might grumble against his taxes, might object to them, might even fight a civil war over them, but once they became law, he would feel obliged to pay them promptly and in full. He was confident that the money was going to be used for some worthwhile object, like the Navy; indeed, the image of the Navy was usually in his mind, as he signed, a little sadly, his check to the Inland Revenue. Somehow to avoid paying his full share might have involved some other taxpayer in having to pay more than his fair share. Worse still, the Navy might have gone short of a valuable piece of equipment. For want of his nail, the battle might have been lost. If he should have succumbed to temptation and, by some means or other, paid less than his fair share, he would later be haunted by remorse, unable to sleep. He would toss and turn in his bed, until finally he would post off an anonymous donation to the Chancellor of the Exchequer. After this, he could sleep in peace and the country would be saved. A day or two later, in the Personal Column of the *Times,* the Chancellor would acknowledge the receipt of fifteen pounds four shillings and ninepence "Conscience Money."

All this was based on the theory of fair shares, the idea that the Chancellor would only take from him as much as he needed to run or defend the country. But since the war, new economic theories have arrived to guide Chancellors: redistribution of wealth, deflation by taxation, siphoning off surplus spending power, reducing general consumption in order to reduce imports. The modern Chancellor of the Exchequer invariably takes far more from the British taxpayer than he requires to run or defend the country, vast as this sum now is. The reasonable man feels this to be unfair; he feels that the government has changed the rules without his agreement, indeed that the government is no longer playing by any rules at all but is making up new rules as it goes along. He therefore feels entitled to protect his money and his standard of living in any way that he can. If he succeeds in paying less than the share which he no longer thinks of as fair, he will feel happy and not remorseful. The public strictures of the chairman of the Board of Inland Revenue will not cause him to lie awake at night or send an anonymous donation to the Chancellor of the Exchequer. It is a long time since the words "Conscience Money" appeared in the *Times.*

The British passion for fair play has its drawbacks in the modern world, resulting in a somewhat schizophrenic attitude toward law and government. There are other drawbacks, too, which have nothing to do with the modern world and have existed through the centuries. The reverence for the rules means that the British can often get obsessed with procedure, the minute regulations and interpretations of regulations, which are so amusing in the committee room of the Marylebone Cricket Club, but often seem trivially unimportant in the world outside. It has been said of English law that "it grew up in the interstices of procedure." To the outside observer it often seems that the House of Commons is largely occupied by the details of its own procedure, the small regulations about which motion may be moved in which circumstances, which subject may be raised or talked out at which time, while the greater problems outside remain unconsidered and undiscussed. The Church of England has been described by one of its more celebrated members as just "a machine for administering itself." Obeying the rules or amending the rules often seems to be more important than playing the game.

Obsession with the rules leads not only to triviality but, more seriously, to inflexibility. The law is the law, and no exceptions can be made, however extenuating the circumstances. An accused man in court is required to answer simply that he pleads guilty or not guilty to the charge. He is not allowed to answer "Yes, but—" or "Yes, and then again, no." But the truth is not usually simple black or simple white. Little, much too little, notice is taken of extenuating circumstances. The British do not like a man who argues with the umpire; if he is given out, then he is out. Courtroom pleas in mitigation are not usually listened to with any care or sympathy. The accused would be wiser to base his defense on some technical point of law; this at least everyone present will understand and approve. It has been observed that French courts of law, which so shock the British with their carefree indifference to the rules of evidence, as they are understood in Britain, or even to the possible innocence of the offender may yet, by their careful probing of the circumstances surrounding the act and the motive for the deed, get closer to the real truth of the case than the bleak and brisk British method.

To the British, it is still unthinkable that any exceptions can ever be made to the rules. But, in a wider context, there are occasions when such exceptions, if not correct, might still be wise. When King Farouk of Egypt wished to train as an officer in the British Army, he sat the entrance exam to the Royal Military Academy at Woolwich. He sat at his desk, waiting for someone to give him the answers to copy out, a procedure which would have been usual in his own country. As he was not supplied with a private copy of the answers, he failed the exam and did not enter Woolwich. Everybody thought it was a good joke against the king and against Egypt. Nobody suggested that perhaps it might have been wise to bend the rules to allow him to become, by hook or by crook, a British officer, and that this goodwill might have been to British advantage in the Middle East during the war which was so obviously imminent. Or again, when Ribbentrop was German ambassador in London, he wished to send his son to Eton. The boy, however, was refused admission, because he was just over the maximum permitted age for new boys, had not passed the common entrance examination and spoke imperfect English. The question of whether it was a good thing to snub the German ambassador at this moment was not even considered, nor, in the wider context, whether it might not benefit Britain for Ribbentrop's son to be at Eton. The rules were the rules, and no exceptions could be made, however great the outside issues involved.

Recently, however, the rules have been broken strangely on a single occasion. The Prince of Wales was admitted to Trinity College, Cambridge, without having the required and very exacting entry qualifications. A popular young man, he suddenly found himself much less popular with the boys and girls of his own generation, who were competing feverishly for the limited number of university places. The question of whether it was desirable for the future king to have a university education was not considered for a moment by his contemporaries; the rules for university entrance existed, and the prince was expected to abide by them as scrupulously as anyone else. In fact, by his evident determination to complete his course and take his degree, he has succeeded in winning back a lot of the goodwill lost by his backstairs entry. But his position would have been much easier if his contemporaries had not been so obsessed by the rules, if it had been accepted that the prince should go to Cambridge in any circumstances, whatever his technical qualifications. The royal family, reacting a little belatedly to outside opinion, declined to pull any strings for their daughter as well, and Princess Anne was therefore unable to go to a university at all. Since she is a young lady who is clearly destined, by circumstances not of her choosing, to play a prominent part in British public life, this may be thought to be a pity.

The third and, perhaps, the greatest disadvantage, is that the British face the outside world one-handed; the other hand holds the book of rules. This is particularly evident in time of war, and indeed wars have been, until 1914, considered sporting events. British history is studded with phrases like "Gentlemen of the French Guard, fire first." And the soldiers who were killed in that first volley lay on nobody's conscience. Ambushes, however, have usually been considered unsporting and therefore to be avoided. William the Conqueror's use of ambushes showed, as was said at the time, that he was of bastard descent and no gentleman. New weapons, such as telescopic rifles, machine guns, gas, submarines, dive-bombing, were also thought to be unfair in the same way that a larger tennis racket would be thought to be unfair. For fair play, both sides must have the same equipment, and it is important that the best man should win, even if he happens to be the opponent. With level equipment, the battle must be fought by fair and rigid rules. At one moment, during the Battle of Waterloo, the British gunners had Napoleon and his staff within their range and sights, but Wellington refused to let them fire; it was, he said, "No business of one general officer to be firing upon another." Even in the heat of that decisive and desperate battle, the rules had to be strictly obeyed. In the same category comes Brigadier Keyes' suicide raid on Rommel's headquarters in the Western Desert. This raid, had it come off, had Rommel been killed, might have hastened the German defeat in the Mediterranean and saved many British lives. But in London clubs, the raid was much disapproved of, for being "unsporting."

The British obsession with fair play often gives the impression that they are innocents abroad, believing naïvely that everyone everywhere will strictly obey the rules, written or unwritten, that signed agreements and treaties will be scrupulously adhered to and that fair play is as important to everyone as it is to the British themselves. Perhaps only hard experience will, in the end, teach the British that there are some people in some countries who have different rules, no rules, rules which can be broken or bent or ignored to suit the needs of the moment, rules which can be laughed at and ignored. After enough painful disillusionment the Britishman may come to understand that he cannot go through life believing simply that it is just a game of cricket.

16

THE SPORTING LIFE

◆§ During many Sunday mornings spent in British pubs, American coffee shops and French cafés, I have noticed a marked difference in international attitudes to the Sunday papers. Many Americans, faced with the jumbo Sunday edition of their favorite paper, will turn immediately to the section of comics should there be one. Grave-faced and careful, they will read the thing through from beginning to end. The average Frenchman, on the other hand, faced with a slim Sunday paper, which has been printed the previous Wednesday, will turn immediately to the crime. He will read, in scarifying detail, the story of an atrocious murderer near Toulouse who may or may not have slaughtered his wife and seven children with an ax.

The Britishman, however, will have none of these things. Later in the day, perhaps, he may look at the few comic strips available in certain papers. Details of recent crimes are likely to be bleak and uninformative, because it is a fiercely punished offense to prejudice a case not yet tried. The speeches and examinations at criminal trials may be reported in detail, and he may later glance at some of this, but he will never begin his paper there. His first choice will always be the sporting pages. Should he ever be offered a comic section as thick and varied as the comic section of the Los Angeles *Times,* should he ever be offered the gory details of an atrocious crime in the manner of *Paris Dimanche,* he would still glance first at the sporting pages, at the football and cricket; then, and only then, would he turn to the other important business on hand, which would be (depending on whether the Sunday papers are delivered to his home or whether he has to go out and buy them) his early-morning tea and his Sunday-morning pint of beer.

The Britishman is sport-mad. Whatever else may be going on in the world, wars flaring up, currencies being devalued, satellites being launched or planes crashing, he will prefer both to talk and to think about sport. Although a spectator and in many cases rather a remote spectator, he will worry about the cricket test match between England and Australia currently being played in far-off Sydney. He will discuss with his friends in pub and club and even in his home whether Portsmouth football club has chosen the right players, whether somebody else might not be a better captain, whether a particular horse is at its best over a distance of six furlongs. When, in the evening, a telerecording of a football cup semifinal is shown on television, the pubs in Britain will be almost empty. Sport is the passion of the British, the lifeblood, the compulsive interest. Indeed, it is to the Britishman of today what religion was to the Tudors.

Other nations are obviously interested in sport, too. One thinks immediately of the huge crowds and the bloody battles waged on South American football grounds. One thinks of the French interest in bicycle racing, of the near frenzy caused by the Tour de France. One recalls, a little disdainfully, hot-eyed Spanish enthusiasts trying to beat up the football referee in his hotel after the game. But no other nation shares the British obsession with sport as a thing in itself, the feeling that the game is the thing and that in the long run, nothing else really counts. To play the game is the ambition of every Britishman; no other phrase sums up so succinctly his idea of the good life and the behavior of a gentleman.

But the interest is in the sport itself and in the players, not in their nationalities. The loyalty is either to the idea of cricket, football or racing or, on the smaller scale, to a particular club, team, side, and this will be a local one. He will follow his local football club around the country at weekends; he will turn out in the filthiest wet weather to watch it; he will follow closely the particular fortunes of his county cricket club; he will give time and care to his local village side; he will spend his Friday evenings mowing the grass of his bowls club. But when the game reaches the rarefied air of the international level, the Britishman's interest tends to fade out. The whole thing is becoming too big, too remote, the players becoming too expert —and the Britishman instinctively distrusts experts. This explains the fact that, while the British are obsessed by sport, while they think and talk about it more than the people of any other nation, their international performances have been rather meager.

It has often been said that the British have achieved few international sporting triumphs in this century. The star tennis players, golfers, athletes have belonged to other nations. There are several reasons for this. One is obviously the weather; it is difficult to produce a tennis champion in a British summer. Another is the feeling that, though a professional should be paid for his time, he should not be paid too much. He is, after all, playing for his own pleasure as well as others'. A poor boy in Spain or Brazil may become a millionaire through football. The British regard such rewards with some incredulity. The ambitious son of a mining family may easily become a great England center half or a famous England fast-bowler, but he will not become a millionaire, not, at least, until he retires from sport and takes up some more profitable occupation. The third reason is that, as already explained, though the Britishman can, and often still does, think big in world terms, in sport he prefers to think small and locally. The Olympic Games arouse comparatively little interest in Britain. The cup final between two league football teams is as far as he will go; or the "Wars of the Roses," the Whitsun cricket match between Yorkshire and Lancashire; or a test match against Australia (but then Australia is regarded as being part of the family); or a test match against the West Indies (but then the West Indian players involved all seem to live in Britain). But to play football against a South American country, this is a different matter. There is considerable doubt, both before and afterward, whether the players are playing by the same rules. There is near certainty that they are playing in a different spirit.

Sport is thought of both as a way of life and as a code of conduct. To play strictly by the rules, both in letter and in spirit, to be if necessary a good loser and to show team spirit, these are the great attributes of a British sportsman. Star quality, the blend of talent and brilliance and egoism which produces the heroes of Milan and Madrid and South America, is neither required nor appreciated. A side of individualists is, in the British point of view, a bad side; a well-trained, dovetailed team is basically a good side, and the Britishman is often bewildered and dismayed that foreign teams, which seem to work on totally different principles, are often more successful.

There are, however, signs of a change, beginning perhaps with the British firsts in the four-minute mile and on Everest and Kanchenjunga. After years of retreat on all fronts, the British sportsmen, at least, were turning at bay and learning to enjoy the taste of success instead of gallant defeat. The Britishman, basically a businessman as well as a sportsman, was not slow to appreciate the greater rewards being offered to the successful sportsman overseas, which, finally and incredibly, spread into Britain too. Recent successes by British professional sportsmen in the World Football Cup, the Open Golf Championship, Wimbledon, women's ice skating and boxing may well be due to these new incentives. But whether this will continue is uncertain. It goes right against the traditional British attitude to sport: that it is immaterial whether you win or lose, and indeed that it is probably better for the character to lose gracefully than to win.

The point is essentially one of character training, and the British believe that sport is the finest possible sort of character training. The object of the exercise is to teach the boy to submerge himself in the team and not to show off, and this training, though it may produce a good citizen or even a nice boy, is unlikely to produce a sporting star. This is not a matter for much worry. The British are not great ones for hero worshiping. A father would feel uneasy if his son, by virtue of being a star sportsman, became a millionaire before he was forty. This is not, in British thinking, what sport is for. The boy should have disciplined his talents and his enthusiasm to fit in with the rest of the team.

But at the same time enthusiasm and talent are required—enthusiasm perhaps more than talent. It is usual for a French boy to go through his entire education without taking part in any sporting activity whatsoever. Indeed it is possible that his parents will never mention the subject, either in his presence or out of it. Such an upbringing is unthinkable for a British schoolboy. Almost as soon as he can walk, he will be given sporting equipment. At school, his father will follow his games career far more closely than his academic career. Never mind his performance with French irregular verbs; he must learn to play with a straight bat—and the phrase implies far more than a technical cricketing stance. It implies honesty, conformity, modesty, self-discipline, courage, endurance, humor and, in many sports, love for animals or at least for horses and dogs. It produces the ideal Britishman; it trains his son in all the qualities which he thinks most important to life.

It was thought at one time, too, that sport trained boys both in the art of battle and in endurance of war as a whole; this theory is now somewhat out of fashion. The slightly more modern theory of the educationist Dr. Kurt Hahn is, on the contrary, that sport, in particular such activities as mountaineering, sailing and athletics, provides a good release for otherwise warlike instincts. But it is still thought that sport encourages boys to be heterosexual—a rather strange piece of thinking, unsupported by facts. And above all, it teaches the boy not to cheat. Sport, like love, is played by the rules, and it is better to lose honestly than to win dishonestly.

The British have accordingly put more time, thought and energy into drawing up the rules of sport than any other nation, and no other country in the world has given so much effort to keeping sport straight and clean. The extremely distinguished men who sit on the committees of the Jockey Club, the National Hunt Committee, the Marylebone Cricket Club, the Football Association and other controlling bodies have one and one thought only in their heads: to make sure that the sport is played cleanly and according to the rules. And with the exception of professional wrestling and greyhound racing, which are widely thought to be beyond hope, they have succeeded fairly well in their single high-minded ambition.

This obsession with sport is of very long standing. Julius Caesar remarked on it in his dispatches. As an Italian, he naturally found it odd that barbarians should rear edible animals for sport, instead of for food. Cockfighting, bullbaiting, bearbaiting were evidently popular at that time and continued to be popular for many centuries. It is possible to see the baited bear or bull behind the inspiration which created some of Shakespeare's tragic heroes. In due course many of these blood sports were suppressed by the British love of animals and by the Puritan streak, both of which are essential parts of the British character. The hunting of stags and the coursing of hares have not quite died out, but both are much attacked, and it is probable that both will be controlled, perhaps made illegal, during the next few years. Fox hunting, however, continues, partly because, as already explained, foxes kill chickens and are thought to be vermin rather than animals and partly because the hunting-field tradition is deeply entrenched not only in British literature but in British life.

The British make a distinction between hunting and shooting. The French lump both sports together under the title *La Chasse,* but the British see a great difference between them, a difference not only in the type of quarry and in the methods employed to kill it, but also in the type of person who participates. Of the two, shooting is supposed to be the more gentlemanly, the more upper-class. Farmers and minor country gentry may be members of the local hunt, may indeed provide the hard core of those who actually go hunting in the field, as opposed to those who merely attend the annual hunt ball. Fashionable shooting, however, requires money. It is necessary to be a member of a shooting syndicate which controls the shooting rights around the woods and covers or else to be sure of an invitation to the partridge country in East Anglia or a grouse moor in Yorkshire or Scotland. So eclectic and so enviable are these invitations that a grouse-moor image is now a symbol in British life not only of social and financial position but also of political achievement. It became, during the time of Mr. Harold Macmillan and Sir Alec Douglas-Home, a convenient label for the type of politician who had been at Eton, who belonged to the right clubs and who, through political acumen, or worth of character, or connections, or all three, finally achieved the top political position. Being British, the popular label attached, that of "grouse-moor image," was, of course, a sporting label.

Shooting is used as a litmus test of the social standing of the sportsman. A hunting man does not have to do anything except subscribe and learn to ride; but not only has a shooting man to join the right shoots and the right syndicates, to buy the right clothes from Savile Row, the right guns from Holland & Holland, but he has, when the moment arrives, actually to hit and kill the bird. The ability to shoot and kill birds in the air can be acquired, like a correct accent, only in early youth, and it is therefore, like the voice, the acid test of a person's social status. It implies children brought up in the country in fairly prosperous surroundings, at least second-generation wealth.

The same point applies also to fishing. Salmon and trout fishing on the more expensive rivers of England needs not only money but also training in the skills of the rod and the fly. But the test is not quite so acid; good and valid excuses can be found by even the most expert fishermen when they fail to catch a trout, excuses which would not be acceptable when a shooting man fails to hit a low-flying pheasant which has been deliberately driven over him. In any event, fishing usually takes place in total privacy, while a display of shooting skills is made under the admiring or critical eyes of fellow guests, beaters and gamekeepers. It is felt, too, that fishing is something which owes something to luck and which can be learned in later life, while the good shot owes nothing whatever to luck and began to learn his craft at the age of six.

However, the British preoccupation with sport is less concerned with expensive blood sports than with games or forms of exploration: one man or one team against another, one man or one expedition against a natural object. The point, the impetus, is largely creative. Britain has, without doubt, contributed its full share to the great literature of the world. Its contribution to art and to music is much less impressive, far below that of France, or Germany, or Italy. The reasons for this are highly debatable; it is perhaps something in the national heredity, a basic Puritanism or Philistinism, an instinctive Norman feeling that a man should be out of doors when he has nothing else to do. But a further reason may be that so much of the British creative impulse has gone into things other than art and music, has been channeled into political and social thinking, industrial inventions and development, and, above all, into sport.

The record of British inventiveness in sport is indeed astonishing. It was the British who gave the world association football (the most widely played game in the world), Rugby football (the father of American football), cricket, rounders (the father of baseball), golf, skiing, mountaineering, whist (the uncle or perhaps the cousin of bridge), darts and such attractive pub games as shove-ha'penny. Not all these sports originated in Britain. Golf, it is thought, was started in the Low Countries, where it died out, but it was the Scots who took the game up, kept it alive and finally spread it around the world. Skiing, of course, was an ancient form of communication in Scandinavia, but it was a Britishman, a Colonel Napier, who first brought a pair of skis to the Alps, to Davos in 1888, followed the next year by Sir Arthur Conan Doyle. The Swiss, seeing them for the first time, were, it is recorded, surprised and incredulous. Later, it was a Britishman, Sir Arnold Lunn, who invented the Winter Olympics, the slalom and, indeed, most aspects of modern ski racing. Mountaineering, of course, developed from chamois hunting, but the record of British firsts, both in the Alps and in the Himalayas, is amazing for a country whose whole area lies completely below the snow line.

But to invent is not the same as to succeed. To create a new sport or game, to nurse it through its fledgling years, to promote it and to propagandize for it is one thing; to win gold medals or championships 50 or 100 years later, is something else, and as has already been pointed out, British interest and performance tend to fade out at the top international level.

Social distinctions, once again, have played an important part here. There has always been a carefully marked distinction between the master and the huntsman, between the gun and the gamekeeper, between the owner and the jockey, the amateur and the professional. Perhaps the most unfortunate event in the whole British sporting calendar was the now-defunct cricket match "Gentlemen-v-Players." Not only was the distinction invidious, but there was also the chagrin when, as often happened, the Players won. Sport is, in the Norman mind, so indissolubly connected with character that it was felt that the Gentlemen, with their public-school-trained characters, their carefully fostered dedication and leadership, possibly their Norman blood, should have had a natural advantage.

The British have a very soft spot for amateur sportsmen, owing not only to these reasons but to an innate distrust of professionalism, of trained experts. The common, reasonable man, at sport as at everything else, is an untrained amateur. Peers who ride their own horses in the Grand National, maharajas who score centuries at Lord's are popular figures, not only with their own class, but with the public as a whole. British fiction is full of heroes who, with no recent practice or training or indeed apparent effort, score sudden and spectacular successes in the boxing ring or the cricket field or on the athletic track.

The dream was bound to fade. In the second half of the twentieth century it is not possible for the occasional amateur to be superior to the whole-time professional. It is a century in which, to misquote Drake, the gentlemen have to work beside the mariners. In a time of rising standards it is not possible for anyone, unless he works full time, to succeed at anything. The amateurs were having to work full time at some other occupation; the sporting journalists, if not the overall public, were on the side of the professional, riding or playing cricket or football for his living. The ending of the Gentlemen-v-Players cricket match was not only the writing out of a less popular cricket fixture, but a symbolic act. Lord Hawke, at one time president of the Yorkshire Cricket Club, said, in a famous and unfortunate phrase, that he hoped a professional would never be captain of Yorkshire. It was the sort of last-ditch remark which is always doomed to a prompt refutation. And distinguished Yorkshire professionals who have captained both Yorkshire and England (one thinks of Sir Leonard Hutton and Mr. Brian Close in this category) are witnesses of a changing attitude.

The last decade has also been remarkable for the rise of the "shamateur," the illegitimate offspring of earlier prejudices, the natural result of modern economic and professional pressures. The idea of the "shamateur," the sporting man who earns his living indirectly through the game, is not, of course, peculiar to the British. It applies obviously to such sportsmen as Austrian skiers, Australian tennis players, French cyclists, Russian chess players, American skaters. But the British, for all their passion for amateurs, find the idea of a shamateur especially regrettable. Somebody is, if not breaking the rules, at least bending them, and since the professional and economic standards can no longer be ignored, clearly it was time that the rules were altered. Britain was not the only country to find the credo of Olympic amateurism, as recently restated in its most rigid and religious form, to be no longer relevant. The British went further. They opened Wimbledon, the world's most prestigious tennis tournament, to all comers irrespective of economic status. It was a trend-setting moment, a trend which other countries have not always felt able to follow, but the British were confident they were upholding the true sporting ideal. Under the new regulations, amateurs, shamateurs and open professionals could play good tennis on equal terms, without bending or avoiding any rules or principles. The decision did not in any way benefit British players, but the sport, the abstract ideal, had been saved.

The average Britishman, of course, does not shoot grouse on grouse moors or ride in the Grand National or play tennis at Wimbledon or play cricket at Lord's or football at Wembley. He is a spectator sportsman: He cheers his team in the rain in Manchester; he schemes and saves up for tickets for the big events; he reads about it in the sporting columns of the papers; he watches it all on television. There is nothing especially British about this. Other nations have their sporting enthusiasts who remain firmly spectators, who would be filled with misery and consternation if they should find themselves in the same ring as the world heavyweight champion or a fighting bull.

But the most popular sport of the British is one which involves total audience participation, has a certain element of risk, requires a certain nerve: gambling. The British are, in fact, a nation of gamblers, an idea which to some foreigners often seems to conflict with "the Beefeater image," but this is to misread history and tradition. Most, if not all, of those who ended as prisoners in the Tower of London were gamblers on the highest level and for the highest stakes, gamblers who had lost. When, a few years ago, by a minor and irrelevant adjustment to the current gaming laws, London suddenly found itself the gambling capital of the world, far ahead of Las Vegas or Monte Carlo or Beirut, the people least surprised were the British. There was a moment's pause while the Britishman learned or perhaps relearned such foreign casino games as American craps or chemin-de-fer, and then he took to it with a will. It is a mistake to imagine that the numerous gambling clubs which have mushroomed in Mayfair during the past decade are frequented only by tourists from overseas. The British have always been a nation of gamblers; according to statistics, 75 percent of the nation are regular gamblers.

The idea, of course, of casino gambling in London is novel, though many Britishmen have been brought up to or learned to find their way around the casinos in France. The gambling holiday at Le Touquet or Deauville or Monte Carlo is part of the British aristocratic tradition and, as such, was bound to find its way down through the classes to those less privileged. My grandfather lost 10,000 pounds in one weekend at Monte Carlo, and he was by no means untypical of his social world or his generation. Before him were the Regency bucks staking their whole fortunes and perhaps even their daughters at cards or backgammon in the clubs of St. James's. And these games still exist, though not usually so spectacularly or romantically.

But the bulk of British gambling takes place on the performances of horses or football teams or, to a lesser extent, greyhounds. In one year the British public poured out about 2.5 billion pounds on horse racing alone. Many will have visited the races to do it, betting with bookmakers or on the totalizators; others will have placed their bets in betting shops by telephone or telegram, though the professional punters (those who make a steady though, it is said, modest income from their racing wins) do it on the course themselves. Further vast sums are poured out on football pools, in smaller bets, though in greater numbers. Many families spend a substantial proportion of their weekly income, a tenth or even a seventh of their pay packet on the pools. This is in no sense a spectator sport; no man can watch all the football teams on which he is betting. He will probably not bet on his home team, which he may go to watch. He is hoping, shouting that his own team should win, but the teams on which he has put his money he hopes will draw, in order to gain the maximum number of points. Pencil in hand, he will watch the results of the day's games on television, obligingly provided by the operating companies. He is participating actively; his money and his hopes for the future are fully engaged.

It is important to distinguish between the rich or moderately rich man gambling out of boredom or traditional hedonism and the small man investing a substantial proportion of his income on football pools or races. The former is passing the time, testing his luck or showing off to his friends; the latter is investing in hope. He firmly believes that winning requires not only luck but skill. Britain has always been a trading nation, and it is well understood that trading is partly a matter of luck and not only of economic laws. Exploration and enterprise have always involved an element of gambling. And such heroic figures as Drake and Raleigh have been, in the truest sense, gamblers. Perhaps the theme is seen at its simplest in *The Merchant of Venice,* where Antonio is gambling that his ship will come in before he is called on to redeem his debts. The phrase "when our ship comes in" was one which I often heard in my childhood, though my father, untypically a most unenthusiastic gambler, used the phrase in a strictly business sense.

But in the modern world, ships rarely come in like that, bringing wealth or riches for all, and if they do, much of their proceeds will be taken by the Inland Revenue. Luck and enterprise in the commercial world are heavily taxed, and the British feeling for trading enterprise, the instinct of "let's have a go," is often underrewarded. The whole instinct has turned, unfortunately but inevitably, in on itself. It is difficult to get rich in business, but a lucky win on the football pools may bring in thousands free of tax. Trying to make money by luck from your fellow citizens may not promote the wealth of the nation, but it may well prove more successful than hazardous and overtaxed ventures elsewhere. But it is possible to feel that if all the time and the care and the energy, not to mention the money, which are at present spent on filling up football coupons or placing racing bets could be devoted to some more creative and outward-looking purpose, Britain might yet be, as in the past, the richest country in the world.

A further factor is involved in this British passion for gambling. Active and intelligent participation is required. It provides in the modern world an opportunity for showing traditional skills, an understanding of the probable performances of a team, a knowledge of horseflesh, an inside knowingness of technical details. It also provides the Britishman with a chance to use his carefully learned training in arithmetic. British boys (this does not apply to girls) are proud of their arithmetic. A child educated in a state primary school will have spent far more time studying arithmetic than any other subject, and his standard will accordingly be much higher when he leaves, aged eleven, than his equivalent in other countries or in other British schools. A class difference is involved once again here. A boy trying to get into a boarding school will have spent most of his time, when not playing games or dodging bullying, in swotting French or Latin, since these are the esteemed subjects of his future select public school. This is traditional because Latin and French were the languages of the Norman nobility. His counterpart at a state school will barely glance at French, at Latin not at all. It is his tackling of arithmetical problems (not to be confused with mathematics) which will determine which stream he is placed in at his secondary school and whether he advances toward higher education. These skills, unlike Latin and French, are Saxon skills, skills of the shopkeeper and the draper, the baker and the small farmer. These boys are proud of their skill and continue to be proud in later life.

Only a people addicted to the techniques of the finer arithmetic could have tolerated for so long the British system of currency, weights and measures, the shillings and pence and guineas, the pounds and bushels, the rods poles and perches, the long tons and short tons, the stones avoirdupois and the pounds troy weight, the pecks and bushels, the drams and gills, the sea miles and the knots. The complication is deliberate. A young Saxon, ancient or modern, will relish the difficulties, will show off his ability to add simultaneously three columns of pounds, shillings, and pence with three fingers without carrying from one column to the other. These skills do not belong to his Norman neighbor, who may well be winning the race which he is timing or laying down the financial policy for which he is keeping the accounts. Many of these traditional skills will, of course, be wiped out with the introduction of the metric system, but there is a widespread feeling that the purchasers will find themselves as much at sea in the new system as the shopkeepers, that a meter and a quarter of cloth at sixty-three new pence a meter may be almost as difficult to calculate quickly as the good old-fashioned problems of a yard and three-eighths at eighteen shillings and elevenpence a yard, while on the other side of the counter the men and women educated in Latin will be protesting that their knowledge of dead languages gives them an advantage, if not in shopping, at least in other spheres of life.

These distinctions, these prides, are transferred to sport. They underlie the self-respect of the bookmaker and the man who can understand the permutations and combinations of the football pool coupon and can fill it in to his best advantage; the scorer, amateur or professional who can work out, throughout the day's play, the bowling average; the knowledgeable spectators at a cricket ground, who applaud when a bowler bowls his fiftieth consecutive maiden over; the soccer fan who knows to two points of decimals the goal average of Newcastle United. All this is not merely active audience participation; it is part of the game for the batsman himself, with one eye watching the ball flying toward him at a terrifying speed and the other eye looking inside at his batting average to date. Or the captain controlling his team on the field, but with half his mind given to the problem of runs per minute, to the calculation of the exact moment when he should declare his innings closed and allow the other side to "have a go." Such calculations are a basic part of the British attitude to sport, as intrinsic and as important as actually winning the match or hitting a six. Arithmetic is an indispensable part of it and rightly so, for the British regard sport as seriously as work, as a form of work and, in many ways, as superior to work.

17

MEN AT WORK

Early in the 1950's, finding myself to be, so far, unsuccessful as a writer, short of money and without any adequate source of income, I signed on at the nearest Labour Exchange. The man who interviewed me there and took down my details was kind and encouraging, but I was considerably dashed to discover that after an expensive classical education, I was barely employable. Far from being skilled or even semiskilled, I was plain unskilled. I was offered a job in a glass bottle factory. "It's a hot job," the man at the Labour Exchange said to me. "Hot?" I queried. "All the bottles are red-hot," he answered. "Do you want it?"

It was no moment for being choosy. I accepted the job gratefully.

"You'll pick it up pretty quickly," said the man, handing me a card. "Best of luck."

I went along to the factory, showed my card to somebody in personnel and was taken on with almost alarming alacrity. No questions were asked about who I was, why I wanted the job, what my previous experience had been. I was simply assigned to a shift, told to report to the shift engineer before seven o'clock the next morning. I spent the rest of the afternoon trying to sort out my Income Tax Code Number and my National Insurance card, both of which were rather complicated, as this was my first job in England.

I clocked in before seven o'clock the next morning, and while waiting for the shift engineer to tell me what to do, I stood on the iron catwalk and looked at the factory. I shall never forget that moment, my first practical experience of British industry: the bleak sodium lighting from the girders, the gray daylight beginning to seep through the skylights overhead, the noise of the machinery, the hiss of the steam, the workmen moving about silently in their overalls and cloth caps, the smell of metal and, most extraordinary of all, the red glowing bottles emerging from the molds, moving steadily down the belts till they were lost to sight beneath me. I felt a great sense of excitement, of adventure, of togetherness with the Industrial Revolution, of the romance of machinery.

In due course I was assigned to work at a machine which was, at the time, making milk bottles. I was glad about this; the big, glowing bottles had a beauty of their own, and I felt that a milk bottle was a useful thing to make, something which was necessary for the national well-being, even if it had no export potential. The machine itself was vast and black and hot, something between a dragon and an old-fashioned steam engine. The raw, molten glass, called the metal, was held in large overhead tanks on the far side of the factory. How it got there I never discovered. From there it was piped down into the twenty-odd machines which stood on the factory floor and which clanked around and around with a rhythm which soon penetrated into my subconscious. The molten glass, carefully measured, was poured into one of the molds on the machine and then blown out by compressed air to make the bottle hollow. With a clank, the machine would then turn, bringing a new mold under the inflow pipe. Three clanks later, the mold would spring open; automatic tongs would take the red-hot bottle out by its rim and put it on a conveyor belt. The bottles traveled along the belt some eight feet to a long hot metal tunnel called a lehr. In lines of six or eight, depending on their size, they would move on into the lehr like an endless squad of waddly soldiers and disappear from our sight. They were carried through the lehr on a slow belt, and it took them about forty-eight hours to reach the far end, during which time they cooled slowly. At the far end, they were checked, sorted, packed, crated and then disappeared.

The process was automatic. The function of the operators, standing there with their double gloves and their tongs, was to supervise and maintain the machines and to be at hand if anything should go wrong. The operator on the machine to which I was assigned was a middle-aged man called Green. He had been in that job for about twenty-five years, for most of the time on that one machine. A child of the Depression, he had been lucky to get the work when jobs were scarce and had had neither the opportunity nor the wish to try anything else. He would no doubt remain on that machine until he retired at the age of sixty-five. He would have spent the better part of fifty years in one factory, on one machine. For a restless young man like myself, it was an awe-inspiring thought. I did not, however, learn these details of his career from him, as he was a silent and morose man. I was told them in gossip in the canteen by the other machine operators.

In principle, I was Green's assistant, a trainee learning the work, doing odd jobs and preparing for the time when I would be promoted to being in charge of a machine myself. However, to appease my dignity as a British workman, I was given a more dignified title than assistant operator or trainee operator. I was known as a weight controller. My specific duty was to take bottles at random from the belt with my tongs and weigh them on a pair of scales, to check whether too much or too little glass was going into the bottles. Young and keen, eager to do my best for the factory and for British industry, I weighed the red-hot bottles furiously, worrying anxiously if a bottle should be a fraction over or under the specified weight. Green watched me with disapproval.

"You don't want to do that," he said, "that's labor in vain." And, indeed, I soon saw that he was right. Once a red-hot bottle had been put on the cold scales it would probably crack and have to be thrown away. The harder I worked, the more bottles I lost.

Another of our duties was to grease the molds with graphite at intervals, to prevent the bottles from sticking. This was rather an exciting maneuver. When the mold tripped open to release the new bottle, Green or I would move in and, with a gloved hand, press the mold open and brush the surfaces vigorously with a brush dipped in liquid graphite. At some moment, which could not always be accurately predicted, the mold would snap shut as it moved on around to receive its fresh charge of liquid glass, and it was important not to have your brush or your glove, still less your hand, caught in the mold as it moved on. There was a one-armed young man to be seen around the factory; he had been a machine operator before his accident and was now employed in the wages office. He was pointed out to me and to the other weight controllers as an example of what happened to you if your hand was caught in the mold. However, accidents were, it seemed, infrequent; only once were my fingers caught in the mold as it snapped shut, and happily, it merely pulled my glove off. A few seconds later, the glove, still in the mold, was covered by molten glass and incorporated in a new milk bottle. Green picked the glove bottle off the belt and threw it away in the wastebin.

"That's labor in vain," he commented briefly.

However, the slight spice of danger added something to the long shifts watching the bottles. Keen to play hard, to do my best for my factory, for my side, for my house, I would brush the molds with graphite every few minutes, until Green warned me off.

"That's labor in vain," he said briefly. He vouchsafed no further explanation, but eventually I discovered from the foreman that too much graphite didn't do the bottles any good.

The factory didn't cease production by day or by night, midweek or weekends. We worked on a shift system, each shift being of eight hours, except that, for general convenience, an extra hour was added to the night shift, so that the morning shift started at seven, not six, in the morning. There were four shifts, three on duty during a twenty-four-hour period and the fourth resting. By a rather complicated roster system, the shifts were rotated so that nobody worked the night shift more than three nights running. We thus worked a forty-two-hour week, which is exactly the national British average working week. But as some of this period was worked by night, and the exact hours varied from week to week, with the turning of the roster, we were deemed to be working a forty-five-hour week, in order to allow us the overtime pay to which we were entitled. We also received a bonus which depended on the output of the factory as a whole and which was reduced by the percentage of faulty bottles which the packers found and discarded. In view of the time lag of about forty-eight hours between making the bottle and packing it, it was difficult to attribute any particular faulty bottle to any particular operator or machine, and the percentage was therefore spread evenly over the whole factory in an impersonal way. It was impossible to feel that there was much connection between the production of my one particular machine and the weekly bonus which I later received.

The sorters and packers, though they were members of the same shift, were no friends of ours, we felt. They worked at the far end of the lehr, where it was much cooler and quieter, and we often felt that they discarded bottles which were perfectly good, just to exercise their right of selection, and this, of course, harmed the bonus. On reflection, this seems to me an unfair criticism of their selectivity. In rejecting a bottle, they were harming their own bonus as well as ours.

I had worked in a factory before, but in different circumstances. I had been the chairman's nephew, learning the business from the bottom up, or down, and though I often felt myself to be suffering from inverted nepotism, I was nevertheless aware, and everyone else was aware too, that I was only going to spend a limited time in the factory before moving on to some other area of work, probably in an office. But this time, making my glass bottles, I was aware that I had no concealed privileges, that I was there, not to learn the business, but to make bottles, and that I was not going to be moved after some months or years to any office.

As I had no technical qualifications, it seemed unlikely that I would ever be promoted to foreman or shift engineer. Unless I was dismissed for bad behavior or redundancy, I would remain on that factory floor in front of that machine, if I chose, for the rest of my working life. It caused a considerable change in my mental attitude toward work and my fellow workers. I became aware of the great divide between "us" and "them." In the other factory, I had definitely been one of "them," even though I was for the moment slumming on the factory floor. But now I was genuinely and properly one of "us," becoming indoctrinated with the attitudes of mind and the mental habits of the British workingman. I was a Labour supporter, a trade union supporter, a hater of Tories and privilege. My mind, like those of all my fellow workers, was fixed upon three things —the end of the shift, the weekly pay packet and the possibility of redundancy. We looked no higher, no wider.

Politicians might make speeches, calling on us to increase our production for the sake of the British economy. We did not often discuss such orations in the canteen, in the mold shop or beside the lockers. But if we did, it would be done in sarcastic tones. There was nothing we could do to increase production. We could not work longer hours with the next shift waiting to take over at two o'clock or ten o'clock. The speed of the machine and of the belt was set by the production engineer, who had no doubt worked in consultation with the sales manager. Should, for some reason, the machines and the belt be set to work faster for a particular job, there was likely to be a slight increase in the number of faulty bottles, so that the harder we worked, the less was our bonus. However, we had no say in this. The factory's production was decided in advance by the production engineer on the basis of the orders he had received. We could do no more than watch the bottles go by.

After a few weeks, I was promoted from weight controller to machine operator. This was a proud moment. Not only was my weekly pay packet bigger, but I was now in sole charge of the huge machine. It clanked and hissed and ate gloves and spewed out red-hot glass like a dragon, and I never lost my awe of it. Whether any of my workmates saw their machines in such romantic terms, I do not know. If they had such private thoughts, they gave no public expression to them, and naturally I never even considered starting that sort of dialogue. I was anxious to be exactly the same as the others. But I wasn't completely successful. My mates, who were not unappreciative, noticed some difference about me, in particular my accent, though there were probably other points, too, of which I was unaware. I was the focus of a certain curiosity, which I would gladly have avoided. The foreman would ask me about my home, my background, where I had been at school, the names of my children. I would dodge and evade these questions as much as possible, producing some lame and unconvincing story. The foreman would laugh and bang me on the shoulder.

"All that education and look where it's got you, eh?"

On one occasion, when I was being evasive about what I had been doing before I came to the factory, he said: "You've done a stretch, haven't you?" And indeed, it was the most obvious explanation of me: that I had recently come out of prison.

Despite his unwelcome curiosity, the foreman was a friendly and genial man. He, too, had started on the floor as a weight controller many years before, but despite his promotion, he had remained one of "us." I always felt that he was on my side, even when my dragon proved temperamental and troublesome and started producing monstrous bottles like spastic embryos. Sometimes he would come up and say, "Feel like a breath of fresh air? Like to take these molds over to the mold shop?" I would put on a special pair of mold gloves, the third pair, lift the hot, heavy molds onto the trolley and wheel them out of the hot, noisy factory into the cool afternoon, across the yard to the mold shop, while he would watch my machine in my absence. I would gossip briefly with the men in the mold shop about politics or football and then, feeling refreshed, wheel back a new, cool pair of molds. Or else the foreman would send me to the canteen to fetch him a jug of tea, giving me the opportunity to get myself a cup of tea while I was about it. On my return he would tip me a penny halfpenny for my services, which I would accept gratefully.

Above the foreman was the shift engineer. He too had started on the factory floor, but he had crossed the divide. He had become one of "them." He would stalk around the factory floor, aloof and impartial, supervising us and our work. He would bring us our pay packets on Friday and would organize the details of the shift. We were allowed a half-hour break in the middle of the shift, to go have a meal in the canteen, while a relief operator minded our machines. "You go for grub at two," he would say to me. "Jack'll mind your machine."

But in the main, his job was to supervise us and the production of bottles, and he was a stickler for things being done in the proper traditional way. One of our problems was that sometimes the bottles would get stuck at the end of the belt and not move on into the lehr. This caused a blockage on the belt and the probable loss of many bottles. Until the fault could be rectified, it was the operator's job then to move the bottles into the lehr one at a time with his tongs. Like the other operators, I soon discovered that the best way of doing this was not one at a time with tongs, but with a broom from which all the bristles had been removed. With this I could push the bottles into the lehr gently, four at a time, in an even line, and the wood, though it might get slightly charred, did not damage the bottles. I provided myself with this wooden implement and used it discreetly and effectively when necessary, but it was too good to last long. Turning around once after pushing a hundred or so bottles into the lehr, I found the shift engineer standing behind me like a disapproving schoolmaster.

"That's the lazy man's way of doing it," he said. "You use your tongs." He held out his hand for the broom and sadly I gave it to him.

Above the shift engineer was the production engineer. He wore a gray flannel pinstripe suit, and unlike the rest of us, he was a qualified engineer. He was occupied in difficult technical problems, and he only spoke to me once in the whole time

I was in the factory. Shortly before Christmas, he came along the factory floor, shaking hands with each operator in turn. I pulled off my gloves and shook hands with him.

"Merry Christmas," he said.

"Merry Christmas, sir," I replied.

"Happy New Year."

He moved on to shake hands with Green. I found the foreman standing beside me. "Well, that's your Christmas present," he said, smiling. "Don't spend it all at once."

Above the production engineer, far, far above, was the managing director. He would sometimes escort important visitors or customers through the factory, explaining how it all worked. He also had the disconcerting habit of turning up at three o'clock in the morning to see that all was going well. He never spoke to me. It was with the other members of "us" that I felt solidarity, though the opportunities for conversation were surprisingly limited. On the factory floor we all were busy with our own machines. Only the operators and their weight controllers had the chance to speak to each other, and the taciturn Green had not exactly encouraged idle talk. Nor, since we went for grub one at a time, did we meet over our roast beef and cabbage in the canteen. The best opportunities for conversation were while changing at the lockers, or while waiting at the end of the shift for the moment to come to clock out, or while walking away through the factory yard in the wet dawn. Even then, we did not speak much. The operators of long standing had little wish to talk to newcomers like myself; our solidarity —our sense of togetherness—was forged in silence. The newer operators, the weight controllers, who had been taken on by the factory about the same time as myself would, however, sometimes speak. They would talk about other places where they had worked, other jobs they had done. More often we talked about the job on hand, the problems of different sorts of bottles. Milk bottles, particularly the quart size, were hot and often troublesome. On the other hand, the machine and the belt were set to move slower for such big bottles, so the operator had more time if anything should go wrong. At the other end of the scale were little shampoo bottles. They would come fast out of the machine, and the automatic tongs would often pull off their small necks. The decapitated bottle would then be stuck on the belt, causing a block, a pileup of bottles and a possible loss of bonus. The favorite bottles were the middle-sized ones which would later hold medicines or cleaning fluid. These gave little trouble, and the operator could often go through an entire shift without losing a single bottle, apart from the ones he chose to weigh. "The less trouble, the better" was our spoken motto, and it was on topics like these that we conversed while we waited for the moment to clock out.

The shift usually changed over about twenty minutes before scheduled time. It was an unwritten law that nobody was ever late on a shift. The previous operator had been there, standing at his machine, for eight hours, and naturally he wanted time to clean up and change before he left the factory. When you took over from the operator on the previous shift, you did so without speaking; occasionally you might mumble, "OK. I'll take over now," but the words would probably be lost in the noise.

Time moved slowly on. Damp autumn gave place to gray winter, though this was barely noticeable inside the factory or indeed in the yards outside. Christmas came upon us and with it the experience, already recorded, of exchanging a few words with the production engineer. The factory closed down for the two days of the holiday, but since the lehrs and the crude metal tanks had to be left switched on, a skeleton staff was required to patrol the factory and keep an eye on possible fires. For this undemanding and somewhat boring task the men were to be paid double time and a half. There was accordingly much competition to be selected for the skeleton shifts. As a comparatively newly arrived workman, I was not, of course, even considered for this select band. This did not distress me as, almost alone on my shift, I wished to spend Christmas with my family.

As a gesture to the festive season, the canteen, a few days before Christmas, provided turkey and plum pudding for our mid-shift grub. This was sold at a slightly higher price, though it still seemed quite modest to me. However, the increased price caused much grumbling in the shifts and many of my workmates preferred to go without. The Christmas spirit, it will be seen, did not play a very large part in our way of thinking. Money was more important. New Year's Eve and New Year's Day were normal working days, but I noticed that several of my mates did not turn up for their shift on New Year's Day. These were the only cases of absenteeism which I noticed during my time in the factory. The shift engineer was prepared for this, and some of the weight controllers found themselves temporarily promoted to acting machine operators.

Winter moved slowly on into a late, cold spring. "The later, the better," said the foreman to me. "In the summer, it gets hot in here." With the British summer usually being about the same temperature as the British winter, I felt that the distinction was more in the mind than on the thermometer. But I politely let him curdle my blood with stories of heat stroke.

I was becoming accustomed to the factory, to the attitudes of mind and the way of life. I was becoming accustomed, too, to the rhythm of the shifts, which ignored the normal week and had a pattern all their own. Three consecutive morning shifts, a break, three consecutive afternoon shifts, a break, three consecutive night shifts, a break, three consecutive morning shifts, and so on to the day of retirement. The morning shift involved getting up very early in the morning to take over the machine at twenty to seven, and this I did not find easy. But once there, and at work, it was, in many ways, the pleasantest of the three shifts. For one thing, it was only seven hours, and, when we came off duty at two o'clock, a whole free afternoon and night stretched out before us. For the more poetically minded there was the dawn creeping in through the overhead skylights. Later in the morning there might easily be girls to watch, secretaries, wages clerks, filing clerks, carrying papers from the production engineer's office to the shift engineer's office. The last hour was spent thinking about our thirsts, thinking about the beer which we could drink when we came off shift, for the pubs in that part of England did not close in the afternoons until half-past two.

The afternoon shift lasted eight hours, from two until ten, but somehow it seemed to take up the whole day; there seemed little time for any outside activities. But in other ways, it was similar to the morning shift. There was the occasional girl to be seen, the parties of visitors being escorted around by the production engineer or one of the directors, twilight falling on us through the skylights. At five thirty the white-collar workers, the clerical and administrative staffs who worked normal working hours, would go home, and we would be left alone in the night with our machines. It was said that the clerical staff outnumbered the shift staff by two to one. I don't know if this was true or not, but the thought gave us wry amusement, increased by the thought that though our work might be hot and dirty, in general we were earning more than they were. I was also pleased by the fact that I was actually producing the goods, the bottles, and not simply making entries in a ledger. But this aspect of the situation did not seem to interest my workmates.

A sad feature, however, of the afternoon shift, was that we had to resist thinking about beer during the last hour. By the time we were out of the factory the pubs would be shut. The factory in fact ran a club, which had different licensing hours to suit the needs of shift workers, but few of us ever went there. We had no wish to stay and drink on the factory premises. We would prefer to forget our thirsts and go straight home.

The night shift was the hardest of all. It lasted for nine hours. Even though I had become accustomed to the rhythm of the shifts, it is difficult not to feel tired and low at four o'clock in the morning. There were no distractions, no dawn, no dusk, no girls, no visitors—unless the managing director should happen to walk around in the middle of the night. The molds, the types of bottles were not changed at night. If the machines were running smoothly, if the bottles were moving evenly along the belt to the lehr, there was little to do, little to occupy the thoughts. Every twenty minutes or so, we would weigh a bottle and brush the molds with graphite, but I had long since learned not to do that too often. Time would move very slowly. I would think it must be already five in the morning and then find that it was not yet two. I would stand there and listen to the endless thumping rhythm of the machine, watch the endless line of glowing bottles moving forward on the belt, and I would try to empty my mind of all thoughts.

We were provided with stools to sit on while we watched the machines and the belts. This was a concession gained for us by our union, but it was not popular with the management. A sitting operator might easily become a sleeping operator, one who would not be alert if the bottles should suddenly start coming out deformed from the molds or if there should be a logjam on the belt. Some of the stools had disappeared for repairs and had not yet been returned. If the shift engineer caught me sitting on the stool, he would wave me to my feet with a jerk of his thumb. "That's the lazy man's way," he would say. Indeed, I sometimes felt myself to be crushed between the two conflicting philosophies of "That's the lazy man's way" and "That's labor in vain." Perhaps this is the basic dilemma of all industry.

Eventually I knew it was time to leave, time to move on before I succumbed completely to the rhythm of shift work, before I became irrevocably hypnotized by the steady beat of the machine. It was time to do something else, to try a different way of earning money, to write a book, to learn to live again in the world outside the factory. To ease my departure, I invented a story about a relative who was ill and how I had to go and look after his work while he was in hospital. I don't know if the shift engineer believed me. The foreman seemed to believe me, or at least he pretended to.

"Farmer Giles," he said jokingly. "You'll find milking cows a bit of a change after all this."

"At least I'm used to getting up early," I answered.

He even suggested that I might return to the factory when my brother-in-law was better and able once again to run his own farm. I was touched and said that I certainly hoped that would be possible. The others were less credulous.

"He won't come back," said one. "They never do."

Another said, "I don't blame you. It's not much of a job, is it?"

I maintained stoutly that it was an excellent job and that it was only family matters that were taking me away. At the lockers, an older operator, a friend and mate of Green, under whom I had worked as a weight controller, said to me, "Didn't think you'd stay long." Long, in his thinking, meant at least twenty years. I collected my last pay packet; I handed in my gloves; I put on my raincoat and my cap. My last action was to give back to Green the blue denim coat which he had lent me on my first day at the factory. I had worn it, shift after shift, for months. I thanked him and said I would have the coat cleaned and posted to him, if he would let me have his home address.

"That's labor in vain," he said, taking the coat from me.

18

CHAIRMEN AND CLUBMEN

☙ I had discovered by practical experience the conflict in the British attitude toward work, the endless dichotomy between "labor in vain" and "the lazy man's way": the basic wish to make things as easy as possible for the workman or alternatively as hard as possible for him; the irreconcilable opposition of interests and opinions between those who wish to give as little as possible in return for as much as possible and those who wish to get as much as possible in return for as little as possible; the endless unsolvable dilemma of "them" and "us."

These are, of course, the permanent problems of management and labor, and the British have their fair share of them. Between the two permanent enemies, between the two organized and probably militant minorities, the typical Britishman finds himself rather bewildered. A reasonable man, playing by the rules, dedicated to the idea of fair play, he believes that a fair day's work deserves a fair day's pay and equally that a fair day's pay involves a fair day's work. Any departure from this principle one way or the other shocks him as, in my industrial experience, it had shocked me. But granted the wish to play by the rules, the reasonable Britishman feels that the only problem is to decide the amount of work and pay which can fairly be said to balance each other. It is the problem of fixing these values permanently or even temporarily which makes the reasonable man feel so unhappy and often so desperate.

This attitude toward work and wages is not, of course, unique to the British, though it is by no means universal. But alongside it go two other attitudes to work, which must be borne in mind; the object of work to the Britishman, or perhaps one should say to the modern Britishman, is to do something—produce something, repair something, complete something. The work is an object to an end; it is not an end in itself. A Britishman works either to earn a living or to do something he particularly wants done, or both. The act of work in itself has little or no importance. This is of course at variance with the attitude of, say, the Germans or Swiss, who value work as something in its own right, whether it produces anything useful or not. It is a misunderstanding of this attitude and indeed of all the attitudes referred to which sometimes gives to foreigners the impression that the British are lazy or work-shy or tired.

It is not easy to generalize accurately about this difficult problem. In Victorian times the gospel of work, the idea that work in itself was important and indeed noble, was widespread in Britain as well as in Germany. The Victorian print contrasting the Sunday of diligence (a bustling, busy family, in their best clothes, admiring a small girl playing the piano, probably rather badly) with a Sunday of idleness (a couple lying beside a river bank on a sunny afternoon and perhaps being tempted into sin) is now reproduced on tea towels as "camp" humor for tired housewives washing the dishes. But the cult continues in many places, particularly the North of England, and among many people, especially those who are not members of the working classes. Admiration of the Germans, the Japanese, the Swiss for their dedication to work is often expressed. The habit of the Swiss bankers of being at their desks by eight o'clock in the morning is recalled with some awe, though the British tourist in Switzerland, trying to cash a check at lunchtime, often finds this awe evaporating when he finds that Swiss banks close completely for two hours for lunch. In fact, the Britishman works as hard and as long as other people.

About 93 percent of men of working age, that is to say, between the ages of fifteen and sixty-five, are at work, the remaining 7 percent being mainly students or men who for various reasons, usually medical, are unemployable. This gives a working life of fifty years. The average working week is forty-two hours, the hours which I worked in the glass factory, and this is longer than in some other nations. Overtime is popular on top of the normal working day, and employers wishing to attract labor to a new factory or project have to advertise that ample overtime is available. For manual workers overtime increases the average working week to forty-six and a half hours. There are also a considerable number of cases of moonlighting, of men fitting in two jobs into the twenty-four hours, often at some danger both to their health and to their family life. For others, the second job is in their home, either redecorating it in a do-it-yourself manner or gardening. Both these activities are considered to be work rather than hobbies and indeed are referred to as work. In fact, the Britishman is likely to get more satisfaction from his unpaid work than from his job. Perhaps this is because such a rugged individualist is bound to dislike working for a master. Even the most enlightened of modern managements raises his hackles (especially if it happens to be foreign, which is increasingly probable). Working for a government department frustrates him even more. He dreams of starting up on his own and being independent. Meanwhile, he pours unlimited energy into his hobbies.

When the British meet in the pub for a Sunday morning drink, they will often ask each other jocularly what work they have been doing that morning. They do not, of course, mean the work of making milk bottles or writing books or even delivering the Sunday newspapers. They mean pruning the roses, mowing the cricket pitch, repapering the spare bedroom or even cleaning the car. These are, for the Britishman, typical examples of work, no less meritorious for being unpaid, as valuable in his own estimation and to the country as his other work in the garage or insurance office.

The wives, during this refreshing occasion, will, of course, as already explained, be working in the kitchen, but they are very likely to have jobs outside the home as well. A man may achieve independence through his hobbies, but his wife finds it through having an income of her own. More than half of all British women have jobs, and half of these employed women are married. This is a factor which aids the national productivity and greatly assists the family income (most of the women's pay packets get spent on the family), though it may be damaging to their relationships, in particular to the children. There are a great many "latchkey children," who, arriving home from school, have to let themselves into an empty house and get their own tea before starting on their homework.

The second British attitude to work arises from the feeling that a man needs to do something useful, if not for the nation, at least for his image and his self-respect. This, once again, is not confined to the British, but it is also far from universal. A rich Spaniard does not work, is not expected to work, and indeed his image requires it of him that he should be seen not to work. "Of course he does not work; he is a millionaire," they explain, even if it is only a million pesetas. When I explain to them that in Britain a well-to-do man, perhaps a hard-pressed managing director, works harder and longer hours than his employees, my Spanish friends express incredulity. "What is the use of money," they say, "if it is not to relieve oneself of the burden of work?"

The British see it differently, and from this arises the belief in the importance and usefulness of voluntary work. This covers an amazingly large area of the nation's activities and is widely respected, and it is doubtful if even my onetime colleague Green would regard it as labor in vain. One can give a few examples of this. In no other country in the world are 90 percent of criminal cases dealt with by unpaid amateur magistrates. Considerable burdens of local government are carried by unpaid members of district councils, and indeed it is still felt by many people that parliamentary business should be conducted in the same way. There was much opposition to the comparatively recent decision to pay salaries to Members of Parliament, and this disapproval, instinctive, if irrational, still exists. It would be unthinkable in Britain for a blood donor ever to be paid for his services. One can mention lifeboats, the St. John Ambulance, Boy Scouts and other youth movements, Citizens Advice Bureaus, the various activities of the Women's Voluntary Services, prison visitors and many other aspects of welfare.

It is felt to be right and proper that these services should be organized and run by volunteers, their equipment paid for by private subscriptions if necessary.

In earlier centuries it was felt that education, care of orphans, the sick, and the aged came into this category, too. The wish to found a grammar school for poor scholars in the neighborhood or establish an almshouse for the old or a foundling hospital for unfortunate abandoned children is deep in the British character—the wish, sometimes charitable, sometimes tiresome, to be your brother's keeper.

The most remarkable achievement of this tradition was the prewar voluntary hospitals system. Charitable subscriptions paid the overheads, and the surgeons and consultants gave their services free. Patients were not charged unless they could afford it. As a result of this system, the ordinary Britishman has for a long time had the remarkable benefit of free hospital treatment. He is horrified to hear that there are still foreign countries where a sick person may be left to die because he has no money to pay for an operation.

When the famous postwar welfare state was set up, this tradition was extended to include free medicine of all kinds for everyone, and the burden was removed from the charitable subscriber to the taxpayer. This produced the National Health Service, which was so much envied abroad that it had to be violently denounced almost daily by its opponents in democracies likely to demand a free service too. However, an unexpected snag has been discovered. The British public was so used to its voluntary hospitals, supported by the generous, that the idea of paying for them through taxation was most unwelcome. The taxpayer has proved to be a stingy and cheeseparing patron, grudging every penny. It was calculated a few years ago that British spending on hospitals was among the lowest in

Western Europe. It amounted to 1.75 percent of the average income per head, compared to 1.9 percent (for less comprehensive services) in the United States and 2.5 percent in Canada. Since then, medical expenses, in comparison with all other costs, have risen sharply in the United States, but in Britain, relative to other costs, they have been forced down.

Inevitably, standards have gone down, too. Doctors and nurses are notoriously underpaid, and many have emigrated. But the Britishman's attitude to his health remains the same as to his food; he regards every pound spent on it as good money wasted.

Many other formerly voluntary activities have now been taken over also by the welfare state and are administered by local authorities or government departments, and following this, there has been a slight shift in attitude from "we ought to do something about it" to "they ought to do something about it." But the wish to do voluntary service, while frustrated in some earlier directions, is continually finding new outlets. There are few, indeed one may say no, contemporary problems, either national or worldwide, which will not arouse in British hearts the urge to do something about it and, in particular, to form a committee.

Committees proliferate through British life. They may vary from the serious to the cranky, from the learned and respectable to the frivolous and ephemeral. It is impossible to organize a village fair without first forming a committee and the British have a deep and long-established wish to do both.

The desire to form a committee, to be a member of a committee, derives partly from the idea of helping, of being a do-gooder. The phrase does not generally have in Britain the sneering connotations which it sometimes has elsewhere, though of course, the urge to do good in Britain is sometimes inspired, as elsewhere, by a liking for being interfering and important, perhaps, if the committee is major enough, by the hope of a knighthood or other honor. A second reason for becoming a member of a committee is the wish to belong—to belong to a small, select group of men and women with the same interests and the same purposes. The British committee and society are social organizations which find few counterparts in other European nations where all do-gooding has traditionally been left to the church. In this, Britain is closer to America than to the Continent.

The committee cult has become a built-in aspect of the British social scene. The reasons why the British should have this passion to belong to small groups are a matter for speculation. It is, perhaps, the result of family untogetherness, the anti-family. If a family prides itself on never being seen together, on never, in fact, being together, then its members will need, for human companionship, to rely on the other members of the Horticultural Society, the Darts Club, the Labour Club, the Conservative Supporters' Club. If a man may not enjoy the company of his family, he will take pride in his membership or patronage of the local Liberal Club or Bowls Club or Dockland Welfare Club. If a woman has no one to talk to at home, she values her work for the Women's Institute or the United Charities Bazaar Committee or the local troop of the Girl Guides. Apart from providing her with an image, the image of someone who is doing good, doing something to help the less fortunate or perhaps to help the country, these clubs or groups or committees provide a much-needed companionship, and the storms and the rows and the arguments which go on in them, though sometimes the result of genuine disagreements about points of detail, are more probably the extrovert expression of conflicts and tensions in British family life, which, by the British code, can never be expressed at home.

The committee is, then, not simply a means of improving the world, or the small part of the world which it may be able to affect, or even merely a substitute for the family for those who either have none or feel their home life to be inadequate. It is partly a safety valve for those who have something to do and cannot do it, who have something to say and cannot say it, who want people to organize and cannot find them.

Most of this may be attributed to the untogetherness of the British family, but there is another, deeper racial reason why the British should seek always to belong to small groups. This may be found in the piecemeal conquest of the country, as a result of which the neighbors in the next county, the next valley, perhaps even the next farm, belonged to a different racial group or came from a different tribe. When the Vikings landed in Britain, chiefly in the eighth and ninth centuries, they landed in the drakkars, large open ships led by one man, to whom they owed their allegiance. When they landed and conquered and settled, they founded a drakkar-type community, and this ideal persists even in the changed world of the present day. The American may seek to discover and, in a sense, try to identify with his racial origins, the Frenchman may wish to define and to conform exactly with his social level, but the Britishman, at heart, wishes to be once more a member of the jolly crew of a drakkar.

He has therefore to find a drakkar substitute, wherever he may go, to divide up large organizations into small groups to which he feels he can safely belong. Oxford and Cambridge, for instance, are less universities than multiple groups of colleges, competing against one another in sport and, it must be fair to say, academic achievement. An Oxford graduate will tell you, should you ask him, that he has been at Balliol or Christ Church or Trinity, rather than that he has been at Oxford. In big amorphous universities like Columbia or Berkeley or the Sorbonne, a British student would feel lost. He wishes to belong to something smaller and then, traditionally, to compete against a rival small organization. British boarding schools, the melting pot and anvil of so many future distinguished citizens, are naturally divided into houses, so as to pander to and indeed encourage this spirit.

A sailor will feel loyalty, of course, to the Navy as a remote and abstract organization, but his detailed and practical loyalty will be to his ship and to his shipmates, temporary though they may be. In a naval regatta he will burst himself to row faster and harder than his opposite number from another ship, for comradeship with one group involves rivalry with another. The British Army is wedded to the idea of regiments; other armies of course have, or have had, their *corps d'élite*—the French Old Guard, the German Storm Troopers, the American Marines —but no other army in history has divided itself up into penny packets like the British Army. No other soldiers have thought it so necessary to identify with a limited group, a restricted number of friends and colleagues, drawn, if possible, from specific regional areas.

A recent book, entitled *Morale* by John Baynes, studied the ideas of the members of a battalion of an ordinary regiment of the line which went into battle in France during the First World War, some 700 strong, and lost, within a few days, 500 men. The remaining two hundred were, however, still a coherent and important fighting unit, and the author was attempting to discover what it was that kept them going in the face of those terrible casualties and of the near-certain prospect of sudden death. He interviewed the survivors and questioned them about their motives and their ideals. The answer was unanimous, both among officers and other ranks: The idea that kept them going through everything was not primarily loyalty to their king or country, or belief in the rightness of their cause, or religion, or faith in their commander in chief who would lead them to victory—these qualities belong to the soldiers of other nations. What held this small, battered group together was the idea of their regiment. This was something they could understand and see; this was something they could fight and die for. A member of the battalion, a private soldier who had often been in trouble for his drinking habits, later wrote to his commanding officer that he knew he had often been "on the wallaby" but he hoped he had never done anything to let the regiment down. His commanding officer, another survivor of the battle, naturally treasured the letter forever. Both men, commanding officer and private soldier, were speaking of the ultimate British loyalty.

The result of these experiences has been to strengthen and support the British belief in the importance of *esprit de corps*, a French phrase which embodies much that is important in British thinking and relationships, but which, I have observed, plays no part whatsoever in French public or private life. *Esprit de corps* is thought by the British not only to be essential to *morale,* but also to be the *raison d'être* for the *amour propre;* on these deep and embarrassing attitudes, the British often prefer to express themselves in French, though no Frenchman would begin to understand their meaning. *Esprit de corps* is to be fostered at all costs and despite all disadvantages. The idea of the British Army was much less important to the British people than the idea of the Argyll and Sutherland Highlanders. When the government recently decided to disband this old and famous regiment, to fit in with the modern concept of a small mobile army, there was an outcry. A committee to fight the move was, of course, organized; posters appeared in windows and on car bumpers; a petition received more than a million signatures. These signatories did not, obviously, come only from the counties of Argyll and Sutherland, or from present and past members of the regiment, the total populations and numbers of which would not nearly approach this figure. The signatories felt that the Argylls were symbols of an *esprit de corps* which should not be lightly cast aside and represented something worth retaining, despite its inconvenience in the modern nuclear-defense world.

This feeling, of course, is not confined only to the army or to organizations with long and distinguished histories but applies also to groups with more modest and less notable achievements. One may cite as an example, perhaps, a girls' boarding school on Speech Day. The fathers, or some of them, will have been conscripted into a tug-of-war match. They will have protested and perhaps tried to avoid this duty. They will be chosen for one side of the rope or the other at random, but once committed, they will try their damnedest, not because they wish to win, but because even at moments like this, they do not wish to let down their *ad hoc* side. It is better to risk a stroke or a rupture than to be accused of lack of team spirit.

At the Guards' Depot, where the recruits of five different regiments of Guards train together on the same parade ground, a curious daily ritual was enacted. The officer taking the parade would walk along the line of smart recruits standing at ease. He would select a recruit at random and ask him the question "What is the best regiment in the British Army?" The recruit would then leap to attention and reply with the name of his own regiment. The officer would nod approvingly and walk on. This odd dialogue was intended to inspire the recruit with *esprit de corps.* It would have been no use his demurring and insisting that all five regiments were really as good as one another, when you came down to it, still less to attempt tact and give the name of the inspecting officer's own regiment. A clever recruit answering thus would have been immediately placed in arrest and marched to the guardroom.

In the same way, though on a more frivolous level, team spirit is brought into activities where it might be thought to be superfluous or irrelevant. On my arrival in a holiday camp in Britain, I found that all campers were immediately allotted to one of two imaginary houses, "Kent" or "Gloucester." Cheerleaders taught us to shout out: "One two three four, who are we for? K E N T—Kent. Hurray!" We would go round calling out "Kent" and blowing kisses or alternatively "Gloucester" and making an obscene gesture. The points which we gained for our achievements at ping-pong or bathing-beauty competitions or knobbly-knees contests were points gained by our house. The objects were not only to have a good and relaxing holiday, but to beat "Gloucester," for even at a holiday camp, playing for the side has its honored and traditional place, without which a holiday would not be a holiday and a Britishman would not feel himself.

Although regimental loyalty was apparently a crucial factor in the First World War, it can be maintained that it was much less valuable during the Second World War and could, in fact, be more damaging than beneficial. Pride in your own unit cannot, it seems, be achieved without denigration of the rival, and this denigration is often both unfair and undeserved. I was once, as a subaltern, severely rebuked in the officers' mess when I suggested that perhaps the Coldstream Guards was not as bad a regiment as I had been told. My not ungenerous remark, it seemed, smacked of disloyalty to my own regiment. Such uncharitable attitudes are comparatively harmless and unimportant in the serene atmosphere of a mess far from the battle, but in battle itself the attitude of denigration may easily lead to bitterness and noncooperation. The Navy and, in particular, the RAF suffered from the same thing. It was not a harmonious factor when squadrons had to share the same airfield.

The logical result of the British wish to belong to a small, select community has been the invention not only of the committee but of the club. Invention is perhaps too strong a word for something so derivative. No doubt there were clubs not only in drakkars but in ancient Babylon. But no nation seems to have popularized them, venerated them and created a mystique about them as have the British. That area of London comprising parts of Piccadilly, St. James's Street, Pall Mall and Mayfair is still referred to as Clubland. The cult has to some extent spread to North America, and distinguished and select clubs are to be found in both New York and Washington, but there is no part of either of these cities which is referred to popularly as Clubland, and the institution of the club barely exists in Paris or Rome.

By clubs I do not, of course, mean nightclubs or gambling clubs or supper clubs, which are to be found also in abundance in Mayfair. I am referring to those august and intimidating premises, possibly with charming eighteenth-century architecture, possibly with heavy Victorian mock-classical porticoes. They have courteous uniformed hall porters who know every member by sight, by name and probably by private life, walls hung with old prints (probably sporting prints), or portraits of distinguished and deceased members, or possibly even stuffed salmon and stuffed rhino heads complete with glassy eyes. The subscriptions are high and the excellent meals relatively inexpensive; the newspaper table will be as well stocked as the bar; and the conversation is supposed, usually wrongly, to be brilliant and full of inside information. Future and hopeful members may have to wait three months or three years or ten years or even forty years, depending on the club in question.

The London clubs (there are also clubs in Edinburgh, Glasgow, Manchester, Cardiff and other cities, but I have little personal experience of these) are relics of the past. Their origins go back perhaps not to drakkars or village moots, but to the coffeehouses of the seventeenth century and the gaming clubs of the eighteenth century. They thrived on the British wish to get away from dull women, all women, and above all from the family. As the fashion for belonging to a club grew, so did the selectivity, the social importance of the clubs themselves. They became the third point of the triangle, the country house, the town house, the club. Now, when the country house has been converted into apartments or opened to the public, and the town house pulled down and replaced by a modern hotel, the club alone remains. Its elegance is still preserved in the beautiful rooms of White's, Brooks's and Boodle's, its glamor in the high stakes for bridge and the marathon backgammon games.

I speak with some expertise on these matters. An uncle of mine was a collector of London clubs and would often talk to me at great length about the difference between one club and another, where another man might discuss the differences between one stock, one racehorse, one symphony orchestra, and another. When I became twenty-one, he felt it was his duty to me, apart from introducing me to his tailor and his wine merchant, to propose me for six of his London clubs. This, when I was finally elected to them all, I found to be most damaging to my bank balance. On one occasion, at the bar of White's, unable to afford a martini on my wages as a machine operator, I asked for a glass of water. The barman gave it to me immediately, politely and, of course, without comment, but it must have been the only glass of water ever served in the bar of White's.

In due course economy forced me to shed several of my clubs, but my experience had been sufficiently widespread to observe the different types of members, their different interests. In one club it would be racing, in another music, in a third cricket, in a fourth politics, in a fifth the stock market, in a sixth Army affairs. You would no more expect to hear the latest opera discussed in White's than you would the prospects for the Derby in the Savile Club. The interests of the members were deliberately as restricted as the membership itself.

One of the consequences—and indeed one of the attractions of a select ingroup—is to foster a strong wish among those outside to join. With this goes a fixed belief that important things are going on there, that influential contacts are being made. Outsiders, particularly women, still fondly believe that the route to a Cabinet office or important directorships or success generally lies in being a member of the right club. It is reported now, and it was believed at the time, that the British wartime intelligence and security services were largely recruited in White's and that the postwar counterintelligence services were run (though not, it is now realized, with total success) from the bar at White's. But the idea that a young hopeful had only to appear in the right club to be offered immediately a seat in Parliament, or a directorship, or the command of a battalion was never more than a romantic fallacy. Many men have stood in their clubs for hours, drinking alone, eating, staring out of the window, reading the papers in the morning room, without being offered a post in the City.

Indeed, the professional clubman, the haunter of clubs, is usually the club bore and is carefully avoided by those busy, influential men who have just dropped in for lunch. As steps on the ladder of professional success, as opposed to social success, clubs are not what they were, and indeed one wonders if they were ever as crucial in a man's career as they were popularly supposed to be. Nowadays the whole shine is going off the system of clubs, many of them struggling to pay the wages bills of their expert and accomplished staff, their members struggling to pay the higher and higher subscriptions out of their taxed incomes.

Clubs retain their popularity as convenient places for lunch, but the idea of dining at your club convivially with like-minded friends (or perhaps, at some clubs, choosing in preference the dining table where conversation is not permitted) is clearly going out. Fewer and fewer members have the opportunity of falling asleep in one of the huge club armchairs in the morning room after lunch. A man has his work to do, and in the evening he wishes to return to his home, which may be some distance from Clubland. The other members of the club in the evening, dining and drinking until the bar closes, are likely to be members who have moved into the club until their divorces come through. The ordinary member will probably wish to return to his home, to his garden, his television and his wife, and in this trend one may notice, perhaps not unhopefully, a slight change in the Britishman's attitude toward his family. Perhaps wives are less boring now that women have the same education as men.

But on the day when the last London club closes, when the last old club servant is pensioned off, when the pictures and the furniture are sold at Sotheby's, and the beautiful eighteenth-century building is pulled down and replaced by a modern office block, something will have gone out of British life; something will have disappeared from British social life. The fund of British funny stories will be the poorer.

I may perhaps end this chapter by recalling one of the most pleasant of them. Toward the end of the last war, Field Marshal Alexander returned from Italy to London on leave and went, of course, to his club. An elderly member greeted him in the coffee room: "Hello, Alex, haven't seen you for a long time. What are you doing these days?" The field marshal replied simply, "I'm still soldiering."

The story can be told from many angles: as an example of Alexander's modesty, for he had been much in the news after the Battle of Cassino and the capture of Rome, or as an example of the unawareness of current affairs of some elderly club members. But it is possible to think that one or both members may have had their tongues in their cheeks and that the dialogue was a deliberate example of British humor by understatement. It is also an example of the sort of conversation which can still be heard from time to time in London clubs.

19

THE GLORY OF THE GARDEN

☙ Of that great British trinity, the town house, the country house and the club, the country house is by far the best known. The others may struggle against increasing costs and eventually be sold, but the country house, whether divided into flats or open to the public at half a crown a visit, plus teas and any amount of gimmicks, continues proudly. It is fortunate that this is so, because English country houses are without doubt the most beautiful in the world, with a greater range of date and style and proportion and size than French chateaus or German castles.

Between them, they span a huge gap from the large Elizabethan houses of Knole and Penshurst, the eye-catching and rather strange vastnesses of Blenheim Palace and Welbeck, the Palladian symmetry of Chatsworth, down to the small manor house, which may be a gem of Jacobean or Georgian architecture. And the curious visitor, whether his interest is historical or artistic or simply a wish to see how the great and the rich once lived and sometimes still live, will be able to visit it and, in doing so, contribute a little to the formidable bills for upkeep.

Evelyn Waugh in his wartime novel *Brideshead Revisited*

was writing, among other things, a dirge for the end of the English country house and the spacious and elegant way of life which it represented. Later he was forced to admit that his prophecy had been wrong, and in a preface to a subsequent edition, he commented that in the modern age, Brideshead, far from being torn down, would have been carefully preserved, restored where necessary and opened to the public. By this means, he felt, the conquering forces of Philistinism had been held at bay a little while longer, an attitude which perhaps does less than justice to the British people, tramping down the long Elizabethan corridors on their holidays, thirsty for proof of civilization and culture.

But it is not only twisted chimneys and Elizabethan windows and Palladian pediments which attract the public, any more than it is sideshows or motor museums or even the line of Kneller portraits in the Long Gallery. The great attraction will be, for most people, the gardens, huge splendid famous gardens, probably laid out by Capability Brown and tended to this day by a large army of gardeners. The gardens will attract the public, which is only mildly interested in the Allan Ramsay portraits or Regency mantelpieces. Indeed, in some cases, the house inside will not be on view. Every Saturday the *Times* publishes a list of gardens which will be open to the public at the weekend. The houses themselves may be modest and indeed modern, many of them in the middle of London or other cities. The owners open their gardens in return for a small fee (which will probably be given to charity) partly, of course, because they wish to be admired for their gardens, partly because they wish to give pleasure to other gardeners, partly because they wish to share something which is individual, indivisible and very precious to the British. The British, it must be admitted, are garden-mad.

Every man will have his favorite garden, his favorite type of garden, and his preference will be personal depending on a private interest or perhaps a private association. There is no space here to give a list of the beautiful gardens of England, and indeed such a list would be highly invidious. But I may perhaps mention three gardens which have given me, in my time, great pleasure: Luxmoore's garden at Eton, emerging each summer like a beautiful debutante, after its annual flooding by the Thames; the gardens of Cadogan Place in Sloane Street, London, with their ancient mulberry trees planted in the time of King James I and still in full leaf and vigor; and Glyndebourne in Sussex, the country-house-opera-house, hidden in a valley of the South Downs, which has proved such an irresistible magnet to the British and to visitors from abroad.

There are many reasons for going to Glyndebourne: One is obviously an enjoyment of opera and, in particular, Mozart opera; another, equally obviously, is the wish to participate in and be seen at a summer social occasion; another is the British delight in excursions to the country, picnics, garden parties, *fêtes champêtres*. There is the pleasure of visiting an old English country house, even if, in this case, much of it is closed to the public. And finally, there is the garden, the typical English country house garden, surrounded by a ha-ha, under the Downs. A garden with great trees and lawns and yew hedges and herbaceous borders, a lake, a rookery, a croquet lawn. Even those who are tone-deaf or care nothing for opera can find pleasure at Glyndebourne.

The music correspondent of a leading London paper has recalled how, emerging after the first act of *Rosenkavalier,* he heard two very British ladies discussing the work. One asked who wrote the opera, the other replied firmly, "Mozart, of course, you can tell by the clothes." But the two ladies in question, who had evidently never heard of Richard Strauss, would have been able to identify accurately every single plant in every herbaceous border and might well have recognized the name of the head gardener, which was printed in the program, alongside the conductor, the producer and the singers.

The basic principle of an English country garden is that it must be carefully planned to look as unplanned and as natural as possible. There must be no formal symmetry. The trees, except for yew hedges, must be unclipped and unpollarded, allowed to grow as that sort of tree would grow. There will be secluded corners, suitable for assignments for courting couples; there will be shrubberies, rockeries, waterfalls. Depending on the size of the garden, there may be an avenue giving a carefully contrived vista of the house itself or of a hill, but which will seem as if it happened purely by accident. There will, of course, be lawns, miles and miles of carefully tended green lawns, which become so green in the wet English spring and the wet English summer; one thinks particularly of the lawns of the Oxford colleges, which have been rolled and mown for hundreds of years, to produce a texture of green velvet. And above all, there will be herbaceous borders.

More than the lawn, more than the rockery, more than the great elms, the herbaceous border is perhaps the heart of the English garden. It requires an enormous amount of thought and an enormous amount of work. The gardener planning one will have to take into account the heights of the various flowers and shrubs, the different times of year at which they will flower, so that there may be a succession of flowers. He will even consider the time of day at which the border is intended to be seen, whether in the blaze of an afternoon garden party or, as at Glyndebourne, glimmering through the dusk of the long interval.

The object is to make the garden appear as if it were part of the landscape and not an artificial pattern imposed by man. Nature must be given, or seem to be given, its head and not cut down to size, a size smaller than human beings. Even in the middle of London, a garden is intended to be a country garden. But within this framework, which is instinctive rather than theoretical, an immense amount of variety is possible. The differences are sometimes historical: The Elizabethans were formal with their clipped yews, their Italian gardens (a result of the Renaissance). Later came the idea of parks, lakes, follies, gazebos, small temples, belvederes and the trappings of Romanticism. Fir trees were imported from Germany; mazes were resurrected from earlier days, as were ruins of abbeys or Roman baths. All the trappings of romantic love and romantic despair had to be present. The concept was entirely different from what one might expect to find in a time of imperial glory, the ideal far removed from the formal classical avenues and vistas of Rome and Versailles.

Formality, however, returned to some extent under the Edwardians, with their rose gardens, deodars, statues and silver tea trays carried out onto the lawn. Peacocks spreading their tails in their pride were undisturbed by the click of croquet balls being propelled inexpertly over shaved lawns by fair men with mustaches, wearing straw boaters.

The differences are not only vertical but lateral, not only historical along the stream of time, but also cut at cross sections across the social scene. Class differences are as much evident in the British gardens as they are in British eating, drinking, holiday-making and other habits. The most upper-class garden in Britain is the one the nearest to nature. It requires a stately home or a university college, many gardeners, much money and several centuries to produce one of these gardens, a garden designed to imitate nature so closely and with such careful art that it transcends nature completely. Andrew Marvell, in the seventeenth century, was describing a typical English garden when he wrote:

> Stumbling on melons, as I pass
> Ensnared with flowers, I fall on grass.

A rustic garden indeed!

Much of the art lies in the planting of trees, and these cannot be conjured overnight. In calculating the contrast of one tree with another—one may cite as an example the combination of yew with autumn chestnuts at Fountains Abbey, Yorkshire—the gardeners were planning for a time which they would probably not live to see.

Time, as much as foresight, is of the essence of an English garden. Instant gardens, such as those created for the kings of Egypt, planted in one night, removed the following night, would not be appreciated in Britain. When I planted an oak in the garden of my Hampshire cottage, I planted, naturally, an acorn. Fifteen years later the tree is now some five feet high.

An American friend visiting me exclaimed, "Oh, you British! If you'd planted a sapling, you'd have saved twenty years." But being British, I could not see that in growing an oak there was any need whatsoever for haste.

As natural as trees and as important in an English garden are wild flowers. Owners of British country houses will open their gardens or probably the surrounding woods specially so that visitors may come and enjoy the early aconites or the bluebells. The visitors themselves will travel for miles to see these small accidental, uncultivated flowers. The passion for wild flowers goes very deep in the British. Illustrated books of rare wild flowers, costing many guineas, still sell in the thousands. Stern female civil servants traveling in a car from one city to another will suddenly stop the car, leap into the nearest ditch or hedge and gather huge bundles of old-man's-beard or Queen Anne's lace.

Down the social scale, the passion for naturalism and wildness grows progressively less. Time and trouble will be more obviously spent, though it will probably not be any greater than that employed and carefully concealed in a landscape garden. In the crowded and affluent area of Surrey, we will find such exotic flowers as stockbrokers' orchids. These are obviously expensive to grow and are likely to win prizes in the more glamorous sections of the horticultural shows. While requiring little space, they produce an immediate image of luxury and wealth.

Moving on down, we find the suburban garden, which is likely to be even smaller and where all the work will be done by the owner. This is the world of the flowering double cherry and the laburnum, roses and wisteria, Virginia creeper and chrysanthemums. Finally, we reach the cottage garden, so often photographed for Christmas cards and calendars, flower beds ablaze with hollyhocks and lupines and delphiniums and Canterbury bells, small flower beds surrounding a small lawn. This is the world of seeds and annuals, for cottagers, after the tradition of centuries of summary eviction, do not have the wish to plant for eternity. Work, loving work, is more important here than money. The object is to produce the biggest blaze possible with as much time and effort, but as little capital expenditure, as can be contrived. This, of course, applies to the front garden; the back garden will be devoted to potatoes and cabbages and turnips, probably far too many to be consumed by the household itself, but some of which may win prizes in the local horticultural society's annual show.

But common to all gardens of all dates and all classes is the herbaceous border, the *sine qua non* of the English garden, whether it is a large and imaginative border at New College, Oxford, or a small flower bed at the side of the front lawn. The herbaceous border requires infinite care and, apart from its own intrinsic beauty, is a visible and outward symbol of the gardener's time and work. Those foreigners—and there are many of them—who consider that the British are intrinsically lazy or weary or disinclined to get on with the job should consider the millions of herbaceous borders in Britain. This is where the energy and the time and the care have gone.

The Britishman has chosen to spend this energy and this time in his garden because, above and beyond his sense of social obligation to the community, his wish to impress his neighbors, his longing to win prizes at flower shows, his garden is an expression of his creative personality. One man may love asters; another may love roses; a third may detest wallflowers; a fourth may despise lilacs. ("Just had to cut it down," the owner explained to me after the massacre. "Just couldn't do anything with it.") A neighbor of mine in Hampshire chose to fill his garden completely with mauve flowers, and though I personally found it difficult to be enthusiastic about them when he invited my admiration, I felt bound to acknowledge the authentic and perhaps original creative taste.

If the garden is the expression of the gardener's creative urge and his personal taste, it follows that public gardens will excite much less interest. Few people glance at the dull beds of massed tulips, all of one color, outside Buckingham Palace. Rose lovers do not murmur Latin names at the roses in Regent's Park. A municipal garden, however skillfully planned and carefully tended, has no more interest to the Britishman than any other outpouring from the government spokesmen. Except for crocuses and daffodils, which are both wild flowers and harbingers of spring, the British prefer their parks to be without flowers, simply large expanses of grass with occasional huge trees, perhaps tame rabbits, a lake, ducks. On these expanses of grass, the British can walk or read the paper, or cuddle their girls, or play with their small children. Their indestructible gardening interest will be kept for their garden at home, even if this is only a window box in Fulham.

Artificial conceits such as the celebrated flower clocks of Ostend, Geneva or Interlaken are popular tourist attractions in those resorts, and the Britishman on holiday may glance at them with curiosity. But it is difficult to imagine a flower clock in Hyde Park, difficult to imagine, too, that if a misguided Office of Works should ever install one it would meet with deep enthusism from the British. The unfortunate North Country district council which planted its flower beds in patterns to spell out the words DON'T DROP LITTER received short shrift. The flowers were torn up at night and scattered over the lawns. This was later attributed to young vandals and hooligans, with no sense of civilized behavior or social conscience. But is seems just as likely that it was done by ordinary Britishmen, outraged at the misuse of their favorite flowers.

The English garden is so intrinsic a part of the British character, such a readily identifiable key to the British attitude to life, that it is instructive to compare it with the gardens of other nations. The Italian garden is an elaborate and symmetrical pattern of small hedges a few inches high, interspersed with gravel paths and fountains. The waves of Italophilia which have spread over England at intervals from the Renaissance onward have caused many Italian gardens to be constructed in England, but these are more exotic and historical curiosities than clues to British gardening tastes. They reflect, perhaps, the British love of travel and foreign parts. The Spanish garden, designed to spread shade and coolness, as in the greenery and the fountains of the Generalife in Granada or the enclosed patios filled with geraniums and carnations, finds no counterpart in Britain. The American front garden is usually a plain, carefully tended lawn with a flagpole, bereft of color or individuality. The French garden relies on artificiality, on clipped chestnuts and formal, symmetrical, distant views of the chateau. The ideas of Le Nôtre at their most splendid are incomparable, but they are a long way in style and in taste from the equally ambitious ideas of Capability Brown. The *jardin anglais,* when it is found in France, is as much of a curiosity as the Italian garden in England.

A few years ago, one of the foremost British public schools decided that its senior French teacher should no longer be an Englishman, but henceforth a Frenchman. Accordingly, when the current French master retired, a highly qualified Frenchman was engaged to take his place, and in due course he moved into the house traditionally reserved for the senior French master. This house had a large and beautiful garden, which had been the pride of his predecessors, but the Frenchman could find little to admire in it. Accordingly he started to work on it, hiring gardeners and tree cutters at his own expense, working there himself in his spare time. He had the large trees pollarded, the smaller ones clipped or removed altogether, the shrubs taken away, the large flower beds and borders transformed into small geometrical beds, largely composed of bare earth, the lawn changed into a fine expanse of gravel path. The school watched this transformation, appalled, but of course silent. Later the Frenchman admitted to the school chaplain, who had become a friend of his, that he felt that he was unpopular in the school and did not understand this, as he was trying his best in his French classes. The chaplain dodged and hedged but finally admitted reluctantly that perhaps it might be due to the Frenchman's treatment of his garden. The Frenchman was amazed and incredulous. "But I have made it so much more beautiful!" he exclaimed. The other side of the medal is perhaps the garden of the British Embassy in Paris, a beautiful garden of large wild trees and shrubs, asymmetrical herbaceous borders and long, undulating lawns, French visitors, garden-partying there, look at it in amusement and say, "How English!"

It is a mistake to regard the Britishman's gardening habits and tastes as a foible, an eccentricity, the equivalent, perhaps, of cars and photography. Most Britishmen, of course, either in *Who's Who* or when answering questions from social surveyors put down gardening as their hobby, photography coming a very poor second, followed eventually by the traditional occupations of stamp collecting, riding and fishing. But gardening to a Britishman is more than just a hobby, more even than a passion. It is a code of moral values, almost a religion, and in fundamental dedicated moments like these, he reveals himself in his own true colors. It is in his garden that a Britishman drops his carefully cultivated reserve, allows his stiff upper lip to curl into a smile and takes off his stuffed shirt. His tastes, his behavior in his garden reveal his identity and his character more truly than any autobiography. He will show his deep love of nature, which in his view should be as unclipped and undisciplined as possible. One may note his love of art, which never has found adequate expression in painting, or sculpture, or music but which bubbles out irresistibly at the thought of *Cotoneaster horizontalis.* In his feeling for rockeries and waterfalls and ruined temples beside lakes, he betrays a romanticism which he was careful to conceal from his wife during their courtship.

The hours of his precious weekends which he will spend energetically mowing the lawn, or bedding out pansies, or digging in extra fertilizer belie the idea of the indolent and weary Britishman, exhausted by too many wars and too many empires. The sight of an elderly and aristocratic Britishwoman, in her raincoat and rubber boots, her gardening hat and her rubber gloves, weeding the border in the pouring rain is one that should be seen by all those who wish to understand the British character. It is in their gardens that the British reveal themselves, at their most dedicated, their most tireless and even at their craziest.

Failing such private, keyhole glimpses, the inquisitive visitor would be well advised to attend a village flower show. These are experiences where the blaze and color of the flowers, the enormity of the vegetable marrows will be matched only by the enthusiasm and the expert knowledge of the exhibitors. This is the world of those flower growers, professional and amateur, who paper their potting sheds only with first-prize cards, tearing up the second and third prizes discreetly when the flower show is over. In this world enthusiasm remains undamped by the weather, which is almost certain to be wet and which indeed forms such an integral part of British summer outdoor activities. The damp smell in the marquee at the annual Horticultural Society's show—wet flowers, wet vegetables, wet people—is as much a part of an English summer's day as the stumbling and probably inaudible opening speech, the tired children and the pride of the exhibitors. Perhaps the most glorious of English summer events, better than the Derby or Ascot or Wimbledon or Glyndebourne, is the Chelsea Flower Show, that splendid and highly professional exhibition which adorns London during May, attended, of course, by the queen and other members of the royal family. It is the meeting place of all those, professional or amateur, who care about gardens. It is difficult to find a bedroom in London during that week, for all will have been reserved the year before by growers and enthusiasts up from the country. They will speak to one another esoterically in gardener's Latin, and the delphiniums will blaze like the delphiniums on a birthday card.

It is estimated that there are about 20,000,000 active gardeners in Britain, the large majority of them keen amateurs. This figure approaches half the total population. If young children, the elderly crippled by arthritis, the ill and those who live all their lives in gray slums and have never seen anything green are excluded, it will be seen that practically every Britishman is an enthusiastic gardener, and probably his wife, daughter and mother, too. In urban areas where gardens are not possible, the Britishman will fall back on balcony plants, window boxes and, failing all else, an aspidistra in the front-room window. Plants are as necessary to the British way of life as dogs or budgerigars, and should a small patch of land be available, it will be immediately turned into one of the world's best-kept gardens. The work will be done lovingly and for free by the family themselves, for except in a few of the largest and richest households, gardeners have gone the way of butlers and head housemaids and scullerymaids. The lady of the household, be she duchess or auctioneer's wife, will herself do the work of four gardeners, partly because she cares so passionately about it and partly because, unlike the employees of earlier generations, she is not afraid to garden in the rain.

Her enthusiasm indeed may even transgress the normal codes of behavior or morality. A lady, the wife of the headmaster of one of Britain's most esteemed preparatory schools, invited herself to stay with the parents of one of the boys. The boy was, in the British tradition, being given rather a tough time at the school, and the parents thought that it was a good opportunity, not to ease the boy's path, but to discuss his progress and to establish a good relationship with the headmaster and his wife. However, it soon transpired that the lady had no intention of discussing the boy. The parents were puzzled at the purpose of her visit. But the reason soon became apparent. She was noticed very early in the morning in her gardening clothes, digging up a rare plant by the roots and tucking it away in a brown paper bag. Being a lady of position and means, she would never, of course, have stooped to stealing the teaspoons, but to a single-minded gardener all is fair, even theft or, as in this case, kleptomania.

She was not, of course, stealing a pansy, but one of the exotic plants which had been brought to the garden from some remote part of the globe and carefully nurtured. One of the characteristics of a typically British garden is that so many of its plants, shrubs, even trees come from every part of the world. In this the British garden has something in common with the British diet. Imported from the four corners of the earth, it becomes typically British, both in its setting and in its associations. Mixed together, it acquires a flavor to be found only in Britain, and in its entirety, it becomes typical of the British mentality, as, say, spaghetti and bolognese sauce on toast with tea, the ingredients of which are also wholly foreign in origin. The British, that great traveling nation, have delighted through the centuries in bringing home, as evidence of their travelers' tales and as souvenirs of their adventures, ingredients for their gardens, though these are sometimes at odds with the setting to which they are transplanted.

Take for example that typically British tree the cedar of Lebanon. The story is told of the first man to bring a cedar home from the Middle East to Britain. He carried it home as a seedling in a pot, nursing it carefully on the long, dry journey. His ship at sea was much delayed by contrary winds, and fresh water ran dangerously short, the ration being halved and then halved again. Nevertheless, he shared his meager water ration on equal terms with the sapling, valuing it above his own life. When he finally reached Britain, he was very ill and the damage to his kidneys great. Indeed, he did not long survive the voyage. The cedar, however, did survive and is no doubt still alive and well, living in southern England. The interest in cedars of Lebanon had begun and has continued fruitfully ever since. There are more cedars of Lebanon in my Hampshire village than there are in Beirut. On a visit to Lebanon, I did not succeed in finding a single cedar. I did not feel like taking a long drive to see the remaining clump of cedars; it seemed silly to go all that way just to be reminded of Hampshire.

It isn't, of course, only cedars of Lebanon. Among the oaks and the elms of Sussex, in the shadow of the South Downs, it is incongruous, but not unusual, to find gardens with monkey puzzles, or Japanese magnolias, or Indian water lilies. If the garden is particularly sheltered, the owner may well try growing hibiscus or frangipani as souvenirs of his adventures farther afield. California redwoods (termed Wellingtonias) are highly prized in Britain, as much, or perhaps more, than they are in California, and there is a singularly fine specimen in Kew Gardens. Indeed, Kew Gardens provides the ultimate climax in British exotic and romantic gardening. The informal layout, the lawns, the shrubberies, the trees, are typically British. The trees and the shrubs come from the far ends of the earth, the point being emphasized by the Japanese pagoda which serves the twin purposes, both British, of a romantic folly and a teashop. The domestication of foreign exoticism is one of the British attributes, and it finds some of its clearest examples in an English garden.

The tendency is not always beneficial. The forebears of a friend of mine had a water garden, which they specially prized. As an addition to this valuable and unusual showplace, they brought home a rare Indian plant called snakeweed. In the wet Welsh climate the plant, accustomed only to dry India, thrived and grew. It rapidly took over the whole area, which became almost solid with huge, giant snakeweed, and the efforts of the family to cut it back, to eradicate it, to put back the clock to the days before it was imported, failed totally. The garden is now a mass of giant snakeweed, unique in its way, but displeasing both to the eye and to the nose. The other plants, of course, have died.

One can cite other, larger-scale examples. There was the unfortunate passion of the British, returning from long careers in India, to bring with them Himalayan rhododendrons, which now provide somber backgrounds for so many British gardens and cemeteries.

There was the Victorian weakness for fir trees, led by the prince consort, which has provided so many damp British country houses with a note of Gothic gloom. There is the more recent wish of the British Forestry Commission to cover large acres with plantations of conifers; theoretically they are intended to be a commercial crop, providing timber for building, pit props for the mines and the annual family Christmas tree, but with the introduction of other building methods and the decline in importance of coal mining, the Christmas-tree market is now the only commercial justification for these vast Germanic plantations. An official of the Forestry Commission frankly admitted that he liked long miles of fir trees, that they reminded him of the Black Forest and that the rest of us would, in the end, have to learn to like them, too. He no doubt felt the same sense of pride and pleasure as a builder or a town planner feels when he dominates and changes a landscape. But those who love the typically British landscape of hedges and oaks and beeches may sometimes feel that planning, however romantic or utilitarian, can be carried too far.

It is important to consider why gardening has such an important place in the British way of life. Other writers have written long and thoughtful books about the Americans, the Italians, the French without needing to dwell on the subject. But it is impossible to consider the British character without dealing at some length with the British passion for gardens and gardening. Why should a people drawn from many races, living in a chilly northern climate, where it rains on so many days, living mostly in cities, working mostly in an industrial environment, have become so besotted by gardening? Why does it form such an important part of the British character and the British way of thinking? Why should the British be crazy about gardens?

Several reasons can be put forward. Gardening, at least cottage gardening, is in England a survival of the feudal system. A serf or villein was required to work so many days a week on his lord's land; in his spare time he was expected to work on his own. If he neglected this duty, his family would starve in the winter. Gardening was, therefore, a moral duty, a symbol of thrift and farsightedness, a public example of the care a man would take of his family. This tradition still continues. It is felt to be vaguely immoral to buy vegetables or fruit at a greengrocer, when they ought to be homegrown. The result has been that British vegetable gardens, the millions of British vegetable gardens, are the most highly cultivated of any agricultural areas in the world. So much intelligent love, so much expensive fertilizer have gone into them that the final product far exceeds the family's capacity to consume it.

There is, I am constantly assured, nothing like a homegrown cabbage, a homegrown carrot, a homegrown pea, but since no marketing organization exists to handle this amateur and seasonal production, much of it is, of course, wasted. A neighbor of mine, after a frenzy of gardening, admitted that he had five hundred lettuces on his hands and asked if I could help him dispose of them. I had to admit to him that our own consumption of lettuces was comparatively limited and that, as a writer, I had no knowledge of marketing vegetables. In the end, he was forced to dig most of them back into the ground. His achievement, however, remained a source of steady pride to him and no doubt boosted his morale during a rather less successful business career. Gardening is thus thought to be a moral duty. The more hours a man spends in the garden, the more worthy he and his friends feel themselves to be. It is thought to be good for the character, for the reasons given in Kipling's regrettable poem "The Glory of the Garden":

> Our England is a garden, and such gardens are not made
> By singing "Oh how beautiful!" and sitting in the shade
> While better men than we go out and start their working lives
> By grubbing weeds from gravel paths with broken dinner-knives.

(There is no reason to believe that Kipling himself ever did any actual gardening.) Army recruits, it was decided, would benefit from regular weekly gardening, as well as from other forms of physical training. They passed too rapidly through the depot ever to see the results of their labors, but they were still required to put in a specified number of hours gardening each week. However, no plants or seeds were provided by the authorities. This, in fact, meant weeding and raking some empty flower beds over and over again. These were inspected every week by the sergeant major; no one made any comment.

A second reason is that the British do it to get away from their wives. If a woman's place is in her kitchen, the man's place is in his garden, and neither presumes to intrude on the other's domain unless invited. They are thus kept desirably far apart. But it is also a substitute for the family. A Britishman is allowed to pour the same love and care on his garden as he gives to his animals, but which he is discouraged from showing to his family. A man may be as proud of his garden as of his home or his dog and will not be afraid to say so, but though he may be proud of his children, he will be cautious about mentioning it, in case the children themselves might hear. Gardening is one more outlet for the affection which he feels in his heart but cannot show.

The third reason, a more recent one, is that the garden is a defense against increasing urbanization. The British were the first nation to move to the towns, to live largely in an urban environment. Eighty percent of the British nation lives in streets, with pavements and sodium street lighting and polluted atmosphere. But deep in British hearts is a feeling for the soil and the countryside from which they came less than 200 years ago, and by tending a small area of suburban garden, a cabbage patch, a window box, they are trying, perhaps unconsciously, to keep the link with the soil alive. Failing all else, they will tack up on the wall colored photographs of gardens to remind themselves that Eden was once a garden and not a factory compound.

Behind these historical and sociological reasons lies the simple basic truth. The British just happen to love flowers, in the same way that they love animals. They see no reason to explain or justify this. They do not regard them as status symbols, corsages to be given to girls. Indeed, the British do not give flowers to girls when they take them out on Saturday nights. They grudge the high prices of wedding bouquets and funeral wreaths, feeling that somebody is making a great deal of money out of something which he ought to be proud to do for free. Flowers, the Britishman feels, are not suitable for commercialization. He rarely buys them to put in his living room. If he cannot cut them in his own garden, he prefers to go without. He may, if he is lucky, sell his spare cabbages, but he will not, unless he is a professional market gardener, sell his flowers. His flowers are something to be loved, cared for and admired. They have nothing to do with the tough commercial world the other side of the hedge.

The Britishman's passion for flowers and gardening is admirable—or so he thinks. But an outside observer may feel that the British passion for gardening is not an unmixed blessing. There are several reasons for this, and the first is that it takes too much of his time and his concentration. In the days when a rich man had a large household which included several gardeners and when he himself had a wide variety of shallow interests, gardening was no more important to him than his collection of silver teapots or Roman coins. Today the man is an advertising-account executive in London, the gardeners have gone with the rest of the house servants, but the garden remains the same size. He is therefore forced to do the whole thing himself, on his weekends.

He makes no complaint about this; he explains to his friends on Saturday evening at parties or on Sunday mornings over drinks that it is great fun, his greatest hobby, good for his figure, good exercise and a wonderful way of relaxing after a busy week in town. This is, of course, self-deception. His former gardeners, could they hear his words, would shudder to hear that their former life's work was no more than an idle hobby, a remedial exercise. But the fact remains that it is not possible to take something from something else without leaving an imbalance, and the businessman will return to his Monday morning work more exhausted than refreshed. He will have packed into his weekend the work of several men, and though he may feel proud of his morale, his body will not forgive him. He may persuade himself and others that gardening is good for his health, but stooping over small plants and half-pruned roses is not particularly good for the heart, and neither his asset to his company nor his life-span is likely to have been increased by his weekend work. His brother businessman and rival in Zurich or Frankfurt, living in a flat with nothing more than a window box, is likely to return to his office on the Monday morning in a more refreshed state.

But the Britishman's belief in the importance of gardening carries him through. Given the chance, he will refuse to move into a modern apartment block. He will prefer his villa in the suburbs with his roses and his lettuces, even though this means an extra hour or more traveling to and from his work each day. This further exhausts him before he even reaches his desk on a Monday morning and, in an international world, places him still further at a disadvantage. And the refusal to live in flats causes the urban sprawl to sprawl still further. There may come a time, if the Britishman has his way, when the whole of the South of England and much of the North will be covered with suburban villas and gardens, each occupying the whole of the spare time of a highly qualified man, assisted, in her spare moments, by his busy wife. It is arguable, in the modern commercial world, whether the destruction of the English countryside and the exhaustion of the British businessman will be adequately compensated by the growing of a few million extra roses.

There are many experts—economists, sociologists, town planners—who look forward eagerly to this state of affairs, when there will be no more British countryside, no more British agriculture, but when England will be not so much a garden as a garden city, cultivated by weekend gardeners, whose professions lie elsewhere. But it is at least debatable whether such a community will be economically effective internationally. Psychologically, the point is equally questionable. A garden gives a man great confidence, as does achievement in any other hobby or spare-time activity, and the confidence is likely to overflow into his normal work. But whether such confidence is always justified or whether it is wise to obliterate all doubts, all diffidence, is another matter. A good gardener is a proud man, perhaps a conceited man, and in the competitive world outside the garden this assurance may be something of a disadvantage.

A dedicated gardener is also a man with his roots in the earth. Being British, he will, of course, travel; being a businessman, he will have his eyes outside the frontiers of his own country. When he flies to Italy to sell detergents, a part, small perhaps, but important, of his thought will remain in his garden, assessing the amount of work which will have to be carried out on his return, the consequences of a few days' neglect of his weeding. He is, in a sense, orientated toward his home plot rather than to the opportunities which await him in the city where he is about to land.

Recently, a friend of mine, the managing director of a metallurgical business, proposed to undertake a prolonged and extensive tour of South America in search of new markets. Discussing this journey with him, I discovered that he did not speak a word of Spanish, and I offered to lend him some records from which I had learned Spanish a few years earlier. He accepted my offer eagerly. Many months later, meeting him again, I asked after his South American trip and gathered that he had been only moderately successful. I asked after his Spanish, but he confessed that he had not had time to play the records. He had had a lot of work to do in his garden before undertaking a long trip abroad. His competitors, living in flats in Milan or Hamburg, would have been under no such disadvantage; they would have had time to learn Spanish. A survey was recently carried out of junior executives in a dormitory suburb near London. The executives came from several social levels, from different educational backgrounds, and no doubt they had slightly different accents. But two things they all had in common; one was their chief hobby, which was, of course, gardening, and the other was that, schoolboy French excluded, they spoke no language except English.

It is possible to say that when a hobby becomes an obsession, it also becomes a danger. And the Britishman's obsession with his garden may blind him to something else he ought to be doing. When he thinks of himself as a gardener first and foremost and as an accountant or a lawyer second, his career is likely to suffer. A nation of gardeners is not likely to be a rich nation.

20

WANDERLUST

The longing of the British not only to bring back exotic plants from remote corners of the world, but to go live there for substantial parts of their lives, is something which should be considered by anyone studying the British character in all its ramifications. This is something other and apart from, say, the traditional British sailors who have roamed the seas since the time of King Alfred or again from the sailors of the merchant navy, who have built up Britain as a trading nation. It is something perhaps derived from the original Viking ancestors, who, having arrived in a place after a long, difficult voyage, liked to remain there for many years, until suddenly the wanderlust struck them again and they moved on somewhere else.

The word "wanderlust" itself is unsatisfactory—a German word which has never been properly incorporated into the English language, but which is far more applicable to the English than it is to their German cousins. The Germans, in the present century at least, are considerable travelers, but their itch to move on is not in the same class as that of the British. Nor is there any special English word for someone who goes to live abroad in a different country. "Exile" means someone who has been ordered abroad against his will and lives only for the day when he will be allowed to return. *"Émigré"* is French. "Expatriate," with its overtones of antipatriotism, is American. The British have no special word for one who goes to live in France or Chile or Japan, any more than they have for someone who goes to live in Devonshire or Argyll. They are simply British, and they are doing what anyone might do, if given the chance. There is no need for any explanation or justification. The other man, whether he is a Treasury official or simply a fellow drinker in the pub, will understand and sympathize. He, too, will have a secret, though perhaps unrealized, wish to get out of the small island and roam the world. As Sir Noël Coward has put it: "An Englishman is the highest example of a human being who is a free man. As an Englishman I have a right to live where I like."

The liberalism of this attitude is perhaps derived from the fact that, for the British, their nationality traditionally does not depend on either where they were born or where they choose to live. If the father is British, his children must be British, too, even if they were born in Tangier and grew up in Finland. In this, their tradition is at variance with most other countries, including America, where the country of birth is a key factor in determining the nationality of the person. I may cite the case of a friend who was born in China, where his parents were missionaries, though his grandparents had lived all their lives in Africa. He chooses to live in France, but he remains a typical Britishman in name, passport, appearance and habits. It would need no crunch to make him declare either his nationality or his loyalty. It is simply that he does not feel less British because he chooses to live elsewhere. The two things are, in his mind and in the general British mind, unconnected.

His case is not the same as those who have determinedly spread the British culture overseas, who have introduced Government Houses and cricket clubs in Ceylon, who used to dress for dinner in the jungle as if they were in Belgravia or who taught the schoolboys of Nigeria the dates of the battles of the Wars of the Roses. These aspects of the British tradition and the British achievement were also part of the national character and of history, but they stemmed from a different cause: the certainty that the British way of life was a good thing, rather than from individual wanderlust.

There is no room in this book to give a list of the famous Britishmen who have chosen to live outside Britain or outside the British Empire and the borders of British sovereignty, but a few random names may be recalled. One may perhaps mention the three extraordinary British women who chose to go live in Arabia: Lady Hester Stanhope, Gertrude Bell and Jane Digby. The first went for the glamor of the East, the second for archeology and the beauty of the desert, the third for sex. All three have a place in English literature. To these striking but very dissimilar ladies, we can add some further names such as Freya Stark, Sir Ronald Storrs and, the most celebrated of all, T. E. Lawrence, who, unlike most of the others, went so far as to wear Arab clothing.

It does not, of course, have to be Arabia. A Scottish family of my acquaintance went to live in Peru and lived there for many years, their children being born and brought up there, though remaining, of course, totally British in all matters. Why they went to Peru, what they did there, why they finally came back are not known, for the reason that nobody ever asked. After all, going to live in Peru is the sort of thing that anyone might do at any time. An ancestor of my wife's, a Welshman with a large property in South Wales, went to live for thirty years in Persia, in early Victorian times, when Europeans were a considerable rarity there. Why he was specially attracted to Persia and how he maintained himself when he was there are, of course, not known, though he seems to have enjoyed a successful love life there. Leaving Persia finally, together with a bevy of beautiful half-Persian daughters, he moved back through Spain, where he spent several years and became instrumental in the founding of one of the big sherry family businesses. After a few more years, he returned to Wales, resumed his position as a landowner and a squire, married and occupied himself with family and country life, though it is reported that he treated his wife as if she were in a harem. His daughters married, too, thus introducing Persian or Spanish blood into the local Welsh strain. The point of this episode is that to his friends and his family, it was unremarkable, typical, just what anyone might be expected to do.

The only aspect of the story worthy of comment in the eyes of his Welsh neighbors was the way he treated his wife, keeping her locked away when she ought, of course, to have been opening flower shows and occupying herself with good works in the county. He had written no letters home during the time he was away, but he had kept a diary, which might have been of considerable interest to historians and Orientalists, but it was casually destroyed. The British are not particularly impressed by travelers' tales from remote parts. Many of them have been in strange places, too. In any group, in a family, in a club, in a pub, there is likely to be someone, perhaps several people who have lived for a considerable time in some foreign country, but it is not likely to excite any particular comment. To go to Iran is, to the British, hardly more intriguing than to go to Scotland, and the man is unlikely to show off his more flamboyant experiences.

To live for a long time in a foreign country does not mean cutting roots or burning boats. The Britishman abroad is quite likely, after a few years or the larger part of a lifetime, to change his mood and return home abruptly, picking up the threads where he dropped them many years before. His return will be greeted with little surprise and less comment. I myself, returning to Hampshire after a spell abroad, perhaps brief, perhaps prolonged, know exactly the welcome that I shall receive: a friendly greeting, an inquiry after the family, followed by the phrase "Well, I expect you had better weather than what we've had."

The mention of the weather is, of course, a polite British conversational gambit, a safe subject where no bricks can be dropped. But it is also an indication of one of the motives which send a Britishman on his travels, the search for better weather. For though the British may feel that their cool gray skies, their chilly, wet atmosphere are good both for their characters and for their gardens, there comes a moment when they wish to see the sun. Almost 5,000,000 of them go abroad each year on foreign holidays, and this figure does not include those who are going to take up work in other countries.

This figure is greater than for any other nation, though the Germans and Scandinavians, for similar reasons of heredity and climate, have a growing wish to take their holidays outside their own countries. But the Italians and the Spaniards feel miserable if they are forced to leave their country and will do so only to emigrate, to seek work and better pay elsewhere. The French have long been celebrated for their stay-at-home preferences, though this is giving way to an increasing curiosity about the outer world, an urge to shop in Carnaby Street or the Kings Road, the growing feeling that travel abroad is a status symbol. The British require no such self-persuasion; the mere sight of a busy airport or Victoria Station is enough to set them dreaming of Spain or Switzerland or Italy. It is partly the wish to see the sun, to acquire a becoming and noticeable suntan, but it is also wanderlust, the longing to roam. Norway and Brittany have their devotees, too, and even Iceland.

When they approach retirement age, the British will think increasingly of retirement in a warm place. This is not, of course, specifically British. Many Americans, facing the thought of yet another New England winter, will dream of retirement in Florida or California, but the displacement is not so drastic. There will be no abrupt change of language or diet or local attitudes. But a considerable number of British are prepared, at a time when many people are thought to be past adventure, to retire to Spain or France or the Bahamas or Jamaica. They will probably choose an area where they have had happy holidays and indeed may well have been planning and saving up for their southern villa for years. One day, they have told themselves throughout their nine-to-five working lives, we'll go live in Majorca or Malta, we'll go be Robinson Crusoe on Tobago or a beachcomber on Tahiti. Even in their sixties, the British are as incurably romantic as ever.

The alternative to this dream is that imagined by those who

have spent the greater part of their working lives in the hot and humid tropics, in Singapore or Guyana or Sierra Leone, with a break for a few months every three years in England, which to them means holidays, relaxation and romance. These sweating administrators and engineers then look forward to retirement in Britain, probably in Sussex, though just possibly, if they are very devoted Scots, in Scotland. Instead of dreaming of spending the last years of their lives in Mediterranean fishing villages or beside palm-fringed lagoons in the Caribbean, these couples will instead opt for village pubs, English gardens, cricket matches and flower shows in the rain. The idea is equally romantic, equally remote and, in the opposite direction, equally far to travel.

The British have a firm idea that while there is no place like home, it is also a fine place to get away from. The pasture on the other side of the fence will always look, if not greener, at least more attractive. The young will hope that it will be less humdrum, full of challenge and adventure and lepers and quarreling tribesmen; the older and more travel-worn will hope for something less demanding, green fields and warm sun, though in the nature of things it is difficult, usually, to find both at once.

The lure of "abroad," then, is equally potent for young and old, for the adventurous and for the weary. But I may perhaps single out a particularly British phenomenon, the British boy or girl who chooses to live and work abroad, temporarily or indefinitely, at far lower wages than he or she would earn at home. The waitress who brings you your canneloni in Rome, the girl who pours your Fundador in Tossa or Torremolinos, or who sells you a silk shirt in a smart boutique in Florence, or who dances on a spotlit platform in St.-Tropez or in Paris are likely to be British. I have bought newspapers from a Cockney boy on a Spanish beach, I have had my watch repaired by a Cockney boy in a Mediterranean jeweler's shop, I know a Cockney ski instructor in the Austrian Tyrol, and I know dozens of young British boys and girls enthusiastically conducting parties of exhausted and bewildered tourists through the holiday countries of Europe. They are not doing this for money; they are working hours which British unions would shudder even to think about; they are earning the small wages of the local inhabitants. It is a British specialty. The waitresses, the barmaids, the shopgirls, the couriers in the more exotic holiday spots of the Mediterranean and the Alps will be, unless they are local, British. They will not be French or German or Scandinavian or American, who would disdain both the work and the pay. They are the Ians and Bills and Janes and Maureens who have gone simply for fun and for wanderlust.

I once asked a girl called Veronica, who seemed to spend sixteen hours a day washing glasses in a small dark Spanish bar in return for a few pesetas and her keep, if she enjoyed her work. "Oh, yes," she replied enthusiastically, "it's much better here than in England." She was not being unpatriotic; she was merely being romantic. When I asked her what was better about it, she merely pointed through the window at a distant view of blue sea and blue sky. In the busy summer season, she can have had little opportunity to spend much time out of doors, but it was enough that it existed and was near at hand and that she in a sense was part of it. She felt exotic and Continental and suntanned, though in fact, she was pale and hollow-eyed from her long hours in the dark.

The Italians have a famous saying: "You cannot eat the view." But the British see it differently. You *can* eat the view. It's beautiful and cheap and slimming; what you cannot eat is baked beans in the rain. Nor is this romantic attitude to travel confined to the very young or the modern generation. The itch to travel and to identify with a foreign people, probably Mediterranean, has been going on for a long time in the hearts of the British, and Byron was only one of the more spectacular examples. Nor are the very young the only ones who can find magic in foreign parts. General Bruce, the leader of two expeditions to Mount Everest, chose to live most of his life in Nepal. When asked why he had done this, he answered, "If you could see the Himalaya when the rhododendrons come into flower, you'd understand."

These wanderers are not to be confused with the American boys and girls taking vacation jobs to help pay their expenses at college. There will, of course, be some trends in common, the wish to travel, perhaps to hitchhike over a continent, to meet new people, have new experiences, but the basic motive is different. The British boy or girl is usually uninterested in the money angle. He (or she) is doing it for the scenery. When a young Britishman decides to become a bullfighter in Spain or a bicyclist in France, he is, of course, partly attracted by the prospect of the wealth and the fame which will come his way if he is successful. But in his heart he knows this is illusory. He is unlikely to be very successful in such exclusively national sports. There will be too much stacked against him. He will, however, be amply consoled in his lack of success by the color and the glamor of the bullring or the Tour de France. When a girl of my acquaintance trained as a nurse with the sole object of going to nurse in Tibet, she was not being drawn by fame or fortune; she had once visited Tibet as a footloose teen-ager and was determined to return there as soon as she had a useful qualification. When I asked her, "Why Tibet?" she replied simply, "I like Tibet." She was no longer very young, but the incoherence of her answer did not disguise the sincerity of her ambition.

One may perhaps compare the opposite point of view, that of the Italians and Spaniards who come to Britain in search of work and money, the German and Scandinavian *au pair* girls who come to learn the language or perhaps to have an abortion, the Asian and West Indian immigrants, whose problems are such a matter of current controversy. Very few indeed of these have come for the romance of the journey or the beauty of the English countryside. The Spanish barman who pours your pint of bitter in a country pub beside a water meadow does not come to England for the trout fishing. He will admit, if he has a moment to speak to you, that he hopes to return to Spain the moment he has earned enough money to support a wife and family. The Pakistani bus conductor in Newcastle is not thrilled by the excitement of the industrial North. He dreams openly of returning one day to his own subcontinent, even though it is obvious to him and to everyone else that this will never happen.

It is not, of course, every Britishman who travels abroad in search of sunshine and romantic scenery. The empire builders and the explorers of other centuries have largely disappeared. These have been replaced by businessmen or engineers or technologists in search of greater opportunities and lower taxation. This exodus, the brain drain, is entirely in British tradition and character, but in its present form it is a matter for some concern. Intelligent young boys from excellent backgrounds and with a fine education are trained at the public expense in, say, medicine or engineering. Their training completed, their hope is to get a rewarding job in the United States or Canada, from which they will probably never return. Their places will be taken in the British population by immigrant unskilled labor from Portugal or the Punjab. It is not educationally a fair swap.

It must not be imagined, however, that 100 percent of those who emigrate are qualified doctors or engineers. A large number who have no special technical qualifications to offer also move to other countries. They go out of curiosity, the traditional British wanderlust, in search of adventure more than wealth or promotion, but with a mental saver on the thought that they may eventually return and pick up their life in Britain where they left it five, ten, fifty years earlier.

A further wave of emigrants, perhaps the most imposing in numbers, though less impressive in quality, wish to emigrate because they are "fed up." A recent public opinion poll showed that almost half of British youth wishes to emigrate permanently, the minority to European countries, the majority to Commonwealth countries. Sample opinions expressed were all of the "fed-up" variety. They wished to go, not because they were passionately attracted by Canada or Australia or the Common Market countries in Europe, but because they were against what they found at home and saw no hope of altering it. One teen-ager after another cited the case of his or her father, who always seemed to have been treated unfairly, the ultimate British grievance. The father had been an unemployed young man in the Depression, had fought in the war, which in its perverse way may have provided the high spot of his life but which is no longer understood, and had followed this by a postwar career of shortages, high taxation, inflation and finally frustration.

Despite the praise and promises showered on them by politicians and university lecturers, a strong skeptical streak remains. They do not wish to end, like their parents, facing rising prices on too small a pension and being told daily that they are no longer wanted in the new Britain. Whether all the young emigrants will manage to find the success and the sense of achievement which have eluded their parents is doubtful, but it is the nature of youth to expect far more than is likely to be fulfilled in any continent. The wish to try something different is something which can never be deplored, even if the motives inspiring it are usually negative.

It is possible to think that an emigrant who is not drawn by the attractions and opportunities of America or Australia but is merely impelled by a wish to protest against his own country, his government, his parents or his society is not likely to make a very positive contribution to the life of his new country. "Againstism," it may be thought, is not a quality which would necessarily be welcomed among immigrants. But then one remembers that the most famous emigrants in British, or indeed in world, history were the Pilgrim Fathers, who were motivated solely by "againstism," who were protesting against certain aspects and restrictions of life in England and who, it is easy to believe, were not particularly attracted by the scenery or climate in the country to which they were going. Their inspiration may have been wholly negative, but they were, because or perhaps despite this, making the most constructive contribution yet made by an emigrant in the history of the world. A jet, unlike a propeller, moves forward by pushing against the air behind it.

A further point may be made: the choice of the country to which the young emigrant hopes to move sooner or later. My little village in Hampshire has its full quota of restless young boys and girls who, from wanderlust or frustration, wish to live in another country. The brainy ones, the ones with high IQ's or with good qualifications, choose Canada; the ones with less impressive academic attainments, the unskilled, the dropouts prefer Australia. The effect which these choices will have on Canada and Australia respectively (and indeed on Hampshire) can be easily, though perhaps not accurately, imagined, and many of those going to Canada will, of course, end up in the United States. The outlook for Australia in this context seems a little bleak.

Granted the wish to go live temporarily or permanently somewhere else, the British have no doubt at all that they will be warmly welcomed and received. This is perhaps surprising, but it is largely borne out by the history of British emigration. Why, one may well ask, do foreign countries put up with the British immigrants?

There is perhaps a double answer to this. In the past, when the British arrived in a foreign country as a regiment, as a fleet, or as a commercial undertaking, they were, on the whole, tolerated for the business and the prosperity which they brought. They were even approved of by many for bringing law and justice, hygiene, the idea of imperial grandeur, of the great family, but without impinging too much on the local customs, traditions and language. This acceptance, like the acceptance of the Roman legions, was bound to be temporary. In the end, the objection to the British ruling classes in the various colonies was not so much that they were ruling but that they were an exclusive elite, that they coexisted alongside the local population (which sometimes, as in Singapore, arrived later than the British) but yet held themselves apart. A growing community, like the human body, eventually rejects a foreign body which cannot be absorbed. The same biological truth works in the opposite sense, and the British, in their history, while welcoming immigrants from abroad who would blend and mingle with the local population, have felt distinctly less enthusiastic toward immigrant groups who have attempted to keep themselves to themselves.

The Britishman, however, who goes on his own, whether it is because of the beauty of the Tibetan landscape or the financial opportunities offered him in New York, is normally far more welcome. The point is that he is alone and independent and willing to merge with his new background. There is a major psychological difference here between the emigrant and the tourist or the traveling businessman; the emigrant will have sold his garden in Britain. He will no longer be thinking about his roses. He is committed to his new environment. Recently in the United States, I talked with an American designer employed by a large aircraft factory. Discovering from my voice that I was British, he told me proudly that he had 1,400 British aircraft designers working with him in Atlanta. He did not feel threatened by such a large, sudden influx into his area of specialists who were not only foreign by birth but potential competitors for his job. On the contrary, he spoke appreciatively of their work and capabilities and seemed proud of the fact that his country should have been able to attract them from Britain and provide them with better opportunities than they might expect at home. Evidently they had fitted in well.

One of the features of the Britishman living abroad is his eagerness and his ability to adapt to his environment. It is not only his appreciation of the landscape and the architecture, to which the local inhabitants may be largely indifferent. It is partly his cheerfulness in a climate which may be very different from that in which he was brought up. He might have been reared in a cool, gray, rainy climate which changes little summer or winter, but he often chose to spend his life in such hot places as West Africa or India or Malaya, frequently wearing hot, thick uniforms in the cause of ceremony or etiquette. At the other end of the immigrant scale the modern longing of the British to lie and toast themselves on hot beaches sometimes causes raised eyebrows among Spanish fishermen, who keep cautiously in the shade during the midday hours of the "three months' hell." "But you are not used to this heat," they comment. "In England you have rain and fog." It is difficult to explain that the attraction is largely the attraction of opposites and that a baking Mediterranean summer beach, like a Malayan plantation or a street in Texas, is attractive partly because it is so very different from Manchester.

As well as his enjoyment of the local climate, the Britishman has at his disposal his flair for recondite languages. This ability may surprise those who have overheard him struggling in schoolboy French in the customs at Boulogne. His terrible French indeed is a worldwide joke, deriving from the fact that he learned it at school as a dead language and resented learning it anyway. One of the most popular schoolboy rhymes begins with the line "No more Latin, no more French," the two languages being, in his eyes, interchangeable and equally useless. But when he has to learn Swahili or Tamil or Chinese or, come to that, American, he will become less inhibited and give his natural talent for languages full scope, something which his French or even American colleagues are not always willing to do. Much of this practice in languages will, of course, be confined to his business and household needs, but many Britishmen have felt inspired to go beyond this and become scholars of considerable erudition in, say, Urdu or Arabic, showing a deep understanding of the language and of its culture and background, which eluded them when they were learning French many years before.

A natural consequence of the wish to admire the scenery and the culture, enjoy the weather, become fluent in the language, study the local history and folklore, and become an expert on the local civilization is a strong fellow feeling toward the local population. "The natives are friendly" is one of the basic phrases of British history, and this basic friendliness which is usually indigenous to the local population, has been amply reciprocated by their British conquerors or guests, as the case may be. There are, of course, exceptions. In some cases British settlers (usually the less admirable and desirable of the species) can find nothing good to say of the local population after ten, twenty or even fifty years of living among them. The local coolie or black or Chinese is, they announce, stupid or lazy or untrustworthy or too clever by half. The abused boy in question may have in fact the unselfishness of a missionary or the dedication of a scholar or the practical ability of an engineer, but this is not likely to be appreciated by his whisky-sodden employer. Such examples of nonappreciation and noncommunication have existed, both in British history and British literature—one thinks of Maugham in this connection—but they are, in the course of events, becoming rarer and indeed are now so rare as to become newsworthy items. In the end it is hoped that such mutual contempt will become extinct.

The large majority of those whose wanderlust has taken them abroad wish to identify closely with the people among whom they have chosen, or happen by chance, to live. A Britishman living for a long time in Japan will probably, in the end, become more Japanese than the Japanese, will admire their people and their culture and their language more than the British equivalent. T. E. Lawrence's admiration for the Arabs became so intense that he saw himself in the end more as an Arab than as an Englishman. His rootlessness when he finally returned to England was not only due to his particular problems of psychology and homosexuality, but also due to the fact that he saw himself as a detribalized Arab.

A friend of mine, an Army officer in difficulties through his racing debts, had himself transferred to a regiment in the southern Sudan for the required seven years, during which time his debts in England would legally lapse. During these seven years, he came so to admire and to love the southern Sudanese that on his eventual return he felt himself lost and would speak of them often as the finest people in the world. His career was perhaps typical of the Britishman in the Army, in all its downs and ups, the highest up being not his medals but his deep understanding of the character of the southern Sudanese. Less controversial, perhaps, was the career of General Bruce, the mountaineer already referred to, who chose to live his life in Nepal, looking at rhododendrons and climbing mountains. His admiration for and, finally, his identification with the

Nepalese, both soldiers and civilians, became so great that in the end he came to *look* Nepalese. On his return to Britain, he was often mistaken for an Asian, and in historical pageants, in which he loved to take part, he was invariably cast as Genghis Khan or Attila the Hun.

The wish to identify with a foreign people is a matter of pride to the British and not one for apology. It can indeed go to extraordinary lengths. Recently I was one of the judges in an international short-story competition, and I became much interested not only in the literary qualities of the stories, but in the settings chosen by their authors. It is well known, for example, that all Italian short stories deal with squalor in the slums of Rome, while French short stories are about problems of human relationships among the well-heeled intelligentsia of Paris. American short stories are usually concerned with adultery in New England, probably on a campus, or social and racial pressures in New York or poverty in the Deep South. But there was no knowing where the British short stories would be set or with what people they would deal. A number were, of course, set in London or in the North of England, describing normal problems of everyday life. But a larger number, the majority, were set in various overseas countries and were about the problems not only of the Britishman abroad, but of the local people themselves. The authors were trying not only to describe the life of a foreign person, but to enter into his mind and often into his speech as well, to see through his eyes and speak through his mouth.

There was considerable overconfidence involved in this. It is not every writer who can hope to speak with the tongue of a French peasant, an American film producer, a German soldier retreating through the snow in Silesia, a Greek businessman, a Portuguese fisherman or an Indonesian civil servant. Such confidence is often misplaced, and, in particular, the British wish to write short stories about comic French peasants should generally be resisted. But still the attempts were gallant, and if one recalls the amazing achievements in literary ventriloquism and in understanding made by some British writers, one may even find the ambition admirable. When we consider the contribution to literature and the understanding of the German character made by Richard Hughes in *The Fox in the Attic* and by Gabriel Fielding in *The Birthday King*—and, even more amazingly, the penetration of the Asian mind achieved by E. M. Forster in *A Passage to India*—we cannot really feel that such proud essays in identification are made in vain.

21

TO THE NORTH

⁂ The sign stands at a junction of the North Circular Road, outside London, TO THE NORTH, and for a long time now the British have found it an exciting sign, an exciting slogan. It has been used as the title of a famous novel. It points the way toward the Great North Road, that ancient, winding, now obsolescent highway, which leads to Yorkshire and Northumberland, to Hadrian's Wall and, beyond it, to Scotland and eventually to the Arctic, to Ultima Thule, to the Final Pole. To all northern peoples, the thought of a region still farther north holds a magnetic attraction, a land of tundras and Eskimos, of Lapps and the sun which shines at midnight. The phrase "To the North" evokes all this.

But it evokes something else as well. To the ordinary Britishman the words "the North" do not imply Scotland or the Orkneys or the midnight sun. They mean Lancashire, Yorkshire, Durham, Northumberland. And within these counties the words do not mean the wide-open spaces, the mountains, the broad acres of the Vale of York, the deserted bleakness of the Yorkshire moors, the lost bareness of the Pennine dales or the rainy beauty of the lakeland fells and cliffs, a landscape of silver and mist inhabited only by wet rock climbers and patient fishermen. These places, these beauty spots, are undoubtedly in the north of England, but this is not what the Britishman thinks of as the North. The North means industry, dark, dirty, grimy industry. It means coal and cotton and wool and steel and shipbuilding. It means power and wealth and prosperity. It means slums and poverty and unemployment and disease. It means the blast furnaces that blaze and roar in the night between Warrington and Wigan. It means the black canals of blacker soot between Salford and Manchester. It means the moment when the train stops at the signals on the curve outside Liverpool's Lime Street Station and the traveler sees an unending vista, a sea stretching as far as the eye can see of wet gray slate roofs.

This was where it all started, the greatest and most lasting revolution in the history of the world, far more profound in its impact than the temporary little upheavals of the French or Russian revolutions, far more fundamental than the discovery of the New World or other worlds, far more somber and significant in its consequences than any war. It was here that the history of the world was changed drastically and forever. It was here in these few acres, in a few cloudy rainy counties, that the revolution began which changed man from wishing to be an agricultural animal to being an industrial animal, which changed the civilization of the world from a rural civilization to an urban civilization. The consequences of the Industrial Revolution can now be seen clearly and simply all around the world and now are no longer even confined to the earth itself. The North of England no longer holds its lead in this amazing transformation. But the spell remains, even now. You do not enter Lancashire or the West Riding of Yorkshire without a shiver of excitement.

It is interesting to speculate why the Industrial Revolution began in the North of England, rather than anywhere else in the world. Coal and iron were a basic part of it, but these natural assets can be found elsewhere in the world. The culture, if it can be so called, was founded on manufactured goods, on cotton and wool, but the raw products for these were not readily available; the cotton came from America, Egypt and India, the wool from Australia and New Zealand. Railways also began in the North of England, but other countries besides Britain possessed steam and steel. What began in the North of England was not an increased production of cotton or wool or railway engines, important though all these became in the history of the world. It was something deeper, an understanding of the importance of the machine in life. A few men—and the revelation was by no means universal—came to realize that what a man can do, a machine can do better and faster and cheaper. To the excitement of some, the alarm of others and the incredulity of many, the machine age had suddenly arrived, with its manifold consequences for good and for evil.

The Manchester *Guardian* of February 11, 1863, quoted from the address of M. Charles Dupin, speaking in Paris:

> Watt improves the steam engine, and this single improvement causes the industry of England to make an immense stride. This machine represents at the present time the power of three hundred thousand horses or of two millions of men, strong and well fitted for labour, who should work day and night, without interruption and without repose, to augment the riches of a country not two-thirds the extent of France.
>
> A hairdresser invents—or at least, brings into action—a machine for spinning cotton. This alone gives the British industry an immense superiority and their wealth is far greater after this great discovery. More than one million of the inhabitants of England are employed in those operations which depend, directly or indirectly, on the action of this machine. Lastly, England exports cotton, spun and woven by an admirable system of machinery to the value of four hundred million francs yearly. The Indies, so long superior to Europe—the Indies, which inundated the West with her products and exhausted the riches of Europe—the Indies are conquered in their turn. The British navigator travels in quest of the cotton of India, brings it from a distance of four thousand leagues, commits it to an operation of the machine of Arkwright and of those that are attached to it, carries back their products to the East, makes them again to travel four thou-

> sand leagues—and in spite of the loss of time, in spite of the enormous expense incurred by this voyage of eight thousand leagues, the cotton manufactured by the machinery of England becomes less costly than the cotton of India, spun and woven by the hand near the field that produced it and sold it at the nearest market. So great is the power of progress of the machinery.

In 1833 the British cotton manufacturer was able to state that the amount of yarn spun in England in a year would, in a single thread, pass round the globe's circumference 203,775 times. After the centuries of the spinning wheel and the handloom, the age of mass production had arrived with a vengeance.

The reason, perhaps, lies not only in the physical and geographical advantages of the North of England, with its coal, its iron, its damp climate and its large ports, but also in the attitude of mind of its inhabitants, in particular, from the unshakable British belief that a problem exists to be solved and that the ordinary, simple common sense of the reasonable, average inexpert man should be quite enough to solve it. The Industrial Revolution was not created by professional engineers or qualified technologists, though these, of course, arrived later to develop and expand the original ideas. The Industrial Revolution was the product of the mind of inventive amateurs, some of them totally unqualified in any subject, some of them experienced in fields far removed from machinery. It was the supreme example and perhaps the justification of the British belief in the ability of the sensible amateur, particularly if he happens to be oneself, coupled with a distrust of those who imagine themselves to be expert on the subject in question.

In 1785, the Reverend Dr. Edmund Cartwright of Hollander House, Kent, the brother of Major Cartwright, the advocate of radical reform, invented a power loom which may be regarded as the parent of that now in use. He wrote later:

> Happening to be at Matlock in the summer of 1784, I fell in company with some gentlemen of Manchester, when the conversation turned on Arkwright's spinning machinery. One of the company observed that as soon as Arkwright's patent

expired, so many mills had been erected and so much cotton spun as hands could never be found to weave it. To this observation it was suggested that Arkwright must then set his wits to work to invent a weaving mill.

This brought on the conversation on the subject in which the Manchester gentlemen unanimously agreed that the thing was impracticable and, in defence of their opinion, they adduced arguments which I certainly was incompetent to answer or even comprehend, being totally ignorant of the subject, having never at that time seen a person weave. I controverted, however, the impracticability of the thing by remarking that there had lately been exhibited in London an automaton figure which played at chess. "Now, you will not assert, gentlemen," said I, "that it is more difficult to construct a machine that shall weave than one which shall make all the variety of moves which are required in that complicated game."

Some little time afterwards, a particular circumstance recalling this conversation to mind, it struck me that, as in plain weaving, according to the conception I then had of the business, there could only be three movements which were to follow each other in succession, and that there would be little difficulty in producing and repeating them. Full of these ideas, I immediately employed a carpenter and smith to carry them into effect. As soon as the machine was finished, I got a weaver to put in the warp which was of such material as sail-cloth is usually made of. To my great delight a piece of cloth, such as it was, was the produce. As I had never before turned my thoughts to anything mechanical, either in theory or in practice, nor had ever seen a loom at work or knew anything of its construction, you will readily suppose that my first loom was a most rude piece of machinery. The warp was placed perpendicularly, the reed fell with the weight of at least half a hundredweight, and the strings which threw with the shuttle were strong enough to have thrown a concrete locket. In short, it required the strength of two powerful men to work the machine at a slow rate, and only for a short time.

Conceiving in my great simplicity that I had accomplished all that was required, I then secured what I thought was a

> most valuable property by a patent on 4th April 1785. This being done, I then condescended to see how other people wove and you will guess my astonishment, when I compared their easy modes of operation with mine. Availing myself, however, of what I then saw, I made a loom on the general principles nearly as they are now made, but it was not till the year 1787 that I completed my invention and I took out my last patent on August 1st of that year.

Thus was the power loom invented. It is to be noted that it was invented by a clergyman, who lived in Kent, far from Lancashire, who knew nothing of either weaving or machinery, and in defiance of the expert opinion of the cotton weavers of the time. He was inspired by the idea that if it were possible to invent a machine which would play chess, it should certainly be possible to construct a machine which would weave cotton cloth. He was, of course, misinformed about the machine which would play chess—only now, nearly 200 years later, are computers being invented which can play elementary games of chess. But the idea was enough, and he was bolstered by his intrinsic confidence that he was as well able as anyone else to invent a machine of this sort. He was also inspired by the prospect of the large sums of money which he would, and did, earn by patenting such a successful piece of machinery. The longing for wealth, even among country clergymen, and the patent law were among the mainsprings of the Industrial Revolution.

Its consequences were global. Britain became quite rapidly the richest country in the world. The Empire, which had been acquired over the previous century or so, had not been, in the first place, much of a financial asset. A few thousand miles of jungle or scrub were not likely to prove very profitable to people in another continent, despite the history of profitable trading of the East India Company and the eternal search for El Dorado, the legendary city of gold. But with the Industrial Revolution came the idea that the British Empire was perhaps an economic as well as a military and prestige asset, and a certain, though rather limited, amount of money was invested in plantations of sugar, rubber, coffee, cocoa and other primary products. Whether the Empire ever actually paid its way, whether its earnings were greater than the cost of administration and defense, is an arguable matter and one which cannot be measured in cash alone. In any event, the benefits were short-lived, and the Empire became once again a liability in the economic sense, though retaining, of course, its political and strategic purpose. The Industrial Revolution, however, continued to be both the heart and the nerve center of the far-flung plantations and mines, whose produce was channeled back to Liverpool.

The power of the industrial North continued almost unabated until the Great Depression, which destroyed it and so much else in the world. The Empire, however, struggled on like a twitching corpse without a head until it, too, was finally dismembered at the end of the Second World War. Not only was the great imperial dream, the dream of Rhodes and Curzon, over, probably forever, but the industrial dream, the dream of Arkwright and Cartwright and Stephenson, was also over in a world of bankrupt companies, closed mills and long dole queues—only temporarily over, we may now think and hope. But the two events were very much linked, the Industrial Revolution and the Empire. When the first faded, the second was, in the end, bound to fade too.

From the first, the Industrial Revolution was undercapitalized. There was no equivalent then of the International Monetary Fund or the World Bank. A country gentleman who wished to open a mill or make machinery, which he had, perhaps, invented, had also to find the finance himself. He went, of course, to the bankers, to the City of London, which was in the beginning understandably suspicious about these small and hazardous projects. Money for further development had to be found from the profits of the mill or the factory itself. It is little wonder, then, that no money was to spare for the building of amenities or comforts. In Victorian England such standards had low priority. Growth and profit came first then, as they still do.

The British flocked to live in the new towns which were being run up, to work in the new mills and the new foundries. Britain became an urban society, for the first time since the Romans left, and the trend has continued until in 1970 four-fifths of the British nation live in towns. The figure is still rising. The towns themselves, apart from a few huge railway stations and town halls, were a sea of gray, dripping slums, with outside sanitation and no running water. The factories and mines were no better, including as they did such horrors as child labor, children of six pulling huge trucks of coal, on their hands and knees, down the black, wet tunnels of the mines. The British Industrial Revolution not only created the urban society, the mechanized world, the machine-fed community, the economic belief in growth and expansion, but also produced social reform, trade unions, strikes, Socialism and, in the more realistic sense, the class war. The eighteenth-century clergymen, playing with their homemade models of spinning jennies and power looms, little knew what they were starting.

The fact that the money had to be borrowed with some difficulty from the bankers and from the City of London increased the animosity between the North of England and the South. This animosity went back a long way and was in its origins racial, the result of a centuries-old conflict between the Danes and the Saxons. But it was felt that the South was getting rich too easily, lending money and keeping its hands clean, while the North plunged into the grime and did the work. The conflict between the industrial North and the South is, of course, by no means confined to England. America, Italy, Spain and France know it, too. But it is unique in Britain, because, though the North has the assets and prides itself on doing the work, the power and the wealth remain obstinately in the South. The money was lent in Lombard Street in London, and the political power still stayed firmly at Westminster. The North's function was to do the dirty work and, in true Northern spirit, they made it as dirty as possible.

The Northerners prided themselves on their grime and on their capability for hard manual work. The North identified itself with the heaviest of heavy industries, with iron and steel, shipbuilding, coal, railway engines, while the South produced such effeminate and fiddly things as bath salts, baby food and canned dog meat, things that no true Northerner would deign to be seen producing. The heavy industries of the North were much hit in the Depression, and lately there has been a move to diversify northern industry, to bring in light industries and consumer-goods factories. These farsighted and well-intentioned schemes are often much misunderstood. When a large American food company opened a factory in Wigan, Lancashire, it had the greatest difficulty in teaching its laborers to wash their hands before they handled food. Such things went right against the Northern grain. An American toiletries firm was misguided enough to open its British factory in Newcastle. Despite the excellent wages offered, no Northerner would dare work in a factory making men's after-shave lotion. He would be laughed out of his workingmen's club in the evening. People would hold their noses when he walked down the street, no matter how carefully he might have eliminated all possible traces of cologne. In the end, the company was forced to import workmen from the South of England who had no such prejudices.

The cult for dirt came from coal, the fuel that powered the Industrial Revolution and that cannot be mined with clean hands. The later arrival of other, cleaner fuels has not altered the Northern belief that grime, smoke, work, thrift and religion are all roughly synonymous. "Dirt for dirt's sake" came to equal "work for work's sake" and " God for God's sake."

The dirt itself is something special. It is the grime of collieries and heavy industry, and it is worn proudly like a badge or a regimental tie. It is not to be confused in any circumstances with Mediterranean dirt, the dirt of not caring, of casualness. The dirt of a Northerner will be confined to his hands, his buildings and his atmosphere; his underclothes, his home, his kitchen, his lavatory will probably be immaculate.

An unfortunate and perhaps unforeseen corollary of the pride in grime was that it involved a cult for ugliness. Or perhaps it was foreseen and ignored, or perhaps the ugliness became itself a matter for pride, like the grime and the long hours and the grim smile of the potteries and the mills. The vicious circle can be rolled indefinitely. Work equals God equals work equals dirt equals ugliness equals profits equals God equals work. If a new town hall, a railway station, a factory had to be built, it had to be huge, rich, grandiloquent, imposing. It also had to be, such was the mood of the times, very ugly even before the grime was later plastered on by the atmosphere.

It was partly a reaction against the age of elegance, the Palladian beauty of Chatsworth or the Regent's Park terraces. The North has its full quota of beautiful country houses, but these were tactfully forgotten. More in the spirit of the place and the times were the four glories of Liverpool: St. George's Hall, perhaps the biggest and the most shapeless classical temple in the world, and the three huge, weird buildings on the Mersey waterfront—the Royal Liver with its twin towers and bulbous domes; the Docks and Harbour Board Building with its echoes of Italy and St. Paul's, dome and all; the Cunard Building, a vaguely Grecian town house. All inflated far beyond their proportionate size, all pitch black.

In Manchester, we think first of the vast Gothic edifice of the Town Hall, the Gothic towers of the Guardian Building, the mishmash of styles which constitutes the campus of Manchester University. Perhaps the most typical street in the prosperous part of the North of England is Market Street, Manchester, facing the little triangle of the Green. Every house is in a different style, without any regard to the height or the style of the one next door. Some of the street is Dutch, some of it is classical, some of it is Gothic, some of it is Art Nouveau, some of it is plain modern brutal; individually, every one is ugly and every one is black. But it is characteristic of its place and of its taste, and it should be carefully preserved, grime and all. This is the architecture of the rich North, an amalgam of classical columns, dreaming spires, brown polished tiles, granite swags and ferns and leaves. There was no shortage of pride or time or care; all that was missing was taste and elegance. Municipal architecture in the North is so splendidly awful that it has a panache of its own; it is a deliberate act of defiance of those who dare to admire William Kent or Inigo Jones. Where there's brass, there's muck, the North seemed to be saying, and it was proud of it.

Separate from this, but a part of it, was the plebeian architecture of the homes of those who were far from rich: the miles of terraced houses in Sheffield and Rochdale and Oldham; Wigan Pier itself (which is, incidentally, a black wharf beside the black canal). This is the proletarian as opposed to the civic North, and this is the heart of the matter.Together with the cult for ugliness came the cult for the working class or the cult of the self-made middle class. These were the fertile plowed fields for the radical and nonconformist movements. The culture, it was felt, was or, if not, should rapidly become totally working-class.

The great wave of popularity of North of England novelists and playwrights in the 1950's—John Braine, Sheila Delaney, Stan Barstow, Stanley Middleton, David Storey—concerned itself exclusively with the working class or with the self-made man on the make. The word "class" has already appeared many times in this book, and it cannot be left out in considering the North of England. The North has its full share of peers, gentry, upper class, middle class, lower middle and so forth, but most of these keep very quiet. The modern image of the North of England, carefully projected by television producers, publishers, film producers and record companies, is one of a totally working-class population. This is the true Marxist dream and is much fostered by critics and social commentators. The fact that so many of these writers and singers choose, the moment they make good, to move to large country houses near London is something of a letdown.

The deliberate ugliness and squalor of the North has produced a definite local culture. It is not only the—perhaps temporary—pop culture of the Beatles or the Scaffold Group; it is not only *Room at the Top* and *A Taste of Honey* and the paintings of L. S. Lowry. It derives, perhaps, more from Northern wealth than from Northern poverty. It came from a feeling that there was more to life than a black canal and a pub. It was the other side of the Industrial Revolution, the natural expression of a frustrated but eloquent people. It found its most obvious outlet in music, in the great choirs of the North. Nowhere in the world is *The Messiah* sung as it is sung in those grim Northern towns. The world's greatest choir is still unquestionably the Huddersfield Choral Society, and the singer who wishes to join it has not only to have a fine, well-trained voice, but to be a deep, intuitive lover of music and to be willing to wait his turn on the long waiting list. The North boasts two first-rate symphony orchestras and concerts of the highest international standards. Manchester has, in its time, been a great center for opera. Culturally, indeed, the North of England has been the unprovincial province. Part of this was no doubt due to the sudden prosperity of the North in the Industrial Revolution. As a center of wealth and influence it also became the center for intellectual activity. The brain drain of those days drew people toward Manchester and Leeds.

However, the cultural movement of the North remained essentially proletarian. A man went to the Opera House in Manchester to hear the work, not to be seen at the opera. All cultural activities, of course, require rich patrons, but the rich patrons who sponsored choirs or concerts or exhibitions wished them to be fine performances or exhibitions in their own right. The North was not without its own snobberies, but it was never forgotten that work and the workingman were the basis on which it was all founded.

The North produced not only cotton mills and the trade unions, but also the international working-class solidarity movement, the idea which bred international Socialism. It was this idealism which prompted the citizens of Manchester to support Abraham Lincoln during the American Civil War, because they felt a brotherly feeling for the slaves of the South, despite the fact that the American Civil War and the blockade of the Southern states were hitting the cotton mills of Lancashire hard. In January, 1863, the workingmen of Manchester sent an address to President Lincoln:

> As citizens of Manchester, assembled at the Free Trade Hall, we beg to express our fraternal sentiments towards you and your country. We rejoice in your greatness as an outgrowth of England, whose blood and language you share, whose orderly and legal freedom you have applied to new circumstances over a region immeasurably greater than our own. We honour your free state as a singularly happy abode for the working millions, where industry is honoured. One thing alone has, in the past, lessened our sympathy with your country and our confidence in it, being the ascendancy of politicians who not merely maintain negro slavery but desire to extend and root it more firmly.

On February 11, 1863, Lincoln replied as follows:

> A fair examination of history has seemed to authorize the belief that the past actions and influences of the United States were generally regarded as having been beneficial towards mankind. I have therefore reckoned upon the forbearance of the nations. The circumstances, to some of which you kindly allude, induce me especially to expect that, if justice and good faith shall be practiced by the United States, they would encounter no hostile interference on the part of Great Britain. . . . I know and deeply deplore the sufferings which the working men at Manchester and in all Europe are called to endure in this crisis. . . . Under these circumstances, I cannot but regard your decisive utterances upon the question as an instance of sublime Christian heroism which has not been surpassed in any age or in any country. It is indeed an energetic and re-inspiring assurance of the inherent power of truth and of the arguments in universal triumph of justice, humanity and freedom. . . . I hail this interchange of sentiments, therefore, as an augury that, whatever else may happen, whatever misfortune may befall your country or my own, the peace and friendship which now exists between the two nations will be, and it shall be my desire to make them, perpetual.

There was, however, an ironic twist to this brotherly feeling. After the end of the American Civil War and the victory of the North, the City of London, which was financing the North of

England, decided on a change of policy and switched its investments from the North of England to the American North, to help the progress of the American Industrial Revolution. The motives behind this switch are obscure. It was probably partly due to the basic rivalry in England between the South and the North, the feeling that the North had got rich enough for the time being and that the South, which held the purse strings, was being left behind. It was also probably business policy. It was felt that the returns on American investment were likely to be more immediately profitable than further investment in the North of England, which was supposed to have achieved its possible growth potential.

The result of this was drastic. There was a sudden and unforeseen depression in the North of England; further expansions of industry and business were checked, and in one year in Lancashire thousands of prosperous families were forced to sell their carriages and obliged to demean themselves in the eyes of their neighbors and employees by taking hackney cabs or walking on foot. The erection of civic buildings and statues went unabated, but the North had received a shock. It had had its first slump, the first of several, which were in the end to bring it despairingly to its knees.

The industrial boom which started in Lancashire shook the world, but little more than a century elapsed between the bursting ideas of Arkwright and Cartwright and the sullen hunger marchers of Jarrow, the long lines of unemployed at the Labour Exchanges. Modern prosperity hit the North of England before anywhere else in the world; the Depression struck there first, too. One of the unfortunate results of this was to increase the antipathy between the North and the South of England. The South of England, it was felt, though it did no dirty work, still controlled not only the political power but the financial power too. It was resented that great enterprises in the North could be ruined at a stroke by the decisions of men with clean hands in a boardroom in London. What, it was felt, had the South done to deserve such authority and power?

There were, of course, factors other than the policies of the

City of London which contributed to the decline of the North and which helped the far too rapid slide from splendors to miseries. The North was heavily dependent on exports, and these in turn were dependent on world prosperity and an adequate price for the overseas primary product. With the contraction of trade during the Depression and with the prices of such crops as sugar, rubber and cocoa on the floor for year after year, the colonies were able to afford less and less Lancashire cotton. Gandhi's boycott, for political reasons, of manufactured cotton depressed Lancashire still further.

Psychologically it was very difficult for the people in the North to understand the change in their fortunes. They worked hard, usually in very disagreeable conditions, and yet the same work seemed now to be largely unrewarded, even unneeded. In a community which depends for its morale on work, which values hard, dirty work for work's sake above all other values, unemployment is the cruelest of blows. Not only are the income and the interest in a job gone, but worst of all, the image is lost, the sense of self-importance, of being essential to the nation's prosperity. A young man in a Sicilian village will not feel the misery of unemployment so keenly; he will be from an early age already partly adjusted psychologically to spending his days loafing in the village square, being supported by some more fortunate relation. His self-respect depends on other things. But it is not so in Rochdale or Sheffield. If a man's self-respect depends on getting his hands dirty, how does he get them dirty standing on a street corner for sixteen hours a day?

Unemployment was a blow as much psychological as economic, and the North of England has never recovered from it. Other factors, too, have contributed to its lessening importance. There is a great temptation for human beings to stop at the moment of their triumph, to wish to relive that golden moment, to believe that they now know everything about everything, to be impatient of any further progress or fresh ideas. Lancashire has not entirely resisted this temptation. Wandering about the North of England, one finds it is easy to forget which century one is living in. There has been, for instance, a conscientious effort to diversify the industry in the North to bring in light industry. Many of the obsolescent factories at Trafford Park, near Manchester, have been adapted to produce cornflakes, electronic goods and other modern essentials. But this has all been done without rebuilding the original factories, which have simply been gutted and reconstructed inside, partly for financial reasons, partly from nostalgia. There was never any question of creating a bright, new, modern area of up-to-date buildings. The old mills still stand beside the Manchester Ship Canal, with its cranes, docks and swing bridges looming through the murk. Clean air, electricity, automation may have reached Trafford Park, but it still looks like an engraving of Manchester in 1850, somber and very impressive.

The reluctance to change or perhaps to admit change is reflected in business methods and management. A traditional and deliberately inflexible approach by both managements and unions, something which was not only aggravated but perhaps ossified by the slump, has contributed its part to the declining power of the North. Foreign buyers who have wrung their hands over the failure of a British shipyard to produce its tankers by the agreed date should remember the long history of unforgotten bitterness, intransigent misunderstandings and wounded pride. Britain, to borrow a recent phrase, is now picking up the dark, Satanic bills.

All the same, it would be unjust to disparage the great achievement of the North both in industry and in culture, and it should be acknowledged that the North of England has made a unique contribution not only to Britain but to the whole world. This contribution, it is to be hoped, is not yet ended, despite some rather discouraging trends, chief among them the drift to the South, However much he may despise London, the ambitious Northerner, in search of wider horizons and opportunities, is tempted to move into the Golden Triangle, the area, roughly between Birmingham, Düsseldorf and Paris, which, in the opinion of economists and the governments they advise, should henceforth be the center of European industry. Other ambitious and qualified Northerners, filled with frustration and restlessness, are moving farther afield to the big new factories across the Atlantic or in Australia. As has already been explained in this book, this movement and flux are part of the British tradition. But it will be a sad day if the North of England ceases to exist as a coherent and contained culture.

In an attempt to evoke the unique atmosphere of the North of England as it still is and as a tribute to a great achievement, it is relevant to describe three of the North's greatest cities—cities where the splendor and misery may be most clearly seen and identified: Newcastle, Liverpool and Manchester.

Newcastle is very old. It dates back to the Romans and was an important fortress on the great wall which spanned England from coast to coast. The city was important to the Normans, too. But this history is strictly for the librarians. Modern Newcastle is a child of the Industrial Revolution. It is a dirty, grimy city, and the inhabitants are proud of it. A friend of mine, a typical Geordie, told me that it was the finest city in the world, even though, typically, he no longer lives there. The inhabitants of the area, the Geordies, are a different race from the rest of the North of England or indeed anywhere else in Britain. They know this and are proud of it. "We're different when you get across the Tyne" is a popular phrase. They are square, solid, tall, slow-speaking, with little obvious evidence of wit or humor, but respecting themselves and others, slow to take offense and quarrel. They usually get on well with the rest of the British, with the possible exception of the Cockneys from London. Apart from the difference in accent, the Geordie finds it difficult to follow Cockney speed and humor. During the last war, at one moment, a Newcastle sergeant found himself in a company entirely composed of Cockney privates. These appreciated his slow, stolid fair-mindedness, but yet they ragged him mercilessly, and it is difficut to think that he ever understood a word they said during the whole of the time they were serving together. The other sergeant was, in peacetime, an Armenian carpet seller, and once again, it is improbable that the Newcastle sergeant understood either his colleague's language or his attitude of mind. He bore his double misfortune with quiet fortitude. It is possible that he had met, occasionally, such people back home.

The Tyneside area, Newcastle itself, is no longer wholly an enclave of the Scandinavian tribe which settled there many centuries ago. Down the Tyne at North Shields is the largest Norwegian colony in Britain, and at the British terminal of the Bergen Line this is perhaps appropriate. The two peoples, even if they are not exactly the same race, have much in common. Like all seaports, Newcastle has its share of immigrant races, but it cannot be thought to be a multiracial city. There is a definite Geordie attitude to life, slightly different from that in other Northern cities and still largely unaffected by immigration from overseas. It is centered, of course, on heavy work (which in Newcastle means steel and shipbuilding) and on its corollary, beer.

Newcastle brown ale is brewed especially strong. After a heavy day in the steelworks or the shipyards, the Newcastle man will feel very thirsty. A few pints of beer may quench his thirst but will not make him feel that he has had a drink. Something stronger is required to make him feel that he has had a good visit to his local drinking place, which in Newcastle is more likely to be a working men's club than a pub. The clubs, indeed, far outnumber the pubs and provide a rather different atmosphere from the normal British industrial pub. For one thing, there will probably be no women present. Women will be permitted to go only once a week to a Newcastle club to play bingo or tombola; in many clubs they will not be permitted to go at all. Newcastle is very much a man's world. The women are kept in their homes washing, cleaning, cooking, bringing up the children. On the other hand, a Geordie is very polite to women in public, opening doors for them, giving up his seat in buses, raising his cap, behaving with courtesy which is not always found in the more sophisticated cities of the world.

Newcastle is in no sense a sophisticated city. There is little theater or music; the Jews, who have brought so much culture to Leeds, seem to have missed Newcastle. The more affluent classes prefer to live in Northumberland as country gentry and commute into the city only for work. But surprisingly, the city contains one of the most swinging nightclubs anywhere, with cabaret stars who come from all over the world to appear there. This perhaps suggests that the Geordie is not as stolid and humorless as he would like to appear. Another clue perhaps lies in the complementary affinity many Newcastle people feel for the Irish. Ireland represents a touch of magic which the Geordie can appreciate without being able to visualize it in his own city—there are relatively few Irish in Newcastle. The Irishman talks fast and amusingly but does not always mean every word he says; the Geordie speaks slowly and without inspiration and means every word. Irish girls are famous for their prettiness; Newcastle women are perhaps the plainest in Britain. Dublin is a mass of charm, blarney and talk; the opposite may be said of Newcastle. My drinking companion, made slightly more eloquent than usual with Newcastle brown ale, not only admired his home city and Dublin in that order, but also spoke nostalgically of San Francisco, Hamburg, Rome, Bombay. An engineer, he had traveled widely in the world, but there was only one city of which he spoke disparagingly: London. He had been there only twice, and he hoped he would never go there again. In this he was typical not only of Newcastle, but of much of the North of England.

Across the country on the other sea, facing west, the other great port of the North of England provides a contrast. It would be difficult to imagine a city with a more dreadful history than Liverpool: the slave trade; the great Irish emigrations to America which passed through Liverpool, full of bitterness and final farewells, the division between those who left their families behind forever and those who found, at the last moment, that they did not have the fare and had to remain in Liverpool. The racial fighting between the English, the Irish, the Scots and the Welsh; plagues, disease, poverty, depression, slums, crime, the slump in shipping—Liverpool has had everything which a city dweller would least wish to have. And yet from all this ash heap, a phoenix or, to be more exact, several phoenixes have arisen.

One is the enormous sense of civic pride. Liverpool has been, for a long time, aware that it is a great city. In the last century Lord Derby, whose family has a large country house nearby, stated that he would rather be lord mayor of Liverpool than Prime Minister of Britain, and he had experience of both positions. The civic buildings, the great business edifices on the waterfront, the hotels and railway stations are possibly the largest in Britain and the blackest. Everywhere there are statues of Victorian prime ministers (including the opposite figures of Gladstone and Wellington), the prince consort and, above all, Queen Victoria, riding sidesaddle on a horse, wearing a bowler hat with a feather in it, a statue which, comprising both grandeur and panache, epitomizes much that is best in Liverpool.

This feeling for size did not stop with the death of Queen Victoria; it is continuing with the St. John's Precinct. This example of modern urban planning is intended to have 150 shops, an air-conditioned shopping arcade, a theater, a hotel and a 400-foot high tower with revolving restaurant on top. The Liverpudlians appreciate the size and ambition of the scheme, while retaining a North Country suspicion of its gimmicks. The tower, especially, is felt to be unworthy of such a city and is referred to as the monstrosity. Above all, Liverpool is the only city in the whole world which has two large modern cathedrals. The Anglican cathedral, still unfinished, probably the last example of Gothic architecture which will ever be built, is a huge, soaring pile of brown sandstone. A few yards away is the Roman Catholic cathedral, built with the pennies of the Irish poor and only finished in 1967. A bare circular cylinder of concrete, topped with a lantern of beautiful modern glass and a crown of spears, it has sometimes been called a blast-off pad for modern faith or more irreverently "the Mersey funnel," since indeed it does resemble a funnel upside down. The street between the two is named Hope Street, and the symbolic significance of this is emphasized in a weekly sermon in both cathedrals. Cooperation between the two cathedrals is, in fact, strong, not only as a result of the ecumenical movement, but partly out of a wish to discourage the religious feuds and the racial intolerance which form such a grim part of the city's history.

The second source of Liverpool pride is its intellectual life. This is not in the least academic but is based in a great interest in the arts and the idea that the arts are not for the rich alone, but for everybody to enjoy. The petition urging the local council to buy the Royal Court Theatre, which had been sadly turned into a bingo hall, and return it to its proper theatrical purpose was signed by the ordinary shoppers in the center of Liverpool. The Philharmonic Hall has excellent acoustics; the concerts of its orchestra, the Royal Liverpool Philharmonic, are among the best in Britain and attract the cream of the world's soloist performers. The Walker Art Gallery puts on exhibitions which are good enough for every serious art critic.

The Liverpool poets, Roger McGough, Adrian Henri and Brian Patten, are probably the most interesting now writing in Britain. They, and others less known, often read their works at the Everyman Theatre on Hope Street, for poetry is felt in Liverpool to be a spoken rather than a written thing. This theater puts on the plays of Genet or Sartre and was the original home of the Scaffold Group, which cheerfully combines modern poetry with corny and amateur sketches. The conversation in the bistro below is the same as you would hear in Chelsea, and indeed the atmosphere is reminiscent of swinging London—miniskirts, protests and all.

It is not to be supposed that these intellectual activities command universal approval any more than the tower of the St. John's Precinct. The large numbers of poets who use the houses in Canning Street as flophouses and, it is said, have reduced the buildings to near ruins, are not much admired by dockers and bus drivers. The poets are not visibly doing any useful manual work, they are not getting their hands dirty, and indeed one may wonder how many of them are actually writing poetry. But the fact that they exist and are tolerated provides a spice to the city, something which one does not find in Newcastle or Rochdale.

The Lancastrian is a different man from his neighbor in

Newcastle. He speaks faster; he often sits on the edge of his chair, waving his hands to emphasize his point. He talks a great deal, but he will also listen carefully and answer with intelligence. Though he is obsessed by work, he is aware, sometimes dimly, sometimes acutely, that there are other things in the world besides work, that there is an art of living and that the art may include everything from modern poetry and experimental theater to Everton Football Club and fish-and-chips, with beer as the great fuel and lubricant.

But not only is Liverpool part of the North of England, it is also a world of its own inside the North. Many of its characters are typical Lancastrians, but as with all great seaports, there is a large international population superimposed on the original Northerners and by no means integrated with them. The Celtic fringe meets in Liverpool, and the Irish, the Welsh and the Scots fight one another, sometimes happily, sometimes nastily, in the pubs and after closing time in the streets outside. There is also, as might be expected, a considerable seaport population of Chinese, Greek, Italian and Lascar; the immigrant West Indians and Pakistanis have added a new element. Liverpool indeed may be called the San Francisco of Britain, both for its multiracial complexities and for the effervescent brilliance of its culture, though scenically the two cities are in great contrast. San Francisco is justly famed as one of the most beautiful cities of the world, but despite the imposing Victorian waterfront, despite the two new cathedrals on their rises, nobody could say the same for Liverpool, with its broad acres of slums beside the great brown Mersey. Those who think that a multiracial city is the ideal city of the future, the New Jerusalem, should look closely at Liverpool.

The population of Liverpool may be defiantly divergent in its origins; the people may come from Londonderry or Palermo or Port of Spain or Glasgow or Rawalpindi or Piraeus or even from Liverpool itself, but on the other dimension, the class dimension, they are amazingly homogeneous. Liverpool is a totally working-class city. You may occasionally catch a whiff of money in Manchester or Leeds, but never in Liverpool. Anyone who has raised himself by the bootstraps or by a small legacy to the middle class will move out immediately, either into the Lancashire countryside or across the Mersey into Cheshire.

There, across the Mersey, the middle and upper middle classes live an extraordinary life, the men commuting daily to their offices in Liverpool through the Mersey Tunnel, but trying to live the lives of country gentlemen in Cheshire, which is technically not in the North of England. Their wives and children will live in the hybrid and rather gimmicky world of pony clubs and French cooking and Greek wine and Finnish saunas and American barbecues. They will take their holidays in the south of Spain or Portugal, and they will have as little as possible to do with the great gray city across the river, which provides their livelihood. Their menfolk rejoin them in the evening, traveling once again through the Mersey Tunnel, and Liverpool is left to its working-class self. All industrial cities, of course, have their commuter population—London and New York are well in the lead—but no other great city, not even Glasgow, is abandoned so totally by its middle-class population every night.

The result is of considerable interest to sociologists and journalists, and the cultural life is thought, by those who wish to think so, to be as much due to this one-class society as to the mixture of racial origins. The more obvious result has been that the working-class population has split like an amoeba into two; the girls who work in Lewis's Department Store and who kiss their boyfriends good-night so ardently outside the pubs are very different from the girls who discuss Pinget or Roger McGough in the Philharmonic Hotel or the Everyman. They do not even look the same; their skirts, their hairstyles, their makeups are as different as their minds and their interests. The one-class city, it seems, is doomed to instant fragmentation, and this perhaps is the special pride of Liverpool.

There is plenty, however, for the Liverpudlians not to feel proud about, and it would be biased to present too rosy a picture of the city, despite the fact of its being, reputedly, the second cultural center of Britain. Much of it is still frankly an eyesore. Many of the houses, derelict with broken windows, appear to be in the course of demolition, until it is realized that there are still people living there. There has been a good deal of urban renewal around the Bull Ring, but a great part of the notorious Liverpool Eight district is enough to make the heart sink. This contrast between grandeur and poverty may be the key to Liverpool, perhaps more important than the classless society or the multiracial origins. Liverpool is not like Edinburgh or Bath, beautiful cities, reluctantly harboring famous cultural festivals imposed on them by outside promoters. Culture in Liverpool springs from the people and the city itself, with almost no help from outside. It is, in a sense, an act of defiance against the grim surroundings.

It is not possible to write about Liverpool without mentioning its most dazzling and celebrated product, the Beatles. This is not the place to write a critical discussion of the Beatles' work or the cultural origins, Irish, North Country, transatlantic, which formed it. But one may perhaps remark that in modern Liverpool, popular opinion seems to be at variance with the views of the critics of London and New York. Judging from casual conversation in buses and shops, the later, more sophisticated work of the Beatles is admired less than the earlier, simpler songs. One may note, too, that it is a long time since any of the Beatles set foot in Liverpool. The object of those who make good in Liverpool, in song, poetry, in the theater, is to move south to London as soon as possible, and in this they are untypical of their less gifted north country brothers and sisters. The result is an impoverishment of the exciting city which inspired them and an arts drain to the south. The Liverpool satirists who likened the Roman Catholic cathedral to a rocket blast-off pad were perhaps saying unintentionally a great deal about the city itself.

A few miles away lies the great city of Manchester, arguably the capital of the north of England and providing a great contrast with Liverpool. Though many of the people are of Irish or Scots descent, this is no cosmopolitan city like Liverpool.

This is the true North of England at its northernmost. To me it is the city of permanent November. To look out your bedroom window on a June morning and see all the lights on in all the black buildings opposite is to realize that you are in a city with a flavor all its own. Better still, and more usual, is to see it on a dark, rainy day with the streetlamps reflected on the wet pavements and the murky sky lowering overhead, hardly distinguishable from the black buildings beneath it. Other cities, of course, have their rainy skies and black buildings, but none of them is quite as proud of its blackness as Manchester, the image of grime magnified, the great black hands in the sky symbolizing wealth and hard work.

A distant kinship may be found between Liverpool and San Francisco, but it is difficult to find another city like Manchester. Perhaps the nearest analogy would be with an industrial city in West Germany. There would be found the same feeling for heavy, uncomfortable work, the same admiration for work as a thing in itself, the same taste for beer and for heavy orchestral music.

For a long time, the heart of Manchester was the Royal Exchange, that huge black building in the center. Many commodities, including shares and cotton, were traded there, and for a while it could truly be said that this was the nerve center not only of the North of England, but of England itself. More than the City of London, more than Threadneedle Street or Lombard Street, more than the Treasury and Westminster, the country and the world listened to what was being said in the Royal Exchange at Manchester.

The financial prosperity of the city brought with it a sunburst of culture, perhaps unequaled since the Renaissance. Across the street from the Royal Exchange, in another black pinnacled building, were the editorial offices of the Manchester *Guardian,* undoubtedly the most literate daily paper in the country. Here C. P. Scott, Ernest Newman, Sir Neville Cardus and many others wrote some of the longest sentences in the history of English journalism. It was known and accepted here that when the literary reviewer or the drama critic or the music critic or, come to that, the cricket correspondent wrote an essay, he would expect and probably receive many columns, perhaps a whole page for his work. Anything less would have been unsuitable to the stature of the work he was describing, to the authority of the journalist himself and to the dignity of a great newspaper.

Down the road in the Free Trade Hall (and the name itself nostalgically evokes the economic philosophy and the crusade which provided the springboard for Northern prosperity) the Hallé Orchestra under Hans Richter was giving the first performances in England of Strauss' latest tone poems. In the Opera House, Sir Thomas Beecham was conducting some of his famous performances of *Die Meistersinger*. At the other theaters the most discussed plays of their time were being performed to full houses. Owens College, which was housed in Quay Street in the former residence of Richard Cobden, the reformer, provided a standard of learning and scholarship as high as London. It was later transformed into Manchester University. Manchester Central Library contained millions of books and was widely used. At Old Trafford Cricket Ground, A. C. Maclaren was captaining Lancashire, a post he regarded as of more importance than captaining England. Not all the famous names mentioned in this paragraph, of course, were on view at the same time, but they may perhaps evoke a picture of the brilliance that was Manchester during its great eighty years.

There was, of course, a darker side equally famous: the rings of dripping slums which encircled the city; the poverty; the disease; the drunkenness; the brawling. Gin, as recalled in an earlier chapter, was the quickest way out of Manchester, and the choice of the city to be immortalized in that famous phrase is significant. For those who were not rich and cultured and literate, Manchester was horror indeed. The Depression ended the riches and the culture without doing anything for the poverty and slums. Since the war, full employment, the welfare state and town planning have done a good deal to alleviate the latter, but nothing to restore the former. Manchester has changed since 1927, and it is doubtful if Cobden would recognize it today. Much of the change is obviously for the better, but the brilliance and the pride have gone. These are things which cannot be commanded by local government committees.

For one thing, Manchester is no longer totally black. Nothing can, of course, be done about the permanent rain, but the raindrops are no longer filled with little cargoes of soot. Electric trains in the monumental stations, modern industries in the Gothic factories, a cleaner air have helped to clear the Manchester sky. That huge Gothic palace, the Town Hall, has been scrubbed almost white, and though several citizens expressed to me the hope that it would be as black as ever in a few years, this, in fact, seems improbable, a dismaying thought to those who liked it the way it was. The slums are being gradually cleared and the inhabitants rehoused in large apartment blocks built in parkland, a conception which would have delighted Le Corbusier, but which is a little disconcerting to the traditional inhabitants. Long green fingers of parks and gardens are being let into the city to provide grass and breathing space. The Piccadilly Plaza provides a surprising note of gaiety with its curved ramps, its fountains, its sudden orange squares on the façades, its Shinto temples—a feverish brightness, out of tune with the rest of the area. It is all very enlightened and ambitious and expensive, but far indeed from the spirit which made Manchester the great and terrible city it once was.

The Victorian pubs, with their patterned frosted-glass windows, their ornamental tiles and their marble counters, are being pulled down or renovated into modern pubs with plastic flowers. But the effect on drinking in the Manchester area is marginal. To pull down and rebuild a slum does not necessarily remove the wish of some of the inhabitants to get aggressively (or peacefully) drunk on Saturday night. Some problems cannot be solved by fountains and clean stonework.

The new Manchester has many things to its credit besides the clearing of slums and the cleaning of the Town Hall. The university expands continually, and new buildings are being put up beside the blackened yellow brick and stone Gothic pinnacles of the original college. The standard of scholarship continues to rise; the Central Library has a stock of more than 9,000,000 volumes and a Telex system by which the librarians will answer, free of charge, any reasonable request for information from anywhere in the world. The excellent bookshops will provide all the books that the most curious and globe-trotting student could possibly need. Academically, Manchester is thriving; culturally, it has almost disappeared from sight.

Its opera has gone; opera lovers have to make do with occasional short visits by touring companies. The only plays which reach the boards now are amateur productions and brief tryouts of plays before they arrive in London's West End. The Hallé Orchestra certainly continues, but doubts are expressed whether it can maintain its international standard now that Sir John Barbirolli has retired. Most woundingly of all, the Manchester *Guardian* has dropped the name Manchester and moved its editor and its head office to London, perhaps the most symbolic example of the drift to the South. Almost equally upsetting to the sports lover is the proposal that big cricket matches such as test matches should no longer be held at Old Trafford and should be played somewhere where the weather is slightly drier. In the television and jet age, it is explained, the public will no longer sit quietly for several hours, hoping that the rain will eventually clear off for a brief, though cloudy, spell.

Economic conditions cannot, of course, be held responsible for the weather at Old Trafford, for the notices of "Rain Stops Play" on a television screen, though they may perhaps account for some of the impatience. But economic changes undoubtedly account for the rest of the cultural wilderness in which Manchester now stands. The Royal Exchange is no longer the nerve center of the economy. Most of the building is, in fact, let as offices. Cotton is no longer king, and Manchester is outside the Golden Triangle of future European prosperity. Free trade, that battle cry of the 1840's, is no longer thought to be a panacea by those engaged in commerce; indeed Lancashire has just persuaded the reluctant government in London to impose import duties on imported manufactured cotton, a move designed to protect the remains of Lancashire cotton from the competition of Hong Kong and Japan. The wheel has moved a long way since the days of Cobden and Bright; those who built and named the Free Trade Hall must be turning in their graves.

As a consequence of the economic decline, Manchester has become no longer a fashionable place in which to live. The rich and the less rich who rode in their carriages through its streets and patronized its arts and its theaters have now moved out of Manchester and have taken instead, as at Liverpool, the image of country gentlemen, commuting into the city only to earn their daily bread. At night, Manchester is a ghost town, its streets empty in a way which would be unthinkable in London or Paris or New York at the same hour.

I found myself one evening in a pub next door to the old Guardian Building. I was feeling in a nostalgic mood, recalling the past glories of that newspaper and the famous people who may or may not have used this particular pub. The pub was, in fact, full of those working on the *Guardian,* night editors, news editors, printers, porters, all rather sadly aware that they were now only a regional office of a national newspaper which now belonged to London. But being Lancashire men, they all were talking very hard. I asked a journalist what he considered the most typical thing in Manchester today. He replied simply, "This is, this pub." He meant, I think, the great aura of the *Guardian,* which Sir Neville Cardus had likened to Balliol College, Oxford, in its intellectual stature and literacy. But as I looked around the shabby pub, which had not been decorated for many years, the seaside-boardinghouse wallpaper, the cheap ugly mantelpiece, the bleak lighting, the atmosphere of neglect and depression, it was possible to read another, sadder meaning into his words.

There is, however, one place in Manchester which is a matter for pride for every Mancunian and indeed for all Lancashire: the International Airport at Ringway, just outside Manchester. In the railway age Manchester was proud of its stations, and it is right in the jet age that it should be proud of its grand new airport. The airport buildings themselves are modern and pleasing and very like those of most other airports, without being outstandingly original. There is an interesting stained-glass sculpture by Margaret Traherne, an abstract work of browns, greens and blue, recalling the historic fact that the first British Airborne Forces were formed and trained at Ringway. At the other end of the hall is a sculpture of an Icarus-like figure by Elizabeth Frink, in memory of the first men to fly the Atlantic, Sir John Alcock and Sir Arthur Whitten Brown in June, 1919. Manchester is proud that both men came from that city. But some of the passengers expressed regret that the sculptor was not from the North of England; others complained that she was only able to find ugliness in flight and human achievement. Greater satisfaction was expressed in the airport technical equipment, in the length of its runways, the convenience of its baggage handling.

However, the proudest thing about Manchester Airport is that it belongs not to the Airports Authority, but to Manchester itself. It is not owned by anyone down South; it belongs to the North, and, a matter for equal pride, it is possible to fly from Manchester direct to all the principal European cities and to America without having to change planes in London, without having to set foot in that Southern metropolis which has unfairly and inexplicably, it is thought, stolen the wealth and the glory of Manchester away.

22

SMITH, MACDONALD AND JONES

☙§ More English people are called Smith than anything else. It is by far the most popular English name, as a glance at the telephone books of London, Birmingham or Manchester will confirm. Yet considered closely, the name is an unexpected choice. The profession of smith itself, though honorable and ancient, is, one would have guessed, an outside selection for the most respected trade in England. It is, after all, possible to live without a blacksmith. There are, to be sure, plenty of people in England called Butcher or Baker or Carpenter or Thatcher or Tyler or Gardner, but they are not so numerous as to be conspicuous. The Smiths are obviously something special and different.

Earlier chapters in this book have dealt with the British love of animals and vegetables. But in the last resort, it is perhaps the feeling for minerals which has proved the most important and enduring in British history. There has always been in the English subconscious an unspoken idea, usually going against the social and economic conditions of the time, that the smith was the most important man in the village, more important than the squire or his groom, than the priest or the farmer or the hunter. The early history of England is largely a history of metals. The different waves sweeping over England, as recorded in an earlier chapter, each brought with them a new metal, which was perhaps responsible for the success of their conquest. The Stone Age yielded to the Bronze Age, which in turn succumbed to the Iron Age. The native minerals of copper, tin and, later, iron were worked and were blended by the metalworkers of the time into the alloys of brass and finally steel. But the mines were few, and the work was difficult. A metal object, a plow or a breastplate or a cooking pot, was a prized possession, and the metalworker, the smith, was a man of importance and dignity.

Much of this derives from the Celts, who were skilled metalworkers and who brought their craft with them when they arrived and conquered. Even more, perhaps, is due to the Saxons, one of whose gods, Thor, was a smith, and one can say that the smith is the only man in the village who had a day in the week specially dedicated to him. The first Lord Birkenhead took as his family motto "I am the smith of my fortune." By profession he was a lawyer, the foremost lawyer in the country, but he was proud of his original name, which was Smith. Eloping couples fleeing to Scotland from angry parents would be married in haste at the Forge at Gretna Green, married, of course, by the smith, a man who actually commanded greater respect than any parson or clerk and whose marriage ceremony could be felt to be binding in a way that other ceremonies were not. The picturesque practice has now been finally obliterated by modern bureaucracy, but the forge itself is still visited by interested tourists, visible evidence of the British belief that something which is done or sworn over the anvil is specially binding and important.

The feeling of the British for brass and copper, however, continues unabated, and rather to the surprise of overseas visitors, very many British homes and almost all British pubs are cluttered with objects made in the two metals. All of them have to be cleaned and polished almost every day. There are brass candlesticks on the mantelpiece, brass ashtrays and knickknacks on the table, brass or copper bed warmers on the wall. The coal is kept in brass buckets. On small ledges stand brass Buddhas bought in Benares long ago by soldiers of the Indian army and brought home; the Buddhas themselves were probably made in Birmingham. The harnesses of dray horses are festooned with brass decorations and medallions, some bearing the image of Sir Winston Churchill smoking a cigar. The British infantryman used to be covered from head to foot in brass buttons and badges, which had to be cleaned daily and which added considerably, it was thought, to his morale. This has nothing to do with the relics of armor, such as are worn on ceremonial parades by the Household Cavalry. The British soldier's brass buttons, which had no parallel on the uniforms of other nations, were simply a result of the feeling for brass, a desire to clothe one of Her Majesty's soldiers in the worthiest manner. And it is only in England that brass is a slang word for money.

This love of metal, deriving from the Celts and the Saxons, was opposed by the Jutes and later the Normans, with their feeling for animals and in particular for horses. The Jutes, as recorded earlier, worshiped the horse. The Normans, who were ultimately of the same origin, followed the Roman tradition in thinking that the cavalry was naturally superior to the infantry. In the same way the landowner, after the Norman Conquest, became of more importance than the village metalworker; the duke or the squire held court in his castle or manor house, while the smith became a mere artisan at the far end of the village in his forge. But respect for him continued strongly; neither duke nor squire are common surnames in England today. This respect given to the smith not only was an appreciation of his technical skill, but was also wreathed in legendary magic, a relic of earlier gods or sagas. The great hero Sigurd or Siegfried not only conquered and overthrew the existing establishment, strode through fires fearlessly and won the sleeping maiden, but also had to be a smith forging his own sword. Legends such as these are deep in the English race memory and survived all through the period when the ambition of every boy was to be a victorious knight in a tournament, still on his horse at the end of the day.

It is no surprise, therefore, that when the Industrial Revolution started in the world, it started in England. The nation of smiths was recovering its nerve, its prestige and its skill. Among the pioneers of the Industrial Revolution were such great smiths as Henry Cort, who introduced the first grooved mill for making wrought iron in 1783 and in the following year invented the first puddling furnace, two inventions which gave the British steel industry a commanding lead. The furnace was later improved by another great smith, Hall. The cotton industry was the child of such inventors as Arkwright, Crofton, Hargreaves and Cartwright, who perhaps cannot, strictly speaking, be called smiths, particularly if they were clergymen by profession. But Henry Maudslay in the eighteenth century was the first toolmaker to devise machines for mass production, and with his advanced emphasis on precision and finish, he was obviously a smith of extremely high standards. The last of his machines went out of service only recently.

In the nineteenth century we may mention such smiths as Sidney Thomas, who, typically in England, was a police court clerk by profession and a metallurgist only in his spare time; he died at the age of thirty-four a rich man, having invented a process which revolutionized the steel industry of Britain. Even more spectacular, perhaps, was Sir Joseph Whitworth, the master smith of the Industrial Revolution, the chief machine-tool maker of Britain, who made a large number of machines, some of them capable of measuring up to a millionth of an inch, and who created the standard gauges that still bear his name. The smiths had made their comeback with a vengeance, a comeback which has continued into the technological and automation ages. However, the Norman belief in the superiority of the country gentleman was a long time adying. The smiths usually came from humbler backgrounds, and as fast as they made their fortunes from their patented machines, they retired to country mansions and had their children taught to ride.

The Norman Conquest, the Norman superiority, lasted from the Battle of Hastings in 1066 to the Battle of Passchendaele in 1917, nearly a thousand years. The cult of the horse had arrived earlier, with Hengist and Horsa, and still continues among those who are devoted to racing and show jumping. The feeling for land, the innate belief that a landowner was a more important person than a metallurgist, died very slowly. The smiths were fighting not only for the success of their ventures, for wealth, but also for social position. However, in the last two decades the position has been largely reversed; the Norman wave is finally spent. In a modern age horsemanship, bravery in battle, daring in the hunting field are less highly esteemed than being a member of the Institute of Mechanical Engineers, and as the smiths advanced, one can note the retreat of the Normans, from large country houses to small country houses, from small country houses to farms, and so on downward.

This has produced the unique British creation of the gentleman farmer. Recently, in a Swiss holiday hotel, I was sitting with a group made up of an English family, complete with four boarding-school children, and an obviously well-off Dutch couple. The Englishman, when asked, said that he was a farmer, and the Dutchman looked surprised. "You are a big landowner?" he asked. The Englishman denied this indignantly. He was simply a farmer, he explained. The Dutchman shook his head, baffled. "But you are not a peasant!" he protested. Finally, daylight dawned. "Ah, you are a gentleman farmer!" he exclaimed. The Englishman made the usual embarrassed noises which the word "gentleman" produces. "Just a farmer," he said.

The decline of the Normans has raised farming in England to a status level which it does not hold in other European countries or America. The gentleman farmer, constantly in retreat from high taxation, assailed by economists who state that English agriculture should be finally and completely abandoned, still tries to maintain the dignity and pride of the Norman country gentleman, on an income which the Ministry of Agriculture thinks suitable to a small farmer. He has to ride, to shoot, to send his children to boarding school and to pony clubs, to make tennis courts, to give cocktail parties and attend the local hunt ball. Although he and his wife work long hours, he has to hire help instead of using his children. It is little wonder that, even allowing for the free eggs and the station wagon which can be charged to tax, he is usually losing money. The balance has to be found from his capital (or possibly from his wife's capital), which is, of course, a dwindling asset. Eventually the farm will have to be sold; the family will move one notch further down and become smallholders. From these, they will sink to becoming laborers for other people and finally disappear into the soil. A thousand years after the death of King Harold at Hastings, the Saxons will at last have won, though the Norman standards of social behavior will no doubt continue for a long while yet, and the status-symbol grouse-moor image is far from gone.

The general election of 1965 was largely fought about this. Harold Wilson and the Labour Party promised a new deal for technologists and engineers. In the new world, metallurgists were to be important men. The inventiveness of the Smiths had not stopped in the last century. Their more recent inventions and discoveries included television, radar, splitting the atom, the jet engine, man-made fibers, the Hovercraft, the swing-wing plane and a mass of other less spectacular products. They had good reason to think they would be needed in the world of "Let's go with Labour." Simultaneously, the Conservative Party, jumping on the bandwagon, attempted to change its image and follow suit. Its leader, who was much associated in the public mind with grouse moors, was jettisoned, and a new one elected who, it was hoped, would appeal more to the metallurgists and technologists of the modern age. Smith, it seemed, after many years of being the underdog, was at last having it his own way. Whichever party won the election, he was likely to come out on top.

In the event, however, it proved otherwise. The Wilson government was duly elected into power but, for various reasons, introduced the Permissive Society rather than the Technological Society. The metallurgist—he was probably a Puritan nonconformist from Yorkshire—found himself at odds with the Permissive Society; as a technician he found himself not wanted, though praised in principle. He found himself once more on his own. His inventions were termed prestige projects which the nation could no longer afford. Fashionable economic theory was in favor of importing from abroad the machinery, computers, television sets, aircraft and other hardware which Smith was equipped to produce at home. It is scarcely surprising that in the 1970 election the Lancashire vote swung back to the Conservatives. But it may be doubted whether any policy change will result. The City of London has never been Smith's friend, even in the earliest days of the Industrial Revolution. Racially different, a blend of Norman and Jew, the financiers and bankers of the City preferred a different metal—gold. The "invisible exports" of banking and insurance are valued above the actual hardware exports which were once shipped out of the ports. It is suggested more and more in political and financial circles that the true future of Britain is not as an industrial country, but as an offshore entrepôt center, buying and selling on margins and living on its wits, being, in other words, to Europe what Hong Kong is to the Far East or Beirut to the Middle East.

Whether a large and inventive people can exist forever on such a fragile economy, balanced so precariously on a single point, is a debatable question. What is certain is that in such an economy of middlemen, the Smiths will have no more part than the sinking Normans. Refusing to sink, too, they will be forced to emigrate, to augment the increasing brain drain, searching for a technological society where their worth and their skill will still be appreciated and rewarded. For Smith is a good workman. Much has been made of productivity statistics which show, for example, that in 1967 Britain and Germany had the same value of engineering output, but it took the British more than 5,000,000 working hours to achieve it, whereas the Germans worked only 3,600,000 hours. In Japan the production figure was nearly half again as large as Britain's, in spite of shorter hours. This is popularly attributed to a lack of will to work. However, remembering from my bottle-factory days that my productivity had nothing at all to do with my keenness but everything to do with my equipment, I was prepared to believe that the failure to provide new machinery has been the key factor.

Already in 1964, in the top ten industrial companies, each British worker had only $9,000 worth of capital investment behind him, compared with the American worker's $17,700. Since then, instead of catching up, Britain has put less capital into engineering than any comparable country. It had been calculated that by 1967 the German and Japanese rate of investment was more than one and a half times the British rate; France's was almost double, and Sweden's was two and a half times as great as Britain's. In the last three years the Treasury's freeze-and-squeeze policy has discouraged modernization and expansion more than ever. It is still felt by governments, economists, shareholders and even managements that installing up-to-date machinery is extravagant, damaging to the balance of payments and, worst of all, encouraging workers in "the lazy man's way." Easier and cheaper is to lecture them once again on working harder and raising productivity.

It is scarcely surprising that the ambitious Smiths want to go abroad, where they can get the right tools for the job. In their new countries they will probably be financed by bankers of the City of London, who have always preferred lending outside Britain to providing British industry with the capital which it has needed. Their products, probably under American or European labels, will then be reimported under the guidance of the Board of Trade and the London School of Economics. It is possible, indeed, that the system may work, though it will need a great deal of ingenuity and juggling to balance the books. But something will have gone out of the British Isles if England is no longer a nation of Smiths.

The brain drain is something new for England. It is nothing new in Scotland. For generations the young Scot has been accustomed to leaving his Highland croft and his Glasgow suburb and journeying abroad in search of opportunities and employment. It sometimes seems that the entire world is populated by Scottish engineers, building bridges and skyscrapers, dredging harbors, constructing water supplies. The accountant in Paris, the dentist in Johannesburg, the bank manager in Vancouver are likely to be Scotsmen. The population of Scotland is now only 4,000,000, of which nearly 2,000,000 live in Glasgow. The Scottish population in the rest of the world is obviously unknown, but clearly far greater. The Scotsman living outside his country, whether it be in Sydney or merely in Manchester, will speak nostalgically of his village, of his clan, of his tartan or his favorite whisky (if it should not be available locally). He will think about the Western Isles in the silver rain or Glasgow on New Year's Eve. He will preserve carefully his Scottish accent; he will join the local Caledonian Society and dance reels in the most inappropriate climates. He will seek out other Scotsmen, unless they be members of the clan with whom his own clan has a historic feud.

But he will not wish to go back to his own country, except in nostalgia and perhaps in retirement. The Scotsman is, above all things, a technician and a businessman, and he knows that rewards are not to be found in the heather and the granite of the Highlands. He will guide his children in the same paths. All this is remarkable, for any proud race; most remarkable of all perhaps is the fact that Scotland, generation after generation, produces and trains more engineers determined to go out and build the bridges and the factories which the world needs. Scotland is, it seems, an inexhaustible well which never runs dry. The result is a bonus for the whole world, English-speaking or otherwise, with the single exception of Scotland itself.

Scotland has always been a poor country; the sheer difficulty of gaining a living on a wet Scottish hill farm is no doubt responsible for the tough element in the Scottish character. The famous Scottish meanness or, more politely, thrift is a virtue of necessity. For a long time now the central government in London has had a guilty conscience about the large country lying in the north, for which it is responsible. Rather belatedly it has introduced various industries and investment schemes and endowed them more generously than some of the schemes in England. Every Scot costs the British taxpayer thirty pounds a year more than his English counterpart. But the differential is still insufficient, and the Scots continue to seek the trains and the planes out of Scotland as fast as they can. Despite the limited financial help and the unlimited speeches, Scotland remains a poor country, and in the economic systems at present canvassed so energetically, it is likely to become even poorer.

The glamor of Scotland, however, persists and is, it is hoped, inextinguishable. To the overseas and overtly homesick Scotsman, as to the tourist, Scotland means Edinburgh Castle; or Stirling Castle rising through the mist; or the sheets of rain driving across Tobermory; or the traffic in Sauchiehall Street; Scottish pubs; Scottish whisky; Highland Games; gatherings of the clans; kilts, tartans and Mary Queen of Scots.

It must not be thought, however, that these Scottish affairs, Highland Games, clan gatherings, or reels, are simply sheepish fancy-dress charades put on for the benefit of tourists, like a Welsh eisteddfod or a Tyrolean evening in Austria. Gatherings of clans have a definite place in Highland life and would continue, even if no tourists were present. For one thing, the events themselves would have to be considerably better stage-managed if they were taken over by entertainments promoters in London. Nothing, for instance, could have been less impressive than the Gathering of Clan Campbell which I once witnessed in Oban, Argyllshire. For some mysterious reason, it took place early in the morning, and I was the only non-Campbell present. Some twenty people were there, including the chief, the Duke of Argyll, and a number of his chieftains, and we assembled on a street corner of Oban in the wet morning. The Campbells were wearing disused Army camouflaged gas capes against the pouring rain. After about ten minutes, the gathering dispersed, and I wondered why I had bothered to get up for it.

More impressive, later that afternoon, were the games. This was a social occasion like a fashionable race meeting. The women wore expensive tweeds and tartan skirts, the tartan cut, of course, diagonally. The men, Highlanders and Lowlanders alike, wore kilts and carried heavy, damp tartan plaids on their shoulders. It had, for the moment, stopped raining, and we tiptoed around in the mud, greeting friends, being introduced to friends of friends, calling them by their home addresses rather than by their names. Little interest was expressed in the games themselves. It is possible to become enthusiastic about sword dancing and about the splendid presence of some of the pipe majors, but it is difficult to become addicted to throwing the hammer or tossing the caber, events which are so much less impressive to watch than to read about. Most tedious of all, certainly, are those long half hours after it is decided that the caber is too long for the throwers, and that a foot or two of it must be sawed off. It is at these moments that one chats to one's friends or, if one is ill bred, strains for a glimpse of royalty.

In the evening comes the ball, the focal point of the gathering. This is even more of a social occasion: The ladies wear diamond tiaras and tartan sashes over their oyster-colored dresses; the men wear velvet coats and kilts and silver filigree sporrans and look like portraits of Bonnie Prince Charlie. All the dances are reels, and everybody present, duchess or deb or Sassenach, is expected to be foot-perfect, or he will be tapped on the shoulder by a steward and led from the floor. In a party of sixteen, I was the only man to wear trousers, for though I have two Highland grandmothers, this does not entitle me to wear a kilt. In return for this, I had taken special trouble to learn my reels beforehand, and when I found myself leading off in a recondite reel called the Machine Without Horses, I was undismayed. We danced all night, pausing only to drink champagne or eat supper or breakfast. In a Highland ball it is not possible to go home early, or the numbers for the sixteensome will be wrong. The last two hours were danced in broad daylight, the rain drumming down on the skylights of the Assembly Rooms. The last dance finished at eight o'clock in the morning, and we all were still there, remembering our steps, remembering one another's faces and names. It had been twenty-four hours nonstop since the gathering of the clan the previous morning, and it demonstrated that one of the great qualities of the Scots, even more than technical efficiency, is stamina.

In earlier centuries, I would have been allowed to wear a kilt and would have been able to choose the tartan myself. Portraits of clan chiefs by Henry Raeburn or Allan Ramsay in the Scottish National Gallery often show these distinguished gentlemen wearing the wrong tartans. At that time a man chose the tartan he liked best in the same way that today he chooses his tweeds; probably he chose the tartan of the place where he happened to be, because it was available. It was that methodical German the prince consort who, at the same time that he covered Balmoral Castle with miles of tartan carpet, reorganized the tartan system and laid down where and by whom each tartan could be worn. This recent rigidity is, however, giving way to the demands of tourism and export, and it is now possible for the American visitor, the Tanzanian businessman, the Swedish *au pair* girl, to choose and wear the tartan which suits him or her best and to wear it with distinction. French tartans, freely adapted from their Highland originals, are known as *façon écossais* or, in Scotland, Clan Bogus, and French girls, it must be admitted, look very nice in them.

Clan Bogus, indeed, is becoming bigger all the time, but this does not mean that the clan system itself is bogus or dead or even moribund. Alone in Britain, the clan system provides that sense of family relationship which is such a feature of, say, Italy. When a Macdonald from Edinburgh happens to meet a Macdonald from Adelaide, he will feel at once a kinship which he would not feel were both their surnames Smith. Even in the jet age the chief of a clan feels responsible for all its members and requests that they call on him should they happen to be near his castle. He or, in the case of Clan Macleod, she will often organize gatherings of the clan with representatives coming from all parts of the world. The gatherings at Dunvegan Castle, Skye, are justly celebrated, and happy is the Macleod who is able to be present.

As with other groups, clan pride is often founded on mutual hostility and indeed on internecine warfare. The Macdonalds have a particularly unfortunate history, having been massacred both by the Campbells at Glencoe and by the Macleods at the Bloody Stone in the Isle of Skye. Despite these disasters, they seem to have flourished and multiplied and emigrated, and the massacres in the gory past are forgiven, if not forgotten. On a holiday in the Isle of Skye, I was invited by the local laird to spend the day at his house. The hospitality was generous in the Highland tradition. Guests were invited to meet me for lunch, I was to spend the afternoon fishing his loch, and more guests were invited to join us for dinner. Both meals were convivial occasions. The talk was mainly of fishing and rock climbing, for both of which Skye is famous, but I noticed that the guests at lunch were Macleods, those at dinner were Macdonalds. Two centuries after the massacre at the Bloody Stone, my host was careful enough not to mix the members of the two clans, even over the dinner table.

The principal division, however, in Scotland is not between Macdonalds and Campbells or Macdonalds and Macleods but, as in England, between North and South, between Highlander and Lowlander. Like the English, the Scots are very mixed racially; the Romans referred to them as Picts and Scots, and there is no reason to think that either of these were the same as the Gaels or the other Celtic tribes which were pushed into Scotland by the successive waves of invasion farther south. There would indeed seem to be a great racial difference between a small man in Glasgow and a tall, lanky Highlander in Inverness. The position is confused by the fact that most Highlanders live in the Lowlands, probably working in the huge city of Glasgow. Many men in Glasgow or Edinburgh will, after a pint or two of Scotch ale, confide that they are really Gordons or Sutherland Highlanders and despise the Lowlanders among whom they are forced to live.

The same division between North and South exists, of course, strongly in Ireland, where the difference of race (and, following this, religion) between the Orangemen of Ulster and the inhabitants of Eire is even more violent. The clashes in Belfast between Protestants and Catholics stem from this incompatibility of temperament. The division also exists noticeably in Wales. The two halves have a language barrier, for, except in primary schools, Welsh is rarely encountered in South Wales. Even the train service between the two is so notoriously bad that travel from North to South is easier via London. This will involve a change of station in London, as North and South Wales come, rightly, under different regions of British Railways. In Wales, as in England, there is as little communication as possible between North and South.

The causes of this division are historical rather than racial. The Romans raided North Wales in subduing the rebellion of Caractacus and because the sacred isle of Anglesey or Mona was the headquarters of their enemies, the Druids. But they never really subdued it. The pattern was repeated by King Edward I in the thirteenth century. He was the Hammer of the Scots, and he succeeded in conquering Wales, too. But once again the conquest of the North was a token one, and the North Welsh were never really tamed. North Wales accordingly retained its ancient culture and its language and proudly regarded itself as the real Wales, despising the South, which had been truly conquered and occupied by the Normans.

The balance shifted abruptly in the nineteenth century. The demand for coal put the South sharply in the lead. Coal itself was called, with typical Welsh lyricism, black diamonds, and it attracted a sort of gold rush from impoverished hill farmers in other parts of Wales, including the North. The new mines and docks in and near Cardiff were a magnet to Welshmen from all over the principality and to many Irish as well. Eighty percent of the total ratable value of the whole of Wales was concentrated in Glamorgan. Cardiff became the most important city in Wales and was finally declared the official capital, to the dismay of Caernarvon, the ancient capital in the North. The heart of the Welsh was in the Rhondda Valley and the surrounding mining area—the grim, wet, slate-roofed cottages spread along the valleys. Opening up the mines was hard, dangerous work, but it was well paid. Miners drank champagne, which they nicknamed tintops. The North found itself despised and neglected, inhabited only by some sheep farmers, by bards orating and declaiming poetry in Welsh and by university professors celebrated for their extremist views on language, politics and nationalism. North Wales had become something of a joke and much fun was poked at Gorsedds and bardic crowns and ladies with bedgowns and black, tall, conical hats.

Richard Llewellyn's popular novel *How Green Was My Valley* dramatized the change in South Wales, how much was gained by the discovery of coal in the valleys and, in a sense, how much was lost. The Depression, once again, turned the whole account to pure loss. The slump hit South Wales as hard as anywhere else in the kingdom. Rhondda miners and Cardiff dockers were as unemployed and as desperate as Tyneside shipbuilders or Sheffield steelworkers. The North of England, has, in fact, made something of a comeback, perhaps temporarily, with modern textiles and chemicals, but coal has gone forever. As an apology, Britain's largest and most up-to-date steelworks has been opened at Port Talbot in South Wales, and there has been a certain, rather limited attempt to build up light industry nearby; the most spectacular gesture is the transfer of the Mint from the City of London to the ancient village of Llantrisant in Glamorgan, where the Black Prince once recruited a company of his archers. The black diamonds are to be replaced by decimal coins. But whether the new minters of the British coinage will ever be able to afford champagne is another matter.

The pendulum is now swinging back again to North Wales. Not, of course, commercially; agriculture, particularly marginal hill-farming agriculture, remains as depressed as ever, as depressed as coal mining. But owing to an unlikely combination of circumstances, the North has now found itself fashionable again. The cult of minority cultures, minority languages, minority nationalism has benefited the North. The growing popularity of rock climbing has opened up its wild and beautiful landscape; the investiture of the Prince of Wales at Caernarvon Castle has pinpointed both its history and its tourist possibilities. Welsh, the forgotten language, rediscovered and resurrected by earnest nationalistic professors, has become the exciting new language. The Prince of Wales has learned enough to be able to make fluent speeches of some length in it; schools, universities give it a high place on the curriculum; down in the South the rest follow suit. Even the lord mayor of Cardiff, who is an Irishman, admits that he is learning the language, though in his mouth, he says, it sounds like Chinese.

How much of this swing of influence in Wales is a quirk of fashion, a collection of gimmicks, is an arguable point, but it seems fairly certain that North Wales, far from the Golden Triangle, with no industry except slate quarrying and the rather parsimonious visits of campers, will remain poor in spite of its recent blaze of publicity. And despite the Welsh National Opera Company, Wales will remain a largely working-class culture. The Welsh princes were killed in battle a long time ago, resisting invaders, from Romans to Normans, and most of the ancient poetry in Welsh consists of laments for them. One of the first, in the late sixth century, is by Aneirin, mourning Owain, killed in an attack on the English:

Man in might, youth in years,
Courage in battle.
Swift long-maned stallions
Under the thigh of a fine lad.
Behind him, on the lean swift flank
His targe, broad and light,
Swords blue and bright
And fringes of goldwork. . . .
Quicker his blood to earth
Than to his wedding.
Quicker the crows were fed
Than we could bury him.

Seven centuries later Gruffud ab yr Ynad Coch wrote a lament for Llywelyn, the last Prince of independent Wales, killed in 1282.

Since Llywelyn is slain my mortal wit fails me.
The heart's gone cold under a breast of fear;

> Lust shrivels like dried brushwood.
> See you not the way of the wind and the rain?
> See you not oak-trees buffet together?
> See you not the sea stinging the land?
> See you not youth in travail?
> See you not the sun hurtling through the sky?
> And that the stars are fallen?

The princes gone, there is no difficulty nowadays in keeping up with the Joneses, for Jones never rose above the rank of sergeant. I have in front of me as I write the latest regimental list of the Welsh Guards, and I am happy to note that all the warrant officers at regimental headquarters are called Jones, and most of the other ranks in the companies, too. In this, at least, things have changed little since I was a serving officer in that regiment. Those with the surnames of Morgan or Roberts or Thomas were distinguished from one another by the last two figures of their regimental number and were known as Sergeant 58 Roberts, Guardsman 09 Morgan. But if they were simply known as Corporal 15, Guardsman 72, then everybody knew that their surnames were Jones. It was unnecessary to speak the monosyllable yet again. The officers, however—and here the question of class once again raises its head—were not called Jones. Often they seemed to have Scottish names like Wallace or Bruce, for Welsh heiresses, with no aristocracy of their own, liked to marry into the Scottish peerage. Jones, however, was acceptable in a Welsh Guards officer if it hyphened to something else and turned into a double-barreled name. The other half of the name had to be a Norman or Scottish name, as in Jones-Mortimer or Seymour-Jones or even Armstrong-Jones. When Mr. Armstrong-Jones married Princess Margaret, it symbolized the return of the Celts to power and influence in Britain, though the bulk of the Welsh people, radical, Socialist, working-class, nationalist, regretted the Armstrong part of the name.

It is indeed not only the Welsh, but the Celts as a whole who are making a comeback on the British scene. With the decline of the Normans and the frustration of the Smiths, it is more and more the Celts who are finding positions of influence in British life, particularly in intellectual, cultural and political worlds. However, it is a mistake to consider them as being Celts and therefore barely distinguishable from one another, members of the Celtic fringe, refugees from the Saxons or the Normans. Their characters are different; their histories are different; their races are different; the strange wild languages which they nurse like chicken breeders in the universities are different. What the three races (or, more exactly, seven races) have in common is a quick intelligence and a tendency to red hair and freckles, but this is not enough to override the historic animosity between them. The fights and sometimes the murders which go on between them in the slums of Manchester or Liverpool or Londonderry on Saturday nights derive largely from racialism and beer. The conquest of most of Britain by the English had at least the merit of keeping the Celtic races apart for a thousand years, until the great cities began to draw them together again. Without the English to separate them, the others soon come to blows, and this is perhaps the true lesson of the Arthurian legends.

Some of the differences of character may be noted easily. The Scots love to roam the world; the Welsh feel homesick if they have to go as far as London. One of the problems of organizing choral societies or opera companies in London used to be that the Welsh singers, who formed an indispensable part of any such music-making organization, often could not resist the temptation to catch the first train back to Cardiff. This is, of course, now changing, and Welsh singers are learning to move around the concert halls and opera houses of the world with the same confidence as Italians or Austrians. But the homesickness remains. A Scotsman may speak nostalgically of Scotland, but a Welshman will actually wish to return to Wales. The tall, craggy Highlander is not even a cousin of the small, emotional, extrovert Welshman, so easily moved to laughter or tears, enjoying a good joke or a good funeral with equal abandon. The Scotsman may thrill silently at the droning of the pipes, but the Welshman prefers a different sort of music, singing his hymns in four or even eight parts and even now sometimes naming his children Haydn or Handel (not Bach, which is Welsh for small).

The Welsh are a nation not only of singers and organists, but of orators and preachers; they have the gift of the gab. The *hwyl* is a hereditary gift and will move audiences to cheers or tears in chapels or political meetings. It travels well too, even as far as Westminster. Three of the most persuasive and spellbinding speakers in the House of Commons this century have been Welshmen—Lloyd George, Aneurin Bevan and Roy Jenkins. Later it was not always possible to recall exactly, still less to agree with, what they had said. None of them has possessed the gift of the memorable phrase which was Churchill's specialty. The *hwyl* does not depend on that; it is more a form of spontaneous poetry. The Word, which is described in the opening sentences of St. John's Gospel, is identified by the Welsh with the *hwyl,* and this part of the Gospel has always been held to be especially holy. When the Welsh began to take surnames, it is not surprising that most of them took the name of John or Jones.

The Welsh have produced the most famous British lyric poet since Byron—Dylan Thomas. And in their lyric gifts, as in their picturesque and well-publicized private lives, the two men have a thread in common. Interesting, however, is the comment of the Irish film actor Richard Harris when chosen to play the Welsh poet in a film. Asked why he, an Irishman, with no physical resemblance to Dylan Thomas, had been given the part, Mr. Harris replied that the Irish were destroyers but the Welsh were conservers, and in this characteristic, Dylan Thomas was more Irish than Welsh.

Though the intellectuals and professors may hope to keep alive the separate minority cultures of the three Celtic nations, such ambitions do not form part of the projected economic future for Britain. The Celtic fringe will have no place in the Golden Triangle. The European Hong Kong, which, in the town planners' dream, is to spread over the whole of south and most of central England, is intended to be multiracial. This huge experiment in urban environmental design, this giant conurbation (the words "town" and "city" are, it seems, obsolete) is intended to attract all that is best in the English, the Scots, the Welsh and the Irish, not to mention the West Indians, the Asians and others seeking a livelihood. The rest of the British Isles, apparently is to be left to the grouse shooters, the rock climbers, the salmon fishers (if there should still be any salmon) and those catering for the needs of tourism. In the southern conurbation, the Celts will be forced once again to live alongside one another as they do today in Manchester, Liverpool and Cardiff. Whether they will preserve their traditional animosities or whether they will intermarry and merge their separate identities is yet to be seen. Should they succeed in blending their racial qualities, a new and exciting people may yet be born, and this may be the consolation, maybe the only consolation, for being forced to live in the conurbational area.

23

THE TIP OF THE ICEBERG

⁂ This book, so far, has described the ordinary Britishman in his home, his factory, his office, his garden or his pub. It was intended as a portrait of a man who is both extraordinary and ordinary, a man who, though in theory he runs the country, is in practice ignored and unpublicized. He has probably never been to the Kings Road or Carnaby Street, any more than he has seen the changing of the Guard or the Tower of London. Though he will watch television for several hours a day, he is unlikely to have appeared on it. Though he reads his newspaper carefully, he is unlikely ever to see his own name there. He is part of the great submerged mass, the unseen bulk of the iceberg, which cannot be photographed, but which can occasionally make its impact with devastating effect.

It is, however, the glittering tip of the iceberg which attracts the attention and the cameras. Britain is largely judged abroad by the performance and the personalities of a relatively small number of people, who command a prestige and an influence infinitely greater than their weight of numbers. It is on them that the television lights fall. It is their faces which appear in the newspapers and on the magazine covers, and it is their utterances which are taken down by reporters and expanded into widely read interview articles. They are the leaders and the arbiters of taste and opinion and fashion. And because of the effectiveness of modern publicity methods, their views are projected more widely, their names are more likely to be household words than those of their predecessors in earlier decades. There are, it has been said, approximately 100 people in Britain today who make the news and the noise, crowd the headlines and steal the evenings of the telly watchers. Exactly who the 100 select people are is bound to be a matter of some controversy, though many of the names on the list, any list, will be generally agreed. Other names will be less universally acceptable, for every Britishman likes to think he is free to choose, even if the choice is very limited. I am prepared to stick my neck out and lay it across the chopping block as readily as anyone else. I have compiled my own list of the hundred names to drop in Britain on January 1, 1970. It can be found at the end of this book as an Appendix.

There are certain points which can be noted about the list. Every name, without exception, is on the list through the sheer ability of its owner. Hereditary privilege or wealth by itself has little place in Swinging Britain. The list embraces people from widely different age-groups, activities, social classes and political beliefs, but a point in common is that all of them, no matter what part of the country they may be from, achieve their successes and probably live in London. Some of them are British by adoption, others travel so widely that they come to London only at intervals, yet London remains for them the place where, above all, it is necessary to succeed and be known. They all have a flair for publicity and public relations, and they all have personalities which intrigue the public that follows their movements and their words. It would be physically impossible for anyone to admire all the hundred names on my list, though, human nature being what it is, it would be possible, just possible, for somebody to hate them all. But either way they cannot be ignored. Their influence on the British people is almost limitless, and it is they who create the international image of Britain.

The list contains representatives of sport, science, show business, the arts and the four main political attitudes existing in Britain today, attitudes which have little to do with the formal political parties. For convenience, the four attitudes may be labeled the New Left, the New Right, the Old Left and the Old Right. The traditional loyalties have regrouped to meet new situations and new problems, and as the sixties move into the seventies, the differences of opinion are sharp indeed. The conflict between the Old Left and the New Left may be symbolized in the public quarrel between the *Daily Mirror,* representing the Old Left, and the *New Statesman,* representing the New Left, on the subject of whether hippies are valuable members of society. The New Right and the Old Right have their disagreements, too, most conspicuously in the area of colored immigration. The New Left and the New Right naturally disagree on almost all points, though sometimes respecting each other professionally. But the Old Left and the Old Right have tended to draw together, to forget their differences, other than the formal party labels, to coalesce into the vast, submerged and largely despised majority which can be safely ignored by the trend setters and those who operate the levers of power.

Party politics have moved a long way from the days of Baldwin and Keir Hardie. Occasionally new loyalties seem to run diagonally; the New Right has something in common with the Old Left, the Old Right with the New Left. On the last day of 1969 I heard a diehard Tory exploding with fury about the evils of big business and giant companies, for all the world as if he were a dedicated Marxist, and the same evening a steelworker, a dedicated trade unionist and Labour supporter, uttering what were to me the saddest words of 1969, "If only Enoch Powell wasn't a Tory!"

It was Disraeli who coined the phrase "The Two Nations," and Britain is still as divided as it was in his day or in the centuries before him. But it is now divided in a new way: The old divisions have healed, only for new ones to open, often cutting at right angles across the old. Where the original divisions have not healed, they have often been confined to limited areas where they are a local rather than a national problem. Others are covered over with a blend of good manners and tolerance. There is, for example, no further open conflict between Norman and Saxon. The old feud between Celt and Saxon is only apparent at certain times in certain areas of North Wales and Scotland. The division between Protestant and Catholic which bedeviled Tudor England is now only to be found in Northern Ireland, and there the conflict is of racial rather than of theological origin.

Disraeli speaking of the Two Nations was referring to the rich and the poor, but in modern Britain, here, too, the difference is less sharply marked. There are certainly many rich people in Britain today, and many more poor ones, but high taxation, full employment, a rising standard of living, slum clearance and the welfare state have made the differences less marked and less painful. The extremes of great wealth and great poverty, which are so conspicuous elsewhere, are rarer and therefore less noticeable in Britain. The division into color groups—white, black, brown, yellow—has not yet reached the critical scale of conflict to be found in some other countries (though it is possible to feel considerable uneasiness on this point and to wonder if this may not in due course become the next major division in Britain).

Nor is the main division in the country one of class. During and after World War II the hope was often, though not universally, expressed that Britain would become a classless nation. This, as everyone knows, did not happen. Class consciousness was as firmly entrenched in Britain as in every other country in the world. What the British did achieve was to make it possible for an individual to move from one class to another with comparative ease. Much has been written in this book about the various class differences in, say, eating habits or holidays. But these very differences make it easier for a man to move up or down the social scale as he chooses. He has only to change his breakfast beverage and the name of his midday meal, and British tolerance will do the rest. He does not have to change his clothes, as these, whether they are maxicoat or dark suit, are classless. His accent, with a little care, he will be able to move to a mid-British or perhaps even a mid-Atlantic accent, and provided he is careful to stay away from grouse-moors, he will be accepted in whatever class he chooses to join. I myself have found it easy to move down several classes. In my experience on the factory floor I was hardly ever aware of any social differences between myself and my workmates, and the occasional comment was always made with great good humor. I was more aware of the general friendliness. By accepting the job and the conditions, I had become "one of us" and was welcomed accordingly. It is also possible in Britain today to move right outside the class system by being an interesting personality or by having achieved something remarkable. Such a person does not need to change his breakfast habits or his accent. This sort of fame is hard to achieve, harder even than learning to kill grouse in middle age, but the names of a hundred who have succeeded in this are listed in the Appendix, and it will be noticed that they come from every social class.

The Two Nations in Britain today exist, I have said, as strongly as ever before, but the division is not racial or religious or financial or social or political. It is something else, something less obvious, less easy to identify; it is the division between the expert and the nonexpert. One of the British passions, as has been noted in earlier chapters, is the passion for imports. The Britishman likes to fill his kitchen and his refrigerator with the foods of other, more remote countries. He likes to fill his garden with the shrubs and trees of more distant and exotic countries. And within the last twenty years, he has begun importing ideas from abroad, somewhat indiscriminately, as with his plants and shrubs, indifferent to whether they conflict with their new environment or with one another. The ideas which the British have imported during the last decade or two, include light punishments, free love and heavy taxation from Scandinavia; squeeze finance from Switzerland; business efficiency, market research, management training, road design, drugs, pornography, protest and violence from America; Oriental mysticism, nonviolence and sitar music from India; Maoism from

China; and Marxism, though it originated in the British Museum, reimported from the international intellectual circuit. Above all, the British have imported the idea of an expert, the theory that on any given subject, however way out, there is a trained expert with a string of letters after his name, who is more qualified to pronounce on the subject than anybody else.

Many of the ideas imported are, of course, incompatible. The idea of capital growth at all costs does not lie down well beside the idea of world revolution. Nonviolence is not a good partner for violence. Business efficiency is far removed from psychedelic dreams. But for each of these viewpoints there is a body of expert opinion, able to support its arguments with a quantity of equally expert evidence. And the ordinary Britishman, as has also been noted earlier in this book, views expert evidence with the greatest suspicion. He regards warily the expert who assures him that higher taxation is in the national economic interest and the expert who assures him that a wider and freer use of psychedelic drugs is in the national social interest. The two experts, though they may differ on all points, are nevertheless closer to each other than they are to the ordinary Britishman in his villa or his pub. They are the new elite, and the Britishman regards them with the same distrust and, to be fair, the same awe with which he once regarded his Norman liege lord.

The division between the Two Nations is as clear-cut as ever it was and, to the observer, as ominous. Experts tend to form a club, a mutual admiration society. The expert in, say, airport design, while tolerating no other ideas in his own subject, will readily accept expert opinion in a different subject. The town planning expert will respect the psychiatric expert and vice versa. Outside the inner circle of experts the ordinary Britishman is left, bewildered, ignored, uncertain whether he is to protest, to submit or to admire—in the mid-twentieth century, expertise is frequently a matter for admiration. In my appended list of 100 swinging names, all the people are experts in their own subjects. More than their ties with London, more than their classlessness, their expertise is the final bond which ties them all together.

Politically, the cult of the expert has meant the end of democracy in Britain, as it has been known for several hundred years. It has produced a situation where, at a general election, the three political parties produce identical platforms of ideas, because they are all advised by the same experts. On such major issues as British entry into the Common Market, capital punishment and taxation, the British electorate finds that all the parties recommend the same policies. Judging from the public opinion polls, there is widespread misgiving about whether entry into the Common Market will ultimately benefit either the British economy or the individual Britishman, about whether lesser punishments inevitably lead to lesser crimes, and about whether higher taxation helps to reduce the cost of living.

It used to be believed that such widely held opinions, whether right or wrong, should at least be represented in the British Parliament. But no party accepts this principle now. A member of the House of Commons preparing a speech on a technical subject, such as pensions, will consult the experts around him. He will note the official views of his party, which are likely to be the same as the views of the theoretically opposing party. He will keep a cautious eye on the whips. He will turn an attentive ear to the various pressure groups which may be trying to lobby him. Should he receive a retainer or salary from some outside organization or company, he will pay careful attention to its viewpoint. He will read articles on the subject in expert journals until he himself has become an expert. He will not, however, bother to find out the views of his constituents. His speech, when he finally delivers it, will probably therefore be unpopular with them, but if he delivers it effectively, it may increase his chances of promotion within his party.

Many Britishmen thus find themselves in the frustrating position of being, in a democracy, unrepresented at Westminster. Occasionally the suggestion is made that on matters of great public controversy, such as entry into the Common Market, a national referendum should be held. This is, of course, immediately vetoed by all politicians of all parties, by all experts.

It would be, it is said, the negation of leadership. As an exercise in formal logic, it is always instructive to hear a Member of Parliament explaining why a referendum is undemocratic. Far better, it is said, is a massive reeducation of the people through mass media, pop culture and increasing the number of university places. Those of a more revolutionary frame of mind may actually advocate minority government in the interests of the majority. And the ordinary Britishman is left bewildered, half dazzled, half suspicious. He gazes with admiration at the shining tip of the iceberg, proud that it should be so great and so beautiful. He basks in the reflected glamor of the famous and the trend setters. He is tempted to follow them, to be as swinging and with-it as they. Britain has always been a trend-setting nation and the Britishman a trend-setting person, and in the performance of the swinging 100 he will find much to appreciate and admire. But if his traditional instincts or the native common sense, which he prizes so highly, warn him to beware, to be distrustful or even to dig his heels in, nobody will notice or even care.

It has been said that Westminster Hall is the place where democracy was founded. This is perhaps to oversimplify, to underestimate the contributions to democratic thought made in Athens, Philadelphia and Paris. But the point is still valid. The Mother of Parliaments began her sessions in Westminster Hall, and from there her ideas and her system spread throughout the world, not always with equal success; parliamentary ideals were not always appropriate to the new areas and the new conditions. Now it seems that they are hardly appropriate in Britain either. Power has moved from the debating chambers to the Cabinet, the committees, the ministries, the lobbies, the newspaper offices, the television studios, the universities and the organized demos. As historians we can say that British democracy started in the Palace of Westminster in the seventeenth century and that 300 years later, in the same place, it died.

24

AS OTHERS SEE US

⁂ At Expo '67 in Montreal, one of the exhibits in the British Pavilion had the caption "The British are they . . . dignified, stuffed shirt, chivalrous, humbugs, just shy?" The questions were not answered. There are some points, the British feel, which are best decided by an independent jury. The opinions held of them by the citizens of other nations are of somewhat masochistic interest to the British and are usually reprinted as news items in the British papers. The opinions of others are always interesting, never more so than when they differ from the homegrown idea of oneself, positively hilarious when they differ from each other.

Yet the outside view of the British character is revealing, all the more for not being homogeneous. Whether the diversity of views is due to the multifaceted brilliance of the British character, sparkling on all sides and in all lights like a diamond, or whether it is simply due to a failure of communication is a question which naturally the British cannot answer. But to help build a composite cubist picture of the Britishman seen by others, here is a ragbag of impressions.

A tall and aristocratic Spaniard once said to me, "The British are like the Spaniards, because you respect rank." A French girl said to me, "You love your British traditions, your coronations, your Guards. I love them, too."

Georges Mathieu, the French Tachiste painter, in his celebrated series of posters for Air France, portrayed the Britishman as a guardsman, a baroque flourish of scarlet tunic and bearskin. An American girl I met on a transatlantic liner returning from her first visit to Britain, and indeed to Europe, told me that she thought the British lived too much in the past. My cabinmate on the same trip told me about the Ceremony of the Keys at the Tower of London, a ceremony of which I had not previously heard, and gave his opinion that the British spent too much of their time in places like the Tower of London. The new nickname for the British, used by journalists on both sides of the Atlantic, is the Neophiliacs, those who follow crazily after anything new.

The French have a term for the new young generation of Britishmen—*les blousons noirs.* This, in theory, means leather-jacketed young men and girls. These are named after the Rockers, the tough young hooligans, male and female, who roared into southern seaside towns some ten years ago to fight their rivals, the Mods, and caused a considerable amount of havoc. The phrase *blouson noir* used indiscriminately for either Rocker or Mod has now been extended to cover any girl in a miniskirt or a maxicoat, any young man with long hair, any girl in a cat suit, any boy in a military uniform, debutantes in pajama suits, their polite and docile escorts in velvet coats and lace cravats, the Beatles, Lord Snowden, hitchhikers, drug peddlers, round-the-world yachtsmen—just about everybody except the Duke of Edinburgh. A famous and much-quoted American view is that Britain is now sinking, giggling, into the sea.

The views of immigrants who have come to live among us provide many revealing glimpses of our character and way of life. According to a recent poll, the Asians find us lazy, overfond of gambling, drinking and loose living. The West Indian immigrants, on the other hand, find us a dull lot who have lost the capacity for enjoying life. Both immigrant races, however, appreciate the British qualities of fair play and justice. They were, they said, taught to expect this on their arrival in Britain and have not been disappointed. One West Indian stated, "Nobody molests us. Government is freer. Life here is very free." Many of the Asian families criticize British moral laxity as demonstrated in the wearing of miniskirts. They also disapprove of British laws prohibiting child marriages. They criticize the British for their lack of feeling in the family, for the failure of communication between generations and for their refusal to let old people live with the rest of the household. A Union leader in England, a Pakistani, stated, "We are now in a position to paralyze the entire transport and hospital system of the country. Our revenge is reaching out to strike at the eye of the octopus." An American immigrant, a lady married to a Britishman and resident now in England, stated, "I had never realized until I came to live in England what a lot of original eccentrics you all are and what conformists the Americans are."

An American commentator on the social scene has worked out that the basic characteristic of a nation is conveyed in its favorite swearword, as in the French *sale* or *merde*. The British equivalent is "bloody," and this shows the essential bloodthirsty nature of the British people. The British are also criticized for never having, except in wartime, draft or conscription, which handicaps their contribution to NATO and Western defense.

Recently the American Undersecretary of State stated that Britain's trouble was that she had lost her place in the world with the loss of her empire and had not found a new role. Another phrase often heard in the United States is that Britain is currently suffering a nervous breakdown after the loss of her empire. Within the Commonwealth, the Prime Minister of an East African country has stated that Britain's trouble is that she still thinks she is the ruler of a large empire and does not realize that she is simply now one member among others of a commonwealth of nations. An Asian Prime Minister, however, has stated that Britain is now tired and has lost her will to lead and to be the leader of the Commonwealth.

A view often heard in New York is that the British, unlike the Germans or the Japanese, are lazy and won't work. In the

Soviet Union, particularly in the schools of the small towns and villages, the view is freely expressed that the British work barbarously long hours for their pitiless masters, small starved children working eighteen hours a day in the cotton mills or pulling coal trucks down mine tunnels.

Novelists, playwrights, film directors often provide perceptive glimpses of the character of a people, and the British are unfortunate in that so few foreign writers have chosen to describe them. One may however mention that the heroines of Hemingway's first two novels were both British women, both nurses or ex-nurses, both extremely sexy, one sleeping with everyone she could find, the other getting into the hospital bed with her own patient, neither behaving in a way which would have given much pleasure to Florence Nightingale. André Maurois and Pierre Daninos have both described British officers in some detail, showing them as lovable, reserved, eccentric, amused and rather silent men. Françoise Sagan set her play *Le Cheval Evanoui* in an English country house and saw the aristocratic family as being sport-mad, driving their harassed and limping French guests from the hunting field to the tennis court and back. Ionesco in *The Bald Soprano* portrayed the British family feverishly working at their *broderie anglaise* and reasonably cross when their guests were thirty seconds late. The Italian film director Antonioni set his film *Blow-Up* in swinging London and showed the British as a race of frivolous, shallow, flibbertigibbet voyeurs—the current cult of the photographer being the apotheosis of the voyeur.

A waitress in a restaurant in a town in Kansas asked me where we learned to speak English. I explained that we were English and had come from England. She exclaimed, "But you all speak English so well, even the children!" A German girl from the Rhineland wrote to me that she had been taught in her geography lessons that Britain was not yet an industrialized country and that she imagined the sheep following their shepherd through the winding streets of the villages near London. A French farmer assured me that we had no beer in England, naturally, because our weather was too wet to grow barley or any crops. He had been taught this, he explained, by his schoolteacher. The more usual French view of British weather, however, is that we live and work in a permanent pea-souper fog, right through the year. British weather has made two conspicuous appearances in the world of opera: in the second act of Wagner's *Tristan und Isolde,* which is set in Cornwall, and the last act of Verdi's *Falstaff,* which takes place in Windsor Great Park. Both composers have evoked, with great care, the atmosphere of a hot, cloudless summer night.

The reader of this book will by now know how many of the opinions expressed in this chapter contain, in my view, a large element of truth, how many are half-truths and how many are pure fantasy.

25

BLINDFOLD INTO THE SEVENTIES

⁂ Piccadilly Circus at midnight, New Year's Eve. Good-bye to the sixties, hello to the seventies. A cold winter's night with the great neon signs flashing and turning and a carnival atmosphere in the streets. Paper hats, paper streamers, paper whistles. All the cars customized, painted gaily in psychedelic colors, solid to the roof with passengers, like sardines in a tin. All the passengers yelling "Happy New Year" at everybody. A giant council dustcart, incredibly passing through the Circus at this moment, cheered to the echo. Girls in ankle-length maxicoats kissing the patrolling policemen. Myself pointing out the most amorous of the policemen with the words "That's the one that likes the girls." The policeman overhearing, reacting by kissing my wife, shaking my hand and wishing me a very happy New Year, sir. Except for the occasional bellicose drunk, an atmosphere of great good humor and euphoric gaiety. The American hippie who had camped all autumn on the steps of the Eros statue shouting at intervals, "You gotta learn to hate. You British don't understand how to hate," had disappeared together with his followers. Eros, the god of love, survived, and the British, uncertain and uneasy about what the seventies might bring, were responding to the changing decade in typical fashion; they were making a joke of it.

Around the Circus were the newspaper stalls, giving the last editions of the evening papers, the first editions of the new morning papers, all marking the occasion with suitable articles. For some weeks the British press had been sadly saying farewell to the Swinging Sixties, taking their readers on a nostalgic tour through the gayest, the most frivolous and the most outrageous decade for a long time. What fun it all was, they all seemed to be saying, we know we weren't always as serious as perhaps we ought to have been, but we didn't do too badly, we certainly enjoyed ourselves. Good-bye, a regretful, wistful good-bye to the Swinging Sixties.

About the future the journalists were understandably more cautious, some of them recalling the failure of the journalists ten years earlier to forecast the Swinging Sixties. One or two suggested tentatively that the party was over, the champagne going flat, and that, in a year or two's time, the only thing still swinging would be the pendulum on its way back. The new decade would perhaps be the Serious Seventies, dedicated to solemn idealism and long words. Some of the trend setters forecast hopefully that the new decade would finally see the end of the Establishment and of such institutions as family life, marriage, work, the monarchy and war. The more technically informed writers tried to evoke for us the automated, computerized world of the seventies, a world without offices, secretaries, typewriters, filing cabinets, cash, checks, credit cards, factory hands, assembly lines, farmers, farms or hedges—those symbols of Britain which would have been cut down to allow more scope for huge, automatic driverless tractors, controlled remotely from a distant switchboard. Alternatively, the hedges might remain, in a wild, uncared-for state, because the whole of British agriculture would be abandoned during the next decade and all food imported from abroad.

I found that these forecasts were usually received with a certain reserve. Perhaps the imagination of the ordinary Britishman was insufficient for him to envisage such a world, or perhaps the more cynically minded, with longer memories, recalled some of the forecasts of the past—for instance, the assertion made in the thirties that the motorcar would soon be obsolete, as everybody would go everywhere by private plane. Whatever was going to happen in the seventies, people seemed to be saying, and a great deal was obviously going to happen, it would not necessarily be what the experts foresaw. As for those writers determined to enter the new decade on a cheery note, who forecast that the seventies would see the entry of Britain into the Common Market and the consequent end of all her economic difficulties, a satisfactory drop in the crime figures, an increased standard of living and the end of the traffic problem, the Britishman preferred to wait and see. He had had expert reassurance before.

I do not propose to add my voice, however tentatively, to those of the brave men who dare to peer into the future and then commit their guesses to print. But it seems to me that a key factor will probably be the character of the British people, which I have attempted to analyze in this book and which, in a changing world, provides a stable influence. The phenomenon known as Swinging London shook the world. This was not the image which the foreigner had of London and Londoners. Some drastic change, it was thought, must have taken place in the British character. But the historians are aware that such periods of hectic gaiety have occurred in Britain before—for instance, Restoration England and the 1920's—and are part of the pattern of British life. Of course, many of the aspects of London in the sixties were international, and the ideas which inspired them were imported from abroad: drugs, student revolt, demonstrations in the streets, pop art, pornography, nudity on the stage, four-letter words in books, sexual license—London was not the only city to have these and cannot even claim them as her own invention. It is more revealing to consider the aspects of Swinging London which were particular. If we do so, we find that there has been no great change in the British character. The British have always been doing these things on and off.

The two aspects of Swinging London which most shocked the French were long hair for men and miniskirts for girls. But the sixties were not the first time that the length of men's hair was a controversial point. It was, after all, the most conspicuous factor which divided the two sides in the English Civil War. The clothes of the sixties, the miniskirts, the maxicoats, the trouser suits, the parodies of uniforms, turned the West End of London into a bizarre carnival. They may not have been in strictly good taste, but they did make the British girl, emerging from the dark little boutique in the Kings Road or Carnaby Street, deafened by pop music, seem the prettiest girl in the world. The British have always had a taste for extreme fashions. In a pavilion in Isfahan in Iran there is a mural showing the British ambassadress at the court of the shah. The mural shows the English lady naked to the waist, and the guide explains wryly that the Persians had been amazed by the fashions of Stuart England and the amount of bosom which was exposed, and the artist had thought it justifiable to exaggerate a little. Gambling in London was another innovation which shook the world. In no other world capital is gambling permitted as it is in London, and the foreigner found it hard to believe that the gambling center of the world was neither Monte Carlo nor Las Vegas but within a few hundred yards of Buckingham Palace. But here again the British were only following their tradition. They have always been a great nation of gamblers, and it seemed only logical to add roulette and baccarat to racing and football pools.

Less surprising, perhaps, was the discovery that London was now a major center for the arts. The historical pattern is that, when a period of imperial glory ends, there is usually an outburst of artistic creativity; Spain in the seventeenth century and France in the nineteenth century provide clear examples of this. London is a town full of new art galleries, large and small, prosperous and struggling. London is a town where sixty new novels are published every week. London, once known as *Das Land ohne Musik,* has five full-time symphony orchestras, two opera houses and a quantity of less ambitious but equally professional groups. The performer from abroad who wishes to make his international reputation has to succeed in London.

It will be difficult for him or her to find an evening when one of the concert halls is free. If the concert is a success, he may have to wait for two years before the concert hall is free again, by which time his name may have been forgotten among all the others. London is the town with the most newspapers and magazines in the world. As for the theater, London has not known such a flowering of new talent since the Elizabethans.

At the time of the coronation of Queen Elizabeth II in 1953 it was widely suggested that the British were about to become New Elizabethans. The new reign under such a happily named queen would give the British a new start and a new impetus. But then, as one crisis, one humiliation followed another, the phrase was quietly dropped. Too much had been banked upon a single name; not enough allowance had been made for differing circumstances and centuries. The new queen had a very different character and opportunities from those of her namesake; yet another forecast had been proved wrong. But looking back now, we can see that the present reign does, in fact, have many similarities with that of the first Queen Elizabeth. The mistake was in misunderstanding the character of Elizabethan England and confusing it vaguely with Victorian England. Elizabethan England was a small, weak country cut off from Europe and threatened by the greater powers of Spain and France. It had recently lost its last foreign possession, Calais. The country was beset by economic crises, which were only temporarily solved by capturing Spanish galleons; by crises of conscience, the great religious divide; by the unending struggle for power. The country was full of both despair and hope. England, at the end of the sixteenth century, had, to borrow a phrase from another context, lost its old role and had not yet found a new one.

"Tired Britain" is a phrase sometimes heard during the present reign, but the Elizabethans were tired too. One thinks of Sir Philip Sidney's lines:

> With how sad steps, O Moon, thou climb'st the skies,
> How silently and with how wan a face.

But at both times people were able to shake off their weariness and take part in great voyages of exploration. Then, as now, there was the wish to sail around the world in small boats, for reasons which can still not be coherently explained to the outsider. At both times there was a great cult of youth, one of the saddest cults, implying as it does, a long slow decline. I recently heard a young girl saying that she was going to be twenty in a few weeks' time. The thought gave her no pleasure. "The best years of my life will be over," she commented sadly. I thought of Sir Walter Raleigh's lines:

> Even such is time, that takes in trust
> Our youth, our joys, our all we have.
> And pays us but with age and dust.

Elizabethan drama has already been mentioned, but one may perhaps add its poetry, its music and its painting to help draw the parallel with the present day. In considering modern fashion, we can recall Shakespeare's line: "Difference of sex no more we knew." And a little later Donne was able to write: "Full nakedness, all joys are due to thee." The parallels should, of course, not be stressed too strongly, but it seems that the experts who prophesied a new Elizabethan age were not too wide of the mark.

Whether the new Elizabethan age will continue in the seventies is not clear. The British are far from united on their view of themselves. Mr. Edward Heath, the Conservative Prime Minister, said during 1969, "Britain may not be a super-power compared with America or Russia, but we offer the rest of the world an example of achievement through the character of the British people. So long as this is true, we shall have that self-confidence which earns us the respect of the rest of the world." The British are proud of the British character. At about the same time Mr. Kenneth Tynan stated, "England is a much more perverse and decadent country than the United States"—another view of the British character, but spoken with equal pride.

The particular facets of the British character which will

endure most tellingly into the seventies are a matter for conjecture. Will the Permissive Society go farther and wider and higher? Or will it remain stabilized at about its present level, thus far and no farther? Or will there be a backlash of Puritanism? There are advocates of all three points of view, and it is too early yet to say who will win. Will marriage be an obsolete and archaic institution by 1980, to be recalled by historians with mirth? Or will it continue in its present devalued and rather fluid form? Or will it achieve new levels of stability and respectability? Will the monarchy have been abandoned in favor of a people's republic, or will it become more beloved than ever before? We may here note the view of Mr. Arthur Koestler, who forecasts that both marriage and the monarchy will continue in their present forms, largely because nobody can think of anything better to put in their place. The monarchy in particular is patently such an unattractive job that only centuries of hereditary dedication could enable anyone to tackle it.

But the question of whether a new wave of Puritanism is about to arrive is carefully left unanswered by all forecasters. It could well happen, as it happened before, under Henry IV, under Cromwell and under Queen Victoria. The periodic wish for it is an essential and historic part of the British character. But should it recur again, it should be referred to as the Old Puritanism and not as the New Puritanism. The New Puritanism is already with us; it is a built-in flaw in the Permissive Society. It consists of the theory that you may do anything you like, write anything you like—as long as nobody enjoys it. In the Permissive Society, pornography must be as widespread as possible, but nobody must get a kick out of it. I am prepared to risk one forecast for the seventies, and that is that the New Puritanism will not survive through the decade. It is completely out of character for the British.

I am, however, not prepared to guess what will take its place, but it will no doubt be far from boring. Britain is, of course, not the only trend-setting country in the world. But the record of British firsts throughout the centuries has been remarkable:

from parliamentary government to climbing the Matterhorn; from beheading a king to miniskirts. And the world should note carefully and perhaps with some apprehension the British performance in the seventies. It may well follow suit.

Every decade has its particular voice, the voice of someone who embodies the spirit of the times, though this is not always recognizable till later. In the forties the voice was obviously that of Churchill, the historic British voice, growling defiance, invoking heroism. In the later forties, we should notice the undramatic voice of Attlee, who brought about a major social revolution so quietly as to provoke no subsequent backlash. In the fifties the voice was that of John Osborne, the angry young man, frustrated, certain that something had gone wrong, but uncertain just where or why. In the sixties, the voice was that of Paul McCartney, the high whine singing, in a stormy world, about love and flowers.

Who will be the voice of Britain in the seventies? Many people hope that it will be the voice of Mrs. Grundy, severe and disapproving, intent on reintroducing capital punishment, flogging, censorship and stern morality. Others hope that the voice will be that of a homosexual, pot-smoking Indian immigrant, capering naked on an apron stage, screaming obscenities at his adoring public. It is fervently to be hoped that a third voice will be found to speak for Britain in the seventies, one which will avoid either of these extremes. Happily, this may well be the case, for the British have always had, in dilemmas of this sort, a talent for working out an effective compromise, and this should be of great value to them in the uncertain decade which lies ahead.

More spectacular, however, is likely to be that other British talent, which should not be forgotten—the genius for the unexpected. And how this will show itself in the seventies is something which not even the most expert of experts dares guess.

Appendix

THE 100 NAMES TO DROP IN BRITAIN
A PERSONAL SELECTION

Leo Abse
Lindsay Anderson
Sheila Armstrong
David Bailey
Gordon Banke
Daniel Barenboim
Jacqueline Barenboim
The Duke of Bedford
Richard Rodney Bennett
Jane Birkin
Robert Bolt
Christopher Booker
John Bowen
Asa Briggs
Benjamin Britten
Brigid Brophy
Richard Burton
Lord Campbell of Eskan
Agatha Christie
Julie Christie
Petula Clark
Lord Constantine
Henry Cooper
Francis Crick
Richard Crossman
Alan Davie
Colin Davis
Simon Dee
Jack de Manio
Bernadette Devlin
Basil d'Oliveira
Benni Efrat
Barry England
Sir Geraint Evans
Dame Margot Fonteyn
John Fowle
Peter Frew
David Frost
Sir Frederick Gibberd
Denis Hamilton
Gina Hathorn
David Hicks
Lord Holford
Tony Jacklin
Mick Jagger
Maudie James
Roy Jenkins
Ann Jones

Gwyneth Jones
Tom Jones
Sean Kenny
The Bishop of Kingston-on-Thames
Robin Knox-Johnston
Arthur Koestler
Osbert Lancaster
Danny La Rue
Edmund Leach
John le Carré
John Lennon
Doris Lessing
The Earl of Longford
Sir Bernard Lovell
Lulu
Michael McCrum
Roger McGough
Cliff Michelmore
Dom Moraes
Desmond Morris
Earl Mountbatten of Burma, O.M.
Malcolm Muggeridge
V. S. Naipaul
Lord Olivier
Yoko Ono
John Osborne
Peter O'Toole
Brian Patten
Harold Pinter
Enoch Powell
Mary Quant
Frederic Raphael
Vanessa Redgrave
Bridget Riley
Lord Robens
Lord Snow
The Earl of Snowdon
Muriel Spark
John Stephen
Norman St. John Stevas
Lord Stokes
Tom Stoppard
Tarig Ali
Penelope Tree
Kenneth Tynan
Peter Ustinov
Laurens van der Post
The Prince of Wales
Dame Irene Ward
Dame Veronica Wedgwood, O.M.
Anthony Wedgwood Benn
Baroness Wootton

Index

Academics, 327
Addams, Charles, 193
Aeneid (Virgil), 26
Affection, open display of, 157–58
Africa, 41
African immigration, 23
Aged, the, 152–53
Agincourt, Battle of, 38
Agriculture, 67, 344
Ainsworth, Harrison, 57
Alcock, Sir John, 329
Alcoholism, 81
Alfred, King, 19
Amateur sportsmen, 228–30
American Civil War, 311–12
American Industrial Revolution, 313
American colonists, 40
American sexual attitudes, 167
Amery, John, 202
Anemia, 71
Anglo-Saxon language, 21
Animal society, 118
Animals, love of, 110 ff.
Animals in literature, 117
Animosity between North and South, 307
Anne, Princess, 127, 218
Antifamily, 145 ff., 255
Antonioni, Michelangelo, 361
Appetites, 59 ff.
Archer-Shee case, 208
Architecture, 309–10
Aristocratic tradition, 231
Aristophanes, 191
Arkwright, Sir Richard, 313, 333
Armstrong-Jones, Anthony, 346
Army, 206
  regimental loyalty in, 256–59
Arnold, Thomas, 130
Art and music, contribution to, 227
Arthur, King, 19, 27
Ascham, Roger, 202
Asian immigration, 23
Attlee, Clement, 370
Auchinleck, Field Marshal Claude, 28
Austen, Jane, 163
Australia, 41
  British immigration to, 118
Austrians, sexual attitude, 167

Bacon, Francis, 169
Bailey, Trevor, 31–32
Bairnsfather, Bruce, 200–1
Balance of payments problems, 67
Balance of world power, 44
Bald Soprano, The (Ionesco), 361
Band of Hope, 82
Barbirolli, Sir John, 327
Barstow, Stan, 310
Barzini, Luigi, 146, 204
Battles, 25 ff.
Baynes, John, 257
Beatles, 310, 323
Becket, Thomas à, 28
Beecham, Sir Thomas, 325
Beer connoisseur, 94–95
Beer drinking, 78
Beheadings, 48 ff.
Belgae, 18
Bell, Gertrude, 54, 286
Bevan, Aneurin, 348
Bevin, Ernest, 80
Bird watching, 119–21
Birkenhead, Lord, 77
Birthday King, The (Fielding), 299
Black market, 62–63
Blood sports, 225
Blow-Up, 361
Blunden, Edmund, 91
Boadicea, 13, 27, 54

Boarding schools, 129–32
Boleyn, Anne, 49–50, 52, 163
Bohemian immigrants, 22
Boundary disputes, 178–79
Boy Scouts, 253
Brain drain, 292, 311, 336–37
Braine, John, 310
Breakfast, 61, 67, 101–2
Brideshead Revisited (Waugh), 264–65
Britain, Battle of, 37–38
British Broadcasting Corporation, 166
British Forestry Commission, 277
British Pavilion, 72
Britishman, 11 ff., 16 ff.
Britons, 13
Brontë, Emily, 64
Brown, Capability, 265, 272
Brown, Sir Arthur Whitten, 329
Bruce, General Charles, 290, 297
Brythons, 17–18
Buchwald, Art, 191
Budgerigars, 121
Buildings in Liverpool, 309
Burley, Sir Simon, 48
Business methods, 315

Cadbury family, 62
Cadogan Place garden, 266
Caesar, Julius, 18, 37, 225
Cage birds, 121
Canada, and the Empire, 41
Canterbury Tales (Chaucer), 64, 162
Cape to Cairo Railway, 41
Capital investment, 337
Capital punishment, 356
Caractacus, 27
Cardiff, 343
Cardus, Sir Neville, 324, 328
Career of Katherine Bush (Glyn), 150
Carroll, Lewis, 194
Cartwright, Dr. Edmund, 303–4, 313, 333
Celts, 17–18, 20, 112, 331, 346–7
Chaplin, Charles, 191–2
Charles I, 113, 205
Charles II, 114, 201
Charles, Prince of Wales, 59, 113, 127, 217–18, 244–45
Charlie, Bonnie Prince, 27
Chaucer, Geoffrey, 21, 64, 162, 193
Chelsea Flower Show, 274
Chesterton, G. K., 78
Cheval Evanoui, Le (Sagan), 361
Children
  alcoholism, 82
  animals and, 116
  cruelty to, 123 ff.
  discipline, 127–28
  education, 128 ff.
  Industrial Revolution, 82
  home and family life, 123 ff.
  hunger, 137–41
  leaving home, 153–54
  living and working abroad, 289–91
  parental contact, 128
  sex talks for, 166–67
  television programs, 115
Christmas lunch, 72
Christie, Agatha, 125
Church services, 73
Church of England, 216
Church of England Temperance Society, 82
Churchill, Winston, 37–38, 78, 143, 198, 370
Citizens Advice Bureau, 253
Civil servants, 207–8
Clan Bogus, 341
Clan pride and history, 341–42
Clans, 339–42
Class consciousness, 353
Class distinctions. *See also* Social classes
  alcoholism, 83
  drinking habits, 77, 92–93
  eating habits, 68 ff.
  gambling, 231, 233
  gardens, 268–69
  in the North, 310
  sports, 228
  tea, 101 ff.
Class war, 307
Close, Brian, 229
Clothes, 366
Clubs, 260–63
Clowns, 191
Clive, Robert, 37
Coal, 343–44
Cobden, Richard, 325
Cockneys, 316
Coffee, 101–3
Committee cult, 254–55
Common Market, 356
Conan Doyle, Sir Arthur, 227
Congreve, William, 162
Connoisseur, the, 79

Conquerors, 37 ff.
Conservative Party, 335
Constable, John, 73
Contracts, 208–9
Cook, Captain James, 27
Corn Laws, 66
Coronations, 34, 45
Cort, Henry, 333
Cottage garden, 269
Cotton industry, 303
Country house, 264 ff.
Courts of law, 212
Coward, Noël, 285
Crécy, Battle of, 21
Crichel Down case, 208
Cricket, 31–32, 210–11, 227
Criminals, 206–7
Crofton, Henry, 333
Cromwell, Oliver, 29, 62
Culture, 311, 323, 325, 327
Curzon, Lord, 42

Danelaw, 19–20
Danes, 19
Daninos, Pierre, 361
Darts, 91, 227
David, Elizabeth, 65
David Copperfield (Dickens), 124, 163
Death duties, 151
Defeats, military, 25 ff.
Delaney, Shelagh, 310
Democracy, 21, 356–7
Depression, Great, 66, 306, 313, 325, 344
Dickens, Charles, 124, 163
Digby, Jane, 286
Discipline, 126–27, 131–33
Divine right of kings, 205
Divisions
  Norman-Saxon, 21–22
  North-South, 313
  political and racial, 353
Divorces, 159
Dogs, 114–15, 121–22
Donne, John, 162, 368
Douglas-Home, Sir Alec, 226
Drake, Sir Francis, 37
Drakkar substitutes, 256
Drinking habits, 75 ff.
Drobny, Jaroslav, 30
Dunkirk, 28
Dupin, M. Charles, 302–3
Durham, 300

East India Company, 41, 305
Eating habits, 57 ff.
Economy, 44–45, 66–67, 336. *See also* Depression, Great; Industry
  decline of, 328
  future of, 348
  in North, 313
  in Scotland, 338–39
Education, 128 ff.
Educational dilemma, 137
Edward I, 20, 343
Edward II, 169
Edward III, 21
Edward VII, 58, 65, 113
Egalitarianism, 214
Eliot, T. S., 91
Elizabeth I, 49, 113
Elizabeth II, 45, 367
Elizabethan England, 367–68
Elizabethan gardens, 267
Elizabethan taste, 193
Emotion, 32–33
Empire, 306, 360
  acquisition, 41–46
  end of, 44–45
English language, 21
English Civil War, 21–22
Esprit de corps, 257–59
Essex, Earl of, 49
Evans, Timothy, 208
Executions, 48 ff.
Expense-account lunches, 63
Experts, distrust of, 211–12, 228, 354–55
Explorers, 27–28
Exploration, games or forms of, 227
Expo '67, British Pavilion, 72
Exports, 45

Factory work, 235 ff.
Fair play, attitude toward, 204 ff.
Falstaff (Verdi), 362
Family life, 123 ff., 255–56
  animals as substitute for, 122
  committees as substitute for, 254–55
  gardens as substitute for, 279–80
  habits, 146 ff.
  lack of communication in, 122
Far from the Madding Crowd (Hardy), 85
Farm subsidies, 66
Farming, 334–35. *See also* Agriculture
Farouk, King, 217

Farquhar, George, 162
Fawkes, Guy, 28
Feudal system, 20, 65, 278
Fielding, Gabriel, 299
Fielding, Henry, 58
Fishing, 226
Flemish immigrants, 22
Flower shows, 274
Forster, E. M., 299
Fox, Charles James, 77
Fox hunting, 225
Fox in the Attic, The (Hughes), 299
Food, 58 ff.
Football, 35, 227
Francophobia, 21
Free Trade Hall, 325
French
  immigrants, 22
  language, 21
  sexual attitudes, 167
  view of British, 359
Frigidity in marriages, 172–75
Frink, Elizabeth, 329
Frost, David, 191
Fry family, 62
Future of Britain, 363 ff.

Gaels, 17–18
Gambling, 230–34, 366
Gandhi, Mohandas K., 39
Gardens, 264 ff.
Gordon, Charles George, 27
Generals, 28–29
Gentleman farmer, 334–35
Geordies, 316–18
George IV, 58
Germans, sexual attitude, 167
Ghosts, 54–55
Gibbon, Edward, 44
Gilbert, W. S., 191
Gin, 81
Glamorgan, 343
Glendower, Owen, 27
"Glory of the Garden, The" (Kipling), 279
Glyn, Elinor, 149–50
Glynedebourne garden, 266
Golf, 227
Government, volunteer work in local, 252
Grahame, Kenneth, 117
Grammar schools, 133–35
Great Depression. *See* Depression, Great
Grenville, Sir Richard, 26–27
Grey, Lady Jane, 49, 51–52, 202
Grouse-moor image, 119, 226

Hahn, Dr. Kurt, 224
Haig, Douglas, 29
Hair, attitude toward, 183
Hall (inventor), 333
Hallé Orchestra, 325
Hamlet (Shakespeare), 75–76
Hardy, Thomas, 85
Hargreaves, James, 333
Harold of England, 27
Harris, Richard, 348
Harvest Festival Service, 73
Hastings, Lord, 49
Heath, Edward, 368
Hedges, 177–78
Hemingway, Ernest, 361
Henri, Adrian, 320
Henry IV, 21
Henry V, 38
Henry VI, 38
Henry VIII, 50, 52, 163–64, 193
Herbaceous borders, 267, 270
Hereward the Wake, 27
History, 17 ff., 47 ff., 112–13, 178, 330 ff.
History of the Decline and Fall of the British Empire (Gibbon), 44
Hobbies, 251
Hodgson Burnett, Frances, 138
Holloway, Stanley, 54
Homosexuals, 126, 169
Honeymoons, 155–57
Horse worship, 110–13
Hospital services, free, 253
Hospitality, 181–83
Housewives, 65, 70–71, 99–100, 252
Housman, A. E., 91
How Green Was My Valley (Llewellyn), 344
Howard, Catherine, 49, 51–52
Huddersfield Choral Society, 311
Hudson, Henry, 27
Hughes, Richard, 299
Humor, sense of, 190 ff.
  in history, 192
  in literature, 191
  on scaffold, 200
Hundred Years' War, 38
Hunger, attitude toward, 137, 141–44
Hunting, 113, 225–26
Hutton, Sir Leonard, 229

Immigrants
British, 292 ff.
view of British, 359–60
Immigration, 22–24, 118. *See also* individual countries
Imported food, 66–67
Incongruity joke, 194
Indian Empire, 41
Indian Mutiny, 40
Individualist, rugged, 251
Industrial Revolution, 65, 81, 236, 301 ff., 333
Industry, 236 ff., 300 ff., 333, 337
Inheritances, 151–52
Intellectual enlightenment, 42–43
Intellectual life in Liverpool, 320–21
Intermarriage, 21
International image, 350 ff.
Invasions, 17–22, 148–49
Inventions, 335
Inventors, 333
Ionesco, Eugène, 361
Ireland, 342–43
families in, 148
Irish, 321
Italian gardens, 267, 271
Italian sexual attitude, 167
Italophilia, 271

Jacobeans, 162
James I, 11
Jane Eyre (Brontë), 138–39
Jenkins, Roy, 348
Jewish immigrants, 22
Joan of Arc, 38–39
John, King, 205
Jones, history of name, 346–47
Jones, Inigo, 310
Journalism, 324–25
Joyce, James, 194
Jury systems, 211
Jutes, 332

Kent, William, 310
Kew Gardens, 276
Keynes, Lord, 177
Keyes, Brigadier, 218
Khan, Genghis, 37
King Lear (Shakespeare), 13
King, Dr. Truby, 62
Kipling, Rudyard, 34
Kitchener, Field Marshal, 29, 40
Koestler, Arthur, 194, 369
Kut, 28

Labor, 289–91, 235 ff.
attitude toward, 249 ff.
management and, 249
Labour government, 63, 133
Labour Party, 335
Lancashire, 300
Language, 20, 296, 344–45
"Latchkey children," 252
Law and government, attitude toward, 215–16
Lawrence, D. H., 162
Lawrence, T. E., 286, 297
Lear, Edward, 194
Legal aid service, 247
Legal history, 178
Licensing laws, 95–97
Lincoln, Abraham, 311–12
Literature, 298–99, 361
humor in, 191
foreign backgrounds in British, 298
Literary ventriloquism, 299
Liverpool, 318–23
intellectual life, 320–21
urban planning, 319
Llewellyn, Richard, 344
Lloyd George, David, 151, 348
London, 230, 361, 365–67
Loser, cult of the, 25 ff.
Lovat, Lord, 48
Lowry, L. S., 310
Lugard, Lord, 43
Lunch, 63–64
Lunn, Sir Arnold, 227
Luxmoore garden, 266

Maclaren, A. C., 325
Macaulay, Dame Rose, 185
Macdonald, Flora, 54
Macdonald, George, 138
Macmillan, Harold, 148, 226
Magistrates, amateur, 252
Management and labor, 315
Mancaldi, Hugo, 123
Manchester, 323–29
Manchester Central Library, 325
Manchester *Guardian*, 324, 327
Manchester International Airport, 328–29
Manufacturing, 302 ff.
Margaret, Countess of Salisbury, 52–54

Margaret, Princess, 346
Margarine, 61
Marlborough, Duke of, 29, 60
Marlowe, Christopher, 162
Marriage, 154–59, 369
Martyrs, 28
Marvell, Andrew, 268
Mary Queen of Scots, 27
Masefield, John, 116–17
Mathieu, Georges, 359
Maudslay, Henry, 333
Maugham, Somerset, 297
Maurois, André, 361
May, Peter, 32
McCartney, Paul, 370
McGough, Roger, 127, 320
McLuhan, Marshall, 194
Mead, 75
Meals, 58 ff.
Medals, military, 33–34
Memorials, 39
Merchant of Venice, The (Shakespeare), 163, 209, 232
Metallurgy vs. farming, 335
Metals, 331 ff.
Michelmore, Cliff, 43
Midday meal, 68–71
Middleton, Stanely, 310
Mikes, George, 194
Military retreats, 28–29
Milk, free school, 141
Miller, Arthur, 12
Milton, John, 163
Mining, 343–44
Mitford, Nancy, 102
Monarchy, 369
Monmouth, Duke of, 27
Montfort, Simon de, 21
Montgomery, Field Marshal, 29, 37, 199
Moore, Sir John, 28
Morale (Baynes), 257
More, Sir Thomas, 202
Moslem, sexual attitude, 167
Mountaineering, 227–28
Mousetrap, The (Christie), 125
Mrs. Dalloway (Woolf), 150–51
Music, 311
Music and art, contributions to, 227
My Secret Life (Anon.), 162

Names, 27, 330 ff.
Names for the British, 11 ff.
Napier, Colonel, 227
Napoleon, 37, 218
National character, 285
National Health Service, 253
Nationalism, 44
Nelson, Horatio, 37
New Left, 352
New Right, 352
Neolithic Man, 17
Nepotism, 149, 239
Neville, John, 53
Newcastle, 316–18
Newlyweds, 154–59, 164
Newman, Ernest, 324
Nightingale, Florence, 54
Noncommunication in British family, 143
Nonsense in literature, 194
North, the, 300 ff.
  antipathy for South, 313
  culture in, 311
  decline of, 314 ff.
  drinking habits, 83
Northumberland, Duke of, 49
Northumberland, 300
Norman barons, family system, 149
Norman Conquest, 334
Norman traditions, 127
Normans, 20, 27, 332
Norwegian colonies, 317
Norwegians, 27

Old Left, 352
Old Right, 352
Opera, 266
Osborne, John, 370
Othello (Shakespeare), 77
Our Dumb Friends' League, 118
Owens College, 325

Pakistani immigration, 23
Palmer, Samuel, 73
Paradise Lost (Milton), 163
Parliament, 253, 356–57
Party politics, 352
Passage to India, A (Forster), 299
Passing of Arthur, The (Tennyson), 25
Patent law, 305
Patten, Brian, 320
People's Dispensary for Sick Animals, 118
Pepys, Samuel, 62, 162
Permissive Society, 335, 369

Personal relationships, 145 ff.
  in business, 147–51
  in home, 152–59
Perversion, attitude toward, 169
Philistinism, 227
Piccadilly Plaza, 326
Pinter, Harold, 180
Pitt, William, 77
Plants, 276–77
Plays, 125
Playwrights, 310
Poets, 320–21
Political parties, 352
Politics, 356–57
Polo, 113
Pope, Alexander, 191
Population
  density, 23
  international character in North, 321
  Scottish, 338
Poverty, 141
Powell, Enoch, 352
Power loom, invention of, 303–5
Prefect system, 131–32
Prelude, The (Wordsworth), 137
Pride and Prejudice (Austen), 163
Primogeniture, Norman system of, 149
Princess and Curdie (Macdonald), 138
Privacy, desire for, 176 ff.
Professional sportsmen, 228–30
Property Acts, 151
Public gardens, 270–71
Public schools, 130–35
Public speaking, 198–99, 202–3
Pubs, 186–87
  sports and, 90–91
  types of, 87 ff.
Punning tradition, 193–94
Puns in literature, 194
Puritanism, 62, 225, 227, 369
Pursuit of Love, The (Mitford), 122

Quarrels, 158–59

Race, 353
Races, 316
Racial differences, 17 ff., 330 ff., 342
Racialism, 44
Raeburn, Henry, 341
Raleigh, Sir Walter, 26–27, 368
Ramsay, Allan, 341
Rationing, 62–63
Rattigan, Terence, 208
"Recessional, The" (Kipling), 42
Regimental loyalty, 256–57, 259
Religion, 221
Remembrance Day, 34
Restoration comedians, 162
Revenge, The (Tennyson), 26
Reynard the Fox (Masefield), 116–17
Rhodes, Cecil, 41
Ribbentrop, Joachim von, 217
Richard III, 49
Richter, Hans, 325
Rochford, Jane Viscountess, 52
Rochford, Lord, 50
Romans, 343. *See also* Caesar, Julius
Romanticism, 267
Rommel, Field Marshal, Erwin, 39, 218
Room at the Top (Braine), 310
Rounders, 227
Rowntree family, 62
Royal Exchange, 324
Royal Liverpool Philharmonic, 320
Royal Military Academy, 217
Royal Society for the Prevention of Cruelty to Animals, 118
Royalty, 113
Rugby football, 227
Rules
  lovemaking and, 167–68, 174
  respect for, 204 ff.
  sports and, 224–25
Russian immigrants, 22

Sagan, Françoise, 361
St. John Ambulance, 253
St. John's Precinct, 319
Salford, 83
Satire, 191–92
Satirical tradition, British, 193
Sayers, Dorothy L., 149
Saxons, 19, 110, 113, 127, 331
Scaffold Group, 310
Scotland, 337 ff.
  population density, 338
  racial differences in, 346
Scots, 321, 347
Scott, Robert, 29
Scott, C. P., 324
Scott, Peter, 119
Scottish clans. *See* Clans
Secret Garden, The (Hodgson Burnett), 138

Self-esteem and appetite, 70
Sex, 51
  in literature, 162–63
  monarchs and, 163
  rhythm of, 170
  as sport, 167–68, 174
Sex education, 166–67
Sexual code, 164
Sexual habits, 160 ff.
Sexual infidelity, 173–74
Sexual relationships, 155 ff.
Seymour, Jane, 50
Shakespeare, William, 13, 62, 75–76, 162, 193, 368
Shaw, Bernard, 201
Shooting, 119, 225–26
Ski racing, 227
Skiing, 227
Slalom, 227
Slums, 321
Smith, history of name, 330 ff.
Smiths, importance in history, 330 ff.
Smuts, Jan, 27, 39
Social reform, 307
Social classes, 321–22. *See also* Class distinctions
Social distinctions. *See* Class distinctions
Social societies, 82, 253
Social status in sports, 226
Socialism, 133, 307, 311
Soldiers, 27–28
Somerset, Duke of, 49
Spanish garden, 271–72
Spectator sportsman, 230
Spending habits, 60
Sporting life, 220 ff.
Sports, 220 ff.
  cult of loser in, 29–32
  fair play in, 210–11
  in history, 225
  international triumphs, 222–23
  inventiveness in, 227–28
  social distinctions and, 228
Squire, J. C., 91
Stanhope, Lady Hester, 286
Stark, Freya, 286
Starrs, Sir Ronald, 286
Steelworks, 344
Storey, David, 310
Strafford, Earl of, 27
Strikes, 307
Suburban garden, 269
Sunday meal, 71
Sweets industry, 62
Swift, Jonathan, 191

Taste of Honey, A (Delaney), 310
Tarka the Otter (Williamson), 117
Taxation, attitude toward, 214–15
Taxes, 232, 253, 256
Tea drinking, 69–70, 98 ff., 101 ff.
Tea ritual, 107–8
Technological Society, 336–37
Technology, 335–36
Tennyson, Alfred Lord, 25–26
Theaters, 325
Thomas, Dylan, 348
Thomas, Gwyn, 193
Thomas, Sidney, 333
Thurber, James, 60
Tom Jones (Fielding), 163
Tom Jones (film), 58
Tourism, fair play in, 210
Tower of London, history, 47 ff.
Tower of London, The, 57
Trade, fair play in, 210
Trade unions, 307
Tradition, 285
  British satirical, 193
  eating, 58 ff.
  Viking, 58, 75–76, 78–79
Traherne, Margaret, 329
Travel, 284 ff.
  motives, 287–88
  young people and, 289–91
Treaties, 209
Trinity College, Cambridge, 217–18
Tristan und Isolde (Wagner), 362
Tudor monarchs, 149
Tudors, 193, 221
Tynan, Kenneth, 162, 368
Two Nations, 352–55

Ugliness, cult for, 308–9
Unemployment, 313–14
Universities, 135–37
Urban growth, 306–7, 323
Urban planning in Liverpool, 319
Urbanization, 280

Vanbrugh, Sir John, 60, 162
Van der Post, Laurens, 43, 185

Victoria, Queen, 164
Victories, military, 37 ff.
Vikings, 19, 256
  jokes, 193
  traditions, 58, 75–76, 78–79
Vintage port, 80
Virgil, 25–26
Voluntary workers, 252–53
  in hospitals, 253
  organizations, 253

Wages, 59
Wagner, Richard, 362
Wales, 343–49. *See also* Welsh
Wales, Prince of, investiture of, 344–45. *See also* Charles, Prince of Wales
Wanderlust, 284 ff.
War, fair play in, 209–10, 218
War of the Roses, 149
Ward, Dame Irene, 54
Warwick, Earl of, 149
Washbrook, Cyril, 32
Washington, George, 38–39, 206
Waterloo, Battle of, 218
Watson, William, 31–32
Waugh, Evelyn, 191
Weather, 287–88
Webster, John, 162
Welfare state, postwar, 253
Wellington, Duke of, 28–29, 37, 82, 218
Welsh, 321, 347
  ancient poetry, 345
  families, 148
  language, 344–45
Welsh National Opera Company, 345
Wembley, final cup at, 35
West Indian immigrants, 23
Whist, 227
Whitworth, Sir Joseph, 333
William the Conqueror, 38, 58, 192, 218
Williamson, Henry, 117
Wilson, Harold, 335
Wimbledon tennis tournament, 229–30
Wind in the Willows, The (Grahame), 117
Windsor, Duke of, 59
Wine, 75–77, 79–81
Wine houses, 80–81
Wine snob, 81
Wingate, Orde, 37
Winslow Boy, The (Rattigan), 208
Wolfe, James, 37
Women's Voluntary Services, 253
Woolf, Virginia, 150–51
Wordsworth, William, 137
Work, attitude toward, 252
Working-class culture, 345
Writers, 298–99
Wuthering Heights (Brontë), 64
Wycherley, William, 162

Yorkshire, 300